D1563131

Sovereign of a Free People

Sovereign of a Free People

Abraham Lincoln, Majority Rule, and Slavery

James H. Read

 University Press of Kansas

© 2023 by the University Press of Kansas

Published by the University Press of Kansas (Lawrence, Kansas 66045), which was organized by the Kansas Board of Regents and is operated and funded by Emporia State University, Fort Hays State University, Kansas State University, Pittsburg State University, the University of Kansas, and Wichita State University.

Library of Congress Cataloging-in-Publication Data

Names: Read, James H., 1958– author.
Title: Sovereign of a free people : Abraham Lincoln, majority rule, and
    slavery / James H. Read.
Description: Lawrence, Kansas : University Press of Kansas, 2023. | Series:
    American political thought | Includes bibliographical references and index.
Identifiers: LCCN 2022042591 (print) | LCCN 2022042592 (ebook)
    ISBN 9780700634774 (cloth)
    ISBN 9780700634781 (ebook)
Subjects: LCSH: Lincoln, Abraham, 1809–1865—Political and social views. |
    United States—Politics and government—1849–1877. | Representative
    government and representation—United States—History. |
    Democracy—United States—History. | Slavery—United
    States—History—19th century. | BISAC: POLITICAL SCIENCE / Commentary &
    Opinion | POLITICAL SCIENCE / American Government / Executive Branch
Classification: LCC E457.2 .R325 2023 (print) | LCC E457.2 (ebook) | DDC
    973.7092—dc23/eng/20230105
LC record available at https://lccn.loc.gov/2022042591.
LC ebook record available at https://lccn.loc.gov/2022042592.

British Library Cataloguing-in-Publication Data is available.

Printed in the United States of America

10 9 8 7 6 5 4 3 2 1

The paper used in this publication is acid free and meets the minimum requirements of the American National Standard for Permanence of Paper for Printed Library Materials Z39.48–1992.

In remembrance of
Herbert Philo Read (1926–2019),
Charlotte Johnson Read (1929–2019), and
William Philo Read (1965–2018)

Contents

1 | "The Only True Sovereign of a Free People"

A majority, held in restraint by constitutional checks, and limitations, and always changing easily, with deliberate changes of popular opinion and sentiments, is the only true sovereign of a free people.

—Abraham Lincoln, first inaugural address, March 4, 1861

Abraham Lincoln was elected president on November 6, 1860. But by the time he took his oath of office, seven slave states had already seceded from the Union rather than accept the legitimacy of his election. If slaveholders' preferred candidate had won, those seven states would have remained in the Union and demanded that the free states respect the election results. The principal cause of the American Civil War was slavery, which had been a festering, unresolved issue since the earliest years of the republic. But the immediate trigger—the spark that ignited the long-accumulating fuel—was slaveholders' refusal to accept the results of a presidential election that did not go their way.

Democracy means rule by the people. But the people never share identical interests and goals. Instead, as Abraham Lincoln observed in his first inaugural address, "We divide . . . into majorities and minorities" with sometimes sharply conflicting views on matters of great importance.[1] Majority vote is a decision rule intended to resolve such disagreements peacefully. But nothing guarantees that the majority's aims are wise or just. And sometimes opinions on important issues are so diverse and fragmented that no majority position exists at all. Deep and increasingly bitter conflicts plague many contemporary democracies, including the United States, where political polarization is greater now than at any time since the 1870s, when the wounds of the Civil War were still fresh.[2]

The institution of slavery no longer exists in the United States. But willingness to resort to extreme measures rather than accept adverse election results, which in 1860 was the flash point for secession and civil war, has returned as a significant factor in today's deeply polarized American politics.

Today the future of American democracy appears uncertain in the wake of a violent insurrection on January 6, 2021, fueled by a defeated incumbent president's false claims of a stolen election. That insurrection failed to halt the constitutionally prescribed counting of electoral votes in Congress, and in that respect, America's democratic institutions demonstrated their resilience. But the continued acceptance of the "stolen election" narrative by a significant minority of the US population suggests that the degree of trust on which any system of democratic elections depends has suffered significant erosion. Increasing numbers of Americans, especially on the political right but evident at both ends of the political spectrum, regard the resort to political violence as legitimate.[3]

The postelection insurrection of 2021 differed in some obvious respects from the postelection, preinauguration secessions of late 1860 and early 1861. The preemptive secessionists did not invent specious claims of a stolen election; instead, they frankly acknowledged that Lincoln's position on slavery, and the fact that he had been elected almost entirely by northern voters, motivated their act. Moreover, the secessionists were far more numerous, powerful, and consequential than the insurrectionists who assaulted the Capitol on January 6. But the preemptive secessionists of 1860–61 and the insurrectionists of 2021 shared a fundamental unwillingness to accept the legitimacy of an election that turned out differently than they had hoped. Unless citizens with deeply opposed views can agree to play by a shared set of political rules, democracy becomes impossible and is replaced by warfare.

This book examines Abraham Lincoln's thoughtful, hopeful statement of democracy's promise: that popular self-government, through the procedure of constitutional majority rule, is capable of peacefully addressing not merely routine political questions but even the most deeply divisive ones; indeed, that only in this way can the most divisive questions be peacefully managed. But this study also highlights how difficult it can be to assemble a majority capable of acting effectively on critical questions, to prevent a majority from acting unjustly toward a minority, and to persuade members of a powerful minority to accept the results of democratic decisions that do not go their way.

"The Capability of a People to Govern Themselves"

Abraham Lincoln closed his Gettysburg Address (November 19, 1863) by expressing the hope "that government of the people, by the people, for the people, shall not perish from the earth." The address articulated Lincoln's conviction that perpetuating government by the people required both a recommitment to the Declaration of Independence's 1776 "proposition" that "all men are created equal" and a "new birth of freedom"—a tacit but unmistakable reference to the emancipation of human beings held in slavery.[4] By 1863, emancipation had become an official Union war aim as well as a critical strategy for winning the war. When Lincoln delivered this address, he had concluded that winning the war, preserving the Union, and abolishing slavery had all become essential to saving the American Revolution's promise of government of, by, and for the people.

But Lincoln never wanted such a war. His hope had been that "time, discussion, and the ballot box" (as he phrased it in his July 4, 1861, message to Congress in special session) would be sufficient to address even the most difficult and divisive political questions and that slavery could be abolished gradually, peacefully, and democratically. We know that is not the direction American history took. Instead, slavery was abolished in a lethal and destructive civil war. In his second inaugural address (March 4, 1865) Lincoln acknowledged there might have been some terrible but divine justice in "this mighty scourge of war."[5]

Yet we cannot understand Lincoln's political thought, both before and during the war, without taking into account his faith that government of, by, and for the people *ought* to have been able to resolve the slavery crisis peacefully, as well as his commitment to restore a free, democratic political order in which, "when ballots have fairly, and constitutionally, decided, there can be no successful appeal, back to bullets."[6] Lincoln's defense of majority rule, his understanding of its strengths and limitations, and his hope that it could effectively resolve even the slavery and secession crises are the focus of this book.

Both Lincoln's hopes for the perpetuation of America's free political institutions and his fears that American democracy might self-destruct date to the earliest years of his political career. In his Springfield Lyceum address of 1838, Lincoln denied that American democracy could be overthrown by a foreign power; the real threat, he observed, was internal: "As a nation of freemen, we must live through all time, or die by suicide." He identified the prevalence of mob violence—a perversion of majority rule—as American democracy's most dangerous characteristic. But he insisted that violent mobs alone could not destroy America's free institutions. The greater danger was that ambitious, deeply lawless demagogues would exploit mob violence to destroy free institutions by pretending to save them. Lincoln's proposed remedy to mob rule was not elite rule—for elites, too, can act lawlessly—but for citizens to recognize that "*the capability of a people to govern themselves*" requires obeying the laws that they themselves have made.[7] This was the strongest safeguard against democracy's worst impulses.

The most transformative event of Lincoln's political career before his presidency was the passage in 1854 of the Kansas-Nebraska Act, which repealed the Missouri Compromise and allowed the (white) inhabitants of a newly settled federal territory to decide by majority vote whether slavery would be permitted in that territory. Lincoln regarded the Kansas-Nebraska Act "not as a *law*, but as *violence* from the beginning. It was conceived in violence, passed in violence, is maintained in violence, and is being executed in violence."[8] In Lincoln's view, the lawlessness of the act was not limited to the clashes it produced between proslavery and antislavery militias in the territory and the well-documented mass election fraud perpetrated by an early-arriving proslavery minority; it was inherent in the legislation itself and in the process by which the law was enacted.

Lincoln considered the Kansas-Nebraska Act a perversion of majority rule for two fundamental reasons. First, the act legitimated the practice of enslavement by majority vote—not only in southern states, where slavery was long entrenched and difficult to remove, but also in newly organized northern territories, where Congress had previously prohibited it. "The doctrine of self-government is right—absolutely and eternally right," Lincoln acknowledged in his October 16, 1854, speech against the Kansas-Nebraska Act. But allowing a white majority to decide whether Blacks shall be enslaved could be called self-government only if one assumed that persons of African descent were not human beings. "But if the negro *is* a man, is it not to that extent, a total destruction of self-government, to say that he too shall not govern *himself*."[9]

Lincoln's second fundamental objection to the Kansas-Nebraska Act was that it failed, even on its own terms, to establish a fair and legitimate process by which the (overwhelmingly white) inhabitants of a newly settled territory could vote to prohibit slavery. Instead, Lincoln charged, the Kansas-Nebraska Act enabled an early-arriving proslavery *minority* to seize control of a new territory through force and fraud, introduce slavery into that territory, and make it difficult or impossible for a large antislavery *majority* later to remove it.[10] Thus, while the Kansas-Nebraska Act violated the rights of Black Americans by permitting a white majority to vote for their enslavement, it also violated the rights of all Americans, whatever their race, by enabling a powerful minority to dominate the majority.

Lincoln observed during his 1858 US Senate contest with Stephen Douglas that, although he had always been opposed to slavery, before 1854 he had "rested in the hope and belief that it was in course of ultimate extinction," and for that reason, politically it "had been a minor question with me." But passage of the Kansas-Nebraska Act convinced him that slavery "was being placed on a new basis—a basis for making it perpetual, national, and universal," and for that reason, he now "considered that question a paramount one."[11] If slavery became "perpetual, national, and universal," it would be beyond the power of the majority of Americans to contain, shrink, and ultimately extinguish the institution. Slavery became a "paramount" question for Lincoln in 1854 because, in addition to the injustice slavery inflicted on its immediate victims, the expansion and perpetuation of slavery threatened popular self-government for *all* members of the political community to which he belonged. It was in this sense that, as he indicated in the Gettysburg Address, a "new birth of freedom" was necessary to ensure that government of, by, and for the people "shall not perish from the earth." But during the 1850s, Lincoln envisaged the extinction of slavery occurring peacefully and gradually rather than violently.

Thus in 1838 Lincoln raised the possibility that American democracy could self-destruct through mob violence, lawlessness, and demagoguery. In 1854 he perceived an impending threat to American democracy in the Kansas-Nebraska Act, whose moral and procedural emptiness enabled mob violence to disguise itself as law and allowed tyranny of the minority to pass itself off as the will of the people. The Kansas-Nebraska Act was also blatantly incompatible with the Declaration of Independence's proposition that "all men are created equal," a common theme of Lincoln's speeches and writings in the 1850s. During that decade he helped build the new Republican Party, denounced the *Dred Scott* decision (1857), challenged Stephen Douglas (author of the Kansas-Nebraska Act) for a US Senate seat in 1858, and became a contender for the Republican presidential nomination in 1860.

When seven slave states of the lower South seceded from the Union

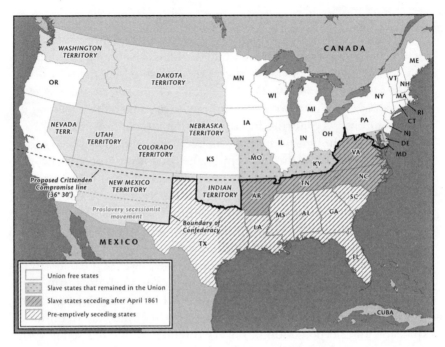

Map 1. March 1861: Free States, Slave States, Seceded States, and Territories.
Map by Erin Greb.

in response to his election as president, all Lincoln's hopes and fears
for the future of popular self-government converged in the crisis (see
Map 1). When an outvoted minority, at the urging of "fire-eating" demagogues, forcibly resisted the results of an election that did not go their
way, coerced dissidents, seized federal property, and declared the Union
dissolved, Lincoln saw it as mob violence on a mass scale. When secessionists pretended that the US Constitution sanctioned their act, it epit-
omized lawlessness disguised as law. Secessionists sought to prevent the
majority of Americans from deciding the single most important question facing the United States: the future of slavery. In doing so, they
nullified a foundational principle of popular government by enabling
the minority to rule the majority. Slaveholders did all this to perpetuate an institution that conspicuously rejected the principle of natural
equality on which, in Lincoln's view, popular self-government necessarily depended. It was under these circumstances that Lincoln defended
majority rule as "the only true sovereign of a free people."

Democratic Principle and Democratic Process

When Abraham Lincoln was inaugurated on March 4, 1861, seven slave states (South Carolina, Mississippi, Florida, Alabama, Georgia, Louisiana, and Texas) had already seceded from the Union in response to his election. No one disputed that Lincoln had won a procedurally fair vote according to constitutional rules. He secured a 59 percent electoral vote majority (180 out of 303), though he received only a plurality (just under 40 percent) of popular votes in the deeply divided four-way presidential contest. But the same was true of his predecessor, James Buchanan, who was elected in 1856 with a 59 percent Electoral College majority (the bulk of his support coming from slave states) but only a 45 percent popular vote plurality in a three-way contest.[12] *Where* Lincoln's votes came from played an important role in the rationale for secession, but the mere fact that he received less than half the popular votes was not what motivated secession.

Nor could anyone claim that Lincoln, prior to taking office, had committed any unconstitutional or oppressive acts justifying secession. Indeed, southern critics of secession argued that only an overt unconstitutional act on Lincoln's part could legitimate secession; his winning a fair election was insufficient justification.[13] But the arguments in favor of *preemptive* secession that prevailed in the lower South were that Lincoln endorsed what slaveholders considered the unconstitutional goal of prohibiting slavery in federal territories; that he had been elected entirely on the basis of northern votes; and that if southerners remained in the Union and treated his election as legitimate, it was only a matter of time before a hostile northern majority squeezed the institution of slavery out of existence. "My friends, delay is dangerous," warned Georgia secessionist Thomas R. R. Cobb, "for ere long you will be imprisoned by walls of free states all around you."[14] Under such circumstances, secessionists maintained, it was perfectly legitimate to dissolve the Union in response to unfavorable election results.

In his first inaugural address (March 4, 1861), Lincoln replied to secessionists by setting forth a principled defense of majority rule as "the only true sovereign of a free people." His immediate aim in defending majority rule was to argue against the legitimacy of a powerful minority forcibly partitioning the United States because it was dissatisfied with the results of a free, constitutionally conducted election. His wider purpose was to establish that a deliberate, constitutionally checked majority, though by no means infallible, was the appropriate ultimate authority not only on routine political questions but even on difficult, deeply divisive questions—such as the future of slavery—that might otherwise trigger violence.

Lincoln did not claim that either he personally or his party *already* enjoyed clear majority support for their commitment to halt the expansion of slavery. He knew he had received only a plurality, not a majority, of the popular vote, and the 1860 election did not produce a Republican majority in both chambers of Congress until secession removed a significant proportion of the opposition. He had secured the Electoral College majority necessary to elect a president. But he did not claim a "mandate" in favor of his or his party's position on slavery, and in the address he acknowledged the ongoing deep disagreement on several slavery-related questions. Yet he emphasized that, as the constitutionally elected president, he had the right and the duty to exercise the constitutionally authorized powers of that office. He insisted that those who rejected his stance on slavery confine their opposition to constitutional channels—which, in Lincoln's view, did not include forcible partition of the country.

Lincoln did not claim that he alone, as president, possessed the constitutional power to halt the expansion of slavery. His view, which he set forth in detail in his Cooper Institute address (February 27, 1860), was that Congress had the authority under the Constitution to prohibit slavery in territories that were not yet states and that it ought to do so.[15] When Lincoln was inaugurated on March 4, 1861, he knew that building an antislavery electoral majority was a task for the future. He recognized that halting the spread of slavery, and gradually squeezing it out of existence, could not be accomplished quickly or easily. But he believed it could be done.

So did the secessionists. They urged *preemptive* secession (before Lincoln took office) to prevent the new president, his party, and the majority of American voters from taking the first critical steps down a path—leading to the eventual extinction of slavery—that secessionists feared would become irreversible unless they immediately and forcefully blocked it. The result of slave states' "submission to the inauguration and administration of Mr. Lincoln," Joseph E. Brown argued in the Georgia secession debate of December 1860, "would be the total abolition of slavery, and the utter ruin of the South, in less than twenty-five years."[16] Whether slavery could have been abolished gradually in the United States without civil war is an open question. What is clear, however, is that many secessionists *believed* this was possible. Preemptive secession, by denying the legitimacy of Lincoln's election, was designed to prevent the first step toward slavery's gradual extinction.

In this book I examine Lincoln's defense of majority rule, his understanding of its capabilities and limitations, and his hope that slavery could be peacefully and gradually extinguished through the action of a committed national majority. I argue that in defending majority rule under the circumstances of the slavery and secession crises, Lincoln was not merely reaffirming an American platitude. Instead, he was offering a fresh, wide-ranging, and in many respects innovative account of the interplay between majorities and minorities in the context of crosscutting issues and shifting public opinion.

Lincoln was not a naïve majoritarian. He acknowledged that majorities could act unjustly, even as he argued for the majority's function as the ultimate arbiter of divisive moral, political, and constitutional questions. His defense of majority rule presupposed that majorities were restrained by constitutional checks. But at the same time, he insisted that majorities legitimately decided constitutional meaning— and not only through the formal amendment process. He understood the phenomenon of cyclical majorities, whereby voter preferences for political decisions generate scissors-paper-rock outcomes: A defeats B, B defeats C, C defeats A. He regarded broad-based political parties as essential to the creation of stable, effective electoral majorities on critical issues. As a Republican Party builder during the 1850s, he sought to construct an enduring antislavery majority able to withstand the disruptive impact of crosscutting issues such as immigration and alcohol prohibition.

Lincoln's Illinois rival Stephen Douglas has sometimes been depicted as a principled advocate of majority rule and defender of local self-government, while Lincoln is portrayed as a centralizing elitist hostile to democracy. Robert W. Johannsen, for example, writes that Lincoln was "suspicious of human nature and distrustful of mass democracy," while Douglas had "an almost transcendent faith in the popular will."[17] I present an alternative picture of the difference between Lincoln and Douglas with respect to democracy and majority rule. In contrast to the image of Lincoln as inherently distrustful of local self-government, he was in fact confident that if slavery were kept out of a territory during its early settlement, and if an orderly and fair vote were conducted among a sufficiently large territorial population, the inhabitants would vote to prohibit slavery. But if slavery established itself early in the process of territorial settlement, "the facts of its presence, and the difficulty of its removal will carry the vote in its favor."[18]

Douglas, in contrast, played a sectional double game with the Kansas-Nebraska Act, leading northerners to believe that slavery could be *prohibited* early in the settlement process, and assuring southerners (whose support he needed to pass the bill) that slavery would be *permitted* from the beginning of settlement and prohibited only—if at all—when that territory entered the Union as a new state.[19] In Lincoln's view, the Kansas-Nebraska Act's deliberate silence about when, how, and by what process slavery could be prohibited in a newly formed territory rendered majority rule practically meaningless:

> The people are to decide the question of slavery for themselves; but WHEN they are to decide; or HOW they are to decide; or whether, when the question is once decided, it is to remain so . . . the law does not say. Is it to be decided by the first dozen settlers who arrive there? Or is it to await the arrival of a hundred? Is it to be decided by a vote of the people? Or a vote of the legislature? Or, indeed by a vote of any sort? To these questions, the law gives no answer.

Lincoln also observed that the law's procedural emptiness encouraged proslavery settlers to kill or drive out antislavery settlers.[20]

Lincoln, in short, was not an opponent of majority rule, either nationally or locally. He believed the ultimate fate of slavery had to be decided by a national majority because slavery deeply affected Americans of all races and backgrounds and threatened to extend its reach to every state and territory. At the same time, he recognized that local antislavery majorities were the indispensable building blocks for any national antislavery majority. And in either sphere, national or local, legitimate majority rule was impossible without paying careful attention to the decision-making process and ensuring that it was as fair and transparent as possible. With respect to slavery in the territories, any meaningful majority vote by territorial residents required that the status of slavery *prior* to such a vote be clarified—a question the Kansas-Nebraska Act deliberately left unanswered.

The difference between Lincoln and Douglas has sometimes been characterized as one between democracy as a *principle* (Lincoln) and democracy as a *process* (Douglas).[21] There is some truth in this observation. Nevertheless, I argue that, in addition to his superior understanding of democratic principle, Lincoln had a better grasp of democratic process, and the role of majority vote in that process, than Douglas did.

The Theme of This Book

Lincoln originally hoped that slavery could be ended peacefully, gradually, constitutionally, and democratically over the course of many decades and election cycles. In his first inaugural address—delivered a month before the assault on Fort Sumter (April 12–13, 1861) irreversibly transformed the situation—Lincoln invoked constitutional majority rule as the only peaceful way of resolving the crisis. Moreover, he argued that even if secession were accomplished, none of the contested questions that motivated it would be resolved. Conflicts over the expansion of slavery into western territories claimed by both the Confederacy and the Union, over access to navigable rivers that flowed through both sections, and over other matters would produce violent confrontations between these legally separate but still geographically intertwined nations, and such conflicts would be even more difficult to resolve after secession.[22] Separation was possible; peaceful coexistence after separation was not.

It was in the context of these two interlinked crises—the long-escalating crisis over slavery and the sudden crisis over secession—that Lincoln articulated his defense of majority rule as the only just and peaceful way of resolving, or at least containing, the deep political divisions that occur in any popular government. That defense of majority rule forms the theme of this book.

I do not positively affirm that the slavery and secession crises could have been resolved peacefully. Many who argue otherwise have made strong cases.[23] At best, peaceful resolution of either crisis was *less probable* than a violent outcome. But the aim of this work is to critically examine Lincoln's political thought. For that purpose, what matters is whether his faith in the capacity of "time, discussion, and the ballot box" to resolve such crises was well or ill founded, given the evidence available to him at the time. In that respect, I argue that Lincoln was overly optimistic but not delusional. I maintain there were plausible grounds for believing that slavery could have been peacefully, gradually, and democratically extinguished. Whether that path would have been *less just* from the perspective of enslaved persons than the rapid wartime emancipation that historically occurred is a different question. I likewise argue that, before Fort Sumter, it was not unreasonable for Lincoln to hope that the seceding states could be persuaded to refrain from initiating a civil war. And even if peaceful outcomes were far less probable in both cases than violent ones, in my judgment, it was reasonable for Lincoln—indeed, it was his moral duty—to give both these nearly impossible tasks his best effort rather than to quickly settle for either the perpetuation of slavery or the terrible path of warfare.

I believe that Lincoln's hopeful, reasoned deliberations on the capacity of majority rule to address deeply divisive questions merit close examination, not only by scholars of American political thought but also by anyone concerned with the capacity of modern democracies to manage the most difficult political, social, and ideological conflicts. If we conclude that American slavery could have been extinguished only by mass violence, this has unsettling implications for the capacity of modern democracies in general, and American democracy in particular, to peacefully manage deep divisions and remedy entrenched injustices in our own time. Lincoln's faith in democracy puts our own to the test.

Majority Rule and the Constitution

When Lincoln called the majority "the only true sovereign of a free people," he made it clear that the majority fulfilled that role only insofar as it was "held in restraint by constitutional checks, and limitations." But the text of the Constitution does not expressly call the majority "sovereign"; nor does it specify majority vote as the ultimate decision rule in Lincoln's broad sense. Lincoln's majority rule argument functioned instead as an extratextual background theory about the Constitution's larger character and purposes, guiding the interpretation of important questions for which the text of the Constitution provides no explicit answer. To call Lincoln's formulation a background theory is not to dismiss or diminish it. All constitutional interpretation, including "strict construction," draws on background theory of one kind or another. Southerners who argued that Congress *must* protect slavery in the territories, and who insisted that states were fully sovereign and had a right to secede for any reason at all, had their own background theories. These were shaped to a large degree by the constitutional thought of John C. Calhoun (1782–1850) of South Carolina.

One intriguing feature of the US Constitution is that simple majority vote functions as the unspoken default rule. The Constitution specifically provides for supermajority decisions in some instances, including overriding a presidential veto, confirming a treaty, removing an impeached president from office, and proposing constitutional amendments. In all cases in which supermajorities are not specified, a simple majority is sufficient. (This includes Senate votes; the filibuster is not a constitutional provision.) The fact that simple majority vote is the decision rule except where otherwise specified invites two very different assumptions about majority rule and the Constitution: (1) that the Constitution institutionalizes a *strong* commitment to majority rule, as a fundamental principle of republican government, to be set aside or qualified only in a limited set of cases; or (2) that the Constitution institutionalizes a *weak* commitment to majority rule, as a decision rule for routine matters, implying that when important rights or interests are at stake, a dissenting minority should be able to block majority action.

Lincoln's first inaugural address expressed a strong theory of majority rule: so long as it respected constitutional processes and did not overstep any clearly specified constitutional limitations, the majority was authorized to decide matters of great political and constitutional importance, even in the face of intense minority opposition. James Madison likewise invoked a strong version of majority rule in his denunciation of nullification in 1830; to prevent a majority in Congress from enacting any law to which the "smallest fraction over ¼ of the U.S." was opposed, he argued, would allow the minority to rule the majority and thus "overturn the first principle of free Gov[ernmen]t." That the majority must ultimately rule (even if the character and tempo of its rule were importantly shaped by constitutional checks) was for Madison, as for Lincoln, the "first principle of free Government"; any other decision rule would create a privileged minority.[24]

In contrast, John C. Calhoun, the principal theorist of nullification, argued that the Constitution nowhere empowered a simple majority of the US population (or what Calhoun called the numerical majority) to enact anything at all. Because *every* piece of legislation had to pass both chambers of Congress—including the Senate, where states with highly unequal populations were equally represented—Calhoun estimated that (in 1850) senators representing 40 percent of the federal population (i.e., the free population plus the slave states' three-fifths augmentation) could defeat legislation favored by 60 percent. Furthermore, as Calhoun pointed out accurately, under certain conditions, the Constitution enabled a minority of US citizens to elect a president over the opposition of the majority. Calhoun also showed that it was technically possible for a numerical minority of the US population (residing in the smallest three-quarters of the states) to amend the Constitution over the opposition of the numerical majority. For similar reasons, it was possible for a *very small* minority of the US population (that proportion living in one-quarter plus one of the smallest-population states) to block a constitutional amendment favored by a *very large* majority. In short, Calhoun vehemently rejected the notion "that the people of these States constitute a nation; that the nation has a will of its own," and that "the numerical majority of the whole was the appropriate organ of its voice."[25] And yet, by the time he died in 1850, Calhoun had concluded that the antimajoritarian provisions of the Constitution were insufficient to assure the perpetuation of slavery, and he argued that secession was unavoidable unless slavery was granted additional constitutional protections.[26]

Lincoln was aware of the countermajoritarian constitutional elements Calhoun emphasized, but he did not believe they negated the principle that, in a republican form of government, a deliberate, constitutionally checked majority legitimately held the final decision-making power. Leaving aside the three-fifths clause (which he characterized as "manifestly unfair"[27]), Lincoln spoke as though constitutional checks and limitations actually strengthened majority rule by rendering it more deliberate and respectful of rights.

Suppose one rejected Calhoun's construction of the Constitution and instead affirmed that majority rule was substantively implicit in the Constitution's provisions and structures. This still left many key questions open. A majority of *whom?* The antebellum Constitution did not specify who was entitled to vote in federal elections; instead, it merely stipulated that whoever was qualified to vote for members of "the most numerous Branch" of the state legislature was entitled to vote for members of the US House of Representatives. In practice, this meant that nearly all women, as well as most free Blacks, were not counted in determining federal majorities. Which branch or branches of the federal government best embodied a popular majority? Was it Congress? The presidency? What function did elections have in communicating the will of the majority? Did elections signify no more than voters' preference for one candidate over another, or did electoral outcomes potentially communicate a "platform" or a "mandate" to officeholders? These were important questions if one subscribed to the notion that the Constitution implicitly empowered the majority to govern. Yet the text of the Constitution answered none of them. These questions were the subject of lively constitutional debate when Lincoln began his political career in 1832 and throughout his years as a Whig officeholder and spokesman. The status of majority rule under the Constitution acquired renewed urgency as the escalating slavery crisis displaced the political issues that had traditionally divided Whigs from Democrats and as the slaveholding minority sought in increasingly aggressive ways to protect slavery from adverse legislation supported by a large, growing, and predominantly northern majority.

The "Ultimate Extinction" of Slavery

In his "House Divided" speech (June 16, 1858), Lincoln called for putting slavery "in course of ultimate extinction."[28] Some have dismissed Lincoln's "ultimate extinction" goal as vague to the point of being empty because he did not explain how the first step (prohibiting slavery in territories that were not yet states, while allowing the institution to remain in states where it already existed) would lead to the disappearance of slavery everywhere on US soil. I argue, however, that even though Lincoln did not specify a precise timeline, his formulation was far from empty.

Nor did defenders of slavery treat it as an empty formula that would permit them to hold slaves indefinitely. On the contrary, they saw the election of a president who spoke such words as an existential threat to slavery's survival, and they considered it no less threatening for being gradual in execution. South Carolina, the first state to secede from the Union (December 20, 1860), listed among its chief justifications "the election of a man to the high office of President of the United States, whose opinions and purposes are hostile to slavery" and who "has declared that that 'Government cannot endure permanently half slave, half free,' and that the public mind must rest in the belief that slavery is in the course of ultimate extinction."[29] Secessionists understood that, despite the gradual pace, the ultimate goal was clear, and the inauguration of a president whose "opinions and purposes" were "hostile to slavery" was the first step.

Though the timing was vague, Lincoln's "ultimate extinction" rested on a clear general strategy, envisaged clear political mechanisms, and included a clear set of political and constitutional criteria. The strategic idea, which Lincoln and many other Republicans embraced, was that slavery had to either expand or die and that halting the geographic expansion of slavery would render the institution increasingly unprofitable as well as politically less powerful.[30] The political mechanisms driving the process—and here Lincoln's thinking was distinctive—were outlined in his "House Divided" speech. That process began with a specific political action, followed by public opinion's response to that action, subsequent electoral reward or punishment, and finally a new disposition of public opinion enabling *new* actions in the same direction that would not have been possible earlier in the process. In principle, this recursive sequence (which I examine in chapter 5) could work in either direction—toward the full legalization of slavery everywhere in the United States or toward its complete extinction—and Lincoln sought to redirect it in an antislavery direction. Among Lincoln's political and constitutional criteria for the "ultimate extinction" process (discussed in chapter 7) were that emancipation had to be gradual, that it had to be accomplished peacefully, that it could not violate any express constitutional provisions, and that slave owners had to be compensated, which Lincoln believed was required under the Fifth Amendment: "nor shall private property be taken for public use, without just compensation."

The most serious objection to Lincoln's "ultimate extinction" scenario was not its supposed emptiness (it was far from empty) but its dubious justice with respect to enslaved men and women. The national majority that Lincoln hoped to build in support of gradually ending slavery was an overwhelmingly white majority. The members of this free, white, nonslaveholding majority had their own interests and reasons for seeking to halt and reverse the growing political and economic power of slavery. Those interests and reasons did not necessarily align with the rights and interests of Black Americans, free or enslaved. Lincoln was aware of the justice problems with his slavery extinction scenarios but did not know how to resolve them.

The most obvious justice problem was that any scenario involving the gradual extinction of slavery inevitably left millions of human beings enslaved for a long time—in many cases, for the remainder of their lives. Moreover, if slavery fundamentally violated a human being's "right to eat the bread, without the leave of anybody else, which his own hand earns," as Lincoln phrased it in his 1858 debates with Douglas, then justice would require paying compensation to the slave, not the slave-holder.[31] In contrast to Lincoln, radical abolitionists demanded that slavery be abolished *immediately*, in the states as well as the territories, and that no compensation be paid to slaveholders. Many abolitionists (notably, Frederick Douglass) insisted that emancipation be coupled with full citizenship, including voting rights, for Americans of all races, including former slaves.[32]

The abolitionists' stance unquestionably expressed a more perfect vision of justice than Lincoln's gradual extinction scenario. But neither the abolitionists nor Lincoln nor anyone else had the power to implement that vision of justice quickly except through a massive civil war, for every slave state would have seceded immediately had it been attempted. Before the war, most abolitionists were unwilling to commence a shooting war over slavery (John Brown being a conspicuous exception). Some took their cue from William Lloyd Garrison, a pacifist abolitionist who urged free states to secede from the Union, thereby absolving themselves of moral responsibility for slavery, serving as a beacon of liberty, and eliminating the hateful constitutional obligation to return fugitive slaves.[33] Many other abolitionists, without relinquishing their moral vision of immediate and complete emancipation, directed their political efforts into legal and constitutional channels and, by the late 1850s, had allied themselves (reluctantly in some cases) with Lincoln and the Republican Party.[34]

Lincoln recognized that several of the Constitution's provisions, including the three-fifths clause, reinforced the injustices of slavery. Nevertheless, he believed (too optimistically, it turned out) that by adhering to the political and electoral processes prescribed by the Constitution, it would be possible to halt, shrink, and ultimately extinguish slavery without triggering a civil war. He also judged that only a gradualist anti-slavery platform could win majority support in Congress and among the overwhelmingly white national electorate.

Race, Colonization, and Coexistence

Lincoln made it clear, both before the war and at least through 1862, that he favored the "colonization" of formerly enslaved persons outside the United States. He insisted, however, that any colonization project

had to be genuinely voluntary on the part of the persons being colonized—a stipulation that practically guaranteed colonization would
never occur on a mass scale.[35] Thus, portrayals of Lincoln as planning
the forced expulsion of millions of Black Americans misrepresent both
his policies and his principles.[36] And unlike many advocates of colonization, including Thomas Jefferson and Henry Clay, Lincoln did not make
colonization a *precondition* for commencing policies of gradual emancipation. Contrary to what many have asserted or assumed, Lincoln was
willing—including before the war—to support gradual emancipation
even if most formerly enslaved persons chose to remain in the United
States as free laborers and property owners. He sought to reassure fearful white Americans that coexistence with free Black Americans could
be peaceful and beneficial to both races.

Lincoln did not believe, however, that white Americans would ever
accept Black Americans as their full political, social, and civic equals.
Believing that a genuinely multiracial democracy was impossible in the
United States, he did not advocate it. Yet at the same time, he affirmed
that persons of all races had an equal right to government based on
"consent of the governed," as promised in the Declaration of Independence. One motivation behind Lincoln's puzzling endorsement of Black
colonization—which he compared to the children of Israel going "out
of Egyptian bondage in a body" to form a self-governing nation—was
that it enabled him to reconcile, if only in his mind, a conflict between
principle and practice that he could not otherwise resolve.[37]

Lincoln's advocacy of colonization is among the most disturbing and
puzzling aspects of his legacy. One can defend Lincoln's support for
gradual rather than immediate emancipation on grounds of political
realism: immediate emancipation was impossible without a civil war. His
support for colonization cannot be similarly defended because the prospect of a voluntary exodus by millions of Black Americans was deeply
unrealistic. Lincoln's support for colonization also raises the much-
debated question of his racial views and his motivation for declining to
endorse full citizenship and voting rights for Black Americans.

In the last public speech of his life (April 11, 1865), Lincoln acknowledged that "the colored man . . . desires the elective franchise."
He recommended conferring it immediately upon "the very intelligent,
and on those who serve our cause as soldiers," and suggested that for
others, the franchise would come in time but not immediately.[38] His
support for Black voting rights may have partly motivated his assassin.[39]

But this was after the war had radically transformed circumstances and reshaped Lincoln's own views. In seeking to understand Lincoln's thinking *before* the war, we cannot sidestep the question why he declined to endorse Black citizenship and voting rights and supported colonization. The antebellum Constitution prevented the federal government from directly abolishing slavery in the states. But nothing in the US Constitution forbade Illinois or any other free state from extending state citizenship and voting rights to free Black residents.[40]

In contrast to many of his contemporaries (including some Republicans), Lincoln never voiced doctrines of inherent Black racial inferiority; nor is there persuasive evidence that he tacitly assented to such doctrines. His unwillingness to support voting rights for persons of all races was premised not on any supposed incapacity for self-government on the part of Black Americans but rather—as Lincoln himself stated—on overwhelming white opposition to political equality with Blacks.[41] During the 1858 Senate campaign, Stephen Douglas, who denied that the natural rights promised in the Declaration of Independence applied to Blacks or any other "inferior race," repeatedly accused Lincoln of supporting full political and social equality for Blacks. Lincoln's response was to positively affirm the *natural* rights of human beings of all races, to deny that he planned to extend citizenship and voting rights to Blacks, and to neither affirm nor deny the premise that Blacks and whites were naturally equal in moral and intellectual endowment.[42]

Though Lincoln did not embrace doctrines of Black racial inferiority, his hedging, defensive response to the claim that he supported racial equality may have reinforced the racial prejudices of his listeners. Lincoln was certainly correct that most white Americans opposed civil and political equality for Blacks. But he also argued that political leaders inevitably shape public opinion, for good or ill. He clearly believed that, with deliberate effort, public opinion on slavery could be moved in an antislavery direction. Thus, we should ask why Lincoln believed white public opinion in opposition to civil and political equality with Blacks was nearly immovable.

Lincoln recognized that for Black Americans to live and work in the United States without possessing equal civil and political rights—to exist as political "underlings," as he phrased it—was a significant injustice. In his 1854 speech on the Kansas-Nebraska Act, in response to Douglas's claim that the act embodied "the sacred right of self-government" because it authorized the (white) majority to vote slavery up or down,

Lincoln replied: "When the white man governs himself that is self-government; but when he governs himself, and also governs *another* man, that is *more* than self-government—that is despotism. . . . Allow ALL the governed an equal voice in the government, and that, and that only is self government." The principle Lincoln voiced here clearly condemned slavery as the most extreme form of ruling others without their consent. But it is equally clear that Lincoln's statement reaches far beyond slavery; it also condemns every form of government that does not accord an *equal* right of consent to *all* those subject to its authority. The conclusion appears inescapable that free Blacks living within the boundaries of the United States and subject to its laws were entitled, according to the principles set forth in the Declaration of Independence, to "an equal voice in the government."[43]

Yet in the next paragraph, Lincoln put the brakes on the radical implications of the principle he had just affirmed. "NECESSITY," he quickly added, prevented "the establishment of political and social equality between the whites and blacks."[44] "Necessity" functions here, as it did for Lincoln's advocacy of gradual rather than immediate abolition, to explain why the prescriptions of justice could not be readily implemented in practice. But in contrast to slavery, where the Constitution, enormous vested economic interests, and the very real prospect of civil war factored into the "necessities" preventing immediate emancipation, no comparable factors prevented nonslave states like Illinois from extending equal civil and political rights to free persons of color.

The obstacles, as Lincoln saw them, lay almost entirely in a certain disposition of public opinion among the white majority. In the same speech, implicitly referring to the abolitionist position that persons of African descent held in bondage should be not only emancipated but also made "politically and socially, our equals," Lincoln observed:

> My own feelings will not admit of this; and if mine would, we well know that those of the great mass of white people will not. Whether this feeling accords with justice and sound judgment, is not the sole question, if indeed, it is any part of it. A universal feeling, whether well or ill-founded, can not be safely disregarded. We can not, then, make them equals. It does seem to me that systems of gradual emancipation might be adopted; but for their tardiness in this, I will not undertake to judge our brethren of the south.[45]

Lincoln thus claimed that among "the great mass of white people" there existed a "universal feeling" in opposition to political and social equality between Blacks and whites. He admitted to sharing this feeling himself while questioning whether it "accords with justice and sound judgment"; indeed, he acknowledged that it may be "ill-founded." Nowhere in this passage or elsewhere in his writings did Lincoln argue that persons of African descent were incapable of participating responsibly in the practice of democratic self-government. Yet, whereas Lincoln could envisage and recommend a gradual abolition of slavery, he spoke here and elsewhere as though white opposition to racial equality was an unalterable social and psychological fact.

Thus, taking Lincoln at his word, both the rule of a master over a slave and the rule by one group of persons possessing political rights over another group that, though legally free, lacked equal civil and political rights were injustices. Slavery was the greater injustice of the two, but in certain respects it was more susceptible to remedy. So long as Black Americans who were formally free (i.e., not enslaved) remained in the United States as a demographic minority amid a white majority that would not accept them as social and political equals, they suffered an injustice without a politically available remedy.

This helps explain, though it does not justify, Lincoln's endorsement of colonization. If Black Americans freely chose to "go out of bondage in a body," like the biblical children of Israel, and form a flourishing, self-governing republic, they would cease to suffer both the great injustice of slavery and the lesser (but still significant) injustice of political disenfranchisement, and white Americans would no longer bear the moral stain of inflicting either type of injustice on the Black race. Yet the notion that millions of free Black Americans would agree to be transported, under the sponsorship of the US government, to some other part of the world to form their own self-governing political orders was deeply impractical from the outset, as Lincoln himself seemed to realize even as he promoted the idea.[46] Lincoln's reference to Africa as the "native land" of Blacks (many of whom, by the 1850s, had deeper family roots in North America than most white Americans) revealed an ignorance of Black communities and their aspirations. Most Black abolitionists agreed with Frederick Douglass that the United States was Black Americans' homeland, and they demanded that the nation treat them justly.[47] Dissenting Black abolitionists like Martin Delaney and Henry Highland Garnet, who urged mass emigration from the United States in the 1850s, did not regard Africa as Black Americans' native land; instead, they had concluded that white Americans would never treat Black

Americans justly and were willing to immigrate to any part of the world where a new self-governing Black community might be formed.[48]

The form in which Lincoln advocated colonization was not marked by the deep injustice that characterized many such proposals.[49] Lincoln recognized the injustice suffered by Black Americans, enslaved or free, in being governed without their consent. *Forced* removal would have violated the principle of consent more radically than continued residence without the franchise. Nor did Lincoln propose that the situation of free Black Americans deliberately be made harsher, as some state laws aimed to do during the 1850s, so that Blacks would be motivated to "voluntarily" emigrate.[50]

Nevertheless, even if colonization were voluntary and the number of participants small, and even if his support was motivated in part by principled opposition to politically unequal status for any group of human beings, Lincoln's colonization scheme would have underscored in another way Black Americans' unequal political voice, for such a policy communicated the message: you are free to stay, but we hope you will choose to leave. That would be sufficient to mark every Black American as politically marginal. Moreover, public funds for colonization likely would have come at the expense of public spending on initiatives, including education, to support Black Americans who chose to remain in the land of their birth.

Though Lincoln declined to endorse voting rights for Black Americans and promoted an ill-conceived colonization idea, in one important respect in the late 1850s he sought to prepare white Americans for coexistence with a growing number of free Blacks. This occurred in the economic sphere. One of the principal fears Lincoln sought to address as a spokesperson for the Republican Party was the frequently advanced claim that the emancipation of Blacks would unleash a zero-sum economic struggle, or even a life-or-death struggle for survival, between the races. White working-class men from free states were especially susceptible to such claims. If the zero-sum premise were accepted, it followed that the economic survival of the white race depended on either keeping the Black race permanently enslaved (so Blacks could not compete with whites in the free labor market) or forcibly removing Blacks from the United States. Lincoln was unwilling to support either course of action.

Instead, he challenged the premise that the two races were locked in such a struggle in the first place. He did so in several public speeches in

1859 and 1860 (and again during the war in preparing white Americans for the Emancipation Proclamation). He rejected the idea that relations between the races resembled "two wrecked seamen on a narrow plank, when each must push the other off or drown himself." In fact, Lincoln insisted, "the plank is large enough for both. This good earth is plenty broad enough for white man and negro both, and there is no need of either pushing the other off."[51]

At the time, Lincoln still supported colonization. But by emphasizing that "the plank is large enough" for both races to coexist without one enslaving the other, he signaled that emancipation *without* colonization was acceptable and workable. This was not the same as advocating for racial equality across the board. Under the circumstances, however, it was a crucial point for Lincoln to communicate to the white, principally northern nonslaveholding majority whose votes were critical to the goal of halting the spread of slavery and gradually squeezing it out of existence.

If the United States had practiced universal suffrage in the 1850s, Lincoln would not have had to focus almost entirely on persuading the white majority to respect the rights, interests, and humanity of Blacks. Black Americans with voting rights would have been their own most effective advocates. Democracy, as a theory of government, does not require that most people be willing to put the interests of others, and especially the most vulnerable, ahead of their own interests. Some people are willing to do this; most are not. Democracy presupposes instead that most individuals are able and willing to stand up for *their own* interests through their voices and votes and that they are able and willing, when necessary, to reach an accommodation with others whose views and interests differ from their own.

But the American democracy in which Lincoln lived and acted was radically flawed with respect to race and slavery. Among those flaws was that those who suffered the greatest injustices did not possess the power of the vote. For that reason, they found it difficult to motivate their countrymen to remedy those injustices or to reward candidates for office who took their side and punish those who did not. If significantly greater numbers of Black Americans had possessed voting rights, Lincoln—who was, among other things, a politician seeking votes—likely would have spoken differently about race, voting rights, and the pace of emancipation. His freedom of action would not have been so narrowly circumscribed by what "the great mass of white people" thought.

But under the actual circumstances of antebellum America, anyone who hoped to remedy the nation's racial injustices was confronted by a horrific dilemma. Apart from violent resistance by enslaved persons on a mass scale, which was difficult, perilous, and uncertain of success, the only way to extend civil and political rights to Black Americans was to persuade the white majority to support that extension. In this respect, those abolitionists publicly committed to equal civil and political rights for persons of all races confronted exactly the same dilemma as Lincoln did: they too had to persuade a white majority. Abolitionists chose to speak the truth without compromise and leave the outcome to God. Lincoln focused on those battles that he believed could be won.

Why Another Book on Lincoln?

"What can you say about Abraham Lincoln that hasn't already been said?" The author of a new book about Lincoln is inevitably asked this question. The question presupposes that a finite number of statements can be made about any subject and that, as the stack of books and articles on a subject grows higher, the number of possible new statements shrinks to zero. The truth is that when a theme is important—ballots versus bullets as channels for political disagreement, for example—there is always something new to say because our own anxious and ever-changing experience drives us to seek clarity and perspective wherever we can discover it. What makes Lincoln significant is the inexhaustible complexity and importance of the crisis through which he lived and acted. That is why so much has been written about him and his times and why there is always room for more.

But there is a more specific justification for the present work. Despite a mountain of books and articles about Abraham Lincoln, there has been surprisingly little extended commentary on his understanding of majority rule.[52] Much has been written about Lincoln's political leadership, political rhetoric, constitutional thought, observations on public opinion, and many other themes relevant to the practice of majority rule.[53] The key passage on majority rule from his first inaugural address is frequently mentioned and sometimes quoted at length but is rarely examined in detail. Some commentaries on Lincoln treat his defense of majority rule as obvious and straightforward, indeed, as a mere platitude of the age. Others rightly emphasize the limits Lincoln placed on majority rule and his desire to prevent majority tyranny,[54] while paying less attention to how Lincoln also sought to *empower* majority rule on the national level to address the slavery crisis. Still other writers use his defense of majority rule to remind readers that Lincoln did not receive a majority of popular votes in the 1860 election. Most of all, I suspect Lincoln's defense of majority rule in the first inaugural address is neglected because subsequent events seemingly rendered it irrelevant: it was not by peaceful deliberation and majority vote but by military force in a horrifyingly destructive war that slavery was abolished in the United States. For this reason, serious engagement with Lincoln's defense of majority rule as the only *peaceful* method of addressing deep political disagreement requires a certain degree of counterfactual speculation. In that sense, my approach is unusual, and I hope readers will judge it to be fruitful.

There is a large literature (both scholarly and popular) on Lincoln and democracy. But democracy and majority rule are not the same thing. Democracy is a multivalent moral and political ideal, typically encompassing the equal worth of all human beings, the promise of a fair chance in the race of life,[55] trust in the capacity of ordinary men and women to deliberate and choose responsibly, and more. Phillip Shaw Paludan calls attention to Lincoln's own concise definition of democracy: "As I would not be a slave, so I would not be a master. This expresses my idea of democracy. Whatever differs from this, to the extent of the difference, is no democracy."[56] The idea that it is best for a human being to live free, neither enslaved by nor enslaving another, exemplifies democracy as a personal, political, and moral ideal. Majority rule, in contrast, is democracy's characteristic decision mechanism but is not an element we typically idealize. Lincoln defended majority rule as the decision method that, *compared to the alternatives* (minority rule, anarchy, violence), best facilitates and least threatens this "neither slave nor master" ideal. It is not my intention to sing hymns of praise to 50 percent plus one or to suggest that Lincoln did so. But I do give majority rule more sustained attention than most other writers on Lincoln have done.

I also pay closer attention to Lincoln's understanding of political parties than do most studies of his political thought. Some historians of American political development have made perceptive observations about Lincoln's efforts and achievements as a party builder.[57] But most studies of Lincoln's political thought neglect his understanding of the function of political parties in a healthy democracy and the specific role he envisioned for the Republican Party in convincing "the public mind" to "rest in the belief that slavery is in course of ultimate extinction." Harry Jaffa, for example, contrasts Lincoln's profound meditations on natural right and the survival of popular government with the many years he spent as "a skilled practitioner of the arts of party politics" and thus, "to put it bluntly, a hack politician"—suggesting that Lincoln's party building, at least during his Whig years, was politically necessary but philosophically uninteresting.[58] Lincoln himself did not view it this way. Here I attempt to do justice to the significant time and energy Lincoln spent *theorizing* about parties as well as organizing them.

The debate over Lincoln's positions on race, voting rights, and colonization has continued for a long time because the matters at stake have lost none of their contemporary urgency and because Lincoln's often evasive statements have been interpreted in sharply different ways. I do not pretend to settle those debates. But I hope my emphasis on Lincoln's effort to build an enduring antislavery majority among an overwhelmingly white electorate helps distinguish between what Lincoln *could* have said or done differently, without crippling that majority-building project, and what would have been impossible for anyone to do under the circumstances, without inviting a civil war. My treatment of Lincoln's attempt to refute the widely shared assumption that whites and Blacks were locked into a zero-sum economic struggle also breaks fresh ground in the Lincoln literature. This theme, too, has enduring contemporary relevance, for in our post–civil rights America, a high percentage of white Americans continue to view Black Americans' social and economic advances as coming at their expense.[59]

Finally, my examination of Lincoln's account of majority rule offers a fresh perspective on his understanding of natural right and its relationship to the practices and processes of electoral democracy. The relationship between natural right and majority rule in Lincoln's thought is a theme that runs throughout this book. In chapter 8 I develop this topic through an extended discussion of Lincoln and John Locke, whose ideas shaped the preamble to the Declaration of Independence, the framing of the Constitution, and much of what was said and done in the early republic. Lincoln probably did not read Locke's *Second Treatise of Civil Government*,[60] but he had secondhand access to Lockean ideas through multiple channels. In important ways, Lincoln's reconstruction of natural right went beyond Locke. The principles set forth in Locke's *Second Treatise* cannot justify the original act of enslaving a free person

in the state of nature, but the application of Locke's principles to an established society where *past* acts of enslavement have long been codified
into property rights is less clear. American slave owners argued that, no
matter how the institution of slavery originally came into existence, to
deprive them *now* of their legal right to hold slaves violated their Lockean natural rights and justified violent resistance to the government.
Lincoln challenged this argument by prioritizing the Lockean natural
right to the fruits of one's labor, which the institution of slavery conspicuously violated, over the right to property in other forms.

Nor did Locke's discussion of natural right offer any solution to
Thomas Jefferson's dilemma, whereby the enslaved person's natural
right to liberty conflicts with the slave owner's natural right to self-
preservation. I argue in chapter 8 that Lincoln relied on majority rule,
in a strong form consistent with Locke's own defense of majority rule,
to modify circumstances through political action and thus eliminate,
or at least minimize, a clash of natural rights that cannot be resolved
at the level of abstract principle.

My perspective on Lincoln, majority rule, and natural right differs in
important respects from that of Jaffa in *Crisis of the House Divided*. Jaffa
rightly emphasized that, for Lincoln, democracy as a form of government depended on a prior commitment to the principles of natural
right, including the natural equality of persons as expressed in the Declaration of Independence. Lincoln understood this; Stephen Douglas,
despite his commitment to the democratic process in other respects,
did not. For Jaffa—and for Lincoln as Jaffa read him—the majority had
a right to rule only insofar as its actions accorded with natural right.
Moreover, in Jaffa's view, the American commitment to Lockean principles unquestionably committed Americans to the position that slavery
was a violation of natural right. Indeed, Jaffa treats the incompatibility
of slavery with Lockean natural right as so obvious as to require only a
brief statement, and he dismisses out of hand the *proslavery* version of
the Lockean natural right to property, which Lincoln himself had to
confront and answer.[61]

Lincoln believed that the principles of natural right should limit and
guide the practice of majority rule. But for Lincoln, the arrow of primacy could simultaneously point in the other direction: majority rule
was necessary to limit and guide interpretations of natural right. In a
political community committed to the principles of natural right, as Lincoln urged the United States to be, there can still be deep disagreement

over what those principles entail in practice. Lincoln's first inaugural address presented a deliberate majority as the ultimate arbiter of *all* deeply divisive questions, including moral and constitutional disagreements. He did so not because he believed majorities necessarily know best but because he recognized that powerful minorities (e.g., a state claiming sovereignty or a Supreme Court) do not necessarily exemplify justice and wisdom either, and their errors and injustices cannot be corrected in subsequent elections as readily as those of the majority.

Moreover, legitimate natural right claims may come into potentially violent conflict with one another.[62] A slave owner might plausibly claim (as Thomas Jefferson did) that under prevailing circumstances, the slave's natural right to freedom clashed with the slave owner's natural right to self-preservation. "We have the wolf by the ear," Jefferson famously said of slavery, "and we can neither hold him, nor safely let him go. Justice is in one scale, and self-preservation in the other."[63] This dilemma cannot be resolved at the level of abstract right. But it might be remedied in practice by persuading the slave owner that his fears are misplaced and/or by *altering the circumstances* such that slave owners can no longer plausibly claim that protecting their own life and liberty requires keeping other human beings in bondage. In Lincoln's view, the majority, through its elected representatives, could enact policies that altered political and social circumstances such that slavery could be "safely" as well as justly abolished. In short, for Lincoln, majority rule was not merely the handmaiden of natural right but, in another sense, an equal partner with a different but complementary mission.

Overview of the Book

This is a critical examination of Abraham Lincoln's political thought, in historical context, with specific attention to his understanding of majority rule. Lincoln did not write treatises comparable to Locke's *Second Treatise of Civil Government*, but he made fresh, concise, remarkably precise statements on fundamental political themes, including his defense of majority rule compared to the alternatives and his argument that natural rights should be understood progressively rather than statically. These statements are worthy of an enduring work of political philosophy. But in Lincoln's case, the rest of his treatise, so to speak, was embedded in his actions and in the wider political crisis to which he was responding.

The narrative principally focuses on Lincoln's words and actions between 1854, when passage of the Kansas-Nebraska Act deeply alarmed him and caused him to fear for the future of the American experiment in self-government, and March 1861, when he was inaugurated president. But I also examine Lincoln's political thinking before 1854, because his sense of both the promise and the fragility of America's free institutions dates to the earliest years of his career and helps explain his response to the Kansas-Nebraska Act.

The onset of the Civil War did not erase Lincoln's commitment to peaceful majority rule nor halt his reflections on the survival of popular self-government. He knew his party could lose its congressional majority in the 1862 elections and that he himself might be voted out of office in 1864. He never suggested that those elections be canceled or postponed because of the war. But the challenges of sustaining a wartime majority within the northern section of a severed Union differed fundamentally from the task of building a peacetime majority within an intact Union that included every slaveholder as well as every enslaved person in the United States. For that reason, I draw on Lincoln's words and actions *during* the war only when they shed light on what he hoped to accomplish *before* the war and how he hoped to do so. For example, I discuss Lincoln's (wartime) observations in his July 4, 1861, message to Congress in special session on "time, discussion, and the ballot box" as the legitimate channel for resolving political disagreements because they continue and expand on his defense of (peacetime) majority rule in the first inaugural address.

Chapter 2 is an extended commentary on Lincoln's defense of majority rule in his first inaugural address. It examines, among other things, what Lincoln meant by calling the majority sovereign; the dual character of majority rule as both restrained by and the ultimate judge of the Constitution; how Lincoln's understanding of majority rule compares with James Madison's analysis of factions and John C. Calhoun's diagnosis of majority tyranny; Lincoln's observations on the problem of cyclical majorities; his stipulation that majorities be both "deliberate" and "easily changeable"; his response to the argument that a *sectional* majority was inherently illegitimate and oppressive; and his (ultimately unsuccessful) appeal to "time, discussion, and the ballot box" for peaceful resolution of the secession crisis.

Chapter 3 explores Lincoln's political thought during the Whig phase of his political career (1834–54), when he denounced mob violence, helped build a Whig Party with a broad popular base, supported a positive role for government in promoting economic development, criticized untethered presidential power, opposed the Mexican War, and took several public stances against slavery without making that issue his priority. I suggest that Lincoln did not place opposition to slavery at the center of his political efforts during this period because he did not yet perceive slavery as a fundamental threat to republican self-government for the (overwhelmingly white) political community to which he belonged. From 1854 onward he did perceive slavery as a fundamental threat of this kind and, for that reason, merged his antislavery politics with his long-standing hopes and fears about the survival of popular self-government.

Chapter 4 describes the evolution of Lincoln's understanding of majority rule from 1854, when he denounced the Kansas-Nebraska Act as a perversion of majority rule, through 1858, when he delivered his "House Divided" speech. In 1854 Lincoln still hoped southern leaders would agree to restore the Missouri Compromise in a "spirit of mutual concession"—that is, as a pact between free states and slave states.[64] By the time he delivered the "House Divided" speech in 1858, Lincoln recognized that no North-South pact could resolve the slavery crisis. That would be the task of a national, principally free-state majority, and the Republican Party as the vehicle of that majority.

Chapter 5 describes how Lincoln sought to overcome the obstacles to organizing a national antislavery electoral majority. He believed the majority of America was antislavery in sentiment. But transforming antislavery sentiment into effective antislavery action required cooperation among many mutually hostile constituencies, including former Whigs, former Democrats, politically oriented abolitionists, immigrants, nativists, temperance activists, and others who had little in common beyond their opposition to the continued expansion of slavery. The chapter also examines the political dynamics underlying Lincoln's "house divided" thesis, whereby an act affecting slavery (in either a proslavery or antislavery direction) is tested in a subsequent election, the results of which reshape public opinion and enable new actions in that same direction.

Chapter 6 examines Lincoln's troubling stances on political equality across racial lines and colonization. I argue that even as he endorsed colonization, Lincoln sought to reconcile white Americans to the reality that most formerly enslaved men and women would choose to remain in the United States.

Chapter 7 describes Lincoln's belief that slavery could be extinguished peacefully, gradually, democratically, and constitutionally through a long, slow territorial squeeze. I locate Lincoln's reasoning within the broader context of how other Republicans thought and spoke about this question. I also suggest that Lincoln's fear that slavery, if not urgently resisted, would ultimately be nationalized throughout the United States was realistic, not overblown or paranoid.

Chapter 8 describes how Lincoln both revitalized and transformed the Lockean natural right tradition. I examine slaveholders' politically influential claim that they had not only a constitutional right but also a natural right to hold human beings as property. I argue that, on the basis of abstract principle alone, Lockean theory was insufficient to resolve the clashing natural right claims that a long-entrenched system of slavery generated. I believe that the degree of authority Locke entrusted to the majority, which parallels Lincoln's case for majority rule in important respects, provides a better foundation than natural right alone for the peaceful, democratic extinction of slavery envisioned by Lincoln. The chapter closes by examining secessionists' unconvincing claim that both the US Constitution and the Lockean right of revolution provided adequate justification for their act. I also describe secessionists' efforts to explain why slaveholders possessed a natural right of resistance, while the persons they held in bondage did not.

The conclusion returns to the question whether democracies are capable of addressing especially difficult and divisive issues such as the future of slavery in the United States. The actual course of events from 1861 to 1865—preemptive secession, followed by a civil war and emancipation by military force—might appear to demonstrate that democracy as a form of government is incapable of peacefully resolving fundamental disagreements. I suggest that the historical record leaves this question hanging: it was not that a democratic solution to slavery was attempted and failed, but rather that the attempt itself was forestalled because its opponents believed it might succeed. I then turn to our own troubled time, when American democracy is afflicted by bitter, increasingly dangerous divisions. I raise the question whether Americans' declining faith in their own democracy, and their increased unwillingness to accept electoral results that do not go their way, indicates that "government of the people, by the people, for the people" is once again at risk of "dying by suicide," as Lincoln feared in 1838, 1854, and 1861.

2 | "We Divide into Majorities and Minorities"

Lincoln's most precise statement on majority rule came in his first inaugural address (March 4, 1861), where he described a deliberate, constitutionally checked majority as "the only true sovereign of a free people." His immediate purpose was to defend the legitimacy of majority rule in the face of a powerful minority's effort to partition the United States because it was dissatisfied with the results of a free and fair election. His broader aim was to argue that the majority, though by no means infallible, was the appropriate ultimate authority not only on routine political questions but also on difficult, deeply divisive questions—such as the future of slavery—that could otherwise trigger violent contests.

In this chapter I examine Lincoln's defense of majority rule as set forth in his first inaugural address and explore several themes and critical questions in historical context. Lincoln did not claim that he or his party *already* enjoyed clear majority support for their position on slavery. Lincoln had received only a plurality (just under 40 percent) of the popular vote in 1860's four-way presidential contest, and the Republican Party lacked a majority in Congress until secession depleted the ranks of the opposition. Lincoln defended majority rule as a constitutionally regulated *process*, not as a presidential or party mandate. He knew that building a clear majority in Congress and in the American electorate in favor of halting and reversing the spread of slavery was a task for the future, but he believed it was possible. The secessionists likewise believed it was possible—indeed, probable—and took forceful evasive action to foreclose the attempt.

Constitutional Context of the Argument

Lincoln's defense of majority rule in the first inaugural address immediately followed his discussion of a series of disputed constitutional questions. We typically think of a written constitution as limiting the scope of majority decision, and the US Constitution served this function for Lincoln. But he opened this section of the address by reversing the roles: he argued that when the meaning of the Constitution itself is deeply disputed—as it was during the political crisis that triggered secession— the only peaceful and legitimate way to resolve these disputes is through the decision of a deliberate majority formed in accordance with clearly specified constitutional processes.

"All profess to be content in the Union, if all constitutional rights can be maintained," Lincoln observed. But it was precisely the nature and extent of those constitutional rights, particularly on matters related to slavery, that were in dispute. Such constitutional disputes cannot be resolved simply by invoking the Constitution itself, as though its meaning is always clear. Instead, Lincoln distinguished between two categories of constitutional provisions: "plainly written" provisions, whose meaning he presumed was not in dispute, and other critical questions that the text of the Constitution "does not expressly" answer. He then asked whether "any right, plainly written in the Constitution, has been denied." He granted that, "if, by the mere force of numbers, a majority should deprive a minority of any clearly written constitutional right, it might, in a moral point of view, justify revolution—certainly would, if such right were a vital one." Lincoln denied there was a *constitutional* right of secession but acknowledged a *natural* right of revolution, which could take the form of secession if it occurred in response to clear and persistent violation of fundamental rights. But Lincoln hastened to add that "such is not our case." Instead, "all of the vital rights of minorities, and of individuals, are so plainly assured to them, by affirmations and negations, guaranties and prohibitions," and none of these express guarantees had been violated (certainly not by Lincoln, who had just taken office). Lincoln did not here specify these vital, expressly affirmed rights, but under the circumstances, such a list would likely include the constitutional rights and processes necessary to conduct free and fair elections, freedom of speech and the press, citizens' right to peacefully oppose the policies of the government, and the minority's right to contest future elections in the hope of gaining the majority. None of these rights had been denied to citizens of the seceding states.[1]

Lincoln also highlighted one politically important rights claim that, though not expressly affirmed in the Constitution, he wanted to emphasize had not been violated: "the right of each State to order and control its own domestic institutions according to its own judgment exclusively"—meaning a state's right to practice slavery within its own boundaries. "I have no purpose, directly or indirectly, to interfere with the institution of slavery in the States where it exists." He quoted from the 1860 Republican platform, which denounced "the lawless invasion by armed force of the soil of any State or Territory, no matter under what pretext, as among the gravest of crimes."[2] Lincoln thus acknowledged that if the federal government used armed force to attempt to interfere with slavery within the boundaries of a state that had peacefully respected the Constitution and the laws, that would be a clear violation of the Constitution. The platform language also implied, however, that lawless resort to armed force *by a state* constitutes a grave crime that the federal government could legitimately suppress by armed force if necessary.

Lincoln then posed three specific constitutional questions, all connected with slavery, that the text of the Constitution did not answer: "Shall fugitives from labor be surrendered by national or by State authority? The Constitution does not expressly say. *May* Congress prohibit slavery in the territories? The Constitution does not expressly say. *Must* Congress protect slavery in the territories? The Constitution does not expressly say."[3] All three questions were central to the slave states' public justification for preemptive secession in the wake of Lincoln's election.[4] The position of most slave states, and of the 1860 states' rights Democratic presidential candidate John Breckinridge (who finished second, with seventy-two electoral votes but only 18 percent of the popular vote), was that Congress was constitutionally *obliged* to *protect* the institution of slavery in federal territories. This position was opposed not only by Lincoln and the Republicans but also by regular Democratic presidential candidate Stephen Douglas, who finished second in popular votes (with just under 30 percent) but won only twelve electoral votes.[5]

In contrast, it was Lincoln's position, and that of the Republican platform, that Congress *may* constitutionally *prohibit* slavery in the territories. This position was opposed not only by Breckinridge but also by Douglas, who argued that only the inhabitants of a territory could decide whether to permit or prohibit slavery.

With respect to fugitive slaves, the antebellum Constitution (Article IV, section 2) stipulated that "persons held to service or labor" who escaped to another state "shall be delivered up," but it did not specify whether the constitutional power and obligation to do so lay with the federal government, the government of the state into which the enslaved person had escaped, or both. Slave states argued that both the federal government and the free states were constitutionally obliged to assist in returning fugitive slaves, and they cited free states' personal liberty laws as one justification for secession.[6] On the other side, many citizens of free states considered the Fugitive Slave Act of 1850 unconstitutional. That law required not only the federal government but also private citizens of free states to cooperate in apprehending and rendering fugitive slaves, while denying the alleged fugitives any of the "safeguards of liberty known in civilized and humane jurisprudence" (as Lincoln phrased it in his inaugural address) designed to prevent "a free man" from being "surrendered as a slave."[7]

Lincoln himself had taken public stances on all three constitutional questions. His Cooper Institute address of February 27, 1860, for example, presented a well-researched, closely reasoned argument for Congress's constitutional authority to prohibit slavery in the territories. In the inaugural address, however, it was not Lincoln's aim to reassert his own or his party's position on these disputed constitutional questions; rather, he wanted to advance a more fundamental claim about *how* they ought to be decided and by *whom*. His defense of majority rule comes immediately after his third iteration of the phrase "The Constitution does not expressly say":

> From questions of this class spring all our constitutional controversies, and we divide upon them into majorities and minorities. If the minority will not acquiesce, the majority must, or the government must cease. There is no other alternative; for continuing the government, is acquiescence on one side or the other. If a minority, in such case, will secede rather than acquiesce, they make a precedent which, in turn, will divide and ruin them; for a minority of their own will secede from them, whenever a majority refuses to be controlled by such minority. For instance, why may not any portion of a new confederacy, a year or two hence, arbitrarily secede again, precisely as portions of the present Union now claim to secede from it. All who cherish disunion sentiments, are now being educated to the exact temper of doing this. Is there such perfect identity of interests among the States to compose a new Union, as to produce harmony only, and prevent renewed secession?
>
> Plainly, the central idea of secession, is the essence of anarchy. A majority, held in restraint by constitutional checks, and limitations, and always changing easily, with deliberate changes of popular opinions and sentiments, is the

only true sovereign of a free people. Whoever rejects it, does, of necessity, fly to anarchy or to despotism. Unanimity is impossible; the rule of a minority, as a permanent arrangement, is wholly inadmissible; so that, rejecting the majority principle, anarchy, or despotism in some form, is all that is left.[8]

The commentary that follows explicates, historically situates, and critically evaluates this statement.

"Sovereign of a Free People"

Lincoln calls the majority "the only true sovereign of a free people." In Anglo-American legal thought, the sovereign is the ultimate decision maker on all contested political questions. In William Blackstone's *Commentaries on the Laws of England* (with which Lincoln was familiar),[9] sovereignty is described as "a supreme, irresistible, absolute, uncontrolled authority" whose acts "no power on earth can undo." The sovereign is free to change its mind, but its decisions cannot be overruled by any separate, higher authority. Blackstone himself, within the English system as modified by the Glorious Revolution of 1688, located sovereignty in Parliament, an elected body, rather than in the person of the king. One great innovation of the American Revolution was to reject the notion that *any* government body, even an elected one, possessed sovereignty; instead, sovereignty was located in the people as a whole, who, in theory, created all governing bodies and whose powers were prescribed and limited by written constitutions authorized and ratified by the people themselves. Though the word "sovereignty" appears nowhere in the US Constitution, either in its original form or as amended, the preamble holds that "We the People of the United States . . . do ordain and establish this Constitution for the United States of America." This, in substance, expresses the principle that the people of the United States are sovereign.[10]

The notion that sovereignty inheres in the people as a whole means that citizens, as constituent units of the sovereign power (each citizen possessing an equal share), have the right to engage in peaceful forms of opposition (e.g., freedom of speech and the press, the right to peacefully assemble, the right to contest elections) that a sovereign king or sovereign parliament might be inclined to suppress. Thus, under popular sovereignty as Lincoln understood it, acts of government could be

opposed through peaceful, legal means; laws could be changed or repealed; and government was controlled through elections and other
constitutional checks and processes. The people could change the Constitution itself through an amendment process specified in the document. The authority of the people, acting deliberately in accordance
with constitutionally prescribed processes, was "supreme" and "uncontrolled" in the sense that the people's decisions could be overruled only
by the people themselves, not by any superior person or body.

But "the people" taken collectively are never in agreement on every important question. Unlike a sovereign monarch, who can act as a
unitary decision maker, popular sovereignty is practically meaningless
without a set of procedures for deciding questions on which one part of
the people strongly disagrees with another part of the people. In calling a constitutionally checked majority sovereign, Lincoln was offering
a specific interpretation of the *process* by which the will of the sovereign
people is expressed and institutionalized. Alternative versions of that
process are conceivable. One might argue, for instance, that the people
of the United States express their sovereignty only insofar as their collective will is *not* sharply divided—such as by meeting high supermajority
thresholds like those required to amend the US Constitution. Thus, in
calling the majority sovereign even in matters on which the people are
sharply divided (as long as that majority respects "clearly expressed"
constitutional limitations), Lincoln was taking a highly contestable position, not merely voicing a platitude.

One might argue that, insofar as the majority is checked and limited
by the Constitution, it is the Constitution itself, not the majority, that is
sovereign. Article VI proclaims that "this Constitution . . . shall be the
Supreme Law of the Land . . . any Thing in the Constitution or Laws
of any State to the Contrary notwithstanding." But accepting that the
Constitution is the supreme law of the land is not the same as agreeing
on its meaning in contested cases. A constitution consisting of phrases
on parchment cannot resolve disputes over the meaning of its phrases,
especially on important matters not expressly addressed in the document. Lincoln, in effect, argued that a majority, formed and acting in
accordance with clearly specified and relatively uncontested constitutional processes, acts when necessary as the ultimate judge of less clearly
specified and more contested constitutional questions.

In calling the majority sovereign, Lincoln did not mean that majorities can do no wrong, that the will of the majority is always just, that the

voice of the majority is the voice of God, or anything of the kind. (Blackstone's own formulation of sovereignty—as the authority whose acts "no power on earth can undo"—indicates that human sovereignty in the political sense should not be confused with the sovereignty of God.) In this regard, Lincoln, though a majoritarian, was not a "populist" majoritarian in the mold of Andrew Jackson.[11] Lincoln meant only that in any form of government, if descent into anarchy is to be prevented, the final resolution of disputed questions—the power of sovereignty—must be placed *somewhere*, and in popular government, the only appropriate location is in the majority. Though vesting final decision-making power in the majority does not guarantee justice, neither does it guarantee justice to place this final power in the hands of any particular minority, whether it be a king, a supreme court, or an individual member state. And giving such power to a privileged minority introduces the additional injustice of violating the natural equality of persons.

In his critique of Stephen Douglas's version of popular sovereignty—which authorized the white inhabitants of a territory to decide by majority vote whether the Black inhabitants of that territory would be enslaved—Lincoln made it clear that natural rights, including the natural right not to be enslaved, had *moral* priority over the will of the majority. This meant in practice that the majority, to avoid committing injustice, *ought* to be guided in its decision making by the principles of natural right. But no *other* person or body had any inherently superior claim to understanding what the principles of natural right prescribed. Even people with a shared belief in the principles of natural right can disagree deeply, and potentially violently, about their application—just as people who believe that all human law must follow the commands of God have, over the course of history, sometimes disagreed violently about what God has commanded. To say that natural right has moral priority over the will of the majority is not the same as authorizing some other agent (whether president, court, congress, member state, or privileged minority) to decide, finally and irrevocably, how best to embody natural right in decisions and laws. In short: majorities are not infallible, but neither are minorities.

On the issue of slavery, Lincoln believed that the majority of human beings, including most slaveholders, possessed natural sympathies and moral intuitions enabling them to perceive the injustice of slavery. But he knew that these natural sympathies could, under certain circumstances, be overcome by fear, economic self-interest, habituation, shifting public opinion, or the words of demagogues. Lincoln also recognized that this same white majority who (he believed) implicitly recognized the injustice of slavery was unwilling to treat Blacks, whether enslaved or free, as social and political equals. A majority, then, might be morally right about some matters related to slavery and race and morally wrong about others. And even if Lincoln was correct about the majority of individuals having natural antislavery sympathies, he knew that translating this moral uneasiness into effective political commitment would be an enormous task.[12] He believed the majority could be persuaded to decide slavery questions in accordance with natural right, but this would not occur simply by aggregating voter preferences (especially when those with the most at stake—enslaved persons—were excluded from the franchise).[13]

Under the circumstances of the slavery crisis, the principal candidates for sovereignty, both of which Lincoln mentioned and rejected, were the individual states, each claiming to act as final judge of all constitutional questions, as in John C. Calhoun's constitutional theory, and the US Supreme Court, which, in effect, asserted sovereign power over constitutional meaning when it ruled in *Dred Scott* (1857) that Congress had no legitimate authority to restrict slavery in the territories. Lincoln acknowledged that states had constitutionally guaranteed rights, powers, and immunities, but in his view, an individual state, as part of a larger whole, could not justly function as the final judge of contested constitutional questions that affect all states, free and slave alike. Whether slavery would be permitted or prohibited in federal territories was a question of this kind. Thus, in calling the majority sovereign, Lincoln specifically meant a *national* majority, at least when deciding disputes over the meaning of the US Constitution.

Unlike a state claiming full sovereignty, the US Supreme Court is a national institution. Lincoln's inaugural address implicitly treats the Supreme Court as the most plausible alternative claimant to sovereignty under the Constitution because constitutional questions inevitably come before it. In the paragraph immediately following Lincoln's "only true sovereign" passage, he acknowledged that "constitutional questions are to be decided by the Supreme Court" and that "such decisions must be binding in any case, upon the parties to a suit" and are "entitled to very high respect and consideration, in all parallel cases, by all other departments of the government." Nevertheless, he continued, "If the whole policy of the government, upon vital questions, affecting the whole people, is to be irrevocably fixed by decisions of the Supreme

Court, the instant they are made," then "the people will have ceased, to be their own rulers, having, to that extent, practically resigned their government, into the hands of that eminent tribunal."[14] Lincoln's critique of the sovereign status of the Supreme Court thus rested on the distinction between the court deciding a constitutional question for the present and in a particular case versus deciding it permanently and "irrevocably" in all future cases.

Indeed, federal courts fulfilled an important, if ultimately secondary, role in Lincoln's understanding of how and under what conditions majorities can legitimately decide contested constitutional questions. If a majority must be "held in restraint by constitutional checks and limitations" to function as the "true sovereign of a free people," then courts clearly have important, though not exclusive, authority in safeguarding the constitutional processes under which such majorities form and act.

Even if a constitutionally checked majority is sovereign—that is, the final judge of contested questions in a free society—this does not mean that a question, once decided, cannot be reopened. On the contrary, the same processes that legitimize the majority's authority to decide a contested question at one point in time enable a future, perhaps differently constituted majority to revise or overturn that decision. Lincoln specifically speaks of a *changing* majority as sovereign, which makes his understanding of popular sovereignty fundamentally different from the Supreme Court's assertion of judicial supremacy in the *Dred Scott* case. Chief Justice Roger Taney's sweeping ruling attempted to impose a final settlement, beyond the reach of electoral politics, of the most politically divisive slavery questions.[15] For Lincoln, in contrast, the majority is the ultimate decision maker in a free society not because its decisions cannot be changed but precisely because they *can* be changed. Lincoln himself hoped for the gradual but permanent extinction of slavery in the United States. But such an outcome depended on persuading the American public that slavery was wrong and to act on that conviction over an extended period of time, not on the irreversibility of any particular decision or law.

Majority Rule and Constitutional Checks

Lincoln describes the majority as the sovereign of a free people insofar as it is "held in restraint by constitutional checks, and limitations."

Lincoln's claim here is in some respects straightforward and relatively uncontroversial. In other respects, his argument is complex and contentious.

The straightforward part of Lincoln's claim is that he was not proposing to replace constitutional processes with government by plebiscite. Instead, electoral majorities exercise sovereignty in Lincoln's sense only when they come into existence and act through constitutionally specified processes. If a majority that gained control of the government in one election attempted to perpetuate its power by canceling or postponing future elections, enacting laws that could not be repealed by future majorities, or driving out opponents and threatening to kill dissenters, such a majority would cease to act as the sovereign of a free people and its acts would lose all legitimacy. Though this point appears obvious, it was not without political significance in Lincoln's time. The proslavery faction in the Kansas territory—an early-arriving, violent, temporary majority—attempted to do all these things and almost succeeded in getting Kansas admitted to the Union as a slave state, despite a growing antislavery majority in the territory.[16]

The legislative process established by the US Constitution includes voting rules of various types. These rules are a complex combination of simple majorities (to pass ordinary legislation in the House or Senate), supermajorities (to approve constitutional amendments and treaties and to override presidential vetoes), and concurrent majorities (passage by majorities in both the House and the Senate and signature by a president selected by an Electoral College majority). To what degree the Constitution's supermajority requirements (which allow a sufficiently large minority to block action favored by a majority) and the equal representation of unequally populous states in the Senate can be reconciled with Lincoln's claim that a deliberate majority is the ultimate decision maker under the Constitution is an open question. But in any event, Lincoln did not suggest that the majority can legitimately circumvent any of these constitutional processes.

Nor was Lincoln calling for the centralization of all political power in the national government. Instead, he recognized the federal structure of the Union as an important constitutional check on the action of a national majority. Lincoln observed near the beginning of his inaugural address that he regarded "the maintenance inviolate of the rights of the States" as "essential to that balance of power on which the perfection and endurance of our political fabric depend."[17] He made it clear that he considered slavery one of those matters constitutionally reserved to the states. A national majority was the ultimate decision maker only on those issues that lay within the constitutional powers of the federal government; matters reserved to the states would be decided by state majorities.

But where the line is drawn between federal and state authority is not clearly specified in the Constitution. Jurisdictional questions of this kind had been contested since ratification of the Constitution and were dangerously contentious in Lincoln's time. Moreover, none of the alleged grievances motivating the preemptively seceding states—the prospect of banning slavery in federal territories, free states' reluctance to return fugitive slaves and refusal to suppress abolitionist societies, the election of a presidential candidate deeply opposed in the South—involved the violation of rights reserved to the states under the Constitution. Instead, these matters clearly fell outside the jurisdiction of any single state but indirectly affected the stability and prosperity of slavery in the states where it was already established. From slaveholders' perspective, policies eroding slavery from outside their states' boundaries violated states' rights and for that reason gave slave states a constitutional right to block those policies. From Lincoln's perspective, these were national matters to be decided by national majorities.

Though many of the constitutional checks and limitations inscribed in the Constitution facilitated the practice of popular sovereignty as Lincoln understood it, some clearly did not. Lincoln regarded the Constitution's three-fifths clause as a fundamental violation of republican principles. "Five slaves are counted as being equal to three whites," he complained in 1854. "The slaves do not vote; they are only counted and so used, as to swell the influence of white people's votes." As a result, 274,567 voters in South Carolina had as much power in the US House of Representatives as 581,813 voters in Maine. The three-fifths clause gave the slave states an additional twenty seats in Congress and thus ensured passage of the Kansas-Nebraska Act, which passed in the House by only seven votes. Lincoln observed that "all this is manifestly unfair," and in his view, it justified efforts to prevent the addition of new slave states to the Union. Nevertheless, the three-fifths clause was part of the Constitution and "already settled," and once a slave state had entered the Union, it could not be infringed.[18]

If Lincoln's only point about majority rule and the Constitution was that majorities cannot override constitutional limitations, he could have said so in one sentence. His claim would then have been indistinguishable from countless other such statements over the course of American constitutional history and completely forgettable. But Lincoln was also making a more interesting and disputable claim about majorities and the Constitution.

To argue, as Lincoln does, that a national majority should ultimately decide contested constitutional questions that are not expressly answered in the text of the Constitution is to confer a very significant power on the majority. Lincoln's argument here presupposes two things: that it is possible to distinguish between what is plainly written in the Constitution and what is not; and that a popular majority can be trusted to understand and abide by those plainly written constitutional checks and limitations, even as that same majority makes potentially far-reaching decisions about important constitutional questions that are not expressly answered in the document. One could compare this to an unorthodox baseball game in which the shortstop is also sometimes the umpire.

Lincoln's sovereign majority argument might seem to violate republican principles by enabling the majority to act as judge in its own case. But that is part of what sovereignty means. The judge-in-one's-own-case problem would not be eliminated if this power of ultimate constitutional judgment were instead conferred on the US Supreme Court; it would merely be shifted. Supreme Court justices are also in the position of simultaneously following and deciding the constitutional rules—by majority vote among the justices themselves. One might argue that Supreme Court justices, by virtue of their legal training, selection process, or independence from popular opinion, are far more capable of fulfilling this complicated dual role—both player and umpire—than ordinary citizens are. Lincoln, especially in light of the *Dred Scott* decision, saw the matter differently. Placing ultimate responsibility for deciding contested constitutional questions (e.g., permitting or prohibiting slavery in federal territories) with a national majority does not guarantee a just and impartial decision, but it at least treats all citizens as equals and presumes them capable of rationally deliberating on constitutional questions. And the unwise or unjust constitutional judgments of a deliberate majority are more readily correctable than the unwise or unjust rulings of the Supreme Court after it has "irrevocably fixed" (as Lincoln phrased it) a vital constitutional question.[19]

Lincoln's case for vesting sovereignty in a deliberate majority restrained by constitutional checks and limitations had another controversial dimension, one that modern-day readers can easily miss but would not have been overlooked by slave-state leaders in 1861. Lincoln pledged to abide by all clearly expressed constitutional protections for slavery, but he also promised to provide *no more* protection to slavery than what was specifically required in the Constitution. From slaveholders' perspective, this was a radical and deeply alarming stance. For decades, leaders in slave states had demanded, and generally enjoyed, far *more* protection for slavery than the Constitution provided.[20] Many of the most important protections for slavery were embodied in extraconstitutional practices such as the "balance rule," which operated from 1820 until 1850, whereby every new free state entering the Union was balanced by a new slave state; the "gag rule," which from 1835 to 1844 prevented the public presentation of antislavery petitions in Congress; and the tacit cooperation between the Democratic and Whig Parties to compete nationally over economic issues such as banking, tariffs, and internal improvements and to marginalize slavery disputes as much as possible. John C. Calhoun regarded the Constitution as a wide-ranging compact characterized by an extratextual commitment to sectional consensus. It followed from Calhoun's theory that the institution of slavery was entitled to as much protection as the slave states judged it needed. If the existing constitutional checks were insufficient for this purpose (and Calhoun argued that they had already failed), additional constitutional protections were needed to guarantee slavery's long-term survival against any direct or indirect threats. In Calhoun's view, if northerners were unwilling to extend these additional constitutional protections, slave states would be justified in seceding from the Union.[21]

Therefore, in pondering Lincoln's assurance that the acts of a national majority would be bound by *clearly written* constitutional checks and limitations, we should attend to the unspoken corollary: that the majority was *not* bound by much more restrictive checks and limitations that a vocal minority believed *ought* to be included in the Constitution but were not.

Majorities, Factions, and Political Parties

Lincoln begins his "sovereign of a free people" passage with this statement: "From questions of this class spring all our constitutional controversies, and we divide upon them into majorities and minorities." His tone here suggests that a political community's division into majorities and minorities is natural, normal, and inevitable, not a political pathology requiring a remedy. What was pathological, in Lincoln's view, was the notion that the appropriate response to peaceful political disagreement was *separation*, in the unrealistic hope that redrawing the political boundaries would cause fundamental disagreements to disappear.

In the inaugural address Lincoln was most concerned with defending a national majority because the flash points of secession concerned disagreement over unavoidably national decisions. But his analysis and defense of majority rule would apply to majorities at all levels—state and local no less than national. Fundamental disagreement potentially characterized politics at all levels, and for this reason, it was an illusion to believe that partition along state or sectional lines would create some "perfect identity of interests . . . as to produce harmony only." Instead, secession would simply displace the arena of conflict and encourage disappointed internal minorities to attempt secessions within secessions. (Lincoln's scenario here closely resembles the actual course of events set in motion by secession during the 1990s in the ill-fated former Yugoslavia.)[22] Lincoln's portrayal of majority-minority divisions thus displays a fractal character: the same basic patterns are found at all scales.

For Lincoln, democratic disagreement went "all the way down" with respect to political scale, but he did not claim that politics consists of *nothing but* radical disagreement. That would be warfare, not democratic politics, in which case it would be pointless to attempt to persuade a defeated minority to respect the legitimacy of the outcome. Lincoln acknowledged in the address the existence of some "persons in one section, or another who seek to destroy the Union at all events, and are glad of any pretext to do it." For such persons (who would certainly include fire-eaters like Robert Barnwell Rhett of South Carolina), any appeal to common interest or shared values was bound to fail, and for this reason, Lincoln said, "I need address no word to them." He reached out instead to those "who really love the Union" and who "profess to be content in the Union, if all constitutional rights can be maintained," but who deeply disagreed with their fellow citizens from a different section of the country about how that shared Constitution should be interpreted and what specific rights it protected.[23]

Despite his appeal to common interests and shared values, Lincoln acknowledged that disagreements ran deep. "One section of our country believes slavery is *right*, and ought to be extended, while the other believes it is *wrong*, and ought not to be extended." Lincoln did not pretend this dispute could be resolved anytime soon. He instead appealed to the priority of other values: reverence for a shared Constitution (even if differently interpreted on some key points); shared commitment to the principle of free elections; the social and economic interdependencies that would be radically disrupted by partition of geographically interconnected sections ("Physically speaking, we cannot separate"); sentimental connections ("mystic chords of memory"); and the enormous, nonmystical interest both sections had in avoiding "the momentous issue of civil war."[24] (As it turned out, Lincoln clearly overestimated the degree to which common interests and shared values could counteract the deep division on slavery.)

Lincoln's defense of majority rule thus presupposed the persistence of both deep differences and strong common ties. He did not relegate majority rule to merely routine questions; nor did he promise that political disagreement on important matters would disappear. The tone of normalcy with which Lincoln describes a community's division into majorities and minorities invites comparison with James Madison's treatment of faction in Federalist 10. Madison defined faction as "a number of citizens, whether amounting to a majority or minority of the whole," who were "united and actuated by some common impulse of passion, or of interest, adverse to the rights of other citizens, or to the permanent and aggregate interests of the community." Madison argued that factions were inevitable in popular government because they thrived in an atmosphere of political liberty and could not be prevented except by eliminating liberty itself. Madison, like Lincoln, rejected the supposed remedy of homogeneity—the notion that with the right kind of policies, or by creating small enough political units, political division could be replaced by political harmony. It was impossible, Madison argued, to give every citizen "the same opinions, the same passions, and the same interests." He believed that factional battles would be more violent and bitter in state or local communities, where "the smaller the compass within which they are placed, the more easily will they concert and execute their plans of oppression," than at the national level, where the multiplicity of factions would tend to prevent any one faction from dominating.[25]

Madison and Lincoln agreed that both majorities and minorities could act unjustly. They also agreed that, despite the risk of majorities acting unjustly, in a popular government there was nowhere else that the final decision-making power could legitimately be placed. In Madison's words, "Yet the parties are, and must be, themselves the judges; and the most numerous party . . . must be expected to prevail."[26] Both Madison and Lincoln refused to remedy political conflict and injustice by (as Madison phrased it in Federalist 51) "creating a will in the community independent of the majority, that is, of the society itself."[27] (Placing final authority in a monarch would be one example of a "will . . . independent of the majority"; in Lincoln's view, placing final authority in the Supreme Court would be another.) Instead, what was essential for both Madison and Lincoln were the institutions and processes that, though not guaranteeing that majorities would act wisely and justly, at least increased their probability of doing so.

But if Madison's and Lincoln's analyses converge in some important respects, they differ in others. For Madison, a faction was, by definition, unjust. Madison acknowledged—indeed, his republican principles depended on—the possibility of just, nonfactious majorities. In Federalist 51 he wrote, "In the extended republic of the United States, and among the great variety of interests, parties, and sects, which it embraces, a coalition of the majority of the whole society could seldom take place upon any other principles, than those of justice and the general good."[28] But for Madison, the emergence of a nonfactious majority presupposed the existence of a large number of factions over the extended territory of the Union, none of which enjoyed a majority. "Extend the sphere, and you take in a greater variety of parties and interests; you make it less probable that a majority of the whole will have a common motive to invade the rights of other citizens." Thus, elected representatives at the national level would be able to legislate with relatively greater impartiality.[29] Madison, at least in 1787, did not foresee the advent of national political parties (though by the 1790s he played a key role, along with Thomas Jefferson, in creating the first national party system).[30]

Lincoln's analysis of majorities and minorities does not necessarily contradict Madison's, but Lincoln's approach and emphasis are certainly different. Lincoln's opening statement, "We divide . . . into majorities and minorities," does not necessarily imply that the aims of either the majority or the minority are unjust. Of course, they *might* be unjust. Lincoln refrained from saying this in the inaugural address, but elsewhere he made it clear that he believed the powerful proslavery minority harbored unjust aims. For Lincoln, however, political division as such did not indicate unjust motivations on either side. During his career as a Whig opposing Democratic policies on banking, currency, public lands, internal improvements, and constitutional interpretation (see chapter 3), Lincoln never claimed that the Democrats' goals or motives were inherently unjust, although he often characterized them as ill-considered and shortsighted. To recall Madison's terminology: for Lincoln, neither the Whigs nor the Jacksonian Democrats nor, later on, the Republican Party counted as factions in Madison's sense, although members of any party could act in factional ways on occasion. Nor did Lincoln argue (as Madison did) that national majorities would seldom form except on the basis of "justice and the general good." The Democrats dominated national government through most of Lincoln's career. He regarded that party's aims as honestly intended, but he rarely believed they advanced the general good.

Thus, Lincoln's understanding of majority rule as "the only true sovereign of a free people" was fully compatible with the existence of strong political parties—though no political party could legitimately claim to possess sovereignty. In his July 6, 1852, "Eulogy for Henry Clay," Lincoln praised Clay, a committed Whig who nevertheless acted "for the whole country." Lincoln saw no contradiction there. "A free people, in times of peace and quiet—when pressed by no common danger—naturally divide into parties. At such times, the man who is of neither party, is not—cannot be, of any consequence. Mr. Clay, therefore, was of a party."[31] Lincoln presents partisanship as a quality that political leaders should be able to rise above in critical times but that, during "times of peace and quiet," contributes to the common good by making it possible for citizens to act with "consequence." Lincoln did not merely adapt himself to the presence of organized political parties: he believed in them, helped build them (the Whig Party in his early career and the Republican Party in the 1850s), defended them, and considered them essential to the vitality of popular sovereignty.[32]

Critical to Lincoln's strategy for the gradual extinction of slavery was to establish the Republicans as a "normal" political party, with the right to express its views, publicize its platform, appoint postmasters and other public employees, and run candidates for election anywhere in the United States, including in slave states, where they had no prospect of winning. To normalize the Republicans as a party would at the same time normalize the type of antislavery speech and antislavery organization that leaders in slave states had sought for decades to prevent, delegitimize, and suppress.

The Cyclical Majorities Problem

Lincoln's phrase "We divide . . . into majorities and minorities" does not mention a third possibility: that on some important matters, there may be no clear majority position. Instead, there may be three or more positions on a question, each supported by minorities of varying sizes, one of them larger than the others (the plurality) but none commanding majority support. This was clearly the case with popular votes for the four major presidential candidates in the 1860 election, and it was almost certainly the case with popular support for their positions on slavery in the territories.

Lincoln was not a naïve majoritarian; he understood that opinions about important matters did not necessarily sort themselves into clear majority and minority stances. Lincoln's Electoral College majority made him president of the United States, but he did not claim that the results of the 1860 election proved that his own (and his party's) position on slavery in the territories enjoyed clear majority support. He certainly believed Republicans' stance against the extension of slavery could win the support of a national majority in the future. But in his inaugural address, Lincoln did not claim any "mandate" on slavery; he claimed only the right to exercise the constitutionally prescribed powers of the presidency.

What Lincoln did instead in the inaugural address was to pose a set of contested constitutional questions, framed in such a way as to elicit clear majority and minority responses. "*May* Congress prohibit slavery in the territories?" "*Must* Congress protect slavery in the territories?" Because these questions are phrased as yes-or-no choices, the responses would sort themselves into majority and minority positions (except in the case of a tie). Assuming that votes for Lincoln, Douglas, and Breckinridge represented support for their respective positions on slavery in the territories, the results of the 1860 election suggested that a strong majority answered "no" to the question "*Must* Congress protect slavery in the territories?" Both Lincoln, with 39.82 percent of the popular vote, and Douglas, with 29.46 percent (for a total of 69.28 percent), strongly and publicly rejected southern demands for a congressional slave code. In contrast, John Breckinridge, who favored that position, won 18.10 percent of the vote. Even if the percentage of votes for the fourth candidate, John Bell (12.61 percent), who took no public position on slavery in the territories, were added to Breckinridge's, the resulting 30.71 percent comes nowhere near a majority.

But the true shape of political opinion on slavery in the territories could not be adequately captured by a single yes-or-no question. Lincoln recognized this, so he posed a second yes-or-no question: "*May* Congress *prohibit* slavery in the territories?" Of the four candidates, only Lincoln (39.82 percent) answered a clear "yes" in 1860. Bell's percentage can be classified as representing "no opinion" voters. Votes for Douglas and Breckinridge, both of whom—though in very different ways—rejected the position that Congress should ban slavery in the territories, totaled 47.56 percent. Given these results, although it was not unreasonable for Lincoln and the Republicans to hope to secure clear majority support for their position sometime in the future, they could not convincingly claim that their stance on slavery was *already* a national majority position.

Instead, the results of the 1860 election suggest a tendency toward what public-choice theorists call cyclical majorities. Wherever there are more than two voters and more than two issue positions, voter preferences can be distributed such that *any* position can be defeated by a majority coalition of the others: thus, position I defeats position II, II defeats III, and III defeats I.

For example, suppose there are three voters (A, B, and C) and a decision in which three outcomes are possible (I, II, and III) over which these voters have ranked preferences (first, second, and third choice). If their preferences are ranked as shown in table 2.1, even though no outcome receives a majority of first-place votes, a potentially stable majority emerges through a series of pairwise votes. Outcome II defeats outcome I by a two-to-one majority in a head-to-head vote, and outcome II also defeats outcome III by a two-to-one majority in a head-to-head vote. If the voting rules provide for multiple pairwise votes, such that each of the three outcomes goes head-to-head against each of the others, then outcome II (voter B's first preference) comes out on top. Voter A and voter C, assuming their respective preference rankings remain unchanged, will not form a majority coalition against voter B to overturn outcome II because voter A's first choice is voter C's last choice, and vice versa.[33]

If, however, preferences are ranked as in table 2.2, no stable majority exists. In this case, outcome I defeats outcome II in a head-to-head vote, outcome II defeats outcome III, and outcome III defeats outcome I. For this reason, the majority coalition of voters A and B in favor of outcome II may be overturned by a majority of voters A and C in favor of outcome I; in turn, this majority may be overturned by a coalition of voters B and C in favor of outcome III. This cycle could continue indefinitely if every

Table 2.1. Stable Majority

Preference Rank	Voter A	Voter B	Voter C
1	Outcome I	Outcome II	Outcome III
2	Outcome II	Outcome I	Outcome II
3	Outcome III	Outcome III	Outcome I

outcome can be reversed by a future majority and preferences remain unchanged.

Lincoln described precisely such a cyclical majority with respect to slavery politics in the 1850s. In 1859 he wrote:

> It is probable that no act of territorial organization could be passed by the present Senate; and almost certainly not by both the Senate and House of Representatives. If an act declared the right of congress to exclude slavery, the Republicans would vote for it, and both wings of the democracy [i.e., the northern and southern wings of the Democratic Party] against it. If it denied the power to either exclude or protect it, the Douglasites [northern Democrats] would vote for it, and both the Republicans and slave-coders [southern Democrats] against it. If it denied the power of either to exclude, and asserted the power to protect, the slave-coders would vote for it, and the Republicans and Douglasites against it.[34]

We could formalize Lincoln's observation as follows: There are three principal groups in Congress with respect to slavery in the territories: Republicans, Douglasites, and slave-coders. Republicans and Douglasites formed a majority against slave-coders, Douglasites and slave-coders formed a majority against Republicans, and Republicans and slave-coders formed a majority against Douglasites. The last of these majority coalitions, Republicans and slave-coders against Douglasites, might seem to be an improbable alliance of the two poles against the middle,

Table 2.2. Cyclical Majorities

Preference Rank	Voter A	Voter B	Voter C
1	Outcome I	Outcome II	Outcome III
2	Outcome II	Outcome III	Outcome I
3	Outcome III	Outcome I	Outcome II

but if one believed that Douglas's position was unprincipled and incoherent, as Lincoln did, it would not be unreasonable for Republicans and slave-coders to form a temporary alliance to eliminate the Douglasite middle position in favor of a clear, dichotomous choice. Indeed, as noted in chapter 5, one principal purpose of Lincoln's 1858 "House Divided" speech was to eliminate the Douglasite middle position and force a clear yes-or-no vote on extending slavery to the territories.

Political scientist William Riker has written extensively on the difficulty and sometimes impossibility of aggregating voter preferences into a clear expression of the popular will. He has described the fractured American politics surrounding the 1860 election and analyzed Lincoln's political tactics (although he overlooks Lincoln's observations on cyclical majorities). In *Liberalism against Populism* Riker argues that in the 1860 presidential election, "Lincoln, Douglas, and Bell were in a cycle, and all three clearly defeated Breckinridge." Riker describes a fluid scenario in which, given voters' positions on slavery in the territories, Lincoln, Douglas, or Bell could have come out on top, depending on which set of voting rules were employed. As a result, so far as aggregating the popular will was concerned, "there was complete disequilibrium in 1860." In this case, the peculiar rules of the Electoral College secured the win for Lincoln. A single-round election with a plurality winner also would have given the victory to Lincoln. In contrast, other available methods for aggregating preferences, such as ranked voting and approval voting, might have elected Douglas or Bell.[35]

I do not dispute Riker's claim that the 1860 election revealed no clear majority position on slavery or that different voting rules might have resulted in the election of Douglas or Bell. But the results of the 1860 election, even as Riker presents them, were far from meaningless as an expression of the popular will. If Riker's book could have traveled back in time and fallen into Lincoln's hands, he would have noted Riker's admission that Breckinridge's position—that Congress *must* protect the institution of slavery in all federal territories—could not have prevailed nationally in 1860 under any set of plausible voting rules. The election results suggested a clear and sizable national majority against this position.

The impossibility, under certain conditions, of forming a stable majority presents some challenges to Lincoln's argument that a constitutionally checked majority can effectively function as the sovereign of a free people. If majority rule is paralyzed by instability and unable to make clear decisions on important matters, to that extent it ceases to function as a sovereign. Lincoln's 1859 observations about cyclical majorities in Congress reveal his frustration over the difficulty of forming a stable majority on slavery. But he clearly hoped the results of the 1860 elections would break the deadlock.

The theory of cyclical majorities, like rational choice approaches to politics in general, presupposes that the preferences of each agent remain fixed throughout the process: indecisiveness is a property of the collective decision, not of the individual agents participating in it, who are presumed to have unchanging, coherently ranked preferences throughout.[36] Rational choice theorists do not deny that voter preferences can and do change, whether through reasoning, persuasion, the passage of time, new issues, or some other cause. But rational choice theory takes *given* preferences as its starting point; preference change falls outside the scope of the theory. Rational choice theorists have argued that much of both stability and instability in political life can be accounted for by strategic manipulation of given preferences, without any modification of voters' underlying interests and values.[37]

Riker applies this method to Lincoln's tactics in his debates with Douglas. In *The Art of Political Manipulation* Riker describes a political technique he terms "heresthetic," meaning the strategic manipulation of fixed preferences, in contrast to "rhetoric," meaning the art of persuasion. Riker characterizes Lincoln as a politician "equally skilled as a heresthetician and a rhetorician," but it is Lincoln's heresthetic skill that interests him most. Riker retells the story of Lincoln's famous question to Douglas at the Freeport debate (August 27, 1858): "Can the people of a United States Territory, in any lawful way, against the wish of any citizen of the United States, exclude slavery from its limits prior to the formation of a State Constitution?"[38] Lincoln's question was an especially pointed one because Douglas had framed the 1854 Kansas-Nebraska Act to be deliberately ambiguous on this point, such that northern supporters of the act could argue that residents of a territory could vote to exclude slavery from the very outset of that territory's settlement process, while the act's southern supporters could insist that "pure nonintervention would prevail, with slaveholders free to enter the territory at will" up until the time a constitutional convention was "called to prepare for statehood.[39] By the time of the 1858 debates, Douglas's effort to present popular sovereignty in these Janus-faced terms had been complicated by the Supreme Court's *Dred Scott* decision, which asserted that neither Congress nor a territorial legislature had the constitutional power to prohibit slavery in the territories.

Lincoln's purpose at Freeport was to end Douglas's double game. If he answered yes to Lincoln's question, Douglas would consolidate his support among northern voters and improve his reelection prospects in Illinois, but he would alienate southerners whose support he would need if he ran for president in 1860. (Lincoln's question was phrased such that if a territorial legislature could keep slavery out simply by refusing to enact a slave code, it would count as an affirmative answer to Lincoln's question and thereby cost Douglas support in the South.) Conversely, if he answered no to Lincoln's question, Douglas would keep the support of southerners but risk his reelection to the Senate, without which his presidential prospects were nil. In the event, Douglas responded with a somewhat finessed yes to Lincoln's query in 1858, claiming that, by declining to enact positive legislation, territorial legislatures could effectively prohibit slavery without violating the Supreme Court's decision.[40] In response, southern Democrats engineered a fateful party split in 1860 rather than support Douglas's presidential nomination.[41]

For Riker, Lincoln's query was a brilliant heresthetic act. "In the heresthetical dilemma Lincoln posed to Douglas the purpose was to force Douglas to put himself in an undesirable position for winning some future election." Whereas the purpose of rhetoric is to persuade, the purpose of heresthetic is "to structure the decision-making situation to the speaker's advantage and the respondent's disadvantage."[42] In Riker's analysis, Lincoln's query was effective precisely because it did not depend on persuading anyone to change their minds; it simply brought the already opposed minds of Douglas's northern and southern supporters into direct confrontation.

Lincoln was unquestionably a skilled political tactician. But I suggest that his purpose in posing this question to Douglas was rhetorical—that is, directed toward persuasion—and not just heresthetical in Riker's sense. Recall that in his inaugural address Lincoln spoke of a majority "*changing easily*, with *deliberate* changes of popular opinions and sentiments" (emphasis added). Of course, unstable and cyclical majorities can occur without any alteration of popular opinions and sentiments. Alternatively, popular opinions and sentiments can change in undeliberate ways (e.g., when played upon by a demagogue or acting on a sudden fear). Lincoln was aware of both possibilities. But his defense of majority rule emphasized the majority's capacity for *deliberate* change of opinions and sentiments.

Lincoln's purpose in the Freeport query, for example, was to persuade voters that, however attractive Douglas's "popular sovereignty" doctrine may have sounded, it did not and could not function as a formula for sectional peace on the slavery question, which was Douglas's most important claim in its favor. Lincoln observed after the 1858 election that, despite the disappointing results, he had sown a seed "that will yet produce fruit . . . Douglas managed to be supported both as the best means to *break down,* and to *uphold* the slave power. No ingenuity can long keep those opposing elements in harmony."[43] Lincoln's tactical skill was unquestionably helpful in making this point, but his success ultimately depended on persuading voters to reason more carefully about the true character of Douglas's doctrine.

Lincoln was realistic about the possibilities and limits of public persuasion. He did not believe that voters whose first preference was to legalize slavery in every federal territory would be convinced in any significant number to support the Republican platform of nonextension. But he could realistically hope to persuade some voters who ranked Douglas's popular sovereignty first, Republicans' nonextension second, and the congressional slave code last to change their minds and rank nonextension first and popular sovereignty second. Such a modification of preference rankings would fundamentally alter the decision dynamic, effectively eliminating the Douglasite middle position over time and enabling the voting public to make a clear, dichotomous choice about whether to prohibit or permit slavery in the territories.

How Lincoln envisioned such a shift in public opinion occurring and, assuming a dichotomous choice were presented, how he believed secession and civil war could be prevented are important questions that I take up in later chapters. The key takeaway here is that Lincoln's defense of majority rule depended on the assumption that majorities, and the opinions and sentiments of the individuals composing them, were capable of deliberate change.

The Entrenched Majorities Problem

Lincoln described a majority as "always changing easily, with deliberate changes of popular opinions and sentiments." This compact formulation combines at least three separate ideas: (1) that the composition of governing majorities can and does change, (2) that majorities can easily change, and (3) that majorities can change as a result of reasoned public deliberation, not just unthinking passion.

In short, Lincoln's defense of majority rule assumed that majorities and minorities were not rigidly fixed. A critical mass of voters might shift their support from one party or one coalition to another, depending on the arguments presented to them, thereby transforming a former minority into a current majority, or vice versa. The majority-turned-minority, in turn, can hope to restore its fortunes in future elections. The fact that majorities are changeable—whether because of new elections, shifting legislative coalitions, the advent of new issues, demographic changes, or other reasons—provides an important check on the potential for majority tyranny. A governing majority has an incentive to respect the rights and interests of the minority if members of the majority know the tables might turn and relegate them to minority status.

But such conditions do not always hold true in practice. Under certain circumstances, entrenched majorities and minorities might emerge and endure over time, even if all members of the political community possess voting rights, political opposition is legal, and constitutional processes are respected. Rigid divisions might occur, for instance, where voting decisions always follow some ascriptive, prepolitical aspect of the individual—his or her ethnicity, race, language, or religion. In the literature of comparative politics, terms such as "plural," "segmented," and "deeply divided" are employed to describe societies of this kind.[44] Yet entrenched majorities and minorities can also emerge among citizens who are relatively homogeneous in terms of race, religion, and language because of geographic factors (extensive territory, difficult communication) or diverse, regionally concentrated economic interests. It should be emphasized that it is not the existence of ethnic, religious, racial, linguistic, geographic, or economic diversity that undermines the preconditions for healthy majority rule but the degree to which those differences control the political behavior of both elites and ordinary voters.

If, for whatever reason, majority and minority are never likely to exchange places, the potentially transformative effects of deliberation would be weakened. A permanently outvoted, relatively powerless group might retain the right to speak, but members of the majority, secure in their power, would have little motivation to listen. Members of the permanent majority, without violating constitutional rules, could calmly and rationally pursue policies systematically disadvantageous to the minority. The problem of entrenched majorities is widely recognized in contemporary democratic theory, though there is little agreement on the appropriate remedy.

The most obvious instance of entrenched majorities and minorities in Lincoln's time was the gulf between a free, enfranchised white majority and an oppressed, overwhelmingly disenfranchised Black minority. Because enslaved persons and most free persons of color were denied voting rights, this type of majority tyranny could be remedied only by emancipating everyone and extending voting rights to all, regardless of race. In Lincoln's time, such fundamental transformations could not be readily accomplished without civil war. But from the perspective of democratic theory, the fact that majorities oppress minorities when the latter are deprived of political and legal rights is an utterly unsurprising result. In theory, the remedy is obvious: enfranchise everyone. What was not obvious in Lincoln's time was how to accomplish this.

A more complicated *theoretical* challenge to Lincoln's defense of majority rule arises from the fact that majority tyranny can develop even when members of the minority continue to enjoy the right to vote, speak, publish, hold office, and organize political opposition. John C. Calhoun of South Carolina, with whose writings and speeches Lincoln was familiar, set forth this argument in its most comprehensive form. Calhoun was a slaveholder and a defender of slavery, but his critique of majority rule should not be dismissed. The logic of Calhoun's critique as well as his proposed remedy—the minority veto—have been applied to challenges faced by outvoted minorities in a number of modern-day political contexts, including Catholics in Northern Ireland and African Americans in the contemporary United States.[45] Moreover, politically, Lincoln needed to reckon with the power of the white, southern slaveholding minority, whose sense of its constitutional rights and privileges had been significantly shaped by Calhoun. Thus, politically as well as theoretically, Lincoln had to answer Calhoun.

Calhoun's critique of majority rule did not begin with the existence of deep social, linguistic, or cultural divisions. Nor did Calhoun initially target majority rule principally for the threat it posed to slavery, although safeguarding slavery motivated his thought to some degree throughout his life, and from 1837 until his death in 1850, it became an all-consuming commitment. Instead, his starting point was the negative impact of the 1828 "tariff of abominations," designed to shield northern domestic manufacturers from foreign competition, on southern states whose economy was tied to growing and exporting cotton.[46] This protective tariff raised production costs for southern planters and, at the same time, diminished the purchasing power of English textile manufacturers, the chief consumers of southern cotton. Sectional divisions over the 1828 tariff were not principally racial, ethnic, or religious but were rooted in the kind of distributional conflicts that exist in every modern political community, no matter how homogeneous. Calhoun argued that the political process itself and the actions of government under majority rule would inevitably create and subsequently reinforce deep and permanent divisions between majority and minority.

Calhoun's most concise version of this argument came in an 1833 speech in which he dramatized the problem by means of a simple model. Suppose a political community consists of just five persons. The community decides democratically, by a vote of three to two, to levy a tax on all five members. It then decides, again democratically by a vote of three to two, to distribute all the benefits of the tax to the three-person majority, leaving nothing for the other two. By repetition of such action over time, a selfish majority could systematically transfer to itself the wealth of the minority.[47] Even though the process was democratic, the laws applied equally to all, and no constitutional rights were directly infringed, from the perspective of the minority, the result was equivalent to being ruled by the most absolute of tyrants. Territorially extensive political communities like the United States were especially susceptible to majoritarian pathologies of this kind because the citizens directly benefiting from the governing majority's policies were their own neighbors, whose interests they understood and shared, while the losers resided thousands of miles away and made their living in ways that members of the majority could barely comprehend.

To this elementary model Calhoun added the workings of political parties to explain how a unified majority could emerge over time in a diversified society where no single interest initially enjoyed a majority. Put another way: he attempted to explain why Madison's solution in Federalist 10—which sought to prevent majority tyranny by increasing the number and diversity of interests—could not work in the long run. Calhoun admitted that the interests constituting modern political parties may initially be diverse and subject to internal conflict. But once the political-economic bargain was struck, all the favored interests would unite and lock the deal into place, at the expense of those interests and geographic sections excluded from it. In this way, a sectionally based majority coalition, temporary at first, would become a disciplined, unified majority party eventually capable of securing control of all branches of the federal government.[48]

In Calhoun's view, the same pattern was in play when antislavery agitation replaced the tariff as the chief source of conflict between North and South. The northern campaign against slavery, Calhoun believed, was caused by an unholy alliance between a northern majority motivated (as all majorities are) by economic and political self-interest and a small but potent abolitionist minority inspired by religious fanaticism. The abolitionist minority was just large enough to give it leverage in northern states where two roughly equal parties, looking to secure a majority, competed for its support. In this way, Calhoun feared, the workings of party politics would eventually place all three branches of the national government in the hands of a majority that was fundamentally hostile to the slave-based economy and social order of the South.[49]

Calhoun argued that each individual state in the Union was fully sovereign, and as such, it possessed the constitutional right to nullify within its own borders any federal law, court ruling, or executive act with which it strongly disagreed. He also insisted that states had a constitutional right to secede from the Union. And he believed that if antislavery agitation continued, the slave states would be forced to resort to secession.

Nevertheless, Calhoun was realistic about the enormous human and economic costs of secession, which he compared to a bloody knife passing through a living body.[50] He conceived his political and constitutional theory as a peaceful alternative to secession for alienated, geographically concentrated minority interests. Such minorities would not be driven to the extreme remedy of secession, he maintained, if each "section" or "interest" of the political community (especially including the slaveholding interest) had the power to block any federal law, court decision, or executive act to which that section or interest was strongly opposed. Near the end of his life, Calhoun insisted that the Constitution be amended to create a kind of dual presidency, with one co-president representing the North and the other the South, each of whom possessed veto rights over legislation and actions of the other co-president.[51] More generally, Calhoun argued that the remedy to majority tyranny was a decision rule he called the "concurrent majority," whereby each important "portion" or "interest" of the community enjoyed veto rights over collective decisions. Calhoun did not believe such an arrangement would generate deadlock or anarchy. Instead, he claimed, the threat of anarchy and the urgent need for common action would force all interests and sections to work together for the common good—which, in the American context, included what Calhoun regarded as the good of protecting and perpetuating the institution of slavery.[52]

As I have argued elsewhere, Calhoun's proposed remedy to the pathologies of majority rule is a cure worse than the disease.[53] But his analysis of how majority rule can degenerate into entrenched domination by one section of the country at the expense of another should be taken seriously. The failure of the remedy does not disprove the diagnosis.

Lincoln and Sectional Majorities

When Lincoln, in his defense of majority rule, asserted that "unanimity is impossible" (so the only alternative to majority rule was minority rule or anarchy), he was in substance responding to Calhoun. Lincoln regarded Calhoun's constitutional doctrine of nullification as a disguised form of minority rule.

But Lincoln did not dismiss the objection that sectional majorities were oppressive. On the contrary, he took it seriously and sought to answer it. He observed in 1856, "It is constantly objected to Fremont & Dayton [the Republican presidential and vice-presidential candidates that year] that they are supported by a *sectional* party, who, by their *sectionalism*, endanger the National Union. This objection, more than all others, causes men, really opposed to slavery extension, to hesitate. Practically, it is the most difficult objection we have to meet."[54]

The sectionalism charge was also key to the justification for preemptive secession by the slave states of the lower South in response to Lincoln's election. In the secessionists' view, Lincoln's election was illegitimate not because he did not win a majority of the popular vote but because all his electoral votes and the vast majority of his popular votes came from the free states. This made him, South Carolina secessionists claimed, the candidate of a "sectional party": "A geographical line has been drawn across the Union, and all the States north of that line have united in the election of a man to the high office of President of the United States, whose opinions and purposes are hostile to slavery."[55] Even if Lincoln had received a majority of the popular vote, South Carolina would have seceded before he could take office.

It did not violate the Constitution to win a presidential election entirely on the votes from one section of the country, but such a result was deeply unsettling. In democratic politics, practices essential to governing in the common good—including listening, learning, persuading, compromising, and demonstrating respect—are closely connected with vote getting. Conversely, if candidates or political parties know they can win without receiving any votes from an entire section of the country, they have little motivation to listen, learn, persuade, or respect the voters living in that section. Given Lincoln's own emphasis on *deliberate* majorities, a democratic process that inhibited substantive political communication between different geographic sections would be problematic even if it did not violate the Constitution. Lincoln considered it essential that Republicans field candidates, solicit votes, and engage in public debate in the slave states, even if the party was unlikely to win an election there in the foreseeable future.

Lincoln examined the sectionalism objection in his July 1856 "Fragment on Sectionalism" (on which he based his public speeches during the 1856 campaign) and again in his Cooper Institute address in February 1860. In both documents Lincoln sought to answer the charge that the Republican Party was inherently sectional. In "Fragment on Sectionalism," Lincoln wrote: "The thing which gives most color to the charge of Sectionalism, made against those who oppose the spread of slavery into free territory, is the fact that . . . the Extensionists [those who favor extending slavery to the territories] can get votes all over the Nation, while the Restrictionists [the Republicans] can get them only in the free states."[56] In the Cooper Institute address, Lincoln, rhetorically addressing the South, stated: "You say we are sectional. We deny it. . . . You produce your proof; and what is it? Why, that our party has no existence in your section. The fact is substantially true, but does it prove the issue?" Lincoln admitted that, at present, the Republican Party received nearly all its votes from the free states. But he denied that Republicans were a "sectional party" in the sense of designing to "wrong your section for the benefit of ours."[57]

In his replies to the sectionalism charge, Lincoln made three basic points: (1) that in a presidential election, the sectional distribution of votes does not affect the constitutional legitimacy of the result; (2) that in the contest over whether slavery would be prohibited in the territories, neither side was any more or less sectional than the other; and (3) that the Republican Party was quite willing to speak and listen to voters in the slave states, but leaders there would not permit the rightness or wrongness of slavery to be publicly debated.

In the sectionalism fragment, Lincoln made the initial observation that, however "*indignant* and *excited*" some people become over the "manifestation of *sectionalism*," the Constitution itself "remains calm—keeps cool—upon the subject." Republicans' critics charged that it would be "unendurable *sectionalism*" to elect John Fremont (the 1856 Republican presidential nominee) "exclusively by free-state votes." Lincoln pointed out that it was equally true that "[James] Buchanan's friends expect to elect him, if at all, chiefly by slave-state votes."[58] So long as the constitutionally specified process was followed, the geographic distribution of the votes did not affect the legitimacy of the result.

But Lincoln recognized that simply emphasizing the Constitution's silence about sectionalism was not a sufficient answer—otherwise, he would not have called it "the most difficult objection we have to meet." The charge that the Republican Party took a self-interested "sectional" position on a crucial public issue—the future of slavery—could not be dismissed simply by pointing to the Constitution's silence on sectionalism.

Lincoln denied, however, that the question "Shall slavery be allowed to enter into U.S. territories, now legally free?" was a sectional one. Instead, it was a fundamental question of right or wrong in which Americans, no matter where they lived, had a stake and on which they had to take a position. In the 1856 sectionalism fragment he wrote: "I beg to know *how one* side of that question is more sectional than the other?" If "one side be as sectional as the other," then "each must choose sides of the question on some other ground—as I should think, according, as the one side or the other, shall appear nearest right."[59] To claim, as slaveholders did, that the Republican position was sectional because it would "wrong" the South simply begged the central question, which was the rightness or wrongness of slavery itself.

In the 1860 Cooper Institute speech, Lincoln's discussion again turned the question away from sectionalism to one of fundamental right or wrong. He did not condemn the South for taking the position it did. Instead, Lincoln extended an invitation to engage in honest debate:

> If we do repel you by any wrong principle or practice, the fault is ours; but this brings you to where you ought to have started—to a discussion of the right or wrong of our principle. If our principle, put in practice, would wrong your

section for the benefit of ours, or for any other object, then our principle, and we with it, are sectional, and are justly opposed and denounced as such. Meet us, then, on the question of whether our principle, put in practice, would wrong your section; and so meet us as if it were possible that something may be said on our side.

Lincoln then asked, "Do you accept the challenge?"[60]

He knew the answer would be no. Southerners instead demanded that the Republican position be condemned "without a moment's consideration." Rhetorically addressing the South, he observed: "You consider yourselves a reasonable and a just people. . . . Still, when you speak of us Republicans, you do so only to denounce us as reptiles, or, at the best, as no better than outlaws. You will grant a hearing to pirates or murderers, but nothing like it to 'Black Republicans.' . . . Bring forward your charges and specifications, and then be patient long enough to hear us deny or justify."[61]

Lincoln's request appears modest: he asks not that slave-state leaders change their minds about slavery but merely that they "grant a hearing" to Republicans. But Lincoln and his listeners knew that slave states had long suppressed antislavery speech, press, and political organization and blocked the distribution of antislavery writings by US mail. Indeed, southern leaders demanded that antislavery speech and organizations also be suppressed in the North. Moreover, slave-state leaders had tolerated and even encouraged extralegal violence against anyone suspected, accurately or inaccurately, of being an abolitionist.[62] Members of Congress who criticized slavery in congressional debate made themselves targets of duels or other less "honorable" forms of assault.[63] Thus, advocates of slavery had full freedom to press their case in the North, while the opponents of slavery had long been prevented from freely expressing their views in the South and took risks doing so even in the North.

This puts the South's accusation that Republican votes came entirely from the North in a very different light. Insofar as that charge implied that Republicans were unwilling to speak and listen to southern voters, the appropriate remedy would be for Republicans to seek and receive votes in the South. That was indeed the direction of Lincoln's response. Yet from southern leaders' perspective, a Republican Party actively *seeking* votes in the South was far more alarming than the prospect of Republicans simply *ignoring* southern voters. Most slave-state leaders did not believe—nor did Lincoln expect—that Republicans would soon start to win elections in slave states. But for Republicans to field candidates for public office in the South would have legitimized forms of antislavery speech and political organization that slave-state leaders had spent decades suppressing.

In the Cooper Institute address, Lincoln acknowledged that "our party . . . gets no votes in your section." But as he pointed out, if "we should, without change of principle, begin to get votes in your section, we should thereby cease to be sectional." He then added, provocatively, "you will probably soon find that we have ceased to be sectional, for we shall get votes in your section this very year [1860]."[64] As it turned out, even though Lincoln was kept off the ballot in all slave states of the lower South, he received 1,929 votes in Virginia, 2,294 votes in Maryland, 1,364 votes in Kentucky, 17,028 votes in Missouri, and 3,822 votes in Delaware, all of which were slaveholding states in 1860. These totals, though small, might have provided a foothold for future party expansion in the upper South if secession and war had not intervened. Daniel Crofts observes, "Once Lincoln was elected, secessionists persistently accused him of planning to build an antislavery party in the upper South"—which of course was exactly what Lincoln intended. In Tennessee, where Lincoln had been kept off the ballot in 1860, advocates of secession warned that Lincoln and William Seward (who became Lincoln's secretary of state) would employ "postmasterships, mail agencies and government contracts" to build an antislavery party in the upper South; by 1864, "a 'Black Republican ticket' would be 'openly run in Tennessee.'"[65] William Freehling argues that slave-state leaders were less alarmed by John Brown's violent raid on Harpers Ferry than by the prospect of peaceful "invasion" of the upper South by the Republican Party, which sought to turn white nonslaveholders against the powerful, overbearing slaveholding elite that had long dominated the South's economy and politics.[66]

Recall Calhoun's description of a selfish, regionally concentrated majority employing formally neutral political rules and processes to entrench itself in power and then enact policies harmful to the rights and interests of a comparatively powerless, regionally concentrated, chronically outvoted minority. The coalition of interests responsible for the 1828 "tariff of abominations"—the context for the development of Calhoun's critique of majority rule—arguably exemplified a sectional majority pushing its agenda at the expense of the wider community.

But Lincoln convincingly showed that the schema of a selfish sectional majority versus a beleaguered sectional minority did not accurately describe the contest between the opponents and advocates of perpetuating human bondage in the United States. Calhoun had argued that the majority, playing by the same constitutional rules as the minority, could rig the outcome to its own advantage. But in the case of slavery, as Lincoln pointed out, the powerful proslavery minority demanded the right to play by an entirely different set of constitutional rules than the antislavery majority. Advocates of slavery were free to speak, publish, debate, organize politically, and run for office in every state of the Union, free or slave, and were protected by public authorities against mob action. Opponents of slavery were not permitted to speak, publish, debate, organize politically, or run for office in most of the slave states, and in many cases, public authorities actively encouraged extralegal violence against anyone suspected of abolitionist leanings.[67] Thus, the picture of an overbearing northern majority dictating policy to an oppressed southern minority (i.e., slaveholders) is inaccurate. The latter was a powerful, well-organized, potentially violent sectional minority imposing its own rules on a less organized, less powerful, less committed northern majority.

"Palpable" versus "Remote" Sectional Interests

A key component of the sectionalism charge was that those who favored extending the institution of slavery could get votes all over the nation, while those who favored restriction could get votes only in the free states. Defenders of slavery claimed that these voting patterns proved that extending slavery to all territories was genuinely in the common good (otherwise, why would a significant free-state minority support it?), while the Republican policy of restricting slavery was a transparently selfish grab for power and wealth, with no appeal to the presumably more impartial voters residing in the South.

In response, Lincoln offered a different explanation for these geographic voting patterns. He denied (as noted earlier) that either position on slavery in the territories was inherently more sectional than the other. He also denied that there was "any difference in the mental or moral structure of the people North and South" that explained the sectional voting patterns. In other words, southerners were by nature no more or less selfish than northerners. This was a point Lincoln empha-sized often during the 1850s, in contrast to many abolitionists' charac-terization of slaveholders as reprobates and unrepentant sinners.[68]

The real reason, Lincoln claimed, why "extensionists" could get some votes in the North and nearly all the votes in the South, while "restrictionists" could get votes only in the North, was that "the people of the South have an immediate palpable and immensely great pecuni-ary interest" in extending slavery, "while, with the people of the North, it is merely an abstract question of moral right, with only *slight*, and *remote* pecuniary interest added." Lincoln estimated the property value of southern slaves at $1 billion. "Let it be permanently settled that this property may extend to new territory, without restraint, and it greatly *enhances*, perhaps quite *doubles*, its value at once." (Conversely, *restricting* the spread of slavery would *diminish* the property value of slaves. The Republican policy of restriction had real economic consequences, and slaveholders knew it.) "This immense, palpable pecuniary interest, on the question of extending slavery, unites the Southern people, as one man."[69]

In contrast, Lincoln observed in the 1856 sectionalism fragment, "It can not be demonstrated that the *North* will gain a dollar by restricting [slavery]." Instead, "moral principle is all, or nearly all, that unites us of the North. Pity 'tis, it is so, but this is a looser bond, than pecuniary interest. Right here is the plain cause of *their perfect* union and *our want* of it." Moral principle may have furnished a "looser bond" than economic self-interest, but that did not make it altogether ineffective. In his 1854 Kansas-Nebraska speech, Lincoln observed, "The great majority, south as well as north, have human sympathies, of which they can no more divest themselves than they can of their sensibility to physical pain." The advantage of these "human sympathies" is that they are present in nearly everyone (Lincoln admitted that some "natural tyrants" lacked them), so these sympathies can potentially shape the conduct of people of all races, sexes, political persuasions, and economic circumstances. Their disadvantage is that their practical effect can be weakened or neu-tralized when they come into conflict with someone's "great pecuniary interest." That was why southerners could be morally repelled by "the sneaking individual . . . known as the 'SLAVE DEALER,'" yet still purchase his services.[70]

Lincoln did not claim, however, that opposition to the spread of slav-ery was entirely disinterested; nor did he believe that human beings in large numbers would ever act in wholly altruistic ways. Instead, he sought to persuade white Americans that they had a real, if not immediately obvious, interest in opposing the enslavement of Blacks. His oft-expressed ideal of a society freed of the curse of slavery, which would "afford to all an unfettered start and a fair chance, in the race of life," was in a broad sense an appeal to the ordinary white person's economic self-interest.[71] Moreover, if white Americans thought the matter through, they would realize that any argument used to justify the enslavement of Blacks could be employed to justify their own enslavement.[72] But such considerations were "remote," as Lincoln acknowledged. White Americans' self-interest in opposing the enslavement of anyone, of any race, was something that needed to be *explained*—a task for political leadership—in a way that palpable economic gains and losses did not.

Secession and Democratic Deliberation

Thus far, this chapter has examined several critical problems related to majority rule that Lincoln recognized and attempted to address. But there remains one enormous potential objection to Lincoln's defense of majority rule in the inaugural address: secession had already rendered it irrelevant. Because South Carolina, Mississippi, Florida, Alabama, Georgia, Louisiana, and Texas seceded before Lincoln took office, one could argue that citizens of those states had placed themselves beyond the reach of any *United States* majority, no matter how just or deliberate it was. To raise this objection is not necessarily to endorse a constitutional right of secession. It merely recognizes that, whether secession was constitutional or unconstitutional, justified or unjustified, the leaders of those states and a majority of their citizens no longer considered themselves bound by the laws and decisions of the United States, which, in their view, was now a foreign power.

To frame the problem in general form: majority rule presupposes a political community whose boundaries have already been defined. One cannot meaningfully speak of a majority unless one has first determined which people and territories belong to that political community: a majority of *whom*? To reply that the majority itself should decide where and how boundaries are to be drawn begs the question, because majorities and minorities will be manufactured by the very act of line drawing. During the cascade of secessions-within-secessions that accompanied the meltdown of Yugoslavia in the 1990s, a bitter joke was common: "Why should we be a minority in your state, when you can be a minority in our state?"[73]

If majority decisions about who is included and who is excluded are inherently question-begging (because majorities exist only after a community's boundaries have been drawn), then Lincoln's assertion of majority support for the position that "the Union is unbroken" would be arbitrary.[74] *Which* majority supported that claim? But the secessionist constitutional claim (i.e., that the seceding states were no longer part of the United States) would be equally arbitrary. Either way, one could argue that both sides engaged in violent acts of boundary-drawing disguised as democratic acts of consent.

Many contemporary democratic theorists maintain that there is no *principled* answer to the question of who is included in a particular political community, who is excluded, and who draws (or redraws) the lines. After reminding the reader of chronically unresolved boundary disputes in Northern Ireland, India and Pakistan, Yugoslavia, Nigeria, Israel and surrounding territories, and countless other cases, Brian Barry observes that "the majority principle has no way of solving them, either in practice or in theory. In practice . . . every move to satisfy majority aspirations leaves the remaining minorities even more vulnerable." Barry is especially critical of the "so-called 'principle of national self-determination' espoused by the Versailles Treaty of 1919" because it simply begged the question which minorities counted as nations and which did not. Barry comes to the bleak conclusion that regardless of how the lines are ultimately drawn, "the majority principle can offer no guidance." In Robert Dahl's *Democracy and Its Critics*, which features a running debate between an advocate and a critic of majority rule, one of the few points on which they fully agree is that the principle of majority rule cannot resolve disputes of this kind.[75]

In contrast, Lincoln spoke as if even the question of whether Americans would remain a single people or divide into two or more peoples could be decided peacefully, deliberately, and democratically. Indeed, he believed that not only the survival of the Union but also the sustainability of democracy itself were at stake in the people's capacity to decide these most difficult matters (slavery and secession) peacefully. Given the subsequent course of events, Lincoln's hope for a peaceful resolution of the secession crisis may seem especially quixotic. Nevertheless, I believe his reasoning merits examination. Here, I draw from both Lincoln's first inaugural address, delivered before the war began, and his July 4, 1861, message to Congress in special session, at which point all hope of a peaceful resolution had passed.

When Lincoln argued in the inaugural address "that in contemplation of universal law, and of the Constitution, the Union of these States is perpetual," he did not mean the United States could never, under any circumstances, be legitimately divided or dissolved. He meant that any such decision had to be the act of the *whole* people of the United States, not a single state or section. Americans in every state and section, not just those living in seceding states, had an enormous stake in the decision. Elsewhere in the address he remarked: "This country, with its institutions, belongs to the people who inhabit it. Whenever they shall grow weary of the existing government, they can exercise their *constitutional* right of amending it, or their *revolutionary* right to dismember, or overthrow it." A constitutional dismemberment through amendment might be peaceful, if it followed the prescribed process. Lincoln considered it absurd for a constitution to provide "in its own organic law for its own termination," but it is conceivable that the people of the United States could first enact a constitutional amendment specifically authorizing state secession and then act on it. Alternatively, a revolutionary dismemberment of the United States, circumventing constitutional processes, was unlikely to be peaceful. But Lincoln's phrasing implies that if a majority of the people of the United States no longer wanted to belong to the United States, disunion would be impossible to prevent.[76]

Lincoln returned to the abstract possibility of democratically dismembering the Union in his July 4, 1861, message to Congress in special session. He insisted that he had a personal obligation to preserve the Union by all constitutional means in his power. It would be contrary to "so sacred a trust" for a president to consent "that these institutions shall perish." Nevertheless, "the people themselves, and not their servants, can safely reverse their own deliberate decisions."[77] Lincoln implies here that in subsequent elections, the American people might conceivably choose a different president and different members of Congress who *would* consent to the partition of the United States.

However, Lincoln had long been confident that a majority of the American people would never choose to dissolve the Union. This issue had been on his mind since at least 1856: "A majority will never dissolve the Union. Can a minority do it?"[78] Lincoln's judgment on this point was reinforced by the strong support for preserving the Union, extending across party lines, that he observed everywhere in the free states as he traveled eastward from Illinois in early 1861 and headed for his inauguration.[79] Thus, when Lincoln's inaugural address acknowledged that the people of the United States (by which he meant the whole people) might "grow weary" of the Union and decide to dismember it, he meant this as an abstract possibility, not a practically likely one. He mentioned it to underscore that the American people had *not* chosen this outcome. If he had simply asserted that "this Union cannot be dissolved under any circumstances," he would have set himself in opposition to the principle of popular sovereignty. To argue instead that the people could choose to dissolve this Union, but had not done so, is to affirm the principle of popular sovereignty.

But merely affirming that the people of the United States had the right to choose whether to separate or remain undivided did nothing to persuade those parts of the people who had already declared themselves separate or who had not yet chosen to secede but reserved the right to do so if circumstances changed (e.g., the states of Virginia, Tennessee, North Carolina, and Arkansas).[80] For Lincoln's appeal for a peaceful resolution of the secession crisis to be anything more than wishful thinking, the people of the slave states (those that had already seceded and those that were debating whether to do so) would have to be part of that process in some way. This could not be accomplished by simply asserting the unconstitutionality of secession. Even if the Constitution allowed the use of military force to prevent states from exiting the Union, Lincoln recognized that the only *peaceful* option was to persuade the citizens of those states to return.

Here, Lincoln invoked the principle and practice of democratic deliberation. On March 4, 1861, such an appeal was not transparently hopeless in the cases of Virginia, North Carolina, Tennessee, and Arkansas or in the slave states of Maryland, Kentucky, Missouri, and Delaware, which remained in the Union even after Fort Sumter. The seven states that seceded before Lincoln took office (South Carolina, Mississippi, Florida, Alabama, Georgia, Louisiana, and Texas) were a different story. In principle, the people of those states could have reversed their secession vote. But those states had already joined an alternative national project, the Confederate States of America, which had seized nearly every federal fort and other federal property within their boundaries, extensively armed itself for a military contest against an ill-prepared Union, and acknowledged no constitutional right of secession. Thus, a seceding state's return to the Union was difficult to imagine, even if a majority of its voters so desired. But no lethal shots had yet been fired,[81] which, from Lincoln's perspective, meant that the door to peaceful deliberation had not yet closed.

It was under these circumstances that Lincoln made his case for reasoned deliberation in the first inaugural address. The most direct appeal to deliberation comes near the end of the address: "My countrymen, one and all, think calmly and *well*, upon this whole subject. Nothing valuable can be lost by taking time. If there be an object to *hurry* any of you, in hot haste, to a step which you would never take *deliberately*, that object will be frustrated by taking time; but no good object can be frustrated by it." Here, Lincoln set up an opposition between deliberation, which is marked by a measured pace, calmness of mind, and a willingness to examine the "whole subject," and a mood of "hot haste" (a phrase he frequently used to characterize secessionists), which disposes people to immediate, ill-considered action that they "would never take *deliberately*" if they understood the consequences.[82]

One prerequisite of genuine deliberation is accurate, publicly available information. Thus Lincoln, responding to what he claimed were unfounded apprehensions that his administration would threaten the peace, property, and personal security of southerners, observed that "the most ample evidence to the contrary has all the while existed, and been open to their inspection. It is found in nearly all the published speeches of him who now addresses you." He returned to the theme of accurate information a few pages later: "Will you hazard so desperate a step, while there is any possibility that any portion of the ills you fly from, have no real existence?"[83] Lincoln spoke as though southerners had been led incorrectly to believe that he and the Republican Party were violent abolitionists like John Brown and that they might reconsider their decision upon receiving more accurate information. (Lincoln did not acknowledge the possibility that a majority of southern voters might choose to secede even if they accurately understood his position on slavery.)

Genuine deliberation requires time, as well as the absence of any perceived threat requiring immediate action. Lincoln assured his listeners that this precondition had also been met:

> There needs to be no bloodshed or violence, and there shall be none, unless it be forced upon the national authority. The power confided to me, will

be used to hold, occupy, and possess the property, and places belonging to the government; and to collect the duties and imposts; but beyond what may be necessary for these objects, there will be no invasion—no using of force against, or among the people anywhere.

Lincoln's policy before Fort Sumter—that is, holding federal property, while deliberately putting secessionists in the position of firing the first shot—has often been analyzed and debated from the perspective of military strategy. But here, Lincoln characterized the policy principally as a means of ensuring the preconditions for calm political deliberation. The "no invasion" passage is followed immediately by another passage stressing deliberation: "So far as possible, the people everywhere shall have that sense of perfect security which is most favorable to calm thought and reflection."[84]

Furthermore, democratic deliberation requires a willingness to tolerate disagreement, to respect fellow citizens who think differently, even if you cannot persuade them to adopt your point of view and they cannot persuade you to adopt theirs. Respect of this kind is necessary so that citizens with different views on one issue can cooperate in other matters on which agreement might be possible and refrain from resorting to violence when agreement cannot be reached. In this spirit, Lincoln made what might seem a comically understated observation: "One section of our country believes slavery is *right*, and ought to be extended, while the other believes it is *wrong*, and ought not to be extended. This is the only substantial dispute." This was indeed a *very* substantial dispute, and Lincoln did not pretend otherwise. His purpose in naming this centrally important dispute in the inaugural address was not to call for its imminent resolution or to demand that southerners change their minds, both of which were unlikely. Nor was his purpose to reaffirm the rightness of his own (and his party's) position on slavery, which would have been counterproductive under the circumstances. He framed it instead as one of those matters on which (as phrased elsewhere in the document) "we divide . . . into majorities and minorities." Though the dispute was a substantial one, Lincoln insisted that it did not fall outside the range of peaceful, democratic discussion, deliberation, and decision. Disagreement on critical matters did not make fellow citizens into enemies. "We are not enemies, but friends. We must not be enemies."[85]

What is arguably Lincoln's most powerful expression on the theme of democratic deliberation—"time, discussion, and the ballot box"—

appears twice in his July 4, 1861, message to Congress. By this time, peaceful deliberation had clearly failed to resolve the crisis; the Confederates had fired on Fort Sumter, forcing the slave states of the upper South to choose sides. Nevertheless, Lincoln reintroduced the peaceful deliberation theme, this time to emphasize how radically that ideal had been violated by the Confederacy's decision to initiate war and to argue that restoring the conditions enabling genuine deliberation was an important goal of the Union war effort.

The phrase first appears in the message following Lincoln's detailed description of the pre–Fort Sumter policy of holding "public places and property, not already wrested from the government," while refraining from retaking anything already seized and "relying for the rest, on time, discussion, and the ballot box." Here, as in the inaugural address, Lincoln's key justification for this strategy was that it would allow time and space for peaceful deliberation, without conceding the legitimacy of secession. He returned to the phrase a few pages later, this time emphasizing that secessionists fully understood that the small garrison at Fort Sumter "could, by no possibility, commit aggression upon them" and that its purpose was "merely to maintain visible possession, and thus to preserve the Union from actual, and immediate dissolution—trusting, as herein-before stated, to time, discussion, and the ballot box, for final adjustment." The aims of the fort's assailants, Lincoln asserted, were precisely the reverse: to foreclose any resort to time, discussion, and the ballot box and instead to force "immediate dissolution" of the Union.[86]

Lincoln's "time, discussion, and the ballot box" phrases connect to a famous passage later in the message characterizing the American Civil War as a kind of high-stakes test. "Our popular government has often been called an experiment," Lincoln observed. The seceding states, by violently resisting the outcome of a free and fair election, had put that experiment to the test. It is now our responsibility, Lincoln continued, "to demonstrate to the world, that those who can fairly carry an election, can also suppress a rebellion—that ballots are the rightful, and peaceful, successors of bullets; and that when ballots have fairly, and constitutionally, decided, there can be no successful appeal, back to bullets; that there can be no successful appeal, except to ballots themselves, at succeeding elections."[87] Lincoln here restated his claim from the first inaugural address that a deliberate, constitutionally checked majority is the only true sovereign of a free people.

Deliberation and Force

Lincoln's call for calm deliberation rather than "hot haste" invites some skeptical questions. For instance, someone might object (and a secessionist certainly *would* object) that Lincoln was inviting deliberation at the barrel of a gun. The key deliberation passage from the inaugural address—"My countrymen, one and all, think calmly and *well*, upon this whole subject"—is followed by this statement: "In *your* hands, my dissatisfied countrymen, and not in *mine*, is the momentous issue of civil war. The government will not assail *you*. You can have no conflict, without being yourselves the aggressors."[88] From the secessionists' perspective, the federal troops stationed at Fort Sumter became the aggressors by not immediately evacuating the fort as soon as South Carolina passed its ordinance of secession on December 20, 1860. That understanding of aggression depended entirely on whether one embraced secessionist political ideology. An ideologically committed Unionist could claim, with equal justification, that the seceding states were guilty of aggression for having already seized every federal military facility within their reach.

But one can reframe the deliberation-at-the-point-of-a-gun objection in a less ideological, question-begging form. Lincoln stated in the address that "there will be no invasion" of seceding states if they refrained from violence themselves; however, he *would* use military force, if necessary, to "hold, occupy, and possess" federal property. Suppose the leaders and citizens of the seceded states, now accurately informed of Lincoln's intentions, engaged in the unrushed, fully informed debate Lincoln called for. If, after time, discussion, and perhaps new results from the ballot box, the people of those states formally reversed their secession vote or—less improbably—decided not to forcibly challenge the federal government's continued possession of federal property, they would not become targets of federal military force. If, however, after a full and unconstrained debate among the (free white) citizens of the slave states they reaffirmed their original decision to secede, that decision would be empty unless those states also took possession, whether by treaty or by force, of the federal military facilities within their boundaries. Lincoln had already made it clear that this would be resisted by force. In short: if slave-state citizens make decision A, they remain at peace; if they make decision B, they find themselves at war.

This is not exactly an unconstrained deliberation. Contemporary theorists of deliberative democracy typically argue that genuine deliberation requires all sides to agree that contested questions will be decided by reasons advanced in the debate, followed by a fair vote among equals, not by resort to superior power or coercive force.[89] Lincoln himself shared this ideal, as expressed in his remarks about "time, discussion, and the ballot box" and the resolution of disagreements by "ballots" rather than "bullets." From his perspective, it was the secessionists who perverted the deliberative democratic process by responding to the unfavorable results of a free election with armed force. His purpose in resisting secession, he maintained, was to restore the normal deliberative democratic process. Nevertheless, the fact remained that, unless and until the secession crisis was resolved, the deliberations instrumental to resolving it would *not* be unconstrained by threats of force. Instead, all deliberations would be constrained by threats and counterthreats on both sides.

Another skeptical question can be raised: Suppose Lincoln had persuaded the seceded states to refrain from firing the first shot (or they had decided, for their own reasons, not to do so) and thereby secured additional time for "cooling off" and fully informed deliberation. Would more deliberation have accomplished anything?

On the one hand, a piece of evidence that arguably supports Lincoln's optimism about deliberation was that, in every state that seceded before his inauguration, secessionist leaders considered it essential to move forward at breakneck speed ("hot haste," in Lincoln's phrase), as though the consequences of delay would be fatal to their cause. Only in Georgia, where the secession vote was close, was there anything approaching a full public debate.[90] As David Potter observes about the strategy in the lower South: "The secessionists realized that although their cause was a popular one, its ascendancy was transient. Delay, from their standpoint, was almost worse than opposition. They seized the momentum of a popular emotional reaction to Lincoln's election and rode it through with astonishing speed."[91] William Freehling reports that the most committed secessionists in the lower South were a self-conscious minority, even within their own states and section, forcing the majority to respond to the minority's bold, irreversible acts. Alfred Aldrich, a South Carolina secessionist leader, asked: "Whoever waited for the common people when a great move was to be made? We must make the move & force them to follow."[92] Both South Carolina's unilateral secession in December 1860 (forcing other slave states to respond one way or another) and the Confederate decision to fire on Fort Sumter on April 12, 1861 (after secessionist efforts had stalled in the upper South) were action-forcing moves of this kind, placing a premium on speed and minimizing public deliberation. In this sense, a Confederate decision *not* to fire on Fort Sumter would have set in motion a different, not readily predictable chain of events.

On the other hand, it is unlikely that additional time and deliberation would have led many southerners to view Lincoln and his party's platform more positively. Near the opening of his inaugural address, Lincoln implied that his actual position on slavery had been misunderstood. In reply to those who feared that his administration would endanger "their property, and their peace, and personal security," Lincoln reiterated his pledge that "I have no purpose, directly or indirectly, to interfere with the institution of slavery in the States where it exists. I believe I have no lawful right to do so, and I have no inclination to do so. . . . The property, peace and security of no section are to be in anywise endangered by the now incoming Administration."[93] Is it possible that additional time and deliberation and his actual record in office would have enabled Lincoln to eliminate these unfounded apprehensions?

Maybe so, but it is not clear how much difference this would have made. The false notion that Lincoln was a violent abolitionist attained some currency in the South in the aftermath of the 1860 election. It is certainly the case, as Daniel Crofts points out, that secessionist demagogues persuaded many southerners that Lincoln and the Republicans were "bloodthirsty abolitionists."[94] But, as demonstrated in the Georgia secession debate, many of the most politically influential advocates of secession had an accurate understanding of Lincoln's policy commitments.[95] They were willing to risk civil war rather than allow Lincoln and the Republican Party to ban slavery in the territories and initiate a slow but inexorable process of weakening and ultimately extinguishing the institution of slavery. More time, information, and deliberation might have merely confirmed their fears about Lincoln's intentions.

Yet secession and civil war also carried the real risk of destroying the very institution—slavery—whose prosperity and long-term survival secessionists were most eager to preserve. No one in early 1861 could have foreseen the full extent and consequences of the war. But southern critics of secession warned that secession and war could put the institution of slavery at grave risk. If there was any chance that more time and deliberation could have made a difference in the South, it probably would have occurred by emphasizing this plausible (and, in the event, 100 percent correct) argument. For example, Henry Cooper, a Tennessee critic of secession, warned that "a dissolution of this Union is the death knell of African slavery." Secession would be followed by civil war, whereupon "in much blood" slavery "will be swept from the face of the Earth."[96] This proslavery, antisecession, antiwar argument was especially influential in the upper South's slave states, but it was also advanced, unsuccessfully, by critics of secession in the lower South (which stood to lose far more if the prediction proved accurate). Benjamin F. Perry of South Carolina urged that the Union "be saved as a bulwark against abolition." Herschel V. Johnson of Georgia argued that "slavery was safer in than out of the Union," a judgment shared by fellow Georgian Alexander Stephens.[97]

The political effectiveness of this argument, however, was highly conditional. Most southern leaders who made this argument presupposed that Congress or the courts would prevent Lincoln and his party from enacting key elements of their antislavery agenda. Blocking the Republican agenda stood a reasonably good chance in the short term, but blocking it forever was less likely. It is difficult to predict what a fully informed, deliberate southern public would have decided if faced with the choice between risking the sudden, violent destruction of slavery through civil war and accepting an agonizingly slow but peaceful end to the institution.

Finally, the effectiveness of the secession-endangers-slavery argument depended on both sides refraining from the use of armed force, for once war began (no matter who fired the first shot), slavery would be even more directly endangered. Under these altered circumstances, many formerly Unionist slaveholders would choose to fall in line behind the armed secessionists (even if they resented them for engineering an unnecessary war) rather than cast their lot with armed Republicans. Secessionists knew that by firing the first shot, they could end the debate.

3 | "The Capability of a People to Govern Themselves"

By the time he was inaugurated on March 4, 1861, Lincoln had developed a comprehensive understanding of majority rule in connection with the critical challenges of the time, including slavery and secession. But his understanding of majority rule did not spring forth fully formed. Instead, the compact and precise formulation in his first inaugural address synthesized a diverse range of themes and problems he had confronted at different points in his career in response to changing events. To name the most important shift: although Lincoln always considered slavery unjust, before 1854 he did not regard it as a threat to the survival of American popular self-government; from 1854 onward, he did.

My purpose in chapters 3–7 is to trace the development over time of Lincoln's understanding of majority rule and its relationship to slavery. The topics I take up—including political parties, public opinion, violence, natural right, and the survival of free institutions—are the same as those discussed in chapter 2, but now I present them as a moving picture rather than a snapshot. This chapter examines Lincoln's political thought with respect to popular sovereignty, majority rule, and slavery during the Whig phase of his career (1834–54).

In his earliest surviving political statement, an 1832 letter "To the People of Sangamo County" announcing his candidacy for the Illinois General Assembly, Lincoln opened by declaring his commitment to "the principles of true republicanism," which required that he communicate "my sentiments with regard to local affairs." He argued that universal public education was "the most important subject which we as a people can be engaged in" because it was essential that every man "be enabled to read the histories of his own and other countries, by which he may duly appreciate the value of our free institutions." He closed by acknowledging "his peculiar ambition," which was to be "truly esteemed of my fellow men, by rendering myself worthy of their esteem." He confessed, "I am young and unknown to many of you. I was born and have ever remained in the most humble walks of life. I have no wealthy or popular relations to recommend me. My case is thrown exclusively upon the independent voters of this county, and if elected they will have conferred a favor upon me, for which I shall be unremitting in my labors to compensate."[1]

Although nearly every candidate and party during the Jacksonian era declared support for republican principles,[2] Lincoln's letter gave those principles a distinctive and personal stamp. To him, republican principles signified a system of "free institutions" that welcomed the ambition and talents of young men from "the most humble walks of life," so long as they rendered themselves worthy in the eyes of the voters. But those same free institutions were vulnerable unless every citizen was taught to "duly appreciate" their value and to recognize what might threaten them. This was Lincoln's political core, evident through all stages of his career: the institutions of popular self-government were of immeasurable value for the opportunities they afforded to all, yet they could be lost. However, at this early stage of his career, Lincoln did not indicate that the persistence of slavery in the United States posed a significant threat to the survival of republican institutions.

That popular self-government might self-destruct—"die by suicide" as a result of mob violence and disrespect for law—was the theme of Lincoln's most significant public statement from his early career: his January 27, 1838, address to the Young Men's Lyceum of Springfield, Illinois. He described the need to *restrain* majorities from lawless behavior, but as a Whig party builder in Illinois, he also sought to *empower* majorities to act effectively through constitutionally provided channels. This latter element distinguished Lincoln from other Whigs who were suspicious of political parties and nervous about mass participation in politics. Lincoln, in contrast, sought to turn out as many voters as possible.

As a Whig, Lincoln pondered and sometimes publicly debated how and by whom the will of a popular majority was expressed politically. That debate was triggered early in Lincoln's career by Andrew Jackson, who claimed in 1832 that he alone, as president, embodied the will of the national majority, while Congress (which resisted Jackson's efforts to abolish the Bank of the United States) was corrupt and unrepresentative. The Whig Party was born in opposition to Jackson's sweeping assertion of presidential power, and Lincoln shared that Whig stance. As a member of Congress (1847–49) Lincoln denounced James Polk's untethered exercise of presidential power in commencing the Mexican War, as well as Polk's dubious assertion of an electoral mandate for his actions. During his Whig years—and also in 1861 in his first inaugural address—Lincoln viewed Congress as the principal (though not exclusive) institution for implementing the will of a national majority.

As a Whig, Lincoln engaged with constitutional questions, though not to the same degree he did in the 1850s and 1860s with respect to the Constitution and slavery. In the Jacksonian era, the Democratic and Whig Parties divided over substantive policy questions: banks and currency, tariffs, federal funding of roads and canals, distribution of public lands, government's proper role, and more. But those clashing policy commitments were interlinked with competing views of the US Constitution. Partisans typically viewed the opposition party not just as wrong on policy but also as deeply unconstitutional in its aims and a threat to republican principles.[3] Lincoln himself denounced Polk's actions in Mexico as unconstitutional, but he did not view the Democratic Party or its economic policies as unconstitutional; nor did he claim that his own party had a monopoly on constitutional fidelity. Instead—and in contrast to some other prominent Whigs—Lincoln argued that *both* Democratic and Whig economic policies were consistent with the Constitution and therefore legitimate matters for majority decision by the elected branches of government. Lincoln in his Whig years thus anticipated an argument he later developed in the first inaugural address: that democratic debate and decision about constitutional meaning are legitimate, especially on questions that the text of the Constitution does not expressly answer.[4]

Lincoln's focus during his Whig years was political economy and, in particular, his vision of an economy that would "secure to each labourer the whole product of his labour, or as nearly as possible," thereby correcting the inequity whereby "*some* have laboured, and *others* have, without labour, enjoyed a large proportion of the fruits." This expressed Lincoln's wider vision of a political order (as he phrased it in 1861) whose purpose was "to lift artificial weights from all shoulders—to clear the paths of laudable pursuit for all—to afford all, an unfettered start, and a fair chance, in the race of life." The ideal of securing to every individual the full fruits of his or her labor was obviously incompatible with slavery. In his 1858 debates with Stephen Douglas, Lincoln emphasized that persons of all races had an equal right "to eat the bread, without leave of anybody else, which his own hand earns." But during his Whig years, Lincoln principally aimed to enact policies that furthered "a fair chance, in the race of life" for persons who were already free.[5]

"That Lawless and Mobocratic Spirit"

Government of, by, and for the people was the freest and most just of all political orders, in Lincoln's view, so long as it could be inoculated against its unfortunate capacity for suicide. In that spirit, I take up Lincoln's Springfield Lyceum address of 1838, the most significant statement of his political philosophy from the early phase of his career.[6]

Lincoln's Lyceum address has been interpreted in widely varying ways. Some have argued that Lincoln's portrait of a "towering genius" who "thirsts and burns for distinction" prefigures his own future role as president acting amid (and, according to some readings, deliberately initiating) a revolutionary cataclysm.[7] The thesis of a deliberately initiated cataclysm implies that Lincoln ran for president in 1860 with the specific intention of triggering slave-state secession and then provoked the Confederacy into assaulting Fort Sumter so he could realize his own long-standing plan to emancipate slaves in a bloodbath and win lasting fame. None of this fits the facts. It was secessionists like Robert Barnwell Rhett and William Lowndes Yancey who consciously engineered the crisis of 1860–61, and it was Lincoln (among others) who insisted on respecting the results of free elections.

Several scholars have highlighted Lincoln's call for a "political religion" of strict obedience to the Constitution and laws.[8] Others present the Lyceum address as expressing the Whigs' order-loving, tradition-affirming political outlook, in contrast to what they considered the mobocratic spirit of Jackson's Democratic Party.[9] Several commentators have noted that most of the lynchings Lincoln mentioned in the address targeted abolitionists and free Blacks, and they supplement Lincoln's picture with details demonstrating that his concerns about mob violence were well-founded. Daniel Walker Howe observes that during this period, "Not only the South, but even in the North, the early antiabolitionist mobs sometimes enjoyed the respectable leadership of 'gentlemen of property and standing,'" such as President Andrew Jackson and future president John Tyler.[10] As a close follower of national politics, Lincoln certainly would have known that some mob actions were encouraged by respected men in office, although he did not call them out by name.

For purposes of the present work, the Lyceum address is important as Lincoln's earliest statement on the connection between popular sovereignty and majority rule. I acknowledge the possibility that, in warning against the individual of great talents whose ambition "thirsts and burns for distinction," Lincoln may have recognized and sought to restrain such tendencies in himself. More importantly, however, he sought to strengthen the people's capacity for self-government as the surest safeguard against one-man rule, no matter where that danger originated. Lincoln insisted that, in a popular government, majorities must be empowered to restrain themselves and educated to understand why such self-restraint is necessary. Moreover, he argued that a lawless disposition among individuals entrusted with public office—including those who pose as defenders of law—posed a greater threat to the survival of popular government than lawless actions in the streets.

That Lincoln's concerns extended beyond the actions of street mobs was already evident a year before his Lyceum address. In a January 11, 1837, speech as a member of the Illinois General Assembly, Lincoln warned against the dangers of moblike behavior in language that anticipated his Lyceum address. "I am opposed to encouraging that lawless and mobocratic spirit, whether in relation to the bank or any thing else, which is already abroad in the land; and is spreading with rapid and fearful impetuosity, to the ultimate overthrow of every institution, or even moral principle, in which persons and property have hitherto found security."[11] By the date of this speech, abolitionists and free Blacks had been the victims of lawless violence for several consecutive years. (The November 7, 1837, lynching in Illinois of abolitionist editor Elijah Lovejoy made Lincoln's words earlier that year darkly prophetic.)

. But Lincoln's immediate target in his Illinois General Assembly speech was a different type of lawless behavior—one practiced bloodlessly by a legislative faction politically targeting the directors of the Illinois State Bank. Lincoln placed these legislators' behavior in the same category as that of violent street mobs ("that lawless and mobocratic spirit, whether in relation to the bank or any thing else"). This episode helps clarify the difference in Lincoln's mind between legitimate and illegitimate majority rule, and it sheds light on the remedy he proposed in the Lyceum address.

The antibank faction in the Illinois house had introduced a resolution demanding an inquiry into the management of the state bank's affairs. On the face of it, there was nothing mobocratic about state legislators seeking to hold a state bank publicly accountable. It would have been perfectly legitimate for legislators to enact a law for that purpose. But this was the rub from Lincoln's perspective: the resolution initiated not a lawful inquiry but a lawless one. The previous year, Lincoln himself had proposed an amendment to the bank's charter that would have subjected its books to public examination, failing which it would forfeit its charter.[12] Lincoln's amendment was voted down by many of the same legislators who were now demanding an investigation without legal authorization, without any clear public process, and in a transparently partisan way. Addressing the bank's self-appointed prosecutors, Lincoln remarked, "though it would be out of order to call their names, I hope they will recollect themselves, and not vote for this examination to be made without authority, inasmuch as they refused to reserve the authority when it was in their power to do so." Lincoln immediately follows with his criticism of the "lawless and mobocratic spirit . . . already abroad in the land."[13]

The behavior Lincoln condemned here resembles the crime known as calumny in the Roman Republic. David Siemers, drawing from Machiavelli's *Discourses on Livy*, describes calumny as "public accusations against an official made without any formal legal charge." Siemers explains, "The purpose of a calumny is to discredit someone without evidence. . . . Calumnies degrade the rule of law and damage the efficacy of political institutions, because the public presumes there is no legal remedy for the problems that are proffered."[14] There is no evidence that Lincoln read Machiavelli, but he certainly understood the concept of calumny,[15] and in substance, that is what the assembly's antibank faction engaged in when it made charges that could be neither confirmed nor disproved by any legal process. Republican government is strengthened when disagreements are routed into legal and constitutional channels where they can be publicly aired and decided. Republican government is damaged when suspicions fester without any public process for ascertaining the truth.

It might seem a long leap from a legislative faction's ad hoc partisan bank inquiry to the acts of mob violence Lincoln described or alluded to in his Lyceum address: hanging gamblers; burning a free Black man without a trial; hanging Blacks "suspected of conspiring to raise an insurrection," followed by hanging "white men, supposed to be leagued with the negroes"; and choosing to "throw printing presses into rivers, shoot editors [a reference to the murder of Lovejoy], and hang and burn obnoxious persons at pleasure."[16] But in Lincoln's view, both the bank episode and the mob actions exhibited what might be called a popular sovereignty shortcut: the notion that because the majority has the authority to make and repeal laws, the majority has equal authority to act *without* law—or, to put it another way, to make and enforce a law on the spot. Why waste time and squander righteous passion by working slowly and patiently to change the law?

Of the mob actions Lincoln described in the Lyceum address, the lynching of gamblers in Mississippi most closely paralleled the lawless bank inquiry, for in both cases there was an obviously available legal remedy. The Mississippi legislature, Lincoln noted, had specifically licensed gambling the year before. The antigambling constituency, believing that it constituted a majority in the state (which may or may not have been true) could have pressed for repeal of the law, just as bank critics in Illinois could have legislated a fair and transparent process to ensure public accountability. In both cases, when a majority—or, more precisely, a group *believing* itself to be the majority—takes the no-process shortcut, the outcome is not a shorter route to the same result but a rapid route to a very different set of consequences (damaged public credit in one case, dangling bodies in the other) that can go far beyond what anyone foresaw or intended. The Illinois legislature's lawless bank inquiry, though bloodless, was in one sense less defensible than the Mississippi lynchings because, unlike members of the general public, the Illinois legislators were legally authorized to enact appropriate legislation, had they chosen to do so.

Another way to clarify the difference between a legitimate majority and a mob is to ask what kind of majority, if any, a mob consists of. In one sense, a mob is a local, quickly assembled, passionately acting majority. A mob derives its passion and self-righteousness from the feeling that it is acting for the community—indeed, that it *is* the community in microcosm. Shouts of "This is *our* house!" and "Tell them the people showed up!" were heard as the violent mob invaded the US Capitol on January 6, 2021.[17] An angry, self-righteous mob does not trouble itself to take votes or conduct opinion surveys to ascertain whether its own view really represents that of the majority, and it does not treat dissent as legitimate. In that respect, a mob is not a majority at all, in an electoral sense; it represents a kind of imagined unanimity: those who dissent do not really belong to the community and may become targets of violence themselves. In contrast, an electoral or legislative majority, formed in accordance with legal procedures, comes into existence as a majority only by virtue of those same procedures that specify the geographic reach of the majority (local, state, national), who is eligible to participate in decision making, and the rules for conducting and counting votes, including the votes of dissenters. In that sense, a constitutional majority and a mob are not the same kind of agent ("the majority") following a different code of conduct; they are different types of agents altogether.

There is no reason to believe that Lincoln foresaw the critical political events of 1854–61. But his warnings in 1837 and 1838 about the "lawless and mobocratic spirit" foreshadow his understanding of those later events and why they caused him to fear for the survival of popular government. "Bloody Kansas," in Lincoln's view, represented not just typical frontier violence (which occurred in every unorganized western territory) but a toxic political sequence in which a small group of men in high office enacted an especially lawless law, the Kansas-Nebraska Act, whose deliberate silence on political process and timing encouraged political violence and fraud. Many of those same officeholders later sought to legitimize mob violence by accepting the mob's fraudulent handiwork as a legitimate territorial constitution. In 1855 Lincoln strikingly characterized the Kansas-Nebraska Act "not as a *law*, but as *violence* from the beginning. It was conceived in violence, passed in violence, is maintained in violence, and is being executed in violence."[18] As he noted in the Lyceum address, it was not the "direct consequences" of mob action that threatened the survival of popular government but their wider effects on public life. Likewise (as Lincoln described it), the proslavery Missourians who invaded Kansas territory and vowed that "abolitionists shall be hung, or driven away" would not have seriously endangered American political institutions were it not for the presidents, congressmen, and others who licensed, encouraged, and legitimated their acts.[19] Finally, in his first inaugural address, Lincoln described secession itself as a kind of elite-driven lawlessness, "legally void" and "insurrectionary," even though it cloaked itself in the respectable garb of "*resolves* and *ordinances.*"[20] Lawlessness was most dangerous when it disguised itself as law.

"All Sexes and Tongues, and Colors and Conditions"

As stated in the Lyceum address, Lincoln's proposed solution to the danger that America's free institutions might "die by suicide" was to inculcate an ethic of strict obedience to the law and the Constitution.[21] From the perspective of the later crisis involving slavery, secession, and civil war—which could indeed have resulted in the United States' political death by suicide—Lincoln's solution in the Lyceum address was in some respects too simplistic. Strictly obey *which* law when federal and state laws come into conflict? Swear fidelity to which deeply contested version of the Constitution's stance on slavery? Moreover, although Lincoln's narrative revealed that slavery and racial fear were key motivators of mob violence, his recommended remedy was oddly color-blind. Yet in one important respect—in relying on lawful majority action at its best to overcome lawless majority action at its worst—Lincoln anticipated a central component of his defense of majority rule in the first inaugural address.

Lincoln argued in the Lyceum address that if mob rule continued unchecked, then ironically, it would be "good men, men who love tranquility, who desire to abide by the laws," and who fear "seeing their property destroyed"—not the mobs—who would deliberately put an end to free institutions. Such "good men" (one might ask how good they could actually be) "become tired of, and disgusted with, a Government that offers them no protection," and imagining "they have nothing to lose," they throw their support to ambitious men who will "seize the opportunity, strike the blow, and overturn that fair fabric . . . the fondest hope, of the lovers of freedom, throughout the world." One might add, though Lincoln does not specifically point this out, that the ambitious individuals these "good men" authorize to overthrow the republic are themselves lawbreakers on a grand scale.

In answer to the question "how shall we fortify against it?" Lincoln replies:

> Let every American, every lover of liberty, every well wisher to his posterity, swear by the blood of the Revolution, never to violate in the least particular, the laws of the country; and never to tolerate their violation by others. . . . Let reverence for the laws, be breathed by every American mother, to the lisping babe, that prattles on her lap—let it be taught in schools, in seminaries, and in colleges;—let it be preached from the pulpit, proclaimed in legislative halls, and enforced in courts of justice. And, in short, let it become the *political religion* of the nation; and let the old and the young, the rich and the poor, the grave and the gay, of all sexes and tongues, and colors and conditions, sacrifice unceasingly upon its altars.

Lincoln's proposition might initially seem deeply, rigidly conservative, as though existing laws and the Constitution were perfect and all criticism or doubt about their justice should be branded as treasonous. But Lincoln stresses that this was not his intention: "Let me not be understood as saying there are no bad laws, nor that grievances may not arise, for the redress of which, no legal provisions have been made. . . . But I do mean to say, that, although bad laws, if they exist, should be repealed as soon as possible, still while they continue in force, for the sake of example, they should be religiously observed." Legitimate grievances existed, but "no grievance . . . is a fit object for redress by mob law."[22]

It was not the laws as such or even the Constitution that Lincoln proclaimed to be sacred and inviolable. What was sacred was the people's legitimate power and, by extension, that of their elected representatives to pass, repeal, or amend laws through constitutionally specified processes. Lincoln urged citizens to embrace not thoughtless obedience (on the contrary, he emphasized that "sober reason" must "furnish all the materials for our future support and defense") but a patient willingness to make and change the law through legitimate processes. This required efforts to persuade those who disagreed, rather than stringing them from trees, and respect for the results of majority vote when consensus could not be reached. It was precisely such processes and practices that Lincoln meant when he advocated "a reverence for the constitution and laws," and they were endangered when a mob—whether a street mob or a legislative mob—demanded a process-free shortcut to achieve its desired goal.[23]

In the Lyceum address Lincoln did not specifically refer to a deliberate, constitutionally checked majority as the "true sovereign of a free people," but that concept from the first inaugural address was already implicit. Lincoln's proposal in the Lyceum address was majoritarian in several respects: (1) it assumed that disagreements were resolved by voting; (2) it presupposed that most citizens were capable of understanding *why* they should obey imperfect laws unless and until they were changed and could commit to doing so; (3) it invited citizens to take action to change and improve imperfect laws, rather than remaining passive; and (4) it rejected the notion that anyone or anything else—some individual or body *outside* or *above* the people—could remedy the problem of lawlessness. The remedy must come from the people themselves.

This last point deserves emphasis because it distinguishes Lincoln's perspective from that of more conservative Whigs, who placed relatively

greater reliance on the judiciary and on the capacity of a social and economic elite to restrain popular passion.[24] Lincoln did not leave the judiciary entirely out of his narrative in the Lyceum address. He remarked
on the "growing disposition to substitute the wild and furious passions,
in lieu of the sober judgment of Courts." For Lincoln (who made his living as a lawyer), courts clearly played an essential role. But nowhere in
the Lyceum address did he suggest that the judiciary alone was capable
of taming lawless popular passions. Unless citizens first resolved to *restrain themselves,* as Lincoln called on them to do, the judgments of the
courts would simply be ignored. (In 1838 Lincoln did not imagine that
the judiciary itself might pose a threat to popular self-government. Until
the *Dred Scott* decision in 1857, he seemed satisfied with the US Supreme
Court's role in American political life.)[25]

In a broad sense, Lincoln's Lyceum address prefigured his defense
of constitutional majority rule in the late 1850s and his first inaugural
address. But in other respects, the "simple" (Lincoln's word) solution
proposed in the Lyceum address was indeed too simple. Exhorting citizens to swear to obey the Constitution and laws in all particulars does not
ensure civil peace when different groups are deeply divided over what
the Constitution prescribes on some matter of great importance, such
as slavery. Lincoln presumed that citizens would disagree in ways that
should be resolved by voting, but his observations on deep political disagreement appear oddly dogmatic. "In any case that arises," Lincoln remarked shortly after setting forth his obey-the-law remedy, "for instance,
the promulgation of abolitionism, one of two positions is necessarily
true; that is, the thing is right within itself, and therefore deserves the
protection of all law and all good citizens; or, it is wrong, and therefore
proper to be prohibited by legal enactments; and in neither case, is the
interposition of mob law, either necessary, justifiable, or excusable."[26]
Lincoln's objections to mob law were clear, and he never suggested that
abolitionism should be "prohibited by legal enactments," as proslavery
ideologues demanded. But he provided little guidance as to how such a
morally charged and divisive issue ought to be constructively addressed
in democratic politics. The tragedy of slavery in Lincoln's time was precisely that it was *wrong* in principle but so deeply entrenched that "legal
enactments" could remedy it only with great difficulty, if at all.

Lincoln's narrative of mob violence in the Lyceum address, much of
it directed against abolitionists and African Americans, tacitly acknowledged some of the American political community's deepest injustices.

But his proposed remedy—that Americans "of all sexes and tongues, and colors and conditions, sacrifice unceasingly" on the altar of obedience to law—raised a fundamental problem that was unacknowledged in the address. The core of Lincoln's argument, the element that makes the speech of enduring interest, is that it challenges citizens—and here I mean citizens who enjoy full civil and political rights—to take the long, often frustrating, but self-government-affirming route of seeking to change unacceptable laws rather than simply breaking them. But if that is the ultimate source of the obligation to obey laws—not because someone commands us to do so, but because we owe it to ourselves—then it cannot apply in the same way to human beings who are systematically deprived of those rights. This problem is rarely addressed in commentaries on Lincoln's Lyceum address.[27] One might argue that free white women in antebellum America were obligated to obey the law because they enjoyed its protections (though not in all instances) and shaped political life in multiple ways, despite lacking the vote. (Lincoln apparently supported extending the franchise to women, although he never made it a political priority.)[28] Free Blacks were disenfranchised in most states, and in practice, they often lacked even minimal legal protections. As for persons held in bondage, it would have been absurd to argue that enslaved persons were morally obligated never to violate the slave statutes and codes that denied their basic humanity. Nor did Lincoln ever push the argument this far. He considered it natural and inevitable that enslaved persons would resist, violently if necessary, both the institution of slavery and the individual slave owners who held them in bondage.[29]

Lincoln's proposed remedy in the Lyceum address, in short, would be *fully* applicable only to a *fully inclusive* democracy, which was far from the case in 1838. He confronted the same problem in his October 16, 1854, speech on the Kansas-Nebraska Act. In criticizing Stephen Douglas's perverted version of popular sovereignty, Lincoln remarked: "Allow ALL the governed an equal voice in the government, and that, and that only is self government."[30] Lincoln here directly acknowledged the inconsistency and injustice afflicting American democracy, yet he still saw no available remedy, given the nearly universal white opposition to enfranchising Blacks. In the Lyceum address the same problem remained unacknowledged.

These critical observations do not diminish the importance of the Lyceum address, which was an extraordinary statement coming from a young man of Lincoln's background and social environment. It demonstrates his rare capacity to reflect comprehensively on the critical problems of the day. But to understand where Lincoln ended up politically and philosophically by the late 1850s, we need to clarify where he began, the better to trace both continuities with and departures from that initial point.

In 1838 Lincoln was passionately committed to the ideal of popular government and feared for its future. From his earliest years, he also recognized the injustice of slavery. But in 1838 he had not yet connected these two issues. In the Lyceum address he did not recognize—or if he did, he did not say so—that the persistence of slavery on American soil posed a fundamental threat to the "political edifice of liberty and equal rights" enjoyed by the white community to which he belonged. The developing threads of his political thought and experience over time will help us understand how these two concerns—threats to the survival of American self-government and the injustice of slavery—ultimately became one.

"To See Each Man of His Section Face to Face"

The Lyceum address, taken in isolation, might seem to support the claim that Lincoln was "suspicious of human nature and distrustful of mass democracy."[31] But the address clearly affirms majority rule when it follows legal and constitutional processes. Moreover, if "mass democracy" means a government in which the vast majority of ordinary citizens, including those of modest means and limited education, are encouraged to raise their voices, cast their votes by the millions, and thereby determine the direction of national policy, then Abraham Lincoln was no less supportive of mass democracy than Andrew Jackson was, although Lincoln was more ready than Jackson to acknowledge that a majority could act unwisely or unjustly. It is in this spirit that I take up Lincoln's record as a Whig partisan, a grassroots party organizer, and a defender of political parties not merely as an unavoidable evil in a popular government but as a positive good.[32] For Lincoln, political parties directed mass popular participation into peaceful, constitutional channels and helped steer citizens away from demagogues and would-be autocrats. This chapter's discussion of Lincoln and political parties focuses on his Whig years; chapter 5 features Lincoln as a builder, defender, and strategist of the Republican Party.

To better grasp Lincoln's understanding of political parties during his Whig phase, I sketch the wider contours of the Second Party System and describe Lincoln's own early efforts to organize an effective Whig Party in Illinois. I begin with Martin Van Buren, whom Lincoln observed closely and who—more than Andrew Jackson himself—built the Jacksonian Democratic Party.[33]

The Democratic Party, which saw itself as the legitimate descendant of the Jeffersonian Republicans, drew its political energy from Andrew Jackson's personal popularity and his antielitist war on the National Bank. But Martin Van Buren, Jackson's vice president and successor as president, was the principal architect of the Democratic Party as an effective national organization. It was Van Buren who codified the Jacksonians' sometimes contradictory policy commitments into a consistent party ideology.[34] By the late 1820s, Van Buren had created an effective party organization in New York, which was crucial to Jackson's election in 1828 and reelection in 1832. Van Buren was principally responsible for forging the often volatile intersectional alliance between Jackson's southern and northern supporters—"the *planters* of the South and the plain *Republicans* of the North," as Van Buren phrased it.[35] This alliance gave Democrats an enduring advantage in presidential elections from the 1830s until 1860, when the party split over the South's demand for a territorial slave code.

Several aspects of Van Buren's legacy are especially relevant to Lincoln's own party-building efforts as a Whig in the 1830s and 1840s and as a Republican in the 1850s.[36] Van Buren was among the first American leaders to defend political parties as positively necessary and constructively functional, rather than as merely an unavoidable evil. He drew this conclusion from his experience of bitter battles among New York's various Jeffersonian factions and nationally during the so-called Era of Good Feelings in the 1820s, after the Federalist Party had disappeared and the Jeffersonian Republicans were effectively unopposed. The Era of Good Feelings was in fact marked not by harmony but by bitter personal disputes and at least two Union-endangering crises: the Missouri controversy of 1819–20 and the nullification crisis of 1828–33. Though Van Buren never regarded the Whigs' political and constitutional views as legitimate, he considered their *opposition* essential to Democrats' unity of purpose and the success of their political agenda. He understood that to be effective, a party had to be based on organization and shared principles, not merely the popularity of individual leaders. Although he and Jackson supported each other, Van Buren was troubled by Jackson's personalistic style of governing and sought to build a party that would constrain the excessive power of individual party figures. Van Buren worked to transform the *individual* mandate Jackson had claimed into a *party* mandate, an affirmation of its platform.[37]

Finally, Van Buren built the Democratic Party deliberately to suppress organized opposition to slavery, both within the party itself and in the public more broadly. Abolitionism, in his view, threatened the Union, and if it were encouraged by northern Democrats, it certainly would have driven away the party's critical southern wing. Van Buren's strategy (at least before his Free-Soil revolt of 1848) was to neutralize slavery as a national issue and to center the electoral competition between Democrats and Whigs around a set of economic issues (currency, the National Bank, public lands, internal improvements, and the tariff) on which northern and southern Democrats could unite. William G. Shade writes, "By consciously deciding to remove slavery and its abolition from the partisan agenda, the Democrats created the first modern party" and thus made a crucial contribution to "the democratization of the American political system." But, Shade adds, "this was at best a paternalist, *Herrenvolk* democracy."[38]

Moreover, by sidelining slavery and remaining competitive in both North and South, the Democrats gave the Whigs a strong incentive to follow suit and sidestep the slavery question in presidential contests if they hoped to be competitive in both sections. The Whigs were less ideologically unified than the Democrats, however; some outspokenly antislavery northern Whigs (including John Quincy Adams) were starkly opposed to the positions taken by the party's southern affiliates, who often attempted to portray themselves as more proslavery than their Democratic opponents.[39]

Van Buren's party-building strategies shed light on Lincoln's party-building efforts. Though his policy commitments and constitutional views differed markedly from Van Buren's, Lincoln was significantly closer to Van Buren than to most Whigs on the issue of party unity. Like Van Buren, Lincoln emphasized the importance of unifying in the face of the opposition and urged the Whigs to adopt the Democrats' practice of holding state and national conventions to choose a single candidate, rather than scattering their votes among multiple candidates, as they had done in the 1836 presidential election and in many statewide and district contests.[40] Moreover, both Lincoln and Van Buren believed that a party had to stand for something beyond attachment to a popular individual candidate. Here too, Lincoln's approach differed from the Whigs' general tendency: in their only two victorious presidential campaigns, 1840 and 1848, the Whigs emphasized the candidate's military record and remained vague on policy.

Finally, Lincoln, to an even greater degree than Van Buren, envisioned political parties as a means of engaging and mobilizing ordinary citizens to participate in American democracy. In January 1840 Lincoln set forth a detailed campaign plan for Illinois Whigs in that year's election. The centerpiece of the plan was the appointment of one precinct captain and ten section captains in every precinct in the state. It was the duty of the precinct captain "to procure from the county poll-books" a list of "all those persons who voted the Whig ticket in August" (there was no secret ballot in Illinois at the time) and to appoint section captains from among those individuals. Each section captain was assigned three tasks: "to see each man of his Section face to face, and procure his pledge that he will for no consideration (impossibilities excepted) stay from the polls on the first Monday in November"; "to add to his Section the names of every person in his vicinity who did not vote with us in August, but who will vote with us in the fall"; and "to procure . . . additional names" of voters in the section who might be persuaded to support the Whig ticket. Lincoln thus proposed that a party representative personally visit every voter in every precinct who had supported the Whig ticket in the past, as well as every voter who had not previously supported the ticket but might be persuaded to do so in the future. There is no indication that these party workers would be paid for their time. This was a volunteer operation, sustained by commitment to a cause. Lincoln was no political general here, ordering troops into battle from the comfort of an armchair; he was urging all committed Whigs to engage in the same kind of individualized, face-to-face voter contact he had practiced from the beginning of his political career.[41]

Though Lincoln was on the cutting edge of such initiatives, especially amid the organization-resistant Illinois Whigs, his proposal was not unique. Similar documents turned up in other states, including among Democrats, during the 1840 campaign. As a result of unprecedented efforts by both parties to mobilize voters that year, turnout among eligible voters leaped from an estimated 56.5 percent in the 1836 presidential election to 80.3 percent in 1840—the highest turnout by far up to that point and one of the two largest single-cycle upswings in American history (exceeded only by the jump from 26.9 percent in 1824 to 57.3 percent in 1828).[42]

To those with an antiparty disposition, Lincoln's 1840 campaign plan may appear intrusive. Would it be more genuinely democratic to leave voters alone, allowing them to vote (or not vote) for or against anyone they like, uninfluenced by candidates or parties? Lincoln did not see it that way. Instead, his 1840 campaign plan was the practical, down-to-earth counterpart to his democratic idealism expressed in the 1838 Lyceum address. The perpetuation of the "proud fabric of freedom" celebrated in that address depended not only on individual citizens' willingness to *obey* the law but also on their continued participation in *making* the law.[43] Face-to-face and person to person was how Lincoln believed the lawmaking process must begin.

"Our Position Is that Both Are Constitutional"

During the phase of US political history known as the Second Party System (roughly 1832–54), the Democratic and Whig Parties divided over questions of political economy (banks, tariffs, currency, public lands). But equally important were their disagreements over constitutional questions and, more generally, over how and by whom the will of the American people was legitimately expressed and implemented. The contest over the Bank of the United States, for example, was simultaneously a dispute over political economy, presidential power, and who really spoke for the American people. Moreover, adherents of each party tended to view the rival party not just as misguided on policy but also as unconstitutional and antirepublican. The notion that a rival party might be equally attached to a shared yet differently interpreted Constitution, and the recognition that party opposition was legitimate, developed slowly and with difficulty.

These debates were ongoing when Lincoln was first elected to the Illinois legislature in 1834, and they continued in one form or another throughout the Whig phase of his career. Lincoln's interventions in these Whig-era debates shed light on his later understanding of constitutional majority rule as a Republican during the 1850s, as well as his acknowledgment in the first inaugural address that deep disagreement, over constitutional meaning as well as policy, was legitimate matter for democratic debate and decision.

When Lincoln commenced his political career, debate about whether Congress had the constitutional authority to charter a national bank already had a long history. In 1791 Alexander Hamilton argued in favor of the bank's constitutionality, while Thomas Jefferson argued that the bank was unconstitutional because the Constitution did not expressly authorize Congress to charter a bank. The US Supreme Court upheld the constitutionality of the Bank of the United States in *McCulloch v. Maryland* (1819).

President Andrew Jackson dramatically reopened the bank debate. He vehemently denounced the bank, on both constitutional and policy grounds, as an engine of oligarchical economic control at the expense of the common man. In 1832 Jackson vetoed a bill extending the charter of the Second Bank of the United States. Because the bank's original charter did not officially expire until 1836, Jackson took the even more dramatic step in 1834—over the strong objections of Congress—of forcibly removing all federal deposits from the Bank of the United States and placing those funds in a series of state-chartered "pet" banks. Jackson claimed that his 1832 reelection represented a popular mandate to dismantle the bank and that he alone as president—not Congress—represented the American people as a whole. Jackson not only reopened the old debate about the bank's constitutionality but also initiated new debates about presidential power, judicial authority, representation, majority rule, and more. The Whig Party, which began to form during Jackson's second term, so named itself to dramatize what its members regarded as despotic, republic-threatening acts by "King Andrew."[44]

Lincoln's first extensive discussion of federal constitutional questions came in his December 26, 1839, speech on the Subtreasury in the Illinois House of Representatives. Lincoln prepared the speech for publication in pamphlet form, indicating that he intended his arguments to reach a broad public and probably also to shape Illinois Whigs' electoral messaging for the 1840 campaign.[45]

In the Subtreasury speech, Lincoln argued in favor of reestablishing the National Bank and against Democrats' proposal for a nonbank Subtreasury as the depository of federal funds. In contrast to the bank, by whose operations government revenues were "kept almost constantly in circulation," the Subtreasury would "injuriously affect the community" by removing a significant proportion of the nation's specie from circulation, where it would perform "no nobler office than that of rusting in iron boxes." But Lincoln knew he had to address Democrats' claim that because there was "no *express* authority in the Constitution" authorizing Congress to establish it, the National Bank was unconstitutional. He initially responded with conventional Whig appeals to legislative precedent and judicial authority: "the votes of Congress have more often been in favor than against its constitutionality," and the Supreme Court "has solemnly decided that such a bank is constitutional." Lincoln remarked that "these authorities ought to settle the question"—but he knew they had *not* settled the question. He then advanced a constitutional argument "which I have not known to be taken by anyone before."[46]

Lincoln's constitutional argument rested on the fact that although there was "no *express* authority in the Constitution to establish a Bank," there was also "no *express* authority in the Constitution to establish a Sub-Treasury." If (as Democrats argued, following Jefferson) the bank could not be justified under the Constitution's necessary and proper clause because there existed no "*indispensable necessity*" for it (because the new nation had survived its first decade without a National Bank), then, Lincoln argued, it followed that there was no "*indispensable necessity*" for the Subtreasury either, since the nation had survived more than forty years without such an institution. Therefore, Lincoln observed, either *both* the National Bank and the Subtreasury were constitutional or *neither* were constitutional. "Our position is that both are constitutional," Lincoln concluded. Thus, it was legitimate for Congress to decide between the National Bank and the Subtreasury on the basis of their respective policy consequences.[47]

Lincoln's conclusion that both the National Bank and the Subtreasury were equally consistent with the Constitution may seem obvious, but it was not. Fellow Whig Daniel Webster, for example, had argued *for* the constitutionality of the bank and *against* the constitutionality of the Subtreasury proposal, on the grounds that Congress had a constitutional obligation to uphold the integrity of the nation's currency and to "protect and regulate the commerce of the country." If Congress enacted the Subtreasury proposal, Webster charged, it would disrupt both currency and trade and thereby negate "the precise, distinct, original object" for which the Constitution was intended.[48] Thus, Lincoln's stance differed from that of some nationally prominent Whig leaders. Lincoln's argument also differed from that of the Democrats, of course, nearly all of whom maintained that the Subtreasury was constitutional and the National Bank dangerously unconstitutional.

Lincoln's constitutional reasoning legitimized democratic decision making through majority vote, following public debate, on matters about which the express language of the Constitution was silent. This anticipated his argument in the first inaugural address that a deliberate, constitutionally checked majority was the ultimate judge of constitutional questions (such as whether Congress could ban slavery in the territories) that the text of the Constitution did not expressly answer. One important difference between the 1839 and 1861 versions of this argument was that Lincoln's stance on the bank was not obstructed by the chief judicial precedent on that issue (*McCulloch v. Maryland*), whereas his 1861 argument had to contend with the *Dred Scott* precedent on slavery. But in both 1839 and 1861, Lincoln explored relatively uncharted territory in accepting legitimate democratic disagreement, and even partisan competition, over questions of constitutional interpretation.[49] The dominant tendency of Lincoln's age (and by no means absent from our own) was for parties to claim a monopoly on constitutional truth and to accuse the opposition of subverting the Constitution.[50]

Presidential Power and Pretended Mandates

During his Whig years, Lincoln took public stances on presidential power and on the question of when, if ever, a winning candidate or party could plausibly claim the electorate's endorsement of a particular policy. In antebellum US politics, the most significant and controversial mandate claims were made by two Democratic presidents to enhance their power at the expense of a Congress that resisted that president's policies: Andrew Jackson, with regard to the National Bank, and James Polk, who claimed that his 1844 election victory was a mandate to annex Texas in 1845 and to initiate armed conflict with Mexico in 1846. Jackson's and Polk's mandate claims were linked to the argument that, as president, they represented the people of the United States as a whole, while Congress did not.[51]

Lincoln, who was a first-term member of the US House of Representatives during the Mexican War, denounced Polk's invasion of Mexican territory (while withholding key information from Congress) as an unconstitutional exercise of executive power. Lincoln also disputed Polk's supposed electoral mandate authorizing his invasion of Mexico and defended Congress as a genuine representative of the American people. Nor did Lincoln reverse his principles for a president of his own party: when Zachary Taylor was elected in 1848 on the Whig ticket with Lincoln's active support, he hoped the new president would defer to Congress in most matters. As noted in chapter 4, Lincoln likewise rejected President James Buchanan's dubious claim that his 1852 election victory amounted to popular endorsement of the Kansas-Nebraska Act of 1854.

But Lincoln did not argue, as some Whigs did, that elections carried no message at all except to determine which individuals would hold which offices.[52] Both during his Whig years and as a Republican in the 1850s, Lincoln believed that a political party (including but not limited to that party's presidential candidate) should communicate a platform to voters and, if successful in the election, should govern in accordance with that platform. I argue in chapter 5 that the political dynamics underlying Lincoln's "House Divided" thesis of 1858 presumed that policies pushing slavery in one direction or the other would be either endorsed or rejected by voters in subsequent elections. In short, although Lincoln never supported presidential mandate claims like those asserted by Jackson and Polk, he did believe that elections enabled citizens to communicate their views on important issues to policymakers and to hold the latter accountable in subsequent elections. Unless some such connection existed between voters and officeholders, Lincoln could not have called the majority "the only true sovereign of a free people" in his first inaugural address.

Lincoln argued in early 1848 that "the war with Mexico was unnecessarily and unconstitutionally commenced by the President." Polk, Lincoln maintained, had fundamentally misled Congress and the American public by claiming in his May 1846 war message "that the soil was *ours* on which hostilities were commenced by Mexico." By initiating and justifying a war based on public statements later "proved to be false in fact," Polk contravened the intentions of the Constitution's framers, who gave "the war-making power to Congress." Once a president is permitted "to invade a neighboring nation, whenever *he* shall deem it necessary to repel an invasion . . . you allow him to do so *whenever he may choose to say* he deems it necessary for such purpose—and you allow him to make war at pleasure." Polk and his congressional allies compounded this initial act of deception by annexing to a military appropriations bill a preamble "declaring that war existed by the act of Mexico." Lincoln characterized this as an "artfully set trap" because congressional opponents of the war, including Lincoln, felt they could not cut off supplies to American soldiers already in the field. Congressional approval for military appropriations then allowed Polk to claim that, whether the territory "was rightfully *ours* or not," in practice, "*Congress had annexed it*" by appropriating military funds, "and the President, for that reason was bound to defend it."[53]

In truth, Lincoln pointed out, Polk himself had initiated hostilities by sending an army "into the midst of a settlement of Mexican people, who had never submitted, by consent or by force, to the authority of Texas or of the United States, and that *there*, and *thereby*, the first blood of the war was shed." Lincoln acknowledged that the people living in that territory could have exercised their natural right, by majority consent, to break ties with Mexico and join the United States, as Texas had done earlier. "Any people anywhere, being inclined and having the power, have the *right* to rise up, and shake off the existing government, and form a new one that suits them better." (Lincoln here meant a *natural* right, not any legal or constitutional right under Mexican law.) But the members of the community where "the first blood of the war was shed" had in fact never consented by law, treaty, or majority vote to be annexed by the United States. Instead, the US Army's incursion was an act of conquest. Rather than greeting US troops as liberators, the people of the settlement fled "from the approach of the United States Army, leaving unprotected their homes and growing crops." Lincoln elaborated on this point in a private letter: "It is a fact, that the United States Army, in marching to the Rio Grande, marched into a peaceful Mexican settlement, and frightened the inhabitants away from their homes and their growing crops. . . . At the time the army reached it, a young cotton crop was growing and which crop was wholly destroyed, and the field itself greatly, and permanently injured." The inhabitants of the territory were thus deprived of both their natural right to the fruits of their labors and their natural right to government by consent.[54]

Polk then used this initial, localized act of conquest to justify additional, massive acts of conquest. He demanded that unless Mexico agreed to surrender half its national territory (including California), he would be forced to seize "the *whole* of the Mexican territory." Lincoln drily observed that although Polk insisted that "the separate national existence of Mexico, shall be maintained," he failed to explain "*how* this can be done, after we have taken *all* her territory."[55]

In addition to violating the *natural* rights of the Mexican people living in the invaded territory, Polk's actions, in Lincoln's view, violated the *constitutional* right of the American people and their representatives in Congress to deliberate on urgent public questions based on accurate, timely, and honestly presented information. Daniel Walker Howe observes that when Polk presented his war message to Congress, "party managers did everything they could to stifle discussion, questions, and dissent. In the House of Representatives, they allowed only two hours for debate, then used up all but thirty minutes of this having presidential documents read aloud."[56]

In effect, Polk parlayed his 1844 electoral victory into boundless authorization for everything he did as president. According to Richard J. Ellis and Stephen Kirk, "From the moment he assumed office, Polk aggressively claimed to have a mandate from the people to pursue his policies, particularly the annexation of Texas." Polk then converted this supposed 1844 Texas annexation mandate into an 1846 mandate to initiate a war with Mexico and an 1848 mandate to forcibly seize vast new territories for the United States. In his last annual message in December 1848, Polk continued to argue that his policies had been directly authorized by the people. In his view, the president most faithfully represented the people's will. Congress, in contrast, was prone to "combinations of individuals and sections, in derogation of the general interest."[57]

"The Will of the People, as Expressed through Their Representatives in Congress"

Lincoln's defense of Congress came in response to Polk's sweeping claims of presidential power. Besides charging that Polk unnecessarily and unconstitutionally commenced the Mexican War, Lincoln criticized what he regarded as Polk's abuse of the presidential veto power. In most respects, this antebellum veto debate is timebound. But Polk's attack on the representative function of Congress motivated Lincoln to articulate his own view of the respective roles of Congress and the president in expressing the will of the majority.

The Constitution does not specify the reasons why a president should veto a bill. Article I, section 7 requires only that the president's veto be accompanied by a statement of "his Objections." This implies that the veto is not a power to be exercised arbitrarily but an act requiring justification. (In contrast, the Constitution does not require Congress to state its reasons for passing a bill or for overriding a presidential veto.)

George Washington considered it appropriate for a president to veto bills he regarded as clearly unconstitutional; otherwise, he should defer to the judgment of Congress. Secretary of state Thomas Jefferson counseled Washington that if he were undecided about a bill's constitutionality, he should demonstrate "a just respect for the wisdom of the legislature" by signing it. James Madison later maintained that a bill could be vetoed either because the president judged it unconstitutional or because he had policy objections, but he believed these two types of reasons should be distinguished. In 1815 Madison vetoed a bill to reestablish the Bank of the United States not on constitutional grounds but because of specific policy objections that he trusted "the wisdom of Congress" to remedy. Congress did revise the bank bill, and in 1816 Madison signed it into law.[58]

Andrew Jackson's veto of a bill to renew the charter of the Bank of the United States was a key grievance motivating the formation of the Whig Party in the 1830s. Jackson's veto message paid no rhetorical tribute to "the wisdom of Congress," as Madison's had. What Whigs perceived as veto abuse continued through the presidencies of John Tyler and James Polk. Tyler (who succeeded to the presidency upon William Henry Harrison's death), though nominally a Whig, vetoed ten Whig-supported bills, including the recharter of the bank, a protective tariff, and internal improvements (federally funded roads and canals). In December 1847 Polk vetoed an internal improvements bill that passed Congress with support from both Whigs and Democrats. In response to Polk's veto, Lincoln's June 20, 1848, speech on internal improvements set forth a careful and detailed statement of his views on political economy and the role of government.[59]

Lincoln's most prominent public statements on the proper relationship between the president and Congress occurred during the 1848 election campaign, when he praised Whig presidential candidate Zachary Taylor's pledge to carry out "the will of the people, as expressed through their representatives in congress," and not to exercise the veto power "except in cases of clear violation of the constitution, or manifest haste, and want of consideration by congress." Lincoln quoted Jefferson's 1791 advice to Washington that a president should veto a bill only when it is "clear that it is unauthorized by the constitution," and if the president is unsure on that point, he should respect "the wisdom and justice of the legislature." Lincoln claimed that Taylor's view of the matter was substantially identical to Jefferson's.[60]

At times during the 1848 campaign, Lincoln seemed to characterize the president as no more than a rubber stamp for Congress; he rhetorically imagined a future President Taylor saying to Congress, "*Your* will, gentlemen, not *mine*," and "Just as you please." In response to a Democratic House member who argued that "the President is as much the representative of the people as Congress," Lincoln replied:

> In a certain sense, and to a certain extent, he is the representative of the people. He is elected by them, as well as congress is. But can he, in the nature of things, know the wants of the people, as well as three hundred other men, coming from all the various localities of the nation? If so, where is the propriety of having a congress? . . . To thus transfer legislation, is clearly to take it from those who understand, with minuteness, the interests of the people, and to give it to one who does not, and can not so well understand it.

In conceding here that the president was "in a certain sense, and to a certain extent" the people's representative, Lincoln here raised the question, but did not answer it, of what the president's specific role should be in representing the popular will and how it differed from the "minuteness" with which Congress fulfilled this role.[61]

In fact, Lincoln's views on the proper role of the president in relation to Congress were more complex than "your will, not mine." Lincoln was frustrated during the 1848 campaign by Taylor's unwillingness to make any policy statements on key public issues such as the National Bank, the tariff, and the extension of slavery. (However, Taylor's lack of public record on these divisive questions was one reason many Whigs considered him the most electable candidate.)

Lincoln's views were best expressed in an unpublished fragment he penned during the 1848 campaign titled "What General Taylor Ought to Say." Lincoln advised Taylor to say that, as president, he would not urge "reagitation" of the National Bank question, but "should Congress see fit to establish such an institution, I should not arrest it by the veto" unless it were subject to some (new) "constitutional objection, from which I believe the two former banks to have been free." This advice closely matches the deferential presidential role Lincoln set out in his July 27, 1848, speech on internal improvements. Lincoln's advice to Taylor on the tariff question, however, anticipated a more substantive leadership role for the president. He recommended that Taylor, as a presidential candidate, announce that "the national debt created by the war, renders a modification of the existing tariff indispensable," and therefore "I should be pleased to see it adjusted with a due reference to the protection of our home industry," although "the particulars" of the legislation "must and should be left to the untrammeled discretion of Congress." Here, Lincoln envisioned Taylor going before the voters with a clear yet general position on a long-contested public question, but doing so in a way that did not detract from, but instead confirmed, Congress's primary role in drafting and deliberating on legislation. Lincoln's remarks here clarify what he meant in the July 27 speech when he described the president as, "in a certain sense, and to a certain extent . . . the representative of the people." Lincoln thus suggested that a presidential candidate who communicated to voters an understandable, general position on issues could, once elected, plausibly claim "in a sense" to represent the popular will, but only insofar as he respected Congress's primary role in representing "with minuteness, the interests of the people."[62]

On the (still unsettled) Mexican War and the status of slavery in any territories acquired in that war, Lincoln urged a somewhat more prominent role for the president. Taylor's position should be that "it is my desire that we should not acquire any [territory] extending so far South, as to enlarge and agrivate [sic] the distracting question of slavery."[63] Lincoln did *not* suggest that a president could unilaterally decide, without the participation of Congress, whether slavery would be permitted or excluded in the newly acquired territories. But a president could, in Lincoln's view, negotiate a treaty (subject to Senate confirmation) that omitted the acquisition of any territories where slavery was likely to take hold. Additionally or alternatively, as president, Taylor could choose to sign (rather than veto) legislation passed by Congress that, on the model of the Wilmot Proviso, would prohibit slavery in the newly acquired territories.

In his July 27, 1848, House speech, Lincoln admitted that "I do not know what [Taylor] would do on the Wilmot Proviso." But "with what information I have, I hope and *believe*, Gen. Taylor would not veto the Proviso." Here and in other speeches from the 1848 campaign, Lincoln appeared to be frustrated with Taylor's unwillingness to take a stance on slavery in the territories. But Taylor's vagueness on slavery did not affect Lincoln's support, for if Democrat Lewis Cass were elected (an early advocate of the "popular sovereignty" policy later voiced by Stephen Douglas), slavery, in Lincoln's view, would "certainly" go into the territories, and there would be "new wars, new acquisitions of territory and still further extensions of slavery." Thus, as early as 1848, Lincoln expected presidents and presidential candidates to exercise leadership in shaping public opinion, yet in a way that reaffirmed rather than undermined the representative function of Congress. Zachary Taylor in the flesh did not exactly match Lincoln's model, but he came closer than his Democratic opponent.[64]

"A Sort of Forced Consent"

In his July 27, 1848, speech in the US House praising Whig presidential nominee Zachary Taylor and criticizing Democratic nominee Lewis Cass, Lincoln made a statement that might appear to reject not only presidential mandates but also party platforms and even the existence of organized political parties:

> You democrats, and your candidate [Cass], in the main are in favor of laying down, in advance, a platform—a set of party positions, as a unit, and then of enforcing the people, by every sort of appliance, to ratify them, however unpalatable some of them may be. We, and our candidate [Taylor], are in favor of making Presidential elections, and the legislation of the country, distinct matters. . . . We hold the true republican position. In leaving the people's business in their hands, we can not be wrong. We are willing, and even anxious, to go to the people, on this issue.[65]

For Lincoln to denounce the inherent evil of political parties would be markedly inconsistent with his own efforts as a party builder and his party-positive statements on other occasions. I suggest that Lincoln was making neither an antiparty nor an antiplatform argument but instead was advocating genuine public deliberation and intraparty democracy. Lincoln's 1848 critique of Democrats' lack of intraparty democracy illuminates his more fundamental objections, in 1854, to the secretive process by which the Kansas-Nebraska Act was drafted and subsequently imposed on the Democratic rank and file as a test of party loyalty (see chapter 4).

That Lincoln was making neither an antiparty nor an antiplatform argument is clear from the last sentence of the passage quoted above: "We are willing, and even anxious, to go to the people, on this issue." "We" clearly refers to the Whigs, and "go[ing] to the people" on an issue in an election year was, in substance, to describe a platform. (Unfortunately, from Lincoln's perspective, the Whigs' 1848 platform merely praised Taylor's military record and took no position on substantive questions.[66] Lincoln attempted to give the Whigs' vacuous official platform some substance.)

The consensus among the political elite of the early republic was that organized political parties were pernicious and should be discouraged, even if they could not be entirely prevented. Citizens should vote based on their judgment of candidates' personal merit, not as followers of a party, and elected officeholders should display an independence from parties in fulfilling their legislative or executive duties. This antiparty ideal endured even as many of those same leaders, including Thomas Jefferson, James Madison, and Alexander Hamilton, organized the Democratic-Republican and Federalist Parties during the high-stakes political contests of the 1790s. The partisans of the 1790s, on both sides of the ideological divide, saw their party-building efforts as defensive and temporary: because their opponents had formed a party, they too must organize, fighting fire with fire, but with the ultimate aim of abolishing organized parties and restoring true republican practice.[67]

This antiparty mind-set persisted to a significant degree during the antebellum period, despite the creation of the Jacksonian Democratic and Whig Parties. It was especially enduring among the Whigs, who remained less tightly organized and ideologically coherent than the Democrats.[68] Zachary Taylor, a career military officer with a distinguished record in the Mexican War, had never publicly affiliated with any political party prior to becoming the Whig presidential nominee in 1848, and during the campaign he presented himself as above parties: "If elected I would not be the mere President of a party. I would endeavor to act independent of party domination. I should feel bound to administer the Government untrammeled by party schemes."[69]

This was the antiparty perspective that Lincoln appeared to echo in praising Taylor at the expense of Cass in his July 27, 1848, speech. But it is evident that Lincoln was not antiparty; instead, he supported intraparty democracy. As quoted earlier: "You democrats, and your candidate, in the main are in favor of laying down, in advance, a platform—a set of party positions, as a unit, and then of enforcing the people, by every sort of appliance, to ratify them, however unpalatable some of them may be." What Lincoln criticized was not the practice of communicating "a platform—a set of party positions"—for that was what Lincoln himself did at the end of the passage. What he targeted was the practice of party leaders formulating positions "in advance . . . as a unit" and then forcing ordinary party members to ratify those positions, even though they were never consulted and found many of those positions "unpalatable."

In his June 20, 1848, speech on internal improvements, Lincoln furnished specifics on the kind of platform abuse he had in mind. At the Democrats' national convention in May 1848, the party had adopted a platform resolution asserting "that the constitution does not confer upon the general government the power to commence, and carry on a general system of internal improvements." This same provision had been included in the Democrats' 1840 and 1844 platforms. But a growing number of Democrats, including in Illinois, favored federal encouragement of roads, canals, and railroads. In December 1847 President Polk, a Democrat, vetoed an internal improvements bill that had secured the support of many Democrats and most Whigs in Congress. Lewis Cass, the Democratic nominee for president in 1848, endorsed the entire platform as a statement "of our political faith, and I adhere to them as firmly, as I approve them cordially."[70]

Lincoln's question for the Democrats was: where does this leave those Democrats who *favor* internal improvements?

> While I know there are many democrats, on this floor and elsewhere, who disapprove [of Polk's internal improvements veto], I understand that all who shall vote for Gen. Cass will thereafter be counted as having approved it—as having endorsed all its doctrines. . . . In this way, the internal improvement democrats are to be, by a sort of forced consent, carried over, and arrayed against themselves on this measure of policy.[71]

One might characterize Lincoln's remarks as a divide-and-conquer strategy in an election year, and that motive was certainly present. But Lincoln also raised fundamental questions about political parties that were equally relevant to the Whigs and, later, to Lincoln's Republican party-building efforts in the 1850s.

Lincoln raised the important question whether a president affiliated with a party, or a party's presidential nominee, necessarily spoke for the party as a whole, including on new issues or issues on which there was substantial intraparty disagreement. He addressed the Democrats:

> I understand your idea, that if a Presidential candidate avow his opinion upon a given question, or rather, upon all questions, and the people, with full knowledge of this, elect him, they thereby distinctly approve all those opinions. This,

though plausible, is a most pernicious deception. By means of it, measures are adopted or rejected, contrary to the wishes of the whole of one party, and often nearly half of the other. The process is this. Three, four, or half a dozen questions are prominent at a given time; the party selects its candidate, and he takes his position on each of these questions. On all but one, his positions have already been endorsed at former elections, and his party fully committed to them; but that one is new, and a large portion of them are against it. But what are they to do? The whole are strung together; and they must take all, or reject all. . . . If we run our eyes along the line of the past, we shall see that almost, if not quite all the articles of the present democratic creed, have been first forced upon the party in this very way.

Lincoln returned to the theme of intraparty disagreement at the end of the speech: "The democrats are kind enough to frequently remind us that we have some dissensions in our ranks. . . . Some such *we* certainly have; have *you* none, gentlemen democrats? Is it all union and harmony in *your* ranks?—no bickerings?—no divisions?"[72]

Lincoln did not argue here against presidential candidates taking positions on issues. What he criticized was the notion that one powerful individual in the party—its presidential nominee—automatically spoke for the whole and thereby silenced all diversity of viewpoints within the ranks. Nor did Lincoln denounce party platforms, though he clearly recognized their limitations. His point was that precisely because of their limitations, party platforms should be open to continuing debate and revision, not dictated once and for all by some powerful person or faction within the party.

These arcane debates about parties and platforms from a long-forgotten presidential election campaign may strike modern readers as mere historical curiosities. Today, it surprises no one that a party's national platform is drafted by the presidential nominee's campaign operatives. The public's image of political parties is so negative (even though this same public is hyperpartisan in its electoral behavior) that many voters hardly care whether political parties are internally democratic or not. For Lincoln, however, political parties were an essential element of a larger picture. If the majority was sovereign in a popular government, how did such a majority actually form, act, and speak? Lincoln did not want government by an uninformed, undeliberate majority. But neither was he willing to reduce the ordinary voter's role to merely selecting the *persons* who make the laws, while giving officeholders a completely free hand. Ordinary citizens needed the opportunity to vote for or against *something*, not just for or against *someone*. Political parties were, for Lincoln, a key link in the chain connecting the opinions of ordinary voters in cities, towns, and farmsteads with the decisions made by their government.

And yet political parties could betray this trust. Parties could become internally authoritarian, as, in Lincoln's view, the Democratic Party had become. Alternatively, parties could stand for too little, as was the case—to Lincoln's frustration—with the Whigs in 1848, although he was not yet ready to look elsewhere. When in the mid-1850s Lincoln decided to put his energy, skill, and passion into building a very different kind of party, he kept in mind the concerns and warnings he had voiced as a Whig. One of the many things that shocked Lincoln about the Kansas-Nebraska Act was that it was initially opposed by Democratic legislators in Illinois, Stephen Douglas's own state. However, after receiving "Douglas's orders . . . to have resolutions passed approving the bill . . . they were approved by large majorities" because "the party necessity of supporting it, became apparent."[73] Lincoln here described a more extreme and politically consequential instance of "forced consent" than the one imposed on internal-improvement Democrats in 1848.

And Lincoln in the 1850s would again face the challenges of internal diversity within his own party, with much more at stake. In his "House Divided" speech of June 16, 1858, Lincoln described the Republican Party as a body formed "of *strange, discordant,* and even, *hostile* elements . . . gathered from the four winds."[74] Chapter 5 examines how Lincoln sought to ensure that the new party clearly stood for something (more so than the Whigs in 1848), yet without driving out any of its sometimes strange, discordant, mutually hostile elements.

"Founded on Both Injustice and Bad Policy"

In 1858, during his Senate campaign against Stephen Douglas, Lincoln reflected on how passage of the Kansas-Nebraska Act in 1854 had transformed his thinking about slavery. "Although I have ever been opposed to slavery," he stated, he had "rested in the hope and belief that it was in course of ultimate extinction. For that reason, it had been a minor question with me." But when the Missouri Compromise was repealed in 1854 (thereby allowing slavery in territories north of the 36° 30' paral-

lel), Lincoln concluded that slavery had been placed "on a new basis
. . . for making it perpetual, national, and universal."[75] In his earlier
political career, Lincoln had occasionally spoken or acted on slavery
questions. During his term in Congress (1847–49), he voted repeatedly for the Wilmot Proviso (which would have prohibited slavery in the
territories acquired from the Mexican War). He proposed (unsuccessfully) to gradually abolish slavery in the District of Columbia, with compensation paid to slave owners.[76] But his legislative priorities remained
focused on economic development—roads, canals, banking, currency,
protective tariffs, and public lands—and on upholding the vitality of
Congress as an institution. But from 1854 on, Lincoln made opposition
to the spread of slavery central to his political efforts, treating all other
questions as secondary and urging others to do the same.

Why did it take Lincoln so long to see the light? Posing the question
this way portrays Lincoln as a footdragger at best, in contrast to the
abolitionists, who appear to be the true heroes of the drama.[77] I believe
it is more fruitful to ask a different set of questions about the timing of
Lincoln's decision to make opposition to slavery his central concern.
From the earliest years of his political career, Lincoln was intensely attached to America's institutions of popular self-government and, at the
same time, deeply anxious about their long-term survival. Before 1854,
Lincoln identified at least three fundamental threats to America's free
institutions: lawlessness, whether it manifested itself in the streets or in
legislative chambers; erosion of the authority and deliberative character of Congress, whether caused by high-handed presidential actions or
abdication of responsibility by the body's own members; and a policy of
territorial conquest that systematically violated the natural rights of that
territory's inhabitants. During his Whig phase, Lincoln may well have
hoped and believed that slavery was headed for "ultimate extinction."
Politically, he regarded it as a "minor question," indicating that, at the
time, he did not consider slavery a fundamental threat to America's free
institutions. But from 1854 on, he *did* regard it as a fundamental threat.
Before 1854, Lincoln acknowledged the injustice of racial slavery but
did not systematically present it as violating the rights of persons of *all*
races, white citizens included. From 1854 on, he consistently maintained
that the expansion of slavery, and the doctrines advanced to defend its
expansion, threatened the rights of everyone, including white citizens
like himself. Before 1854, Lincoln regarded lawlessness, erosion of the
authority of Congress, and expansionist foreign policy as problems that

were largely separable from slavery. From 1854 on, the urgent threat of slavery's continued expansion merged in Lincoln's thinking with these other concerns.

This suggests two questions I examine in later chapters. First, why did Lincoln regard passage of the Kansas-Nebraska Act as a *new* and urgent threat to the survival of America's free political institutions? (Why, for instance, was it a greater threat than many other slavery-friendly federal policies that preceded it?) Second, how did Lincoln believe these same free institutions, insofar as they still functioned, could be used to contain the growth of slavery and eventually abolish it? Such questions direct us to the evolution of Lincoln's own reasoning about slavery, in connection with the full range of matters he thought and cared about, rather than contrasting him unfavorably with others whose manner of thought was different.

What is arguably Lincoln's most revealing pre-1854 statement on slavery occurs, somewhat surprisingly, near the end of his February 22, 1842, address to the Washington Temperance Society. Lincoln's immediate purpose in the address was to praise the society for rejecting the punitive, drunkard-shaming approach of other temperance advocates, expressed in "thundering tones of anathema and denunciation," and instead favoring "kind, unassuming persuasion. . . . If you would win a man to your cause, *first* convince him that you are his sincere friend." Lincoln opposed the demand in some circles for the legal prohibition of alcohol (which, during the 1850s, complicated efforts to build the Republican Party) and favored a voluntary approach that appealed to the self-interest of the individual targeted for reform. The address features a perceptive discussion of the power of public opinion—"the strong inclination each of us feels to do as we see all our neighbors do."[78]

Near its conclusion the address took an unexpected turn. Because the society's namesake was a hero of the American Revolution, Lincoln compared the *political* revolution accomplished by the patriots of 1776 with the *moral* revolution desired by the Washington Temperance Society. The political revolution of 1776 "has given us a degree of political freedom, far exceeding that of any other of the nations of the earth." But the American Revolution came at a high cost: "It breathed forth famine, swam in blood and rode on fire; and long, long after, the orphan's cry, and the widow's wail, continued to break the sad silence that ensued. These were the price, the inevitable price, paid for the blessings it sought." In contrast, the "temperance revolution" promised to overthrow "a stronger bondage" and "a greater tyrant," yet without the steep human cost of the American Revolution: "By *it* no orphans starving, no widows weeping. By *it,* none wounded in feeling, none injured in interest." Even the dram makers and dram sellers "will have glided into other occupations *so* gradually" as to remove "the shock of change." At this point, briefly but unmistakably, Lincoln introduced the institution of slavery. He predicted the eventual victory of the "Reign of Reason," when "there shall be neither a slave nor a drunkard on the earth"; when "both those revolutions"—the political and the moral— "shall have planted, and nurtured to maturity, both the political and moral freedom of their species."[79]

Lincoln thus (in 1842) placed slavery in the category of evils to be remedied by the gentle moral methods of the temperance revolution, rather than the violent and costly methods of the political revolution of 1776. In suggesting that peaceful moral persuasion rather than direct political action was the key to abolishing slavery, Lincoln echoed a position that had once been voiced by nearly all wings of the abolitionist movement (William Lloyd Garrison and his followers, for example, abjured all political action, even voting, in favor of "moral suasion"). By 1842, however, there were significant divisions among abolitionists over whether the movement should engage in direct political action.[80] In the temperance address, Lincoln did not explain *how* an effective moral revolution against slavery would play out (Would all political methods be ruled out? Only some?). But two things are clear: first, Lincoln recognized the possibility that divisions over slavery might produce a violent political conflict, and second, he very much hoped to avoid this. By the late 1850s, Lincoln no longer believed (if he ever did) that the injustice of slavery could be remedied through voluntary efforts alone, as the evil of alcohol abuse could. But he unquestionably still hoped to avoid civil war.

Lincoln's earliest recorded public statement on slavery was his March 3, 1837, protest in the Illinois legislature, coauthored with Representative Dan Stone. Their protest came in response to antiabolition resolutions that had passed both houses of the Illinois legislature earlier in the session. Leading up to this episode was the abolitionist petition campaign in Congress, which reached its peak at this time, and the intense proslavery backlash against it. In 1836 and 1837 abolitionist societies, mostly in the Northeast, repeatedly pressured Congress with antislavery petitions, some of which contained enormous numbers of individual signatures.[81] These petitions urged Congress to abolish slavery and the slave trade in the District of Columbia, where the Constitution (Article I, section 8) gave Congress the power "to exercise exclusive legislation in all cases whatsoever," in contrast to the states, where (at least according to "mainstream" constitutional doctrine) the institution of slavery fell outside the jurisdiction of Congress. The abolitionist petition campaign provoked a massive defensive response from the slave states. In addition to persuading Congress to enact the infamous "gag rule," the legislatures of several slave states sent antiabolitionist memorials to the legislatures of the free states, urging their support in suppressing abolitionism. In sympathy with the pleas of these slave states, the Illinois legislature passed resolutions holding that "we highly disapprove of the formation of abolition societies, and of the doctrines promulgated by them"; that "the right of property in slaves, is sacred to the slave-holding States by the Federal Constitution, and that they cannot be deprived of that right without their consent"; and that "the General Government cannot abolish slavery in the District of Columbia, against the consent of the citizens of said District without a manifest breach of good faith."[82] (The Illinois resolutions did not actually call it *unconstitutional* for Congress to abolish slavery in the District of Columbia, as slave-state leaders claimed, but calling abolition there a "breach of good faith" came close to the southern constitutional position.)

The Lincoln-Stone protest stated:

> They [Lincoln and Stone] believe that the institution of slavery is founded on both injustice and bad policy; but that the promulgation of abolition doctrines tends rather to increase than to abate its evils.
>
> They believe that the Congress of the United States has no power, under the constitution, to interfere with the institution of slavery in the different States.
>
> They believe that the Congress of the United States has the power, under the constitution, to abolish slavery in the District of Columbia; but that that power ought not to be exercised unless at the request of the people of said District.
>
> The difference between these opinions and those contained in the said resolution, is their reason for entering this protest.[83]

Some commentators have characterized the protest as differing marginally, if at all, from the majority's resolutions.[84] In fact, the Lincoln-Stone protest differed from the majority resolutions on several important points. The most fundamental difference was that the majority resolutions asserted that "the right of property in slaves" was made "sacred . . . by the Federal Constitution." The Lincoln-Stone resolution nowhere acknowledged any federal constitutional right to hold slave property. After the *Dred Scott* ruling in 1857, Lincoln—in common with most other Republicans and many non-Garrisonian abolitionists—positively asserted that the Constitution did *not* affirm a property right in slaves. In this respect, Lincoln's constitutional position was the same in 1857 as it had been in 1837, though not yet loudly proclaimed.

That "the Congress of the United States has no power, under the constitution, to interfere with the institution of slavery in the different States" was a position shared by Garrisonian abolitionists (who regarded the entire Constitution as a "covenant with death") and, for different reasons, by many of the "political" abolitionists who were most active in enlisting the support of sympathetic elected officials.[85] Because the antebellum Constitution blocked efforts to abolish slavery in the states, politically engaged abolitionists focused most of their efforts on abolishing slavery in the District of Columbia and the territories and on opposing fugitive slave laws—domains in which Congress had the authority to act.

The Illinois resolutions to which Lincoln and Stone were responding emphasized what Congress *could not* do, or at least *should not* do, with respect to slavery in the District of Columbia. The Lincoln-Stone resolution emphasized what Congress *could* do—that is, it "has the power, under the Constitution" to abolish slavery in the District—and proceeded to specify the circumstances under which that power might prudently be exercised: "at the request of the people of said District." In contrast to the majority resolutions, the Lincoln-Stone resolution did *not* say that slaveholders in the District of Columbia "cannot be deprived" of their slaves "without [the slaveholders'] consent." If the majority of voters in the District supported abolition, Congress (under the Lincoln-Stone formulation) should override slaveholder opposition and abolish slavery in the District of Columbia.

The Illinois resolutions held that "we highly disapprove of the formation of abolition societies, and of the doctrines promulgated by them," while saying nothing whatsoever about the injustice of slavery itself. The Lincoln-Stone resolution held that "the institution of slavery is founded on both injustice and bad policy"; nowhere did it condemn either the formation of abolitionist societies or their doctrines. However, the line that follows is troubling: "but that the promulgation of abolition doctrines tends rather to increase than to abate its evils." What was it about abolitionist doctrines that led Lincoln and Stone to believe that they would increase the evils of slavery?

If Lincoln offered any explanations on this point, the historical record has not preserved them. But given the enormous, often violent, and potentially Union-threatening southern backlash against the abolitionist petition campaign, it was not implausible to assert that the abolitionists' confrontational approach made a bad situation worse. Yet if Lincoln shared abolitionists' moral condemnation of slavery but criticized the movement's methods, what alternative methods did he think should be adopted? At this stage of his career, Lincoln offered no concrete answer to that question. Instead, his critique of abolitionism apparently depended on his assumption—which he later acknowledged may have been a delusion—that slavery was on a course toward ultimate extinction. In retrospect, slavery—economically, politically, geographically, and with respect to public opinion in the slave states—was clearly *not* trending toward ultimate extinction in 1837 but was heading in the opposite direction. For that reason, Lincoln's 1837 criticism of abolitionists for urgently promulgating abolitionist doctrines missed the mark. From 1854 on, Lincoln shared abolitionists' urgency about slavery, though they continued to differ with respect to methods.

"Using Our Most Intelligent Judgment of the Consequences"

In a July 10, 1858, speech in Chicago (delivered shortly after his famous "House Divided" speech), Lincoln remarked, "I have always hated slavery, I think as much as any Abolitionist." Then he added, "I have always been quiet about it until this new era of the introduction of the Nebraska Bill began. I always believed that everybody was against it, and that it was in course of ultimate extinction."[86]

The documentary record supports Lincoln's claim that he always considered slavery unjust and that before 1854 he believed it was headed for extinction. But early in his career, he does not appear to have hated slavery with the passion of an abolitionist. A pair of letters describing the same incident, one from 1841 and another from 1855, reveal the shift in Lincoln's moral thermometer with respect to slavery. In 1841 Lincoln and his friend Joshua Speed (from a slaveholding Kentucky family) rode a steamboat along the Ohio River on their way to St. Louis.

In a September 1841 letter to Joshua's sister Mary, Lincoln described a gang of twelve enslaved persons recently purchased in Kentucky, all chained together by the wrists, to be sold in the South. "The negroes were strung together precisely like so many fish upon a trot-line. In this condition they were being separated forever from the scenes of their childhood, their friends, their fathers and mothers, and brothers and sisters, and many of them, from their wives and children, and going into perpetual slavery where the lash of the master is proverbially more ruthless and unrelenting than any other where." But Lincoln immediately softened the harsh picture by adding, "and yet amid all these distressing circumstances, as we would think them, they were the most cheerful and apparently happy creatures on board." In contrast, in an 1855 letter to Joshua Speed—the same letter in which Lincoln denounced the Kansas-Nebraska Act as "*conceived* in violence," "*passed* in violence," and "*maintained* in violence"—Lincoln reminded his friend of the violent scene they had witnessed on the steamboat, this time without the conscience-salving sentimentalities of his 1841 letter to Mary. "You may remember, as I well do, that from Louisville to the mouth of the Ohio there were, on board, ten or a dozen slaves, shackled together with irons. That sight was a continual torment to me; and I see something like it every time I touch the Ohio, or any other slave-border."[87]

In his early career, Lincoln viewed the territorial expansion of slavery—at least before President Polk's "unnecessary" and "unconstitutional" instigation of war with Mexico—with relative detachment, as revealed in his 1845 observations on the annexation of Texas. American settlers had planted slavery in Texas before its independence from Mexico, so admitting Texas to the Union did not technically expand the territorial reach of slavery. But the United States certainly could have chosen not to admit a new, large, powerful slave state. Lincoln claimed to be against the annexation of Texas—"I never could see much good to come of annexation"—but his opposition seemed tepid. "I never could very clearly see how the annexation would augment the evil of slavery," since "slaves would be taken there in about equal numbers, with or without annexation." Moreover, Texas was already a free republic "on our own model." Lincoln declared it "a paramount duty of us in the free states, due to the Union of the states, and perhaps to liberty itself (paradox though it may seem) to let the slavery of the other states alone." Yet at the same time, free-state citizens had a duty not to "knowingly lend ourselves" to anything that would "prevent that slavery from dying a natural death."[88] From this perspective, no urgent antislavery action was called for, and even opposing the annexation of Texas was not a high priority. Lincoln was certainly resting on the hope (or rather, the delusion) that slavery would die out on its own. He expressed a much higher degree of moral outrage about slavery's expansion from 1854 onward than he had in 1845.

Nor did Lincoln appear worried in 1845 that the continued enslavement of Black Americans threatened the liberty of white Americans. His comment about slaveholding Texas being a free republic "on our own model" contrasts strikingly with his cry in the 1854 Kansas-Nebraska speech that "our republican robe is soiled, and trailed in the dust," and his warning that in "our greedy chase to make profit of the negro" we may "cancel and tear to pieces even the white man's charter of freedom." Moreover, in his 1854 Kansas-Nebraska speech, Lincoln specifically refuted his own 1845 argument about Texas: that allowing slave owners to transport slaves to a new state or territory did not "augment the evil of slavery" because it did not change the number of people enslaved. In the 1854 speech, Lincoln called this a "lullaby" argument because it ignored the degree to which opening new territories to slavery increased the demand for slaves illegally imported from Africa and because "we know that [the] opening of new countries to slavery, tends to the perpetuation of the institution, and so does KEEP men in slavery who otherwise would be free." Lincoln apparently realized that he had once been fooled by that "lullaby" argument.[89]

During the 1840s Lincoln was critical of the Liberty Party (first formed in 1840) and the Free-Soil Party (1848) because he considered antislavery third parties counterproductive with respect to their own goals. In 1844 the Liberty Party's presidential candidate, James Birney, probably drew enough antislavery voters away from Whig nominee Henry Clay in the key state of New York to allow Democratic nominee James Polk to win both that state and the presidency.[90] Lincoln expressed his frustration in an 1845 letter to a Whig acquaintance with Liberty Party sympathies: "If the whig abolitionists of New York had voted with us last fall, Mr. Clay would now be president, whig principles in the ascendant, and Texas not annexed; whereas by the division, all that either had at stake in the contest, was lost." Lincoln criticized the moral absolutism of "Liberty-men" who refused to vote for Clay because he was a slaveholder, thus resulting in the election of Polk, who in addition to being a slaveholder actively expanded the institution of slavery. "If the fruit of electing Mr. Clay would have been to prevent the extension of slavery, could the act of electing have been *evil?*"[91] During the 1848 presidential campaign Lincoln made a similar criticism of the Free-Soil Party, even though, as a member of Congress, he had taken a free-soil stance by voting for the Wilmot Proviso. Lincoln argued against the moral view that one must "do their duty and leave the consequences to God." The only way to discern what one's duty is, Lincoln insisted, was by "using our most intelligent judgment of the consequences." The abolitionists who refused to vote for Clay in 1844, Lincoln complained, "while they professed great horror at the proposed extension of slave territory," in fact "aided in the election of Mr. Polk." And in that sense, they shared responsibility for the "disastrous consequences" of Polk's election, including the potentially enormous territorial expansion of slavery.[92]

Lincoln's argument here was reasonable but not beyond dispute. On the issue of slavery, most abolitionists saw little distance between Polk and Clay in 1844—especially since Clay failed to take a clear position against the annexation of Texas[93]—or between Cass and Taylor in 1848. But politically focused abolitionists did depend on the cooperation of northern antislavery Whigs, even as they denounced the latter for their membership in a slavery-compromised national party. Liberty Party abolitionists sought to challenge antislavery Whigs vigorously enough to motivate them to take a stronger antislavery stance, but not so vigorously as to cause them to lose their seats to proslavery Democrats. As it turned out, this high-stakes strategy (aided by the extremism of the slave states' response) helped move northern public opinion in an antislavery direction.[94] But such a strategy could also result (and sometimes did) in throwing elections in northern states to slavery-friendly Democrats, which was Lincoln's principal objection.

Lincoln's criticism of antislavery third-party initiatives may seem ironic because, in crucial respects, the Republican Party (though less radical) inherited the work begun by the Liberty and Free-Soil Parties.[95] But what Lincoln criticized about antislavery third parties in the 1840s was not their goals, which he shared, but what he considered their counterproductive political strategies. By the mid-1850s, with the disappearance of the Whig Party and the Democratic Party's increasingly proslavery stance, the strategic circumstances had fundamentally changed. Now, in Lincoln's view, taking responsibility for consequences meant creating and supporting a national, electorally competitive, ideologically inclusive antislavery party. This would maximize the political effectiveness of what Lincoln believed to be a national majority opposed to the extension of slavery. What was irresponsible, in his view, was to divide the votes of this antislavery majority by emphasizing crosscutting secondary issues such as immigration or alcohol prohibition. Lincoln's opposition to slavery may have been much stronger in his Republican phase than in his Whig years. But throughout his career he opposed the practice of defeating one's goals by scattering one's votes.

Conclusion

During his political career before 1854, Lincoln cared about many particular things and one big thing. The one big thing was securing the great promise of popular self-government against several worrisome tendencies that could cause it to self-destruct. His particular concerns included creating economic opportunity, expanding political participation, encouraging respect for law, upholding the vitality of Congress as a representative and deliberative body, building responsive and responsible political parties, opposing reckless foreign policy, and containing the spread of slavery. What changed in 1854 was that one of these items—the spread of slavery—became more important than all the others and in many respects absorbed them all because it now posed a mortal threat to the one big thing Lincoln cared about most.

4 | "Aroused Him as He Had Never Been Before"

From Kansas-Nebraska to House Divided

The Kansas-Nebraska Act, which potentially opened vast new territories to slavery, transformed Lincoln's political thought and gave new purpose to his political career. In a brief autobiography penned for the 1860 presidential campaign, he recalled: "In 1854, his profession had almost superseded the thought of politics in his mind, when the repeal of the Missouri compromise aroused him as he had never been before." Before 1854, Lincoln had believed slavery "was in course of ultimate extinction." But the Kansas-Nebraska Act threatened to make slavery "perpetual, national, and universal," beyond the power of Congress or a majority of the American electorate to halt or reverse. From that point on, slavery became Lincoln's "paramount" concern.[1]

Lincoln was not alone in believing the Kansas-Nebraska Act initiated a crisis of government. Michael F. Holt observes that during the 1850s, "a genuine sense of crisis troubled Americans living in that decade," though they understood that crisis and responded to it in very different ways.[2] The Kansas-Nebraska Act triggered a chain of events that helped destroy one major political party (the Whigs), created another (the Republicans), and ultimately left a third (the Democrats) fatally divided.

The central provision of the Kansas-Nebraska Act was that the (white male) inhabitants of each territory had the power to decide, by majority vote, whether slavery would be permitted or prohibited in that territory. Stephen Douglas, the author of the act, argued that it embodied the most sacred principle of free government: "the exclusive right of a free people to form and adopt their own fundamental law, and to manage and regulate their own internal affairs and domestic institutions."[3] Congress, which had enacted the Kansas-Nebraska Act, would henceforth have no authority to decide whether slavery would be prohibited or permitted in territories belonging to the United States. Douglas's goal in stripping Congress of authority over slavery in the territories was to take slavery off the national political agenda, thereby ensuring peace between North and South. He accomplished precisely the opposite.

The institution of slavery had been expanding, numerically and geographically, long before 1854. Abolitionists had denounced slavery as a moral and political crisis for decades before the Kansas-Nebraska Act. Why, then, did repeal of the Missouri Compromise arouse Lincoln "as he had never been before"? Why were Lincoln and others able to organize a major political party around opposition to the spread of slavery after 1854, when antislavery parties had previously received only a small fraction of the vote, even in those states where abolitionism was strongest? If slavery was a "monstrous injustice," as Lincoln phrased it,[4] merely limiting its spread and phasing it out over decades appeared to be a tiny and tardy remedy.

The matter takes on a different aspect when the point of reference is not the abolitionists (compared to whom Lincoln appears a foot-dragging latecomer) but Lincoln's own lifelong concern for the survival of popular self-government, including the practice of deliberate majority rule. From this perspective, the Kansas-Nebraska Act signified a fundamentally *new* threat in at least three respects. First, the act perverted the principle of government by "the consent of the governed" by legitimating enslavement by majority vote. No system of majority rule can endure if it permits those who win an election to enslave those who lose the election. Douglas could describe the Kansas-Nebraska Act as popular self-government, Lincoln observed, only if persons of African descent were not considered human beings: "if the negro *is* a man, is it not to that extent, a total destruction of self-government, to say that he too shall not govern *himself?*" In practice, slavery had long enjoyed the support of a (white) majority in slave states such as Georgia and Alabama. But the Kansas-Nebraska Act was different, in Lincoln's view, because it enabled slavery to spread to new territories where it had never existed, in contrast to the "necessity" of tolerating slavery (though not forever) where it was long established and difficult to remove. In this sense, the Kansas-Nebraska Act reproduced the original injustice of the transatlantic slave trade by permitting the enslavement of persons who would otherwise remain free. "No argument could be made in favor of a man's right to take slaves to Nebraska, which could not be equally well made in favor of his right to bring them from the coast of Africa."[5]

Modern readers can readily see that the Kansas-Nebraska Act, like slavery itself, conspicuously denied persons of African descent the right to government by consent. Less evident to readers today, but equally important to Lincoln and many of his contemporaries, was that the Kansas-Nebraska Act also violated the principle of government by consent for the (overwhelmingly white) US citizens who enjoyed voting rights in the 1850s, for the act failed to establish any clear *process* by which the inhabitants of a territory preparing for future statehood would decide whether to permit or prohibit slavery. This procedural emptiness potentially enabled an early-arriving, violent proslavery minority to entrench slavery beyond the power of a future antislavery majority to reverse. Lincoln observed in 1854: "The structure . . . of the Nebraska bill is very peculiar. The people are to decide the question of slavery for themselves; but WHEN they are to decide; or HOW they are to decide; or whether, when the question is once decided, it is to remain so, or is it to be subject to an indefinite succession of new trials, the law does not say." Meanwhile, Lincoln observed, advocates of slavery were already moving into the territory and seizing and holding it—violently, if necessary—with the aim of permanently establishing slavery there. Proslavery Missourians, Lincoln reported,

> are within a stone's throw of the contested ground. They hold meetings and pass resolutions, in which not the slightest allusion to voting is made. They resolve that slavery already exists in the territory; that more shall go there; that they, remaining in Missouri will protect it; and that abolitionists shall be hung, or driven away. Through all this, bowie-knives and six-shooters are seen plainly enough; but never a glimpse of the ballot-box.

Lincoln's description of the act's radical emptiness with respect to process was accurate. He also accurately predicted the violence that would follow.[6]

The procedural emptiness of the Kansas-Nebraska Act was no accident. The legislation was deliberately unclear on the critical question of whether slavery would be *permitted* in a territory unless and until that territory became a state and then decided to remove it, or whether slavery would be *prohibited* in a territory unless and until a majority of its inhabitants specifically voted to legalize it. This ambiguity encouraged slaveholders to believe that they could immediately transport enslaved persons to Kansas, entrench slavery there, and prevent its future abolition. Free-state voters, on the contrary, were encouraged to believe that residents of a territory could exclude slavery before the territory was admitted to the Union as a new state. The law's lack of clarity on this high-stakes question made its implementation susceptible to violence and

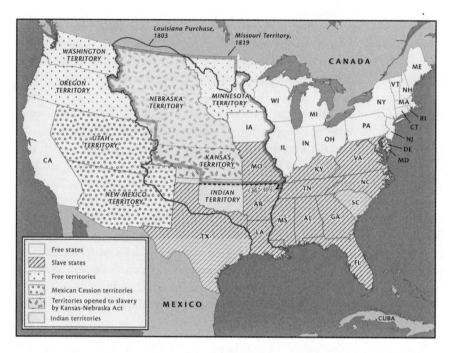

Map 2. States and Territories before and after Kansas-Nebraska Act of 1854. Map by Erin Greb.

electoral fraud, for which "Bleeding Kansas" became notorious. Without clear and effectively enforced procedures, any system of majority rule risks degenerating into mob rule. In that sense, too, the Kansas-Nebraska Act was a perversion of local self-government, not an expression of it.

Finally, the Kansas-Nebraska Act obstructed popular self-government nationally as well as within newly organized territories. To Lincoln, it was obvious that whether slavery would be nationalized and perpetuated or ultimately eradicated was a decision affecting the whole United States, and Americans in each state and section had a stake in the outcome (see Map 2). For this reason, Lincoln saw the Kansas-Nebraska Act as an abdication of popular self-rule because, in passing the law, Congress deliberately stripped itself of the power to decide the most important question facing the people of the United States. In his view, Congress, as the body most responsive and accountable to the people of the United States, was the legitimate forum for deciding critically important, genuinely national questions.

The Contradictions of Popular Sovereignty

Popular sovereignty, as institutionalized in the Kansas-Nebraska Act, had a long history, and none of it was encouraging to those who hoped to prevent the spread of slavery to new territories. The precedent for Congress to establish territories without specifically permitting or prohibiting slavery in those territories dates back to the Southwest Ordinance of 1790. Its earlier counterpart, the Northwest Ordinance (1787), specifically prohibited slavery in territories north of the Ohio River. In practice, the Southwest Ordinance's textual silence on slavery was understood as granting permission to bring slaves into those territories. This same textual silence characterized the statutory language organizing the Louisiana Purchase territories that lay south of 36° 30' under the Missouri Compromise of 1820. Tacitly permitting slavery south of that line was the slaveholders' share of the bargain that expressly prohibited slavery north of that line. Florida, too, was established as a territory in 1822 without reference to slavery. From 1790 through 1850, *every* territory that Congress authorized without reference to slavery entered the Union as a slave state: Kentucky, Tennessee, Louisiana, Mississippi, Alabama, Missouri, Arkansas, and Florida.[7] (Texas, which also entered the Union as a slave state, did not pass through a territorial stage.)

But this pre-1854 textual silence on slavery was not yet popular sovereignty in Kansas-Nebraska guise, because nothing in the enabling legislation stripped Congress of the authority to decide the status of slavery in those territories. (This was an important point in Lincoln's 1860 Cooper Institute address.) The law's silence was construed as Congress tacitly permitting slavery in those territories, not as Congress denying itself jurisdiction over slavery there. However, during the crisis preceding the Missouri Compromise (1820), some proslavery leaders asserted that Congress had no power to ban slavery in *any* territory, regardless of latitude.[8]

Popular sovereignty in the form ultimately inscribed in the Kansas-Nebraska Act was first proposed in 1847 by Vice President George M. Dallas and subsequently taken up by US Senators Daniel S. Dickinson of New York and Lewis Cass of Michigan; the latter advocated this position as the Democratic presidential nominee in 1848. The proposal was an attempt to resolve the crisis over slavery unleashed by the vast new territories acquired by the United States in the Mexican War, most of which lay south of the 36° 30' Missouri Compromise line. Many northern

Democrats and most northern Whigs (including Lincoln) supported the Wilmot Proviso, which would have prohibited slavery in all the territories acquired from Mexico. Slave-state leaders of both parties angrily denounced the proviso; many equated it with abolitionism, and some publicly threatened secession if the proviso became law. One proposal to resolve the crisis was for Congress to extend the 36° 30' line to the Pacific, which would have divided California into a northern free territory and a southern slave territory and would have placed the New Mexico territory (which included the future states of New Mexico and Arizona and part of Nevada) in the slavery column. Extending the 36° 30' line to the Pacific also would have classified any future acquisitions south of that line (e.g., Cuba) as slave territory. John C. Calhoun and Jefferson Davis insisted that slaveholders had a constitutional right to bring slave property to any US territory, but they were willing to accept the 36° 30' extension as a Union-preserving compromise, which would have left at least half of California open to slavery.[9] Popular sovereignty was promoted as a third option, preferable to both the Wilmot Proviso and the 36° 30' extension. Under the Compromise of 1850, the New Mexico and Utah territories were organized without reference to slavery, and California, unpartitioned, entered the Union as a free state. Stephen Douglas, who brokered the final stages of the compromise, later claimed that by organizing the territories of Utah and New Mexico without reference to slavery, Congress also repealed the 36° 30' restriction in the Kansas-Nebraska territory. Others, including Lincoln, strongly rejected that claim.[10]

From the beginning, popular sovereignty was characterized by a fundamental ambiguity that allowed it to be described in different, contradictory ways in the North and the South. In northern states, the policy's advocates argued that the residents of a territory could, at an early stage in the territory's political development, vote to prohibit slavery and thereby prevent the importation of enslaved persons long before the territory was ready for statehood. In contrast, southern advocates of popular sovereignty argued that slaveholders could bring their human property to any US territory and keep it there, unless and until that territory's population grew large enough to qualify for statehood, at which point the territory's citizens could, if they chose, draft and ratify a constitution prohibiting slavery. By that time, of course, the institution of slavery would already be rooted and difficult to remove. Even if future importations were prohibited, slaveholders resident in the territory would certainly resist, by lawsuit, force, or both, any attempt to emancipate the enslaved persons they already held. This debate over the practical meaning of popular sovereignty had been going on, without resolution, for at least six years when Douglas introduced the Kansas-Nebraska Act in 1854. Every attempt by advocates of popular sovereignty to clarify the actual process and timeline for deciding the status of slavery in the territories generated immediate political backlash. Because northern and southern advocates of popular sovereignty realized that their interpretations were contradictory, a third important element was present from the beginning: the expectation that the federal judiciary would resolve the dispute over whether and when territorial residents could prohibit slavery. This prospect appealed to many members of Congress because it relieved them of a political hot potato.[11]

When he introduced the Kansas-Nebraska Act in 1854, Douglas made no effort to resolve popular sovereignty's well-known internal contradictions; on the contrary, he drove them deeper and raised the political stakes. In 1848–50 the status of slavery in the Mexican Cession had to be addressed, and popular sovereignty was one of several proposed solutions to an urgent national crisis. In 1854, in contrast, there was no national crisis regarding the status of slavery in the Louisiana Purchase territories north of 36° 30'. That question had been settled by the Missouri Compromise in 1820 and unaltered by the Compromise of 1850. Douglas's reason for reopening an apparently settled question was to authorize the construction of a railroad proceeding westward from St. Louis, a project in which he was heavily invested both politically and personally. This required formal organization of the territory through which the railroad would run, for which he needed the support of southern members of Congress. Slave-state members of Congress were content for the region to remain Indian territory. But if the lands were opened to white settlement in large numbers and future statehood, southerners had a powerful stake in the status of slavery there.[12]

·The text of the Kansas-Nebraska Act deliberately left unanswered the question of whether territorial settlers could prohibit slavery prior to that territory's admission to the Union as a state. Douglas refused to answer this question when specifically pressed to do so during Senate debate on his bill.[13] But the behind-the-scenes process by which Douglas altered his original bill to win slave-state leaders' support was clearly interpreted by the latter as Douglas accepting *their* interpretation of the popular sovereignty doctrine, and they intended to hold him to it.

On January 4, 1854, Douglas introduced a bill to organize the Kansas-Nebraska territory, and it "said nothing about the Missouri Compromise or about the status of slavery in the territory." He gave no indication that his bill would repeal the Missouri Compromise's slavery restriction, nor did he argue, as he later claimed, that the Compromise of 1850 had *already* repealed the Missouri Compromise. Southern senators pointed out, however, that the 1820 Missouri Compromise's slavery restriction was still in force in the territory, and they refused to "support a Nebraska bill with the Missouri Compromise intact"; they "wanted the Nebraska bill drawn so that it did not exclude slavery from the Nebraska territory." Because he needed these southern senators' support, Douglas added a clause to his bill (which he dubiously claimed had been omitted by clerical error) specifying "that all questions pertaining to slavery in the territories, and in the new States to be formed therefrom, are to be left to the decision of the people residing therein, through their appropriate representative."[14]

Alice Elizabeth Malavasic argues that "physical and circumstantial evidence supports the argument that Douglas was forced by the F Street Mess to add the section." The F Street Mess was a group of influential slave-state senators who roomed at the same boardinghouse; members included David Atchison of Missouri, James Mason and Robert M. T. Hunter of Virginia, and Andrew P. Butler of South Carolina. All members of the F Street Mess had been close political allies of John C. Calhoun (who died in 1850). All of them were fully committed to Calhoun's constitutional argument that US territories were the "common property" of all the states, and for this reason, citizens of slave states had a constitutional right to bring and hold their human property in any US territory, regardless of latitude—a doctrine that was irreconcilable with the notion that a territorial legislature could prohibit slavery during the prestatehood stage. Douglas, who had been neither an ally nor a follower of Calhoun, needed the support of these influential senators to pass the Kansas-Nebraska bill.[15]

But the slave-state senators made it clear to Douglas that this modification of the bill did not go far enough. Unless the Missouri Compromise ban on slavery north of 36° 30' was explicitly repealed, "it would still exclude slaves until the territorial government arrived at the decision to let them in—which such a government could never be expected to do if no slave interest had been permitted to establish itself in the first place."[16] Such an understanding of popular sovereignty was unacceptable to southern Democrats, who instead "viewed popular sovereignty through southern-tinted lenses," meaning that "neither Congress nor a territorial legislature could exclude slavery from a territory during the territorial stage" and that "only a state constitution adopted at the time of statehood could positively disallow slavery."[17] Unless the Missouri Compromise restriction was formally repealed, federal courts might hold that "slave owners . . . were still prohibited from residing in Nebraska with their slaves during the territorial stage." The upshot was that southern senators made their support of the bill conditional on the inclusion of language explicitly repealing the Missouri Compromise slavery restriction. Douglas was apparently reluctant to do this. His own committee report for the bill originally introduced on January 4, 1854, "specifically recommended *against* either 'affirming or repealing the 8th section of the Missouri act,'"—that is, the 36° 30' slavery restriction.[18] But faced with the loss of southern support, he ultimately agreed to explicit repeal of the slavery restriction.[19] From that point forward, Douglas advanced the claim that the Compromise of 1850, which organized the New Mexico and Utah territories without reference to slavery, had also repealed the Missouri Compromise's slavery restriction in Louisiana Purchase territories (see Map 2). No such argument had been made in 1850, even by proslavery members of Congress.

In addition, Douglas needed the support of Democratic president Franklin Pierce—not only to sign the bill if it passed but also, and more immediately, to make support for the bill into a test of Democratic Party loyalty and thus use his substantial patronage powers to pressure Democratic members of Congress to vote for it. Pierce had reservations about repealing the Missouri Compromise restriction, and most members of his cabinet advised him to oppose the bill. But Secretary of War Jefferson Davis, who had been a close political ally of Calhoun, arranged a short-notice Sunday meeting with Pierce at which Douglas, Davis, three members of the F Street Mess (Atchison, Hunter, and Mason), and two other southern Democratic senators (John Breckinridge of Kentucky and Philip Phillips of Alabama) were present. Somehow, this group not only got Pierce to support the bill and make it a test of party loyalty but also persuaded him to write out in his own hand that the Missouri Compromise had been "superseded by the principles of the legislation of 1850, commonly called the compromise measures, and is hereby declared inoperative and void."[20] Because Pierce and the Democrats had run and won in 1852 on a platform of full support for the Compromise of 1850, the president could claim that the voters had, in effect, mandated the repeal of the Missouri Compromise, when in fact that question had not been raised during either the Compromise of 1850 or the 1852 presidential campaign.

It was politically necessary for the bill's passage that it *not* answer any of the crucial questions about slavery. When Senator Salmon Chase of Ohio proposed an amendment providing that "the people of the Territory, through their appropriate representatives, may, if they see fit, prohibit the existence of slavery therein," Douglas opposed it because he knew it would "split the supporters of the bill, since southerners denied that slavery could be tampered with during the territorial period."[21] Moreover, the political imperative of leaving this central question unanswered led Douglas to leave *all other* essential questions unanswered, including when in the process of territorial formation a territorial majority could make a decision regarding slavery, how that decision would be made (e.g., by territorial legislature, territorial convention, territorial referendum), who was eligible to vote, and who would monitor elections to ensure that they were free of violence and fraud—for everyone understood that the stakes would be high. Rather than specifying key processes and providing for congressional oversight, Douglas revised the bill in the opposite direction: ensuring that Congress would have *less* oversight over territorial legislation and elections than it had previously exercised in other territories.[22] Douglas claimed that by stripping Congress of its usual powers over territorial decisions and processes, his legislation would enable popular sovereignty in its purest form. What these revisions actually did was make it easier for an early-arriving faction (crossing the river from Missouri) to seize control of the electoral process, drive dissenters away from the polls with threats of violence, practice blatant election fraud, overrule a territorial governor's attempt to set aside fraudulent results, enact laws criminalizing expressions of disagreement with those laws, draft a constitution that declared its slavery provisions unalterable by any future amendments, and present itself as the legitimate popular government of the territory, despite a growing territorial majority that rejected its actions as illegitimate.[23] In short, in the guise of pure democracy, the Kansas-Nebraska Act produced minority rule, mob violence, and territorial civil war. Four years later, Douglas declared his opposition to the fraudulent, unrepresentative, proslavery Lecompton Constitution. But he never acknowledged that the Kansas-Nebraska Act itself, a law that was both procedurally and morally empty, had contributed to the chaos in Kansas.

The Kansas-Nebraska Act attempted to resolve the divisive question of slavery's future by removing that decision from Congress and transferring it to residents of newly settled territories that lacked well-developed political and legal institutions. It was unrealistic to expect that newly arrived residents of Kansas could peacefully and democratically decide urgently important national questions, free of pressure from powerful sectional interests that, from the outset, placed high-stakes bets on how those residents would act. Moreover, the act failed in its effort to find principled middle ground between two polar positions on slavery in the territories (either free soil from the outset or legalized slavery until the point of statehood). Instead, in design as well as in practice, the act vibrated chaotically and deceptively between these two positions, adding distrust and a sense of betrayal to the already strong sectional passions connected with slavery. When Lincoln spoke in 1858 of a "house divided" that must ultimately be resolved one way or the other, the failure of popular sovereignty as Douglas conceived it was exhibit A.[24]

"Violence from the Beginning"

Stephen Douglas persistently defended the Kansas-Nebraska Act as the purest embodiment of the democratic process. Lincoln saw trouble, and *violations* of the democratic process, in the Kansas-Nebraska Act from the beginning, even before the public reports of electoral violence and fraud in Kansas.

When Lincoln publicly denounced the Kansas-Nebraska Act in October 1854, he could not have known the specific manner by which southern Democrats of the F Street Mess had pressured Douglas to include repeal of the Missouri Compromise and persuaded President Pierce to make support for the bill a test of Democratic Party loyalty. (Had Lincoln known these details, he likely would have featured them in his October 1854 Kansas-Nebraska speech as well as his 1858 "House Divided" speech.) But Lincoln had closely read the act in its final form and ascertained that it was entirely silent about when, by whom, and through what process the inhabitants of a territory would determine the status of slavery. Moreover, Lincoln had closely tracked the significant changes in Douglas's bill between January and May 1854, as well as Douglas's own shifting public statements during that period—first denying that the Kansas-Nebraska bill would repeal the Missouri Compromise and later claiming that repeal was its purpose all along. Lincoln also knew that "the public never demanded the repeal of the Missouri Compromise"—not the general public and certainly not voters in Illinois. Without knowing the full details, Lincoln correctly concluded that between January and May 1854, Douglas changed the text and purpose of the Kansas-Nebraska bill in response to intense, behind-the-scenes proslavery pressure.[25]

What Lincoln knew about the text of the act and the process that produced it enabled him to predict, fairly accurately, the lawless and chaotic events that occurred in Kansas soon thereafter. According to David M. Potter, "When the fraudulently elected [Kansas territorial] legislature met, it acted in the most bigoted and despotic way. Over the governor's veto, it adopted a uniquely repressive set of statutes for the protection of slavery, making it a capital offense to give aid to a fugitive slave and a felony to question the right to hold slaves in Kansas."[26] The provisions of the act not only enabled a fraudulently elected territorial legislature to override the governor's veto but also made it extremely difficult for a territorial governor to prevent or remedy gross election fraud. The presidentially appointed territorial governor, Andrew Reeder, had ordered that special elections be held in May 1855 in several districts where the results of the March 1855 elections were glaringly fraudulent. In response, the proslavery faction of the territorial legislature took advantage of the near-absolute power conferred on it by the Kansas-Nebraska Act and overturned the governor's electoral reforms, expelled the antislavery members elected in the (comparatively fair) May special elections, and reinstated the proslavery members fraudulently elected in March.[27] Here, the proslavery territorial legislature acted precisely as a lawless mob, and the procedurally empty Kansas-Nebraska Act enabled it to do so.

In an August 24, 1855, letter to his old friend Joshua Speed—who supported the Kansas-Nebraska Act but hoped it would be administered fairly—Lincoln replied that the act was being executed in "the precise way which was intended from the first."

> I look upon that enactment not as a *law*, but as *violence* from the beginning. It was conceived in violence, passed in violence, is maintained in violence, and is being executed in violence. I say it was *conceived* in violence, because the destruction of the Missouri Compromise, under the circumstances, was nothing less than violence. It was *passed* in violence, because it could not have passed at

all but for the votes of many members, in violent disregard of the known will of their constituents. It is *maintained* in violence because the elections since, clearly demand its repeal, and this demand is openly disregarded. *You* say men ought to be hung for the way they are executing that law; and *I* say the way it is being executed is quite as good as any of its antecedents. . . . Poor Reeder [the territorial governor who tried to ensure honest elections] is the only public man who has been silly enough to believe that any thing like fairness was ever intended; and he has been bravely undeceived.[28]

This passage shows how the Kansas-Nebraska Act, by needlessly opening vast new territories to slavery, aroused several of Lincoln's principal concerns from the 1830s and 1840s, as noted in chapter 3: lawlessness, not only on the streets but also in the halls of power; disregard for legitimate democratic processes; intraparty authoritarianism; and bogus mandate claims.

Lincoln here characterized the Kansas-Nebraska Act as a kind of deliberately lawless law. The ostensible purpose of the act was to empower territorial residents to "decide the question of slavery for themselves," yet the "peculiar" structure of the law itself—which failed to specify when and how residents might be authorized to *exclude* slavery from the territory—practically guaranteed that any attempt to prohibit slavery prior to statehood would be violently opposed by proslavery forces. Douglas's own persistent refusal to clarify this crucial point added to the act's lawless character. Another senator's attempt "to give the [territorial] legislature express authority to exclude slavery," Lincoln reported, "was hooted down by the friends of the bill." Lincoln later concisely captured the act's deliberate ambiguity in his 1858 "House Divided" speech: "'But,' said opposition members, 'let us be more *specific*—let us *amend* the bill so as to expressly declare that the people of the territory *may* exclude slavery.' 'Not we,' said the friends of the measure; and down they voted the amendment." Lincoln charged that the law's deliberate ambiguity about whether, how, and at what stage territorial residents could vote to prohibit slavery was designed to increase the probability that slavery would secure a permanent foothold.[29]

This was probably an inaccurate description of Douglas's purposes. But it accurately described the purposes of the slave-state senators who persuaded Douglas to radically revise his bill. F Street Mess member David Atchison—by early 1855 an ex-senator—urged proslavery Missourians to cross into Kansas to vote in the territorial elections, bragging that "we can send five thousand—enough to kill every God damned abolitionist in the Territory." And indeed, on March 30, 1855, the first day of elections for the new Kansas territorial legislature, "4968 one day Kansans [from Missouri] overwhelmed the 1210 permanent Kansans who voted."[30] Atchison's activities after the Kansas-Nebraska Act's passage lend credence to Lincoln's charge that the law was both conceived in violence and executed in violence—in this case, by some of the same individuals.

Lincoln's remark that the Kansas-Nebraska Act was "passed in violence" because it "could not have passed . . . but for the votes of many members, in violent disregard of the known will of their constituents," referred to the intense party discipline imposed on northern Democrats in Congress. They were forced to fall in line behind a bill that was strongly opposed by most voters in the states and districts they represented. (Every northern Whig in Congress voted against the Kansas-Nebraska Act.) Lincoln had always been a strong advocate of political parties. But in his view, a strong party was one in which intraparty differences of opinion could be openly voiced and no powerful individual or faction could dictate, prior to discussion, what the party's position would be on some important, newly raised issue. The repeal of the Missouri Compromise's slavery restriction was a new issue of enormous importance. The Compromise of 1850, which both the Democratic and Whig presidential candidates endorsed in 1852 as a "final settlement" of the slavery question, had not touched the Missouri Compromise. Yet, as noted earlier, President Pierce was convinced to make support for the Kansas-Nebraska Act a test of Democratic Party loyalty, on the pretext that the Compromise of 1850 had already repealed the Missouri Compromise and that the 1852 election results endorsed this stance. Lincoln called Douglas out on this dubious mandate claim: "But next it is said that the compromises of '50 and the ratification of them by both political parties, in '52, established a *new principle*, which required the repeal of the Missouri Compromise. . . . I deny it, and demand the proof."[31] Lincoln acknowledged that the Compromise of 1850 was ratified by both political parties in the 1852 elections but denied that those elections ratified repeal of the Missouri Compromise. That was a new and entirely different matter that no one, including Douglas, had suggested at the time.

Lincoln, who was a close observer of opinion trends among Illinois Democrats, claimed that when the Kansas-Nebraska bill was first discussed in the Illinois legislature, only three Democrats (and no Whigs) supported it. But then "Douglas' orders came on to have resolutions passed approving the bill. . . . As soon as the party necessity of supporting it, became apparent, the way the democracy began to see the *wisdom* and *justice* of it, was perfectly astonishing."[32] Those northern Democrats who "violently" disregarded the "known will of their constituents" paid a high political price in the 1854 elections, losing sixty-six of the ninety-one free-state seats they had won in 1852; those northern Democrats who voted for the Kansas-Nebraska Act fared much worse than the northern Democrats who broke party ranks and voted against it.[33] Lincoln interpreted the 1854 results as a strong and clear anti–Kansas-Nebraska message, at least among the northern electorate: the act was "*maintained* in violence because the elections since, clearly demand its repeal, and this demand is openly disregarded." Thus, as Lincoln saw it, a bogus mandate claim—the assertion by Pierce and Douglas that voters in 1852 had endorsed repeal of the Missouri Compromise—continued to be pushed, despite voters' genuine expression of outrage against the Kansas-Nebraska Act in the 1854 elections.

In describing the Kansas-Nebraska Act as *violence* rather than law, Lincoln deliberately employed the term in both a broad, figurative sense ("violent disregard of the known will of their constituents") and a specific, literal sense (e.g., the vow that, in Kansas, "abolitionists shall be hung, or driven away"). He stretched the meaning of the word to make a practical point: violations of the democratic process can produce violent, antidemocratic results.

Slavery and Local Decision

Stephen Douglas defended popular sovereignty as decentralized, respectful of diversity, and Union preserving, and he characterized the position of Lincoln and the Republicans—that Congress should outlaw slavery in the territories—as centralized, hostile to diversity, and Union threatening.[34] Was this true?

Lincoln did regard the continued expansion of slavery as a national concern and held that Congress had the constitutional authority to prohibit slavery in the territories. But he also viewed state, local, and territorial majorities as indispensable components of the enduring national antislavery majority he hoped to organize. He was confident that the people of a territory, if given the opportunity, would reject slavery as long as three preconditions held: that their numbers were sufficiently large to be representative, that they were moved by "ordinary motives," and that slavery was not already established as a vested interest in the territory. "Keep [slavery] out until a vote is taken, and a vote in favor of it, can not be got in any population of forty thousand, on earth, who have been drawn together by the ordinary motives of emigration and settlement. To get slaves into the country simultaneously with the whites, in the incipient stages of settlement, is the precise stake played for, and won in this Nebraska measure."[35]

Lincoln's threshold number for a representative vote (forty thousand) lay midway between the minimum population required under the Northwest Ordinance to form a provisional government (twenty thousand) and the number required under that ordinance for a territory to be eligible for statehood (sixty thousand). In suggesting forty thousand as the point at which residents of a territory could be trusted to vote on slavery, Lincoln deliberately indicated a middle phase between the small, unrepresentative population of early arrivals and the full population needed for statehood. Although his *preference* was clearly for Congress to prohibit slavery until a territory achieved statehood, he was willing to *settle* for territorial residents voting on the issue at an earlier stage, as long as slavery had been kept out until that middle stage was reached. In this sense, despite his opposition to the Kansas-Nebraska Act, Lincoln believed that popular sovereignty could be enlisted for antislavery purposes if certain key conditions were satisfied.

One might be tempted to conclude that while Lincoln *somewhat* trusted territorial residents to decide the slavery question responsibly, Douglas trusted them more. But because Douglas refused to answer the crucial question whether, regardless of the wishes of the territorial majority, slavery would be legal in the territories until statehood (the position of the southerners whose support he needed to pass the bill), we cannot draw any firm conclusions about what Douglas trusted territorial residents to decide and when. Nor can we meaningfully compare Lincoln and Douglas with respect to the number of residents required to make a decision on slavery. Unlike the Northwest Ordinance, Douglas's act did not specify a threshold number for the formation of a provisional government or for statehood. The Kansas-Nebraska Act said nothing about how many territorial residents were required to decide the slavery question, when, and by what process. All we know for certain is that Lincoln stated a threshold number and described a process, while Douglas did neither.

Lincoln's second precondition—that the territorial residents "have been drawn together by the ordinary motives of emigration and settlement"—drew an implicit contrast between those migrating to Kansas principally to set up homesteads and make a living and those rushing to the territory as armed missionaries of the proslavery or antislavery cause. At the date of this speech (October 16, 1854), the principal nonordinary immigrants were the proslavery Missourians who, Lincoln reported, were "within a stone's throw of the contested ground" and "resolve that slavery already exists in the territory." But the "ordinary motives" condition would also exclude antislavery ideologues like John Brown and his sons, who arrived in Kansas and began their violent crusade in 1855.[36] Lincoln assumed that, as the total population of a territory increased, the proportion driven principally by ideological motives would naturally decrease. This is consistent with Lincoln's observation elsewhere in the speech that the percentage of human beings who are "natural tyrants," by which he meant individuals incapable of sympathizing with the suffering of others, was relatively small.[37] Such natural tyrants would likely form a larger percentage of those early-arriving ideologues who resolved "that abolitionists shall be hung, or driven away," than those in the larger pool of later-arriving homesteaders. Natural tyrants would be more numerous among those eager to transplant slavery to a territory where it did not yet exist than among those who accommodated themselves to slavery where it was already rooted.

This brings us to the final and most important of Lincoln's preconditions for a fair territorial vote on slavery: the institution must not yet exist to any significant degree in that territory. It was far easier to introduce slavery into a new territory, whether directly by law or indirectly by the law's silence, than to remove slavery once it was established. If slavery did not yet exist in a territory, there was no *necessity* that it be introduced there. Once established in a new territory, even in relatively small numbers, all the "necessities" that prevented its abolition in Virginia, South Carolina, Missouri, and other slave states immediately began to generate that same necessity in the newly settled territory. Thus, in Lincoln's view, a *free decision* on slavery by a territorial majority could occur only if it was still a *free territory* when that decision was made. Slaveholders, of course, would object that Lincoln's condition deliberately weighted the scales against slavery. But that was the crux of the problem: the scales were necessarily weighted on one side or the other. Either slavery already existed in the territory when the decision was made or it did not. Douglas, in drafting the Kansas-Nebraska Act, simply dodged this problem.

Lincoln spoke often about the obstacles that even a determined antislavery territorial majority would encounter in attempting to abolish slavery once it had been established in the territory. In his 1854 Kansas-Nebraska speech, immediately preceding the passage (quoted above) in which he stated that a territorial population of forty thousand could be trusted to ban slavery if it had *not* already been introduced, Lincoln described the complications that ensue once slavery *has* been introduced. Such complications arise even in the earliest stages of settlement if territorial law is silent on slavery.

> Wherever slavery is, it has been first introduced without law. The oldest laws we find concerning it, are not laws introducing it; but *regulating* it, as an already existing thing. A white man takes his slave to Nebraska now; who will inform the Negro that he is free? Who will take him before court to test the question of his freedom? In ignorance of his legal emancipation, he is kept chopping, splitting, and plowing. Others are brought, and move on in the same track. At last, if ever the time for voting comes, on the question of slavery, the institution already in fact exists in the country and cannot well be removed. The facts of its presence, and the difficulty of its removal will carry the vote in its favor.[38]

Lincoln here, in substance, anticipated and rejected Douglas's Freeport doctrine (1858), formulated in response to the *Dred Scott* decision: that slavery cannot exist except where it has the positive sanction of law. Lincoln's point was that slavery could entrench itself, even in the absence of positive law, to a sufficient degree to ensure its affirmation by law at a later stage. Lincoln also testified here to the empowerment that comes with knowledge and the vulnerability that accompanies ignorance. "Who will inform the Negro that he is free?" Even this apparently straightforward act of communication—telling enslaved persons that there was no territorial law requiring them to remain enslaved—involved legal complications and great personal risk, unless territorial law specifically prohibited slavery.[39]

It was no accident that in Kansas's initial proslavery code of 1855 and in the proslavery Lecompton Constitution of 1857, any attempt to "inform the Negro that he is free" was subject to severe punishment. The Lecompton Constitution also specifically barred any laws or constitutional amendments that would emancipate persons already held in bondage in Kansas, even if laws enacted subsequent to statehood prohibited the future importation of slaves.[40]

In an 1856 speech, Lincoln provided an especially perceptive description of how slavery could gain a foothold in a new territory and eventually win legal recognition, despite majority opposition. Lincoln explained how, even in the absence of violence, a wealthy proslavery minority could defeat an antislavery majority through a process of gradual, corrupting consent:

> Can men vote truly? We will suppose that there are ten men who go into Kansas to settle. Nine of those are opposed to slavery. One has ten slaves. The slaveholder is a good man in other respects; he is a good neighbor and being a wealthy man, he is enabled to do the others many neighborly kindnesses. They like the man, though they don't like the system by which he holds his fellow-men in bondage. And here let me say, that in intellectual and physical structure, our Southern brethren do not differ from us. They are, like us, subject to passions, and it is only their odious institution of slavery, that makes the breach between us. These ten men of whom I am speaking, live together three or four years; they intermarry; their family ties are strengthened. And who wonders that in time, the people learn to look upon slavery with complacency? This is the way in which slavery is planted, and gains so firm a foothold. I think this is a strong card that the Nebraska party have played and won upon, in this game.[41]

Lincoln here assumes that most nonslaveholding human beings start out "naturally anti-slavery," and he described himself in those terms.[42] He observed in his speech on the Kansas-Nebraska Act, "The great majority, south as well as north, have human sympathies, of which they can no more divest themselves than they can of their sensibility to physical pain."[43] These natural sympathies generate the large *initial* antislavery majority Lincoln assumed would exist in a newly settled territory. But if antislavery sentiment was rooted in human nature, so too were the sentiments and interests that enabled these initially antislavery settlers to be corrupted by the presence of slavery over time: gratitude for "neighborly kindnesses," community and family ties, the attractive power of wealth. These counteracting passions might not destroy the original sympathies, but they weakened and muffled their voice. Thus, both antislavery and proslavery sentiments were rooted in human nature; it was the circumstances under which men and women lived and interacted with one another that determined which sentiment gained the upper hand.

Lincoln's observation that "our Southern brethren do not differ from us" echoed his Kansas-Nebraska speech, where he argued that "the Southern people . . . are just what we would be in their situation. If slavery did not now exist among them, they would not introduce it. If it did not exist amongst us, we should not instantly give it up."[44] In contrast to those who condemned slaveholders as sinners and others who claimed that deeply rooted cultural differences accounted for southern slavery and northern freedom,[45] Lincoln rejected claims of northern moral or cultural superiority. In his view, both opposition to slavery and acceptance of slavery revealed the workings of a common human nature under different circumstances.

That all human beings were susceptible to being corrupted by the presence of slavery may seem a darkly pessimistic conclusion. But Lincoln's observations also contained seeds of optimism. He knew that moral and religious denunciation of slaveholders would accomplish nothing, for the same reason this approach failed to reform alcoholics.[46] It is difficult to imagine the North completely remaking the culture of the South except through victory in war. But many of the circumstances that, in Lincoln's view, determined whether human beings retained or lost their natural repugnance to slavery lay within the power of legislators and voters and thus could be shaped through "peaceful ballots" rather than "bloody bullets."

Restoring Missouri Compromise, or House Divided?

If Lincoln believed, optimistically, that political and social circumstances could be deliberately shaped in ways that favored liberty over slavery, the obvious question is: how? What specific political actions could be taken not only to keep slavery out of Kansas but also to place slavery "in course of ultimate extinction" everywhere in the United States? That question is examined in chapter 7. Here, I describe Lincoln's initial steps in that direction, which were marked by false starts and a phase of deep pessimism. What he believed to be an appropriate and effective political response to slavery changed significantly between his 1854 Kansas-Nebraska speech and his 1858 "House Divided" speech.

In 1854, as a Whig, Lincoln's proposed response echoed the time-honored path of seeking sectional consensus. By 1858, Lincoln, now a Republican, expressed the less consensual, more majoritarian, and

more radical idea of a "house divided" in which one side or the other—
"those who are *for*, and those who are against a legalized national slavery"—must prevail. He acknowledged that "the conflict will be a severe
one," adding that it must be "fought by those who *do* care for the result"
(unlike Stephen Douglas, who did not care). Yet Lincoln, more optimistic in 1858 than he had been in 1854, believed that "to give victory to
the right, not *bloody bullets*, but *peaceful ballots* only, are necessary."[47] Even
if Lincoln was ultimately wrong about peaceful ballots being sufficient
to extinguish slavery, his reasoning merits examination. This begins by
attending to Lincoln's initial false start: calling for restoration of the
Missouri Compromise of 1820.

The idea that slavery must eventually be abolished everywhere
was already implicit in Lincoln's October 1854 speech on the Kansas-
Nebraska Act, where he compared the founders' accommodation to
slavery in the Constitution to a man afflicted by "a wen or a cancer,
which he dares not cut out at once, lest he bleed to death; with the
promise, nevertheless, that the cutting may begin at the end of a given
time."[48] Lincoln believed the founders sought to eliminate slavery eventually, and he characterized his own purposes the same way.

Even though the substance of Lincoln's 1854 speech included the
idea of ultimate extinction, he had not yet linked that outcome with the
concept of a "house divided," whereby the advocates of nationalizing
freedom, in a severe but peaceful electoral contest, defeated the advocates of nationalized slavery. Lincoln himself noted that only in 1857
did he come to the "house divided" conclusion.[49] In 1854 he apparently
believed (oddly, in retrospect) that influential southern leaders could
be persuaded to support policies restricting the spread of slavery and,
consequently, that slavery could be gradually phased out through sectional compromise rather than political victory by an overwhelmingly
free-state majority.

The opening sentence of Lincoln's October 16, 1854, speech denouncing the Kansas-Nebraska Act is this: "The repeal of the Missouri
Compromise, and the propriety of its restoration, constitute the subject
of what I am about to say." It is not surprising that Lincoln denounced
the repeal of the slavery restriction, which potentially opened up vast
new territories and future states to slavery. What seems odd, however, is
Lincoln's call for "restoration" of the compromise in its widest sense: not
just reinstating the slavery restriction but, more sweepingly, reaffirming
the compromise as a kind of sacred principle: "the spirit of concession

and compromise—that spirit which has never failed us in past perils, and which may be safely trusted for all the future." He invited slave-state leaders to "join in doing this."⁵⁰

This emphasis on sectional pacts between free and slave states is difficult to reconcile with Lincoln's later "house divided" theme, when he argued that "this government cannot endure, permanently half *slave* and half *free*," and ultimately, that it would become "*all* one thing, or *all* the other."⁵¹ In its broader sense, the Missouri Compromise, including the informal balance rule that developed in its tracks (admitting equal numbers of free and slave states to the Union), seemed to furnish the quintessential "house divided" formula.

Lincoln in 1854 framed his call for restoration of the Missouri Compromise in the language of sectional consensus, balance, and exchange of "equivalents"—bargaining chips, so to speak—among geographic sections as a means of maintaining sectional harmony. He contrasted the Compromise of 1850, in which North and South each got something of value, with the Kansas-Nebraska Act, in which the North gave away something of enormous value—the Missouri Compromise's slavery restriction—"*without any equivalent at all*."⁵² Containing sectional conflict over slavery by exchanging "equivalents" already had a long history by 1854. Both the Democratic and Whig Parties, from their formation in the 1830s until the Whig Party's demise in the wake of the Kansas-Nebraska Act, practiced a politics of sectional accommodation that deliberately marginalized critics of slavery. Lincoln's political rhetoric of "concession and compromise" in the 1854 speech thus seems utterly conventional and difficult to reconcile with his impassioned denunciation of slavery in the same speech. Although repeal of the Missouri Compromise continued to play a key role in Lincoln's diagnosis of the slavery crisis of the 1850s, he ceased to call for its restoration and moved toward a more comprehensive, more principled, and arguably more radical stance on both slavery and majority rule.

To understand this shift in Lincoln's thinking, we should ask why he called for restoration of the Missouri Compromise in the first place. One reason was that he gave the Missouri Compromise an antislavery interpretation that southern leaders did not share. Another reason was that Lincoln, like many political leaders of the time, feared disunion and civil war if the time-honored practice of sectional compromise over slavery was disrupted. Thus, the intriguing question is not why he initially called for restoration of the compromise but how he later persuaded himself that a different political response to slavery could be both effective and peaceful.

The Missouri Compromise resolved, or attempted to resolve, the sectional conflicts that erupted in 1819 over the effort by many northern members of Congress to block Missouri's proposed entry into the Union as a slave state and to prohibit slavery in the remaining territories of the Louisiana Purchase. The Missouri controversy occasioned the first major public debate since 1790 about the future of slavery in the United States. Several issues were fiercely debated, including the meaning of the Declaration of Independence's "all men are created equal" clause, whether the framers of the Constitution envisioned slavery as temporary or permanent, whether the westward movement of slavery would facilitate its ultimate abolition by "diffusing" it or fasten its shackles more tightly, whether slavery inherently violated the Constitution's guarantee of a "republican form of government," and whether free Blacks were entitled to the "privileges and immunities" of citizenship under Article IV. Many antislavery arguments later employed by abolitionists and Republicans were first voiced during the Missouri debates. On the other side, the "positive good" defense of slavery and the claim that slaveholders had a constitutional right to enslave human beings in any US territory also made their appearance during the debates.[53] The Missouri controversy appeared to put the Union at risk because southerners were outraged by northerners' assumption that Congress could make a new state's admission to the Union conditional on its prohibition of slavery, while northerners saw the westward and northward expansion of slavery as an effort by slave states to magnify their already significant, unfair political advantages under the three-fifths clause.

The territories of the Louisiana Purchase composed all or most of the modern-day states of Louisiana, Arkansas, Oklahoma, Missouri, Kansas, Nebraska, Iowa, Minnesota, North Dakota, South Dakota, Wyoming, Montana, and Colorado and smaller fragments of Texas and New Mexico. These territories had been purchased by the federal government and were therefore unencumbered by preconditions imposed by older slave states. The old Southwest territories—Kentucky, Tennessee, Alabama, and Mississippi—had been ceded to the Union by the slave states of Virginia, North Carolina, South Carolina, and Georgia, in some cases (as Lincoln pointed out) on the explicit condition that slavery remain legal in the ceded territory.[54] Slavery was prohibited by the Northwest Ordinance in territories north of the Ohio River and east of the Mississippi River, covering the future states of Ohio, Michigan, Indiana, Illinois, and Wisconsin and part of Minnesota. Because nearly all of Missouri lay north of the Ohio River and directly west of the free states of Indiana and Illinois, its entry into the Union as a slave state signified a significant northward shift in the territorial range of slavery. But the Northwest Ordinance did not apply to Louisiana Purchase territories, and slavery had already acquired a foothold in St. Louis. Missouri pressed for entry as a slave state.

The Missouri Compromise (or, to be more specific, the *first* Missouri Compromise[55]) defused the Union-endangering crisis for several decades. Henry Clay, whom Lincoln admired, engineered passage of this complicated sectional juggling act, relying on predominantly southern congressional majorities to pass some of its parts and predominantly northern majorities for others. Under the compromise, Missouri entered the Union as a slave state and Maine entered as a free state, thereby preserving the balance of free and slave states. In the remaining Louisiana Purchase territories that were not yet states, slavery was prohibited north of the 36° 30' parallel (a line extending westward from the southern boundary of Missouri). Louisiana Purchase territories south of 36° 30' would be organized without reference to slavery, but this was understood by parties to the compromise as authorizing slavery there. Besides Louisiana, which had joined the Union as a slave state in 1812, this southern section included the Arkansas territory. Arkansas entered the Union as a slave state in 1836, balanced by the admission of Michigan as a free state in 1837. This extraconstitutional "balance rule" continued as a political modus vivendi for states not included in the Louisiana Purchase: thus, between 1845 and 1848, two new slave states (Texas and Florida, neither of which were part of the Louisiana Purchase) were balanced by two new free states (Iowa, included in the Louisiana Purchase, and Wisconsin, where slavery had been prohibited by the Northwest Ordinance).

These were the specifics of the Missouri Compromise. But the "spirit" of the compromise was understood very differently by North and South. It is not uncommon for a law to be interpreted differently by the various leaders and constituencies that supported its passage. Typically, such differing interpretations are addressed through judicial construction and legislative revision. But when a law of enormous significance has been repealed long after its initial passage and an effort is made to restore it, widely differing understandings of the law's purpose can be fatal obstacles to its restoration. Such was the case with the 36° 30' slavery restriction of the Missouri Compromise. (Other elements of the compromise, such as the admission of Missouri as a slave state and Maine as a free state, were not subject to repeal.) When Lincoln called for restoration of the Missouri Compromise in 1854 as some type of "sacred" pact, what did he mean?

For Lincoln, the wider principle underlying the specific provisions of the Missouri Compromise could be summarized this way: tolerate slavery where it is already established, but restrict it wherever possible from entering new territories. In this sense, the Missouri Compromise was (at least in Lincoln's historical narrative) the logical westward counterpart to the Northwest Ordinance of 1787, which prohibited slavery in the territories of the Old Northwest but remained silent on slavery south of the Ohio River, where it already had a foothold—just as slavery already had a foothold in Missouri in 1820. Thus, based on Lincoln's interpretation, the slavery *restriction* of the Missouri Compromise expressed a broader national antislavery commitment, while its tacit slavery *permission* south of 36° 30' was an accommodation to necessity that applied only to Louisiana Purchase lands.

For this reason, in Lincoln's view, there was no contradiction between his denouncing the 1854 repeal of the Missouri Compromise's restriction on slavery in Louisiana Purchase territories north of 36° 30' and his voting for the Wilmot Proviso at least forty times during his term in the US House of Representatives (1847–49), even though most of the territory where the Wilmot Proviso would have prohibited slavery lay south of the 36° 30' line. Lincoln claimed that the Missouri Compromise's tacit allowance of slavery south of 36° 30' applied only to US territories included in the Louisiana Purchase, not to newly acquired territories, where Congress remained free to prohibit slavery, regardless of latitude. It comes as no surprise that southern leaders interpreted the Missouri Compromise very differently. Some even justified repeal of its slavery restriction in 1854 by claiming that northern members of Congress (such as Lincoln) had already repudiated the Missouri Compromise when they voted for the Wilmot Proviso in 1848. Lincoln characterized this line of argument as "absurd." But it is clear that the Missouri Compromise meant very different things to different people in different sections of the country.[56]

In contrast to Lincoln's antislavery-slanted construction, the Missouri Compromise could instead be read as simply affirming a sectional balance of power, without implying any judgment for or against slavery. The wider principle here would be, in effect: preserve the Union by maintaining equality of status among its sections. Under this reading of the historical record, each geographic section secured something of value: for northern states, the seedbed of future free states north of 36° 30', and for southern states, the seedbed of future slave states south of that line. Though nothing in the text of the Constitution required sectional equality of this kind, politically, the "equality of sections" principle best matches the one-for-one balance of free states and slave states admitted into the Union between 1820 and 1850.

The most famous practitioner of sectional compromise in this sense was Henry Clay of Kentucky, whom Lincoln had long admired. Clay was one of the chief architects of the 1820 Missouri Compromise; the 1833 Compromise Tariff that ended the showdown between President Andrew Jackson and South Carolina over the state's nullification of federal law; and, in its initial stages, the Compromise of 1850, the actual passage of which was secured by Stephen Douglas.[57] Lincoln implicitly invoked a sectional equality principle when, in his 1854 speech on the Kansas-Nebraska Act, he argued that, in restoring the Missouri Compromise, Americans would thereby restore a "spirit of concession and compromise." Lincoln certainly would have included Clay among these exemplars of "concession and compromise." In his 1852 "Eulogy on Henry Clay," Lincoln credited Clay with saving the Union "on at least three important occasions," including his heroic efforts on behalf of the Missouri Compromise. "As a politician or statesman, no one was so habitually careful to avoid all sectional ground. Whatever he did, he did for the whole country."[58]

But Clay's stance on slavery in the territories was very different from Lincoln's in his 1854 Kansas-Nebraska speech. The 1820 Missouri Compromise brokered by Clay included the 36° 30' restriction as a concession to the North (to buy northerners' support for Missouri's admission as a slave state), but Clay's position was actually similar to that of the elderly Thomas Jefferson: to permit slavery in all territories, on the theory that "diffusion" of slavery would make it easier to extinguish it sometime in the future. (Lincoln dismissed this as a "LULLABY argument" in his Kansas-Nebraska speech.) Nor did Clay, during the 1850 crisis, endorse any position comparable to the Wilmot Proviso. Thus, despite Lincoln's praise of "mutual concession and compromise" and of Clay for embodying that spirit, the two men's political responses to slavery were different from the outset and would become increasingly different by the time of Lincoln's 1858 "House Divided" speech.[59]

Finally, the Missouri Compromise could be given a distinctly pro-slavery interpretation. Under both the Northwest Ordinance and the Missouri Compromise, slavery was banned only where specifically prohibited by law and permitted to spread wherever the law was silent. Arguably, this could imply the principle of slavery national, freedom local—that is, slavery was presumed legal everywhere subject to the US Constitution, except in specified areas where it was expressly prohibited by some act. On this view, a state could prohibit slavery within its borders if it chose to do so (assuming it also faithfully fulfilled its constitutional obligation to return fugitive slaves), but such an act carried no moral or constitutional authority outside its borders.

Congress, a national body, had enacted the Missouri Compromise. The proslavery interpretation of the compromise, however, was that Congress had no legitimate authority to ban slavery in *any* territories but that southerners had agreed to waive the practical exercise of their constitutional rights north of 36° 30' in the interests of sectional harmony and to better secure their right to transport and hold persons in bondage south of that line.[60] Southerners' willingness to waive what they considered their constitutional right to slavery in the territories shrank significantly over time. During the Missouri debate in 1820, John C. Calhoun, who was still a committed nationalist at the time, doubted that Congress had the legitimate power to impose any territorial restriction on slavery, but because he was worried about the Union-endangering potential of the slavery debate, he accepted the compromise and sought to calm southern concerns about it. Later in his career (1848), Calhoun described the Missouri Compromise's restriction on slavery in much more negative terms, calling it a provision with no constitutional legitimacy whatsoever, "carried by the almost united vote of the North against the almost united vote of the South; and . . . thus imposed on the latter by superior numbers in opposition to her strenuous efforts," in which the southern states acquiesced simply because they were averse to "disturbing the peace and harmony of the Union."[61]

Clearly, the underlying principle of the Missouri Compromise, if it expressed any stable principle at all, was interpreted in radically different ways. Lincoln in 1854 did his best to argue for an antislavery interpretation of the Missouri Compromise, whereby slavery was already prohibited north of 36° 30' in Louisiana Purchase territories and, additionally, was subject to future prohibition in any remaining US territories, regardless of latitude. But one must ask: by the 1850s, how many slave-state leaders understood the Missouri Compromise this way? If the answer is none or very few, then it is not clear how it could be restored as an intersectional agreement affirmed by both North and South.

This does not mean Lincoln ever ceased to value concession and compromise. Later, as president-elect in the face of secession, he was willing to retreat on some slavery-related points in the hope of avoiding disunion and civil war. But (as noted in chapter 7) he refused to back down on prohibiting slavery in the territories. Nor would he continue to accept the political ground rules that had governed the Missouri Compromise, the Compromise of 1850, and other sectional bargains in the past: that is, that any slavery-related legislation had to be supported by slave owners and the political leaders of slave states. The latter would continue to be consulted and heard. But if legislation affecting slavery lay within Congress's constitutional jurisdiction, was passed by both chambers, and was signed by the president, the resulting law would be binding even in those sections of the country whose leaders and voters opposed it. This was majority rule in strong form.

"Peaceful Ballots," Not "Bloody Bullets"

Thus, in 1854 Lincoln still accepted the widely shared assumption that any policy affecting slavery had to have significant support in the South. By the time of his "House Divided" speech in 1858, Lincoln recognized that no slave-state leaders currently in office would support policies directed toward not only containing but ultimately eliminating the institution of slavery. Why, then, did Lincoln believe a sectional contest over slavery could, under the right circumstances, be conducted peacefully rather than violently? Answering this question illuminates the constructive and peaceful role Lincoln envisioned for political parties.

In early 1855 Lincoln, at that point still a Whig and making his first unsuccessful bid for the US Senate, drafted resolutions urging Congress to restore the Missouri Compromise's restriction on slavery. But over the course of that year characterized by violence and proslavery election fraud in the Kansas territory, Lincoln increasingly perceived the impracticality of restoring the Missouri Compromise. In an August 24, 1855, letter he wrote: "I shall advocate the restoration of the Missouri

Compromise, so long as Kansas remains a territory; and when, by all these foul means, it seeks to come into the Union as a Slave-state, I shall oppose it." As he began to realize the impossibility of restoring the Missouri Compromise (which southern leaders had always understood very differently from Lincoln), he became more pessimistic about the prospect of peacefully extinguishing slavery. In another letter written that same month (August 15, 1855), he observed that "thirty six years of experience" (i.e., since 1819, the commencement of the Missouri controversy) "has demonstrated, I think, that there is no peaceful extinction of slavery in prospect for us." Henry Clay "and other good and great men" had failed to persuade slaveholders in Kentucky and elsewhere to support gradual emancipation. Lincoln closed this letter by anticipating, but in a deeply pessimistic sense, his "house divided" theme of 1858: "Our political problem now is 'Can we, as a nation, continue together *permanently—forever*—half slave, and half free?' The problem is too mighty for me."[62]

Lincoln's August 15 letter has sometimes been cited to argue that he expected, perhaps even welcomed, a civil war over slavery. This construction mistakenly treats Lincoln's "no peaceful extinction of slavery" as his final word on the subject.[63] He did not welcome civil war. He was sensitive to the enormous suffering such a war would bring and, despite enormous obstacles, attempted to find some peaceful means of ending slavery. By the time Lincoln delivered his "House Divided" speech on June 18, 1858, he had recovered his hope that slavery could be extinguished peacefully, democratically, and constitutionally, without resorting to Missouri Compromise–type sectional pacts. (Whether Lincoln's hope was reasonable or illusory is a separate question.)

I begin with an important and underappreciated element of Lincoln's thinking: the conflict-channeling function of partisan electoral competition. At the time Lincoln penned the August 15, 1855, letter expressing his fear that there was "no peaceful extinction of slavery in prospect for us," the Whig Party had disappeared. In Lincoln's mind, this fear and the collapse of the Whig Party were interconnected. He reflected on "the signal failure" of Whig leader Henry Clay (who died in 1852 and whose antislavery commitments Lincoln tended to exaggerate) "to effect any thing in favor of gradual emancipation in Kentucky" or any other slave state. Lincoln lamented, "That spirit which desired the peaceful extinction of slavery," which had animated the American Revolution and whose latest champion had been Clay, "has itself become extinct." American slaveholders were no more likely to "voluntarily give up their slaves" than the Russian czar was to "proclaim his subjects free republicans."[64]

Lincoln had hoped in 1854 that popular outrage against the Kansas-Nebraska Act would revive the Whigs, at least in the North, in opposition to the extension of slavery. But that did not happen. The Whigs' southern wing, which was essential to the party's competitiveness in presidential contests and to its capacity to broker sectional compromises, had begun to collapse by the early 1850s. This occurred in part because of northern Whigs' support for the Wilmot Proviso and Whig president Zachary Taylor's perceived betrayal of southern interests. By 1853, the Whigs' northern wing was also collapsing due to a confusing variety of causes, including the party's perceived deference to the interests of slaveholders.[65]

In his August 24, 1855, letter to Joshua Speed, Lincoln acknowledged that he had become politically homeless: "I think I am a whig; but others say there are no whigs, and that I am an abolitionist. When I was at Washington I voted for the Wilmot Proviso as good as forty times, and I never heard of any one attempting to unwhig me for that. I now do no more than oppose the *extension* of slavery."[66] The contrast Lincoln drew between Whig and abolitionist is revealing: To be a Whig (as Lincoln viewed it) meant to oppose the extension of slavery. To be an abolitionist—or even to be perceived as one for supporting the Wilmot Proviso—meant to be the kind of northerner slaveholders feared and hated the most and whose policies they would oppose through secession and civil war, if necessary. Thus, when Lincoln remarked "there are no whigs," he meant that the peaceful, gradualist middle position on slavery had disappeared, leaving nothing but extreme defenders of slavery on one side and radical abolitionists on the other. This was how the metaphor of a "house divided" looked to Lincoln in 1855: it was a formula for civil war. (And by the date of this letter, violent conflict over slavery had already begun in Kansas.)

In 1858 Lincoln still referred to a "house divided" in which there was no stable middle position on slavery; indeed, this was the central point of his antislavery message. But he now spoke as though this "severe" contest could be determined by "peaceful ballots" rather than "bloody bullets." Unless Lincoln was disguising his real view and fully expected civil war (an interpretation I do not share), something must have changed in his thinking, in the circumstances of American politics, or in both to justify this greater optimism. The most obvious change, one that Lincoln himself helped bring about, was the creation of the Republican Party as a moderate but firmly committed antislavery party that was competitive throughout the free states and nationally in presidential elections.

Why did Lincoln believe that this new, overwhelmingly northern antislavery party would shift political dynamics in favor of a peaceful rather than a violent contest over slavery? That the Republican platform was moderate and gradualist rather than radical and immediatist in its antislavery commitments is only part of the answer. Southern leaders had repeatedly threatened to dissolve the Union in response to moderate, gradualist antislavery policies.

Historically, in 1860, even the mere election of a president committed to a gradualist antislavery platform was sufficient to trigger secession and civil war. Thus, Lincoln's "no peaceful extinction" observation from 1855 may appear correct in hindsight, and his "peaceful ballots" assurance from 1858 may seem a delusory hope. We are unlikely to take Lincoln's "peaceful ballots" seriously if we assume the historical events leading up to Fort Sumter unfolded with iron necessity. Some preliminary observations may help us loosen the grip of hindsight in critically evaluating Lincoln's faith in the power of peaceful ballots.

First, whatever may have been the merits of the Missouri Compromise and the Compromise of 1850 in containing the explosive potential of the slavery controversy, it would have been extremely difficult, if not impossible, to negotiate another comprehensive sectional compromise on slavery after 1854. The Kansas-Nebraska Act had mortally wounded both compromises, as Lincoln himself recognized by 1855. (And the *Dred Scott* ruling in 1857 was the final nail in the coffin.) Henceforth, *any* restriction on the expansion of slavery would have to be the work of a committed northern free-state majority, not an element of a pact between free states and slave states. By 1858, the only way to politically oppose the expansion of slavery was by building overwhelmingly northern, antislavery majorities in national, state, and territorial politics. This would have been the case even if Douglas's popular sovereignty had effectively functioned to keep slavery out of the territories, for only a sectional northern majority (a coalition of Republicans and northern Democrats) prevented the patently unrepresentative Lecompton Constitution from being accepted by Congress and Kansas from entering the Union with a proslavery constitution.[67] Thus, if Lincoln and others, fearing civil war, had abandoned their peaceful efforts to build a northern antislavery majority, this would have meant capitulating to the nationalization and perpetuation of slavery. Lincoln was not willing to buy peace at the price of both perpetuating slavery and renouncing democratic politics.

Second, although it was certain that any direct attempt by the federal government to abolish slavery in states where it already existed would be met with secession, no one could have known for certain in 1858 that the mere election of a Republican president would be enough to trigger secession. Even fire-eaters like Robert Barnwell Rhett of South Carolina, who hoped the election of a Republican president would serve as a catalyst for secession, could not have known for certain that their efforts would succeed.[68] Thus, it would not have been obvious to Lincoln in 1858 that the political party he helped build would have to deal with secession and civil war as soon as it won a presidential election. Instead, it would have been reasonable to assume that slave-state leaders would wait to see what a Republican president actually did once in office. After Lincoln's election, this assumption held in Virginia, North Carolina, Tennessee, Arkansas, Kentucky, Maryland, and Missouri but not in South Carolina and the rest of the lower South.

Finally, even if it was more likely that the abolition of slavery in the United States would be violent rather than peaceful, probability is not the same as necessity. Given the enormous human costs of a civil war and the unacceptability, to Lincoln and many others, of consenting to the nationalization and perpetuation of slavery, it was not unreasonable for Lincoln to stake his hopes on "peaceful ballots," even if peaceful abolition was less probable than either the full nationalization of slavery or its violent extinction.

With such a historical contingency in mind, let us turn to Lincoln's own observations about how a severe political contest over slavery might play out without widespread violence. The essential elements, in Lincoln's view, were (1) that individual citizens who believed slavery was wrong must be able and willing to vote in accordance with that belief, and (2) that at least one major political party existed that was willing and able to act in accordance with those antislavery votes. In making these claims, Lincoln was standing on its head the oft-repeated warning that a major political party publicly opposed to slavery would make disunion and civil war more likely.[69] Why, in the face of this received political wisdom, did Lincoln believe the formation of the Republican Party made civil war *less* likely?

In his February 27, 1860, Cooper Institute address, Lincoln rejected slaveholders' demand that the Republican Party "break up," based on the (false) allegations that it supported violent antislavery efforts like those of John Brown. Lincoln replied that John Brown–type efforts would become *more* frequent if the Republican Party disbanded:

> Human action can be modified to some extent, but human nature cannot be changed. There is a judgment and a feeling against slavery in this nation, which cast at least a million and a half of votes. You cannot destroy that judgment and feeling—that sentiment—by breaking up the political organization which rallies around it. You can scarcely scatter and disperse an army which has been formed into order in the face of your heaviest fire; but if you could, how much would you gain by forcing the sentiment which created it out of the peaceful channel of the ballot box, into some other channel? What would that other channel probably be? Would the number of John Browns be lessened or enlarged by the operation?[70]

Antislavery sentiments, which Lincoln believed were rooted in human nature, would turn into action one way or another. If "the peaceful channel of the ballot box" was unavailable, "some other channel," likely a violent one, would take its place. In addition to Brown's 1859 Harpers Ferry raid, Lincoln probably had "Bloody Kansas" in mind (where Brown had also been active). The violent contests between proslavery and antislavery militias in Kansas occurred at a time when no legitimate process existed by which residents could communicate their antislavery sentiments through fairly counted votes.

Lincoln here drew a direct connection between "the peaceful channel of the ballot box" and the individual voter's sense of personal efficacy—that is, having both the opportunity and the courage to vote in accordance with one's genuine beliefs. The *opportunity* to vote against slavery depended on the availability of an antislavery political party. The *courage* to vote against slavery depended on a voter's refusal to submit to intimidation. Speaking to the South in his Cooper Institute address, Lincoln said:

> But you will not abide the election of a Republican President? In that supposed event, you say, you will destroy the Union; and then, you say, the great crime of having destroyed it will be upon us! That is cool. A highwayman holds a pistol to my ear, and mutters through his teeth, "Stand and deliver, or I shall kill you, and then you will be a murderer!"

To be sure, what the robber demanded of me—my money—was my own; and I had a clear right to keep it; but it was no more my own than my vote is my own; and the threat of death to me, to extort my money, and the threat of destruction to the Union, to extort my vote, can scarcely be distinguished in principle.

Lincoln urged, in response, not similar threats of violence but a principled and dignified insistence on exercising one's rights as a citizen. "Thinking [slavery] right, as they do, they are not to blame for desiring its full recognition, as being right; but, thinking it wrong, as we do, can we yield to them? Can we cast our votes with their view, and against our own? In view of our moral, social, and political responsibilities, can we do this?"

The closing paragraph of the Cooper Institute address is at once remarkably bold and remarkably modest—bold in its appeal to courageous action, and modest in directing that action toward the peaceful channel of the ballot box: "Neither let us be slandered from our duty by false accusations against us, nor frightened from it by menaces of destruction to the Government nor of dungeons to ourselves. LET US HAVE FAITH THAT RIGHT MAKES MIGHT, AND IN THAT FAITH, LET US, TO THE END, DARE TO DO OUR DUTY AS WE UNDERSTAND IT."[71] In closing the address by emphasizing the right and duty to vote as one thinks, Lincoln rejected the accusation, made by Douglas and others, that Lincoln, along with his party, "advocates boldly and clearly a war of sections, a war of the North against the South."[72] No one, in Lincoln's view, could justly accuse Republican voters of making war on their fellow citizens simply by casting a ballot.

Nor would peaceful resolution of the slavery conflict be advanced through the self-censorship of those on one side of the question, while those on the other side were free to speak as loudly as they liked. Lincoln made this point in his 1858 debates with Douglas, where he confronted those northern Democrats who privately acknowledged that slavery was wrong but followed Douglas's lead in studiously avoiding any public condemnation of the institution. Rhetorically addressing "that Democrat who says he is as much opposed to slavery as I am," Lincoln replied:

You say it is wrong; but don't you constantly object to anybody else saying so? Do you not constantly argue that this is not the right place to oppose it? You say it must not be opposed in the free States, because slavery is not here; it must not be opposed in the slave States, because slavery is there; it must not be opposed in politics, because that will make a fuss; it must not be opposed in the pulpit, because it is not religion. Then where is the place to oppose it? There is no suitable place to oppose it. There is no place in the country to oppose this evil overspreading the continent, which you say yourself is coming.[73]

Lincoln here described citizens who were pathologically incapable of speaking and acting in accordance with what they believed and who deceived themselves (and were encouraged by Douglas to deceive themselves) into thinking that their self-censorship was an act of political and civic responsibility. Lincoln instead described it as a kind of psychic paralysis destructive of democratic politics.

Lincoln also emphasized the one-sided character of Douglas's emphasis on public neutrality toward slavery. Douglas's purpose, Lincoln observed, was "to educate and mold public opinion to 'not care whether slavery is voted up or voted down.'" Lincoln then added a significant qualification: "At least Northern public opinion must cease to care anything about it. Southern public opinion may, without offense, continue to care as much as it pleases."[74] Lincoln did not demand that southerners cease to advocate for slavery (and they would have ignored such a demand in any case). Counterintuitive as it may seem, Lincoln believed the best hope for avoiding civil violence over slavery was to allow all sides to speak and vote freely on the matter.

Moreover, it follows from Lincoln's argument about directing anti-slavery sentiment into peaceful channels that *advocates* of slavery also needed to direct their passions, interests, and fears into peaceful channels. Lincoln nowhere suggested that slaveholders be deprived of such channels. He may have envisioned instead that the Democratic Party, after casting off Douglas's unsustainable popular sovereignty juggling act, would become a predominantly southern, slavery-friendly party facing off against the predominantly northern, free-state Republican Party. Lincoln's observations about parties and voting in the Cooper Institute address suggest that he would have been satisfied with such an outcome and considered it a favorable step toward the long-term extinction of slavery. What Lincoln did not foresee, or perhaps foresaw without fully realizing its significance, was the fatal division within the national Democratic Party over slavery, which occurred between April and June 1860.[75] It followed from Lincoln's own argument in the Cooper Institute address that if the Democratic Party ceased to function as an effective platform for slaveholders' interests and concerns, they would redirect their proslavery passions into violent, extrapolitical channels.

In *The Political Crisis of the 1850s* historian Michael F. Holt argues that secession and civil war in 1860–61 cannot be fully explained as the result of "a basic conflict between sectional interests and values," for the slavery conflict "had long been carried on in peaceful channels." The more important question, Holt writes, is "how the nation could contain or control that division for so long and then allow it suddenly to erupt into war." Holt's answer, which converges in important respects with Lincoln's emphasis on the peaceful ballot box, is that even deep disagreements rooted in conflicting visions of republican government can be peacefully managed so long as there are "competing parties, each with a real chance of winning, to give voters options for political action and an opportunity to remove an unpopular regime from power. . . . Interparty rivalry was necessary to assure divergent groups in society that they had a political voice, a political vehicle through which they could carry on conflict with rival social groups." In contrast, Holt argues, "sectional antagonism was most marked, powerful, and dangerous precisely at those times when or in those places where two-party competition did not exist." Where voters were offered no alternatives, whether because one of the major parties had collapsed within that state or because the parties had become indistinguishable from each other, they "tended to view opposition to their interests in nonpolitical terms, as an external alien threat that required fundamental, nonpolitical solutions"—like secession. "Whatever else secession represented, it was a rejection of the normal political process." This occurred, Holt maintains, because by 1860 there was effectively no party competition in the South. The Whig Party had collapsed in the early 1850s, the Republicans had no presence in the South, and the Democratic Party was fatally divided over southerners' demand for a territorial slave code. In this political vacuum, the secessionist fire-eaters found fertile ground for what was, in essence, "an antiparty, anti-politician movement."[76]

As noted in chapter 2, Lincoln took seriously the criticism that the Republicans were a sectional party, and he sought to broaden the party's appeal, at least in the border states. But he denied that its sectional base of support made the party or its message illegitimate. Moreover, he denied that organizing a major political party around opposition to slavery was a formula for civil war. On the contrary, he thought the creation of the Republican Party should have improved the prospects for sectional peace. By 1855, the Whig Party had collapsed and could not be revived. Lincoln viewed this as a dangerous political situation, fraught with the potential for significant extralegal violence. The Republican Party restored, at least for northern voters, a competitive political environment where deep disagreement could be directed into the peaceful channel of the ballot box. However, the Republican Party could not fulfill any comparable function for southern voters. The collapse of the Democratic Party in 1860, which created a political vacuum where secessionism could flourish without effective opposition, was at least as important as the electoral success of the Republican Party in triggering the Civil War.

Conclusion

Passage of the Kansas-Nebraska Act in 1854 fundamentally altered the course of American political history. It also transformed Abraham Lincoln from a middling Illinois politician into a national leader. Lincoln had always considered slavery unjust, but before 1854, opposition to slavery had not been the principal focus of his political activity. In contrast, the abolitionists had long placed the injustice inflicted on slaves at the center of their petitions and public addresses. It is not unreasonable to ask why Lincoln did not take a stronger antislavery stance before 1854. But I believe the more interesting and fruitful questions are why Lincoln concluded in 1854 that slavery posed a fundamental threat to the survival of republican self-government, including for the mostly white political community to which he belonged; and how his response to slavery from 1854 onward was shaped by his long-standing commitment to the institutions and practices of popular government, including decision by majority vote. The Kansas-Nebraska Act was deeply wrong, not only because it threatened to place additional chains on human beings already held in servitude but also because it enabled a powerful and violent minority, both locally and nationally, to deprive the majority of its legitimate authority to govern. If the Kansas-Nebraska Act had, in Lincoln's words, placed slavery "on a new basis—a basis for making it perpetual, national and universal," then slavery could ultimately become so entrenched that no majority, whether local, state, or national, would be able to uproot it, no matter how morally impassioned and politically determined that majority was.

If a deliberate majority was "the only true sovereign of a free people," then such a majority had to be capable, if it so chose, of halting the expansion of slavery, reversing it, and eventually extinguishing it. How Lincoln believed such a majority could be formed, how he envisioned it acting, and how he attempted to address the explosive question of race relations and racial equality in a postslavery United States are questions taken up in the next three chapters.

5 | "Of Strange, Discordant, and Even, Hostile Elements"

Building an Antislavery Electoral Majority

Lincoln believed that the majority of human beings possessed "human sympathies" that enabled them to "sense . . . the wrong of slavery." This human sympathy—the consciousness "that slaves are human beings; *men*, not property"—could be silenced by self-interest and habituation to the institution of slavery. But even in slave states, Lincoln observed, these sympathies surfaced when slaveholders "instinctively" shrank from contact with that "sneaking individual" the slave dealer (though continuing to do business with him). A slaveholder selling an enslaved human being intuitively knew that this was very different from selling "corn, cattle, or tobacco."[1]

Lincoln also argued that it was in the self-interest of free white citizens to oppose the spread and perpetuation of slavery and to acknowledge that the natural rights promised in the Declaration of Independence applied to human beings of all races. As he insisted, "the class of arguments put forward to batter that idea, are also calculated to break down the very idea of a free government, even for white men, and to undermine the very foundations of free society."[2] However, unlike "human sympathies" that operate "instinctively" and thus prior to reason, enlisting the political self-interest of white citizens in opposition to slavery depended on reasoned persuasion. Self-interest is typically a stronger motive than disinterested sympathy. But to many white citizens, it was far from obvious that the enslavement of Blacks threatened their own rights and interests. Slaveholders were not shy about making the opposite argument: as John C. Calhoun phrased it, the enslavement of Blacks furnished, for white citizens, "the most safe and stable basis for free institutions in the world."[3] This too was an appeal to white Americans' self-interest.

Lincoln firmly believed that the enslavement of some threatened the rights of all. He also believed that most citizens were capable of understanding this. But persuading white Americans of this truth required leaders and political parties that were willing and able to make the argument clearly, persuasively, and publicly. Lincoln knew how difficult it would be to translate the majority's inchoate antislavery sympathies and perceptions into effective political action against slavery. In the slave states there were insuperable obstacles to organizing an antislavery party or movement. But the challenges were formidable even in the free states. By the 1850s, the abolitionist movement had turned public opinion in the free states against slavery to an impressive degree. But in electoral contests, abolitionist candidates and parties won only a small fraction of the vote. This chapter describes how Lincoln understood the obstacles to organizing an antislavery *electoral* majority and how he sought to overcome them.

Much of the chapter focuses on Lincoln's efforts to build an electorally competitive Republican Party. Yet there is a larger theme that extends beyond the specific challenges of constructing the Republican Party: how Lincoln envisaged organizing an antislavery national majority. He understood that if the Republican Party was successful in establishing itself as an enduring major party, this would transform public opinion and party dynamics well beyond the range of the party's committed supporters. In his June 16, 1858, "House Divided" speech, Lincoln characterized the goals of "the *opponents* of slavery" as, first, to "arrest the further spread of it," and second, to "place it where the public mind shall rest in the belief that it is in course of ultimate extinction."[4] Lincoln did not simply identify slavery's opponents with the Republican Party; nor would the public's belief in slavery's ultimate extinction require a mass conversion to Republican Party principles. As noted in chapter 2, Lincoln knew (as did slaveholders) that the Republican Party's public presence in the slave states would fundamentally alter the political discourse on slavery, even where the party's candidates had little chance of winning. What mattered most to Lincoln were these wider transformations of policy and opinion, not the Republican vote count alone. But he believed the Republican Party was an essential catalyst for these broader changes.

Lincoln was convinced, for example, that many northern Democrats were personally opposed to slavery, despite their public support for Stephen Douglas's policy of official neutrality. Lincoln did not expect all Democrats troubled by slavery to immediately leave their party and join the Republicans, much as he would have cheered this development. Instead, he anticipated that an electorally competitive Republican Party in the free states would force northern Democrats off the fence. Some would eventually become Republicans. Others would remain Democrats but find it politically prudent to cooperate with Republicans in halting the expansion of slavery (as in 1857–58, when a coalition of Republicans and northern Democrats in the US House of Representatives defeated the Buchanan administration's effort to force a proslavery constitution on Kansas).[5] Some northern Democrats would make the opposite choice and publicly embrace the proslavery stance of their southern counterparts. Either way, Lincoln believed, Douglas's "don't care" stance toward slavery would become unsustainable. The justice or injustice of slavery would become the central political question of the age.

But realigning the electoral competition between the major parties to make slavery the central question did not occur quickly or easily, and it might not have happened at all. William Gienapp describes the establishment and endurance of the Republican Party as "one of the most striking success stories in American political annals," for it became "a formidable political organization after only a few short years," "elected its first president in just its second national campaign," then "preserved the Union, abolished slavery, and enacted one of the most significant legislative programs in the nation's history." And yet, Gienapp observes:

> It was not obvious at the outset that the Republican party would become either powerful or permanent, and its continued existence was anything but inevitable. . . . Less than five years earlier, defeated almost everywhere and barely organized in half the northern states, the Republican movement seemed destined, like every antislavery party before it, for an early death. Indeed, in view of the fate that befell every antislavery party before it, its survival was in many ways even more remarkable than its eventual success.[6]

Lincoln's own recognition of the organizational challenges helps explain both why he was more reluctant than many others to abandon the Whig Party in 1854 and why he became, from 1856 onward, such a committed and effective organizer of the Republican Party. Near the close of his "House Divided" speech, after noting with pride that the Republican Party had "mustered over thirteen hundred thousand" votes in the 1856 elections, Lincoln observed, "We did this under the single impulse of resistance to a common danger, with every external circumstance against us. Of *strange, discordant,* and even, *hostile* elements, we gathered from the four winds, and *formed* and fought the battle through."[7]

Despite his conviction that most northern voters harbored antislavery sentiments, Lincoln recognized that there was something extraordinarily difficult—indeed, almost unnatural—about founding a major political party principally on opposition to the spread of slavery. Political constituencies with mutually opposing views on most of the important political questions of the day had to be persuaded to put aside their differences and, at least for the foreseeable future, prioritize halting the spread of slavery. The connecting thread of Lincoln's action and thought as a party builder can best be discerned by first surveying the political chaos among the northern electorate immediately following passage of the Kansas-Nebraska Act in 1854.

Abandoning Old Loyalties

The repeal of the Missouri Compromise in 1854, which potentially opened all US territories to slavery, provoked widespread outrage across the North. The Democratic Party suffered significant losses in the 1854 congressional elections in the free states, which could be construed as popular renunciation of the Kansas-Nebraska Act. In the US House of Representatives, Democrats had held 157 of 234 seats (67 percent) in the Thirty-Third Congress; this number fell to 83 seats (35.5 percent) in the Thirty-Fourth Congress. Democrats were hardest hit in the free states, where they lost sixty-six House seats; only seven free-state Democratic House members who voted for the act were reelected. In the slave states, in contrast, where every Democratic House member voted for the Kansas-Nebraska Act, the party lost only four of its sixty-seven seats. As a result, the Democratic Party was permanently weakened in the North and became an increasingly southern-accented, proslavery party.[8]

But in the free states, the many critics of the Kansas-Nebraska Act were unable at first to cooperate effectively. The act's opponents in Congress failed to defeat it, and after its passage, the act's critics in the northern electorate—many of whom, like Lincoln, regarded the expansion of slavery as a grave threat to America's republican institutions—were unable to agree on a specific political strategy beyond the minimal goal of restoring the 36° 30' slavery restriction. Nor could opponents agree on a political vehicle for their antislavery efforts. Should it be a revitalized Whig Party (because every northern Whig had voted against the act)? Should they settle instead for limited cooperation between Whigs and anti-Nebraska Democrats (even though these factions had failed to co-operate in preventing the act's passage)? Or should the act's opponents break with both major parties (for both the Democrats and the Whigs were deeply compromised on slavery) and form new ones?

Gienapp notes that in Congress, despite strong opposition to the Kansas-Nebraska bill, "cooperation among Northern Whigs, anti-Nebraska Democrats, and Free-Soilers was distinctly limited." Each opposition group retained its separate identity and refused to caucus with the others. The opposition also lacked a recognized leader. The bill's passage subsequently produced "a significant change in northern political opinion," marked by a determination henceforth "to resist the aggressions of the Slave Power." But, Gienapp observes, "into what political channel this anger would flow was not clear in the summer of 1854."[9]

One factor inhibiting the formation of an effective antislavery party or coalition was the persistence of party loyalties. Lincoln confronted this barrier in February 1855 when he sought the US Senate seat held by James Shields, a Douglas-supported Democrat who had voted for the Kansas-Nebraska Act. Lincoln was still officially a Whig, but he now placed opposition to slavery at the center of his political agenda. Despite retaining the Whig label, Lincoln was already participating in a broader, loosely organized anti–Kansas-Nebraska coalition in Illinois. In 1854 he corresponded with and attended some public events arranged by a group of political abolitionists who were attempting to form a Republican Party in Illinois and hoped to recruit Lincoln to the cause. Lincoln assured these abolitionist proto-Republicans that his "opposition to the principle of slavery" was as strong as theirs but that "practically," he did not "feel authorized to carry that opposition" as far as the abolitionists hoped.[10] He was also unwilling to dismantle the Illinois Whig organization in favor of a fledgling party with no prospect of imminent electoral success.[11]

Lincoln had carefully studied the results of the 1854 election for the Illinois legislature and determined that an anti–Kansas-Nebraska senator could be elected through an alliance between Whigs and anti-Nebraska Democrats.[12] But this would be possible only if some anti-Nebraska Democratic legislators would vote to send a Whig to the US Senate or, alternatively, if Whig legislators were willing to support an anti-Nebraska Democrat for that seat. This would require at least some Whigs or some Democrats to rise above decades of fierce opposition over presidential candidates, banks, tariffs, internal improvements, public land policies, and other matters whose importance had been diminished but not erased by the Kansas-Nebraska crisis. Gienapp argues that in Illinois the most significant barrier to forming an effective antislavery coalition was "the unwillingness of both Whigs and Democrats to abandon their old loyalties."[13]

Lincoln himself was reluctant to abandon "old loyalties," and yet in the three-way contest in February 1855 for the Senate seat, he demonstrated how and why it must be done. Lincoln was "far and away the strongest candidate, having collected pledges of support from most of the Whig members" of the legislature.[14] The other candidates were Douglas-supported Democratic incumbent James Shields and Lyman Trumbull, an anti–Kansas-Nebraska Democrat. Shields's vocal support for the Kansas-Nebraska Act proved a liability, and he was replaced after the sixth ballot by another Douglas-supported Democrat, Joel Matteson, who privately assured Douglas of his support for the Kansas-Nebraska Act but issued ambiguous public statements on the subject. Lincoln led on the first ballot, receiving forty-five votes to Shields's forty-one votes and Trumbull's five. If the five anti–Kansas-Nebraska Democrats who voted for Trumbull had been willing to vote for Lincoln, he would have been elected senator. But four of these five anti-Nebraska Democrats made it clear that they "could never vote for a whig." Lincoln's vote total fell in subsequent ballots, and Matteson's election appeared likely. Lincoln therefore "determined to strike at once; and accordingly advised my remaining friends to go for [Trumbull], which they did & elected him on the 10th ballot." Lincoln was disappointed but reflected, "On the whole, it is perhaps as well for our general cause that Trumbull is elected."[15]

Lincoln's willingness to cross party lines, and direct his Whig supporters to do likewise, sent a clear public signal that opposition to the spread of slavery—the "general cause" to which he referred—must take precedence over the issues that had long divided Whigs and Democrats. Lincoln's action in securing the election of Trumbull (who later joined the Republican Party) was also Lincoln's first significant act as a builder of the Republican Party, even though he was still a Whig and soon became politically homeless when that party collapsed. Lincoln's disappointment with those who were unwilling to cross party lines to oppose slavery did not convert him from an advocate of strong parties to an antiparty ideologist, although similar experiences might have led others down that path. Instead, Lincoln ultimately concluded that a new major political party would have to be organized, built on an antislavery foundation.

Meanwhile, the antiparty outlook, which had a long history in American republican thinking, made a powerful resurgence in the early 1850s and was a factor in the surprising (and to Lincoln deeply alarming) rise of the anti-immigrant Know-Nothing movement.

Nativism, Temperance, and Slavery

The early 1850s were a time of enormous flux and uncertainty in American politics, for reasons including but not limited to divisions over slavery. Many voters, especially in the North, were concerned about several social and cultural issues that had been largely ignored or marginalized by the major parties, including temperance (in response to antebellum Americans' high levels of alcohol consumption and abuse) and immigration (especially the large influx of immigrants from Ireland and Germany). Differences of opinion over temperance and immigration did not readily align with the traditional Whig-Democratic disagreements over economic development, presidential power, and the role of government. The Whig Party was especially vulnerable to these new, crosscutting issues because its predominantly Protestant and moral reform–oriented supporters were the voters most likely to favor the prohibition of alcohol. Many Whig voters also favored restricting citizenship and voting rights for Irish Catholic and German (both Catholic and Protestant) immigrants. (The Democratic Party, in contrast, was more unified behind its immigrant- and alcohol-friendly stances.)

Adding to the disruptive potential of new issues was the growing perception among northern voters that both major parties, especially the Whigs, had ceased to stand for anything beyond holding office and distributing patronage. By the early 1850s, many of the issues that had once divided the major parties were now either dead (the National Bank) or less important (protective tariffs), or they had ceased to differentiate the parties (in Illinois, for example, both Whigs and Democrats enthusiastically supported railroad development). Meanwhile, the major parties ignored or suppressed other issues of importance to many northern voters. In the 1852 campaign, Whig presidential candidate Winfield Scott attempted unsuccessfully to outflank Democratic candidate Franklin Pierce in courting Irish Catholic voters, despite Irish immigrants' traditionally strong attachment to the Democratic Party and the nativist inclinations of many Whigs. As it turned out, many of the Whigs' traditional supporters sat out the 1852 election, most Irish immigrants remained loyal to the Democratic Party, and voters were deprived of substantive debate on an important emerging concern.[16]

If the 1852 campaign signaled a false consensus on immigration, the major parties and their presidential candidates even more forcefully and deliberately suppressed any discussion of slavery. Democratic and Whig leaders alike insisted that the Compromise of 1850 represented a final settlement of all slavery questions, and the issue must not be reopened. The 1852 Democratic national platform included a plank that stated, "the democratic party will resist all attempts at renewing, in congress or out of it, the agitation of the slavery question, under whatever shape or color the attempt may be made." The 1852 Whig platform affirmed that all elements of the Compromise of 1850, including "the act known as the Fugitive Slave Law . . . are received and acquiesced in by the Whig party of the United States as a settlement in principle and substance of the dangerous and exciting questions which they embrace." Because northern and southern Whigs were sharply divided over slavery, Winfield Scott's advisers urged him to maintain "perfect silence on the issues of the day." But Scott ultimately bowed to pressure from southern Whigs and publicly endorsed the Compromise of 1850, including the Fugitive Slave Act. The Whigs' 1852 platform and presidential candidate thus failed to distinguish their party from the Democrats with respect to the two most important concerns for northern voters: immigration and slavery. Historians disagree about the relative weight of slavery and nativism as factors in the Whig Party's demise, but it is safe to say that both factors played a significant role in its dissolution by the mid-1850s.[17]

Both the enormous political fluidity of the early to mid-1850s and the major parties' failure to distinguish themselves from each other on a range of important issues are critical to understanding how Lincoln envisioned the task of building the Republican Party after the demise of the Whigs. One consequence of this complex, chaotic political landscape in the wake of the Kansas-Nebraska Act was that the *intensity* of northern voters' opposition to the expansion of slavery was not clear. One New York journalist claimed, on the eve of the 1854 elections, "the election tomorrow in this State, turns about as much upon the Nebraska issue as upon the opium trade in China."[18] Lincoln, among others, interpreted the Democratic Party's enormous 1854 electoral losses in the North as voters' negative judgment upon the Kansas-Nebraska Act. But the biggest (and to many contemporaries surprising) winners in 1854 were nativist Know-Nothing candidates.[19] Most northern Know-Nothings, like most northern temperance advocates, were also antislavery to some degree, which multiplies the difficulties of drawing conclusions from the 1854 election results. Holt observes, "There is massive evidence that most Know Nothing voters in the Northeast were also hostile to slavery expansion." But those seeking to build a Republican Party in the northeastern states by opposing the expansion of slavery "could not distinguish themselves sufficiently from the Know Nothings to lure away voters by that strategy."[20] And the Know-Nothings elected in 1854 were not willing to subordinate their own nativist agenda to those who prioritized opposition to slavery.[21]

To Lincoln, it seemed self-evident that halting the expansion of slavery took priority over both the issues that traditionally divided Democrats and Whigs and emerging political concerns such as temperance and nativism. He had long regarded temperance as a worthy object for private associations that relied on voluntary persuasion rather than legal prohibition, which he opposed. Nor, in his view, should voters categorically refuse to support a candidate for public office simply because that candidate sometimes consumed alcohol.[22]

In private correspondence, Lincoln was harshly critical of nativism. "I am not a Know-Nothing. . . . How can anyone who abhors the oppression of negroes, be in favor of degrading classes of white people? As a nation, we began by declaring that '*all men are created equal.*' We now practically read it 'all men are created equal, *except negroes.*' When the Know-Nothings get control, it will read 'all men are created equal, except negroes, *and foreigners, and catholics.*'"[23] Even though Lincoln regarded Know-Nothing principles as "little better" than "those of the slavery extensionists," he recognized that most northern Know-Nothings opposed the extension of slavery. For that reason (as he observed in an August 1855 letter to Owen Lovejoy), securing the support of "the elements of this organization" was essential to defeating the effort to plant slavery in Kansas. But winning over the antislavery Know-Nothings would take time, and "an open push by us now, may offend them, and tend to prevent our ever getting them." Thus, timing mattered. "Know-nothingism has not yet entirely tumbled to pieces. . . . We can not get them so long as they cling to a hope of success under their own organization."[24] In Lincoln's judgment, the Know-Nothings could not ultimately succeed as a major party, precisely because the slavery issue was more important than any other; however, time, persuasion, careful organization, and the force of events would be necessary to draw Know-Nothing voters into the Republican camp. Indeed, when Lincoln penned this letter, the American Party (the official Know-Nothing political organization) was dividing over slavery into a "North" American and "South" American Party.[25] The American Party's fatal split over slavery supports Lincoln's judgment, and that of some historians, that the slavery issue was ultimately more fundamental than nativism to the northern electorate.[26]

Lincoln has often been described as remaining publicly silent about the Know-Nothings during the 1850s.[27] Though true in one sense, it is inaccurate in another. Lincoln voiced *public* support on many occasions for a generous immigration and naturalization policy. Adherents to an anti-immigrant, anti-Catholic agenda would not have mistaken Lincoln as a supporter of their cause.[28] His efforts to attract German immigrants to the Republican Party were no secret. On multiple public occasions he quoted the Declaration of Independence's maxim that "all men are created equal" in contexts that carried an unmistakably immigrant-friendly message.[29] In 1844, nearly a decade before the emergence of Know-Nothingism as a political movement, Lincoln publicly denounced the violence of anti-immigrant mobs.[30] Thus, on the issues central to Know-Nothing political ideology, Lincoln was far from silent and clearly on the opposite side.[31]

Lincoln's "silence" on Know-Nothingism was limited to one important aspect: for the most part, he refrained from publicly attacking the Know-Nothings (except those who engaged in anti-immigrant violence). The distinction between publicly supporting the rights of immigrants and Catholics, on the one hand, and avoiding a public battle with Know-Nothings, on the other, was an important one for Lincoln. He advised against "an open stand against them" because it would "offend them" and thereby "prevent our ever getting them."[32] He recognized the difference between disagreeing with people and publicly vilifying them. In this respect, Lincoln's approach was parallel to the advice he gave the Washington Temperance Society about reforming alcoholics: "If you would win a man to your cause, *first* convince him that you are his sincere friend." If instead, you "mark him as one to be shunned and despised," then "he will retreat within himself, close all the avenues to his head and his heart; and tho' your cause be naked truth itself . . . you shall no more be able to pierce him, than to penetrate the hard shell of a tortoise with a rye straw."[33] In contrast to Lincoln's course of action, William Seward, the Whig-turned-Republican US senator from New York, engaged in a bitter public battle with the Know-Nothings in 1854 and 1855. By 1860, the Know-Nothing movement had lost its momentum, and most of its former northern supporters had entered the Republican ranks—even though the 1860 Republican platform included an immigrant-friendly plank supported by both Lincoln and Seward. But these former Know-Nothings had neither forgiven nor forgotten Seward's public crusade against them, and they refused to support him at the 1860 Republican national convention. Yet they found Lincoln, whose views on immigration hardly differed from Seward's, an acceptable candidate.[34]

Thus, the political fluidity of the early to mid-1850s and the emergence of new issues created three interconnected challenges for Lincoln's efforts to mobilize northern voters around opposition to the expansion of slavery. First, these hitherto suppressed issues, combined with voters' disgust toward major parties that appeared to stand for nothing, helped kill the Whig Party, which Lincoln had initially hoped to revitalize around opposition to slavery. Second, these circumstances made it difficult at first to ascertain how *intensely* northern voters were opposed to the expansion of slavery. Finally, the fluctuating, amorphous political situation made it difficult to achieve effective political cooperation among the diverse constituencies whose support was needed to build a national electoral majority firmly opposed to the expansion and perpetuation of slavery. These challenges illuminate how Lincoln, as a political thinker and an advocate of majority rule, approached the task of party building.

Creating Common Ground

Lincoln was not suspicious of political parties; nor, in the 1850s, did he share the popular revulsion against parties. But he recognized that the Republicans would have to be a very different kind of party than the Whigs had been. He did not abandon the Whigs in the 1852 election, as many others did. But his speeches supporting Whig presidential candidate Winfield Scott are among the dullest, most uninspired performances of his political career.[35] In this respect, even Lincoln seemed to be afflicted by the party fatigue felt by so many voters in the early 1850s. In contrast, once he joined the Republican party-building effort, he became a man reborn; his public speeches and private writings shimmer with excitement and conviction. He expressed this spirit in his observations about the Republican project—"*our great cause*"—that closed his "House Divided" speech of June 16, 1858. He must have conveyed similar excitement in his May 29, 1856, "lost speech" at the Illinois Republican state convention, where listeners were reportedly so enthralled that they dropped their pencils and neglected to record his words. His description of the Republican movement in the "House Divided" speech—"Of *strange, discordant,* and even, *hostile* elements, we gathered from the four winds"—suggests that Lincoln saw the Republican Party as fundamentally different in character than the Whig and Democratic Parties of the Jacksonian era.[36]

Both Lincoln's Whig and Republican party-building efforts reveal elements of his thinking about parties and majority rule. But the differences between these two phases of his experience with political parties are as important as the continuities.

One central thread runs through Lincoln's thinking about parties, evident at all stages of his political career: organized political parties facilitate majority rule. They do so by enabling voters who hold broadly similar views on important public issues (e.g., opposition to the spread of slavery) to unite behind a single candidate on Election Day, rather than scatter their votes among multiple candidates and thereby allow a better-organized minority to elect the majority's least-preferred candidate. To state the point another way: a majority ceases to be a majority if its members cannot cooperate politically. During the late 1830s and 1840s (as noted in chapter 3), Lincoln urged the Whigs to unite behind a single candidate at a nominating convention, as the Democrats did, rather than scattering their votes among a number of Whig-affiliated candidates in the general election, as they did in the 1836 presidential election and in many Illinois state elections. Party primaries did not exist in Lincoln's time. Party conventions, especially at the state and local level, enabled ordinary citizens to deliberate and decide on their party's nominee. To those Illinois Whigs who resisted Lincoln's efforts to institute nominating conventions, the practice seemed antirepublican because it prevented citizens from casting votes on Election Day for whichever Whig-affiliated candidate they preferred. From Lincoln's perspective, conventions advanced republican principles by making majority rule practically effective. Later, as a Republican Party builder in 1858, Lincoln pushed the convention practice further. He persuaded the state party to nominate its US Senate candidate (who ended up being Lincoln himself) at the Illinois Republican state convention in advance of the 1858 election, even though, at the time, US senators were chosen not by voters in the general election but afterward by state legislatures.[37]

Party nominating conventions could not prevent third parties, whether long established or newly emergent, from fielding candidates in the general election and potentially drawing a decisive share of votes away from one or both major parties. In this case, the only option available to those (like Lincoln) who feared a counterproductive scattering of votes was to persuade individual citizens to consider the practical consequences of their choices when they cast their votes. During the 1840s Lincoln warned against casting antislavery votes in a way that could produce proslavery outcomes. He believed that in 1844 the Liberty Party ticket had drawn enough votes away from Henry Clay to ensure the election of James Polk, who, as president, pursued expansionist proslavery policies. In the 1848 presidential campaign, Lincoln argued that antislavery voters should support Whig candidate Zachary Taylor rather than Free-Soil candidate Martin Van Buren, who could not win but whose candidacy might hand the victory to Democrat Lewis Cass, an early advocate of the popular sovereignty policy toward slavery in the territories.[38]

But Lincoln's consequentialist arguments during the 1840s that antislavery voters should cast their ballots for Whigs rather than Liberty Party or Free-Soil candidates were weakened by the Whig Party's notorious sectional divisions over slavery, the complete absence of language on slavery in its 1844 and 1848 national platforms,[39] Henry Clay's support for the annexation of Texas in 1844, and Zachary Taylor's silence on slavery in 1848. Thus, in the 1840s Lincoln was in the peculiar position of urging antislavery voters, on *purely* consequentialist grounds, to support Whig presidential candidates who took no principled stand against slavery rather than third-party candidates who forthrightly condemned the institution of slavery.

Antislavery arguments played a fundamentally different role in Lincoln's party-building efforts in the 1850s, for the Republican Party's central commitment was opposition to the spread of slavery. Lincoln was now able to make both principled and consequentialist arguments about why antislavery voters should support Republican candidates. Indeed, from 1854 onward, Lincoln's principled and consequentialist antislavery arguments cannot be sharply distinguished, precisely because he now emphasized the positive practical consequences of commitment to the principle of natural equality and the destructive practical consequences, for white as well as Black Americans, of rejecting that principle.

This did not make Lincoln an abolitionist—at least not the type of abolitionist who demanded that slavery be immediately abolished everywhere in the United States. Lincoln regarded this stance as just in principle but impossible to accomplish without civil war. In this respect, he continued to distinguish between principled and consequentialist approaches to slavery. The Republican platform and Lincoln's own views were less radical than the position of even the most politically pragmatic abolitionists.[40] Nevertheless, it was far easier, both on principled and consequentialist grounds, to persuade abolitionists to support the Republican Party in the late 1850s than it had been to persuade abolitionists to support Henry Clay or Zachary Taylor in the 1840s. Though some abolitionists scathingly denounced Lincoln and the Republicans for their limited antislavery commitments,[41] many others made a considered decision to make common cause with the Republicans while pushing the party wherever possible to take a stronger antislavery position.[42]

As a Republican Party organizer, Lincoln found abolitionists less troublesome than some conservative Whig-turned-Republicans who sought to drive the abolitionist-turned-Republicans out of the party. In 1856 Owen Lovejoy (whose brother Elijah Lovejoy had been murdered by an antiabolitionist mob in 1837) won election as an Illinois Republican to a US House seat. In 1858, as Lincoln was preparing for his Senate contest with Stephen Douglas, some conservative Republicans (David Davis and Ward Lamon) sought to prevent Lovejoy's reelection and drive him out of the Illinois Republican Party by running an independent candidate against him, thereby ensuring Lovejoy's defeat. Lincoln responded that such a scheme "will result in nothing but disaster all round." It would turn Lovejoy's supporters against Lincoln and "in the end lose us the District altogether." Lincoln wrote to Lamon and urged that the Republican candidate be selected at a convention: "If, in that convention upon a common platform, which all are willing to stand upon, one who has been known as an abolitionist [Lovejoy], but who is now occupying none but common ground, can get the majority of the votes to which *all* look for an election, there is no safe way but to submit."[43] Despite Lovejoy's reputation as an abolitionist, his current stances were consistent with the Republicans' "common platform" and "common ground"—ground that Lincoln considered spacious enough to include radicals like Lovejoy and conservatives like Davis and Lamon. If Lovejoy received a majority of votes at a party convention, Republicans who would have preferred a less radical candidate must accept the convention's choice and support him in the general election. Just five days after he wrote the letter to Lamon quoted here, Lincoln delivered his "House Divided" speech, where he described the Republican Party as composed of "*strange, discordant,* and even, *hostile* elements." He might have had the Lovejoy episode in mind as he spoke these words.

Lincoln is often described as a moderate Republican who staked out moderate antislavery territory. Eric Foner in *Free Soil, Free Labor, Free Men* classifies Lincoln as a moderate rather than a conservative Republican and observes, "In politics as well as ideology, Lincoln represented a middle ground between conservatism and radicalism." With respect to his antislavery principles, Foner positions Lincoln on the side of the radicals because he "made clear that his ultimate goal was not merely the non-extension of slavery" (which many conservative Republicans were willing to settle for) but slavery's "ultimate extinction." Foner also mentions Lincoln's opposition to conservative efforts to deprive Lovejoy of his congressional seat.[44] William W. Freehling in *Becoming Lincoln* describes him as representing "the incrementally moving dead center of northern antislavery inclinations" and observes that Lincoln worked "to convince Radical Republicans to remain in the moderate-dominated party."[45] (It should also be noted that Lincoln worked to convince conservative Republicans to remain in a party that received radicals into its ranks.) The description of Lincoln as a moderate is accurate as far as it goes. But it is important to emphasize that Lincoln did not just *occupy* middle ground in the party; he worked energetically and deliberately *to make middle ground possible* in a newly organized party that could not endure unless party leaders fostered cooperation among its diverse and often mutually hostile constituencies.

Issue Priorities and Stable Majorities

Securing the support of the Know-Nothings posed a different kind of problem for Lincoln and the fledging Republican Party than did mediating differences between radical and conservative antislavery opinions. Republicans who sharply disagreed about whether the party's stance on slavery should be radical, conservative, or somewhere in between at least agreed, in the wake of the Kansas-Nebraska Act, that slavery had become the central political question of the day. Radical, moderate, and conservative Republicans also agreed on the goal of winning elections, which helped diminish the intensity of their ideological disagreements.

The Know-Nothings posed a fundamentally different kind of challenge. Though most northern Know-Nothings were also antislavery to varying degrees, they did *not* agree that slavery was the most urgent political issue of the day. Instead, their priorities were stopping or slowing the pace of immigration and naturalization (especially from Ireland and Germany), limiting the influence of the Catholic Church (which many Know-Nothings regarded as a kind of "slave power"), and reforming what they viewed as corrupt or violent electoral practices by immigrant political clubs.[46] Though their anti-Catholicism could be characterized as simple bigotry, the historically unprecedented influx of immigrants and the irregular electoral practices of some immigrant political clubs were legitimate and important concerns around which major party competition might have realigned were it not for the slavery crisis. Nor were Know-Nothing voters committed to helping Republican candidates win elections. They had their own leaders and party organizers who hoped to relegate Republican leaders, organizations, and issues to subordinate status or, if this did not succeed, to "fuse" with Republicans on equal terms. After the Whigs' demise, it was not clear for several years which new party-building initiative, the Republicans or the Know-Nothings, would win the competition to become the Democrats' major rival in the North. Republicans' effort to win over the antislavery Know-Nothings was complicated by the fact that many of the Republicans' most articulate and committed leaders, including Seward and Lincoln, were strongly opposed in principle to the Know-Nothing political agenda. Seward engaged in a high-profile public fight with the Know-Nothings, while Lincoln strove to keep his opposition from becoming a bitter public battle. But neither of them were willing to concede anything of substance to Know-Nothing ideology in their effort to win over voters who had supported Know-Nothing candidates.[47]

Lincoln recognized that stable majorities on contested public issues did not form spontaneously but required political organization and public persuasion. The surge of Know-Nothingism in the years following passage of the Kansas-Nebraska Act threatened to undo what Lincoln hoped would become an enduring antislavery electoral majority. As noted in chapter 2, Lincoln understood the phenomenon of cyclical majorities, and in 1859 he described the dynamic of cyclical majorities in Congress with respect to three very different policies toward slavery in the territories: a coalition of Republicans and popular sovereignty Democrats defeats the slave-code position; a coalition of popular sovereignty Democrats and slave-coders defeats the Republican position; and a coalition of Republicans and slave-coders defeats the popular sovereignty position.[48] A similar dynamic may have characterized the northern electorate's preferences with respect to the Republican position, Douglas's popular sovereignty, and Know-Nothingism in the mid-1850s. I offer here an elementary model to illuminate the strategic opportunities and constraints that Lincoln (and other Republicans) faced in building a Republican Party focused on opposition to slavery, amid the crosscurrents of other issues. To simplify the model, I omit temperance (alcohol policy), which was decided principally by state and local governments, and focus on slavery and immigration, which involved federal as well as state and local authority.

Suppose that northern voters have preferences with respect to decisions on slavery and immigration but that they also have preferences with respect to which issue, slavery or immigration, is more salient. Judgments about the relative salience of slavery and immigration would be important in shaping voters' decisions about which party to support (Republicans, Democrats, or Know-Nothings) under the fluid political circumstances of the mid-1850s.

Let us assume that northern voters are offered two positions on slavery: the Republican policy to restrict slavery (RS) and Douglas's popular sovereignty policy to permit slavery (PS). (I leave out the proslavery position that all territories must enact a slave code, because that stance had little support in the North.) Assume also that northerners are offered two positions on immigration: permit immigration (PI) and restrict immigration (RI). If every mathematically possible ranking of RS, PS, PI, and RI were included, there would be twenty-four rankings. But many of these combinations are psychologically implausible. For instance, a voter who ranks immigration as the most salient issue and who strongly supports an anti-immigration party or candidate is unlikely to support a pro-immigration party or candidate as his second choice if other options are available. Therefore, I assume that, on the issue most salient to a voter, that voter will rank his own stance on that issue first and rank the opposing stance on that issue last. Thus, a pro-immigration voter for whom immigration is the most salient issue (and especially a voter who is an immigrant himself) would be more inclined to support candidates or parties on either side of the slavery issue, as long as they are pro-immigration, than to support *any* anti-immigration candidates or parties, whatever their positions on slavery.

Assuming that a voter who ranks restrict slavery (RS) first also ranks permit slavery (PS) last, and vice versa, and that a voter who ranks restrict immigration (RI) first also ranks permit immigration (PI) last, and vice versa, the number of psychologically plausible rankings are reduced to the eight listed below. Within each set of preference rankings, stances are ordered from most favored to least favored.

> RS/PI/RI/PS: restrict slavery/permit immigration/restrict immigration/permit slavery (referring to an antislavery, pro-immigration voter for whom slavery is the most salient issue and permitting slavery is the lowest-ranked option)
>
> RS/RI/PI/PS: restrict slavery/restrict immigration/permit immigration/permit slavery
>
> PI/RS/PS/RI: permit immigration/restrict slavery/permit slavery/restrict immigration
>
> PI/PS/RS/RI: permit immigration/permit slavery/restrict slavery/restrict immigration
>
> RI/RS/PS/PI: restrict immigration/restrict slavery/permit slavery/permit immigration
>
> RI/PS/RS/PI: restrict immigration/permit slavery/restrict slavery/permit immigration
>
> PS/PI/RI/RS: permit slavery/permit immigration/restrict immigration/restrict slavery
>
> PS/RI/PI/RS: permit slavery/restrict immigration/permit immigration/restrict slavery

Lincoln's views on these two issues and their relative salience put him in the RS/PI/RI/PS preference set: he was both antislavery and pro-immigration, but slavery was the most important issue. By far his least-preferred outcome was permitting the further spread of slavery. Stephen Douglas qualified as PS/PI/RI/RS: he had staked his career on the Kansas-Nebraska Act, which permitted slavery to spread to new territories, and he took a pro-immigration stance, as Lincoln did. The northern Know-Nothings, whom Lincoln found troublesome because of their anti-immigration views but hoped to bring under the Republican tent because they were also antislavery, were RI/RS/PS/PI. The anti-slavery German Americans, whom Lincoln also hoped to bring under the Republican tent and feared losing if the Republican Party shifted its platform in an anti-immigrant direction, were PI/RS/PS/RI.

It is evident that if each voter preference set included equal numbers of voters (and if voter preferences remained fixed), the result would be a tie on both slavery and immigration. In fact, we cannot know—nor could Lincoln's contemporaries know—exactly what proportion of northern voters fell into each preference set. That was precisely why political conditions in the North were so fluid and confusing in the mid-1850s. We can make some inferences about voter preferences from election results, but the available electoral options did not always allow voters to clearly communicate their preferences on both slavery and immigration or to signal which of the two issues they considered more salient. We can also make inferences about the distribution of voters among these preference sets based on the strategic behavior of leaders, like Lincoln, who hoped to build a party capable of winning elections.

We should not assume that voter preferences on slavery and immigration remained fixed over time or that candidates' and parties' electoral success resulted entirely from the effective manipulation of fixed preferences. As noted in chapter 2, Lincoln considered it essential to persuade at least some voters to *alter* their preferences; he did not believe an enduring antislavery majority could be built if voter preferences remained static. But persuasion does not take place in a vacuum; nor does it necessarily occur quickly. Lincoln believed, for example, that northern voters would eventually recognize that slavery, not immigration, was the critical issue of the day. (For southern voters, slavery had been the critical issue for decades, as southern Democratic and southern Whig candidates competed to present themselves as the better defender of slavery.)[49] Lincoln also believed that northern voters would eventually recognize the inherently contradictory and deceptive character of Stephen Douglas's policy of popular sovereignty.[50] But Lincoln also understood that time, events, careful political organization, and effective public persuasion would be necessary for voter preferences to shift in the direction he hoped. Thus, to alter voter preferences over the long term required taking into account given preferences in the short term.

We can better understand the opportunities and challenges faced by Lincoln and the Republicans by first considering the strategic options available to Stephen Douglas and the Democrats in the North. Douglas

176 I CHAPTER 5

and other pro–Kansas-Nebraska Democrats would obviously have the support of voters for whom slavery was the most salient issue and for whom permit slavery was the preferred policy; thus, both PS/PI/RI/ RS and PS/RI/PI/RS voters would provide reliable support. But the deeply negative results of the 1854 elections for pro–Kansas-Nebraska Democrats indicate that the proportion of northern voters for whom permitting slavery to spread was the *most* preferred option was quite small. The weak support for this position in the North is also suggested by Douglas's own tactic of selling popular sovereignty in the North as a means of *preventing* the spread of slavery (even as his southern supporters promoted popular sovereignty as a means of enabling slavery to expand).[51] In the years following passage of the Kansas-Nebraska Act, Douglas worked vigorously to persuade northern voters that a policy of public neutrality toward slavery was both Union preserving and consistent with the principle of popular self-government. But he recognized the need to tap other sources of support. His words and actions indicate that he regarded a pro-immigration stance as a political strength and that he believed the Whigs and later the Republicans were vulnerable because of their nativist contingents.[52] Thus, if a coalition between the two voter preference groups for whom permitting slavery (popular sovereignty) was the *first* option (PS/PI/RI/RS and PS/RI/PI/RS) constituted far less than a majority of northern voters, a slavery-friendly coalition might secure a majority of northern voters if it also enlisted the two groups for whom a pro-immigration stance was most salient: PI/PS/ RS/RI and PI/RS/PS/RI.

Such a coalition had an additional advantage: the Democratic Party's immigration-friendly stance had decades of history behind it and therefore appeared trustworthy, in contrast to the Republicans, a new party whose supporters were visibly divided on immigration. The 1856 Republican national platform was silent on immigration (reflecting unresolved internal disagreements). In contrast, the Democrats' 1856 national platform affirmed "the liberal principles embodied by Jefferson in the Declaration of Independence, and sanctioned by the Constitution, which makes ours the land of liberty and the asylum of the oppressed of every nation," and it pledged to resist "every attempt to abridge the privilege of becoming citizens and the owners of soil among us."[53]

Lincoln's own alarm about the Know-Nothings suggests that he shared Douglas's judgment that a slavery-friendly, pro-immigration coalition could be a winner for the Democrats and that he thought it would be a strategic error (and wrong in principle) for the Republicans to pursue a nativist strategy by seeking to build an antislavery, anti-immigration coalition that turned its back on immigrants. Instead, Lincoln's strategy in Illinois (and later as a national party leader and presidential candidate) more closely approximated an antislavery, pro-immigration coalition. This required competing head-to-head with the Democrats to win the support of pro-immigration, antislavery voters (antislavery German immigrants in particular). This also placed the two categories of nativist voters, RI/RS/PS/PI and RI/PS/RS/PI, in a kind of political limbo, with neither major party appealing to their first preference and leaving them no choice but to fall back on their second preference: restrict slavery or permit slavery. Lincoln apparently judged that RI/RS/PS/PI (nativist voters with antislavery leanings) constituted a larger group than RI/PS/RS/PI (nativist voters with slavery-friendly leanings) and that the former group could be convinced to vote for Republicans on the basis of their second choice, given that neither Republicans nor Democrats publicly endorsed their first choice. Such a strategy is consistent with Lincoln's sustained efforts to win over German immigrants while avoiding a public confrontation with the Know-Nothings.

But a strategy of leaving the nativists (and especially the slavery-friendly nativists) in limbo could succeed for the Republicans only after the Know-Nothing movement had clearly failed to establish itself as a major political party and the principal rival of the Democrats in the North. Both sets of first-preference anti-immigration voters (RI/RS/PS/PI and RI/PS/RS/PI) would have supported a new, explicitly anti-immigration party if they believed it could defeat the Republicans (also a start-up party) in the contest to replace the now-defunct Whigs as the second major national political party. And it was not known for certain that the Know-Nothings would fail in this effort until the results of the 1856 presidential election (when their American Party candidate Millard Fillmore received only 21.5 percent of the popular vote and only eight electoral votes). Lincoln's August 1855 observation (quoted earlier) that the Republicans could not attract the Know-Nothings "so long as they cling to a hope of success under their own organization" was clearly framed with the electoral calendar in mind.

But Lincoln never believed that an effective antislavery party could be built *only* by assembling coalitions of voters whose preferences remained unaltered. At least some voters had to be persuaded to revise their preference rankings. Committed proslavery voters were unlikely to become antislavery voters, and committed anti-immigration voters were unlikely to be transformed into pro-immigration voters. But it was not unreasonable to hope that some anti-immigration voters with antislavery leanings could be persuaded, through a combination of arguments and political events, to become antislavery voters with anti-immigration leanings (slavery now being the more salient issue).

Moreover, given that Douglas's popular sovereignty was promoted in the North as slavery restrictive in its effects, it was not unreasonable to hope that some supporters of popular sovereignty could be persuaded, as political events unfolded in Kansas and elsewhere, to become re-strict-slavery voters. Conversely, Douglas hoped to convert some restrict-slavery voters into supporters of popular sovereignty. Coalition building and public opinion shaping were essential and intertwined on both sides of this contest for the political support and political soul of northern voters.

It is from the perspective of this interconnected coalition-building, opinion-shaping challenge that we turn to Lincoln's "House Divided" speech.

Opinion Shaping, Election Results, and the Future of Slavery

The central message of Lincoln's June 16, 1858, "House Divided" speech was that the United States "cannot endure, permanently half *slave* and half *free*," but would ultimately "become *all* one thing, or *all* the other."[54] But in making this statement, he was neither advocating nor predicting that this fateful question be decided by civil war (as claimed by Stephen Douglas, his 1858 US Senate rival).[55] In other contexts (though not in the "House Divided" speech) Lincoln acknowledged that civil war over slavery was possible.[56] His hope that the nation could be *peacefully* united in favor of freedom rested on two essential factors, both of which are featured in the "House Divided" speech: public opinion, or what Lincoln called "the public mind" (and elsewhere "public sentiment"), which predominates in the opening section of the speech; and the mission of the Republican Party—the political vehicle of "*our great cause*"—with which the speech closes.[57]

My aim in what follows is to examine how Lincoln understood the interconnection between the shaping of public opinion, on the one hand, and the electoral success or failure of parties and candidates that take public stands on slavery, on the other hand, in grounding the process by which slavery might be gradually, peacefully, and democratically abolished. Lincoln's observations on public opinion, and how it could be shaped for good or ill, have received significant attention from scholars.[58] But the specific process I describe here has not (to my knowledge) been examined in depth in connection with Lincoln's "house divided" thesis. That process involves (1) an initial state of public opinion on slavery, (2) parties and candidates that take stances on slavery, (3) subsequent electoral reward or punishment, and (4) a new state of public opinion that has shifted closer to either the "all slave" or "all free" end of the spectrum.

These two factors—opinion shaping and the role of political parties—were clearly not identical, because what parties and their candidates said about slavery in an effort to win elections was only one element among many that influenced public opinion on slavery. Abolitionist orations, Harriet Beecher Stowe's *Uncle Tom's Cabin,* events in Kansas, the caning of Charles Sumner on the floor of the US Senate, high-profile fugitive slave cases, the *Dred Scott* decision, and other events affected Americans' thinking about slavery in the 1850s and how they prioritized it compared with other public concerns. But the "House Divided" speech, taken as a whole, suggests that Lincoln believed the Republican Party had a critical and specific role to play in the wider effort to eliminate slavery.

The speech's opening famously presented Americans with two radically opposed futures with respect to slavery. Both futures were possible, and one of them, Lincoln claimed, would necessarily come to pass if the other did not. "Either the *opponents* of slavery, will arrest the further spread of it, and place it where the public mind shall rest in the belief that it is in course of ultimate extinction; or its *advocates* will push it forward, till it shall become alike lawful in *all* the States, *old* as well as *new*— *North* as well as *South*." Lincoln argued, moreover, that the "*tendency*" at present was toward the latter of these two futures: the full legalization and nationalization of slavery.[59]

Lincoln also described the *causes* that he believed would bring about one or the other of these two radically opposed futures. The first possible outcome, the ultimate extinction of slavery, depended on "the opponents of slavery" doing two things: arresting the further spread of slavery, and placing slavery "where the public mind shall rest in the belief" that it was headed toward ultimate extinction. The first element (stopping the spread of slavery) would require that specific public *action* be taken immediately, or as soon as possible. The second element (bringing the public mind to "rest in the belief" that slavery would ultimately be eliminated) required an enduring shift in public opinion. Thus, Lincoln's argument was that if (a) the spread of slavery was halted and (b) the public affirmed the goal of its ultimate extinction, then (c) slavery would eventually be eliminated throughout the United States, even if the exact timeline and the specific public actions by which this goal would be achieved were not foreseeable. Conversely, it followed that if the spread of slavery was *not* halted, or if its expansion were only stalled temporarily for reasons unrelated to the public's conviction of slavery's injustice, then slavery would not be on the path to ultimate extinction. For example, the expansion of slavery to western territories might proceed slowly if most slaveholders found it more profitable in the short term to maintain slave plantations in the existing slave states. But if those same slaveholders persuaded the American people they had the *right* to transport enslaved persons to any US territory whenever they chose to do so, then despite any temporary lull in slavery's expansion, the public would *not* have embraced the idea of slavery's ultimate extinction. In this case, by Lincoln's "house divided" logic, slavery would remain on a slow but sure path to full nationalization.

Lincoln's scenario for eliminating slavery thus required both a specific short-term action (a public law or policy enacted for the express purpose of halting the spread of slavery) and a long-term shift in public opinion. The mere belief that slavery would one day disappear from American soil, without public action designed to operationalize that belief, would be insufficient to achieve the long-term goal of ending slavery. Instead, this would simply be "resting in a delusion" that slavery was on the way out, as Lincoln admitted he might himself have done before the Kansas-Nebraska Act shocked him into action.[60] Thus, in speaking of the public mind coming to "rest" in the conviction of slavery's ultimate extinction, Lincoln did not mean "rest" in the sense of passivity; rather, he meant an enduring disposition to support antislavery acts and policies insofar as they were consistent with the Constitution. (One could liken this active type of "resting" to the understanding of rest in Newtonian physics, whereby a body set in motion "rests" in motion unless acted on by some new force.) Whether the shift in public opinion Lincoln envisioned would have signified a return to a public antislavery consensus from the founding era (as Lincoln believed), or instead would have required a new degree and type of public antislavery commitment going beyond the example set by the founders, is an open question. But in either case, the key point of Lincoln's argument was that both specific near-term public action and a longer-term shift in the public mind were necessary.

Moreover, Lincoln regarded public actions and shifts in public opinion as interrelated components of a recursive process, whereby each prepared the way for and built upon the other. In the "House Divided" speech, he made this point most clearly in describing how the process worked on the other side of the divided house. Slavery's ultimate nationalization, which Lincoln feared was the stronger tendency at the moment, would likewise entail a series of specific short-term actions, followed by the effect of those actions on public opinion, followed by new actions made possible by the altered disposition of public opinion. The long section of the speech following the compact opening describes a recursive interaction of public action and public opinion of the kind Lincoln believed revealed a "tendency" to make slavery "alike lawful in *all* the States, *old* as well as *new—North* as well as *South*."[61]

Lincoln also famously asserted that events suggested the existence of a "design, and concert of action" on the part of Stephen Douglas, Franklin Pierce, Roger Taney, and James Buchanan to nationalize slavery, a claim for which Lincoln has been sharply criticized by some of his contemporaries as well as by historians. I take up this issue later. Here, however, I want to emphasize that the narrative set forth in the "House Divided" speech potentially explains how slavery could be fully nationalized *without* a conscious design to do so, even on the part of the key players Lincoln named. Lincoln's observations about how the public mind can shift over time suggests that intentions might develop later in the process that were implicit but not fully conscious at the beginning. In this sense, his "house divided" argument does not depend on the existence, from the outset, of a deliberate plan to nationalize slavery.[62]

Lincoln's narrative begins with Congress's passage of the Kansas-Nebraska Act in 1854, which "opened all the national territory to slavery; and was the first point gained." Lincoln immediately notes, however, that "so far, *Congress* only, had acted; and an *indorsement* by the people, *real* or apparent, was indispensable, to *save* the point already gained, and give chance for more." In short, although passage of the Kansas-Nebraska Act was a crucial first step toward the nationalization of slavery, the degree to which it effectively advanced that goal depended on how the new law was received by public opinion and on efforts by political parties and leaders to shape public opinion about the new law. Lincoln specifically mentions Stephen Douglas's doctrine of popular sovereignty, with its premise that slavery (for Black Americans) was a matter of moral indifference for white citizens: "That if any *one* man, choose to enslave *another*, no *third* man shall be allowed to object." The text of the Kansas-Nebraska Act did not require citizens to be morally indifferent toward slavery. But the public opinion–shaping arguments of Douglas and others, in defense of that act, prepared public opinion to accept *future* actions that went further in a proslavery direction than the Kansas-Nebraska Act did.[63]

The "*indorsement* by the people, *real* or apparent" to which Lincoln refers was the election of Democrat James Buchanan in 1856. As noted earlier, Lincoln believed the 1854 elections signified a clear public *rejection* of the Kansas-Nebraska Act, at least in the free states. But in the years immediately following its passage, the northern electorate divided over both slavery and immigration in ways that complicated attempts to focus attention on slavery as the more important concern. The election of Buchanan, who turned out to be more aggressively proslavery than Douglas, allowed both men to claim the 1856 presidential election results as a popular endorsement of the Kansas-Nebraska Act. Lincoln denied that Buchanan and the Democrats could legitimately claim any such mandate for the act. Buchanan had been serving as a diplomat in England when the Kansas-Nebraska Act was passed, which allowed him to keep his distance from the deeply controversial law during the 1856 campaign. The 1856 presidential election was a three-way contest involving Buchanan, Republican John Fremont, and American Party (Know-Nothing) candidate Millard Fillmore in which no candidate received a majority of popular votes. Thus, Lincoln observed, "the *indorsement*, such as it was . . . fell short of a clear popular majority by nearly four hundred thousand votes, and so, perhaps, was not overwhelmingly reliable and satisfactory."[64] Nevertheless, as Lincoln acknowledged, even an "apparent" electoral endorsement had an impact on public opinion.

Lincoln hypothesized a similar public action–public opinion dynamic in narrating how the 1854 Kansas-Nebraska Act prepared public opinion for the 1857 *Dred Scott* decision, which in turn prepared public opinion (Lincoln predicted) for "another Supreme Court decision, declaring that the Constitution of the United States does not permit a *state* to exclude slavery from its limits."[65] Lincoln's prediction here was conditional rather than absolute. He believed that a Supreme Court decision legalizing slavery in every state followed *logically* from the premise upheld in the *Dred Scott* ruling (and denied by Lincoln) that "the right of property in a slave is distinctly and expressly affirmed in the Constitution of the United States."[66] But the court, Lincoln argued, would be unlikely to push this premise to its logical conclusion unless and until public opinion was prepared for it. "And this may especially be expected if the doctrine of 'care not whether slavery be voted *down* or voted *up*,' shall gain upon the public mind sufficiently to give promise that such a decision can be maintained when made."[67] In short, the *Dred Scott* decision—a specific *public act*—would have limited effect unless, like the Kansas-Nebraska Act, it received the endorsement of *public opinion* in the form of subsequent electoral victories by candidates and parties that, like Stephen Douglas, urged voters not to care about slavery. It followed that if the *Dred Scott* decision *did* receive such an electoral endorsement (especially in 1858, the first national election following the ruling), this increased the probability that the Supreme Court would issue a future ruling affirming the right to hold slave property even within the boundaries of a free state.

Thus, Lincoln outlined fairly clearly in the "House Divided" speech (and in the 1858 debates with Douglas) the recursive interaction between public action and public opinion that could push the divided house to tilt toward perpetuating slavery—in which direction Lincoln feared events were trending at the time. But my purpose in rehearsing this well-known story is to emphasize its converse: that the same type of public act–public opinion interaction also characterized the process by which slavery proceeded toward ultimate extinction. In this speech and in other statements of the late 1850s, Lincoln described this scenario in less detail than he outlined the process by which slavery might be fully nationalized. His vagueness about how the ultimate extinction of slavery might occur has led some scholars to claim either that he intended nothing beyond halting slavery's expansion (in which case the whole argument of the "House Divided" speech becomes incoherent) or that, although he desired slavery's ultimate extinction, he had no clear notion of how this could be achieved.[68]

I argue in chapter 7 that Lincoln and other Republicans had in mind a fairly specific menu of peaceful and gradual middle-range policies designed to weaken and shrink the institution of slavery *after* the initial, critical, and politically difficult step of halting its expansion had been accomplished. These middle-range measures did not directly target slavery in the states where it existed, which was nearly universally regarded as unconstitutional and, if attempted, would have quickly triggered the secession of nearly every slave state. But even Congress's initial step of prohibiting slavery in territories that were not yet states (which Lincoln and the Republican Party supported) would have diminished the portability, and thus the value and profitability, of slave property everywhere in the United States; placed slavery under the bar of public opinion; and eroded slavery's present and future political support. "Ultimate extinction" was not an empty idea.

Here, I want to underscore that *all* antislavery measures—including the first step of barring slavery in the territories, as well as any second, third, and fourth steps that followed—depended for their effectiveness on the same public action–public opinion interaction that Lincoln envisioned for slavery's ultimate nationalization. His "house divided" argument, if one takes it seriously, implies that the political dynamic tending in one direction roughly mirrors the political dynamic tending in the other. This might seem obvious, but there are important, less obvious implications.

First, Lincoln's understanding of the recursive interaction of public action and public opinion over several election cycles helps explain his relative (though not complete) silence about the series of antislavery actions that would follow the first step of halting slavery's expansion. As with the slavery nationalization scenario, whereby the American public would eventually come to support proslavery actions it would not have accepted earlier in the process, the ultimate extinction scenario likewise entailed the American public supporting later antislavery actions that went beyond what it would have accepted in the initial stages. For this reason, it would have been politically self-defeating for Lincoln to dwell on steps two and three when the public had not yet been persuaded to support step one. One might characterize Lincoln's disposition as a "design" to extinguish slavery, except that, in contrast to those who worked secretly to legalize slavery everywhere, Lincoln publicly acknowledged that the ultimate extinction of slavery was his desired outcome. What he was disinclined to discuss, except tentatively and sometimes evasively, was the sequence of actions and shifts of public opinion that would come between the first stage of slavery's nonextension and the final stage of its complete extinction.

Second, the dynamic of the house divided was *active* in both directions. Stasis was impossible. Merely stopping slavery's extension, without taking additional antislavery actions in the future, would simply hand the initiative back to the proslavery side, which Lincoln described as active and determined to win the long game. The antislavery side, conversely, could not achieve its aim by resting at stage one, except in the Newtonian sense of a body resting by staying in motion.

Finally, and most importantly for understanding the key role of the Republican Party in the final section of the "House Divided" speech, the interplay of public action and public opinion necessary to move slavery toward ultimate extinction required a political actor capable of first accomplishing an antislavery action and then having that action endorsed by public opinion in a subsequent election. Only a major political party could do this. Lincoln recognized that abolitionist petitions and writings helped foster what he called in his Cooper Institute address "a judgment and a feeling against slavery in this nation." But abolitionists, or at least those who kept their distance from the Republican Party, did not enjoy enough political power and electoral support to accomplish even the first necessary public act: halting the extension of slavery. And without that first public act, the next crucial stage in the evolution of public opinion in an antislavery direction, its electoral endorsement, could not occur. Abolitionists played an indispensable role in cultivating a "feeling" and "judgment" against slavery, but it was Republicans' mission to demonstrate that a major political party could win millions of votes by campaigning on an antislavery platform. Despite the moderation of the Republican platform in contrast to the more radical commitments of abolitionists, the Republican Party was positioned to enact initial antislavery policies that abolitionists could not (and, in many cases, scorned as insufficient). Thus, in the long run, the Republican Party, through a series of gradual steps endorsed by voters over a series of election cycles, was best positioned to move public opinion irreversibly toward the goal of ending slavery. At least that was Lincoln's hope in his closing sentence of the "House Divided" speech: "*Wise councils* may *accelerate* or *mistakes delay* it, but, sooner or later the victory is *sure* to come."[69]

"House Divided," Dichotomous Decision, and Majority Rule

In *Prelude to Greatness: Lincoln in the 1850s*, Don E. Fehrenbacher argues persuasively that Lincoln's purpose in the "House Divided" speech was not to express an "apocalyptic vision of the bloody years ahead" but to maintain "the unity and purpose of the Republican party" against what he viewed as "an ill-considered retreat" by some Republican leaders "to the lower ground of popular sovereignty" and, in conjunction with that retreat, to support Stephen Douglas's reelection to the US Senate (at Lincoln's expense). Douglas had recently made common cause with congressional Republicans in opposing the Buchanan administration's effort to force a proslavery constitution on Kansas against the known wishes of the territorial majority. Lincoln's "house divided" thesis had the effect of "eliminating the middle ground" on which Douglas stood (i.e., his moral indifference toward slavery) and committing the Republican Party to restricting slavery "*because* it was wrong"—a stance that also ensured Lincoln's relevance as Douglas's opponent in the upcoming US Senate contest in Illinois.[70]

I agree that maintaining the unity and purpose of the Republican Party was Lincoln's aim in the "House Divided" speech and that he viewed Republicans' flirtation with Douglasite popular sovereignty as a threat to that unity. But Lincoln's "house divided" thesis also functioned to counter a wider range of threats to the party's unity and purpose. One reason the fledging Republican project was susceptible to being co-opted by Douglas was the party's great internal diversity. It depended on cooperation among former Democrats and former Whigs, immigrants and Know-Nothings, abolitionists who reluctantly tempered their radicalism and conservatives who were deeply alarmed by abolitionists. I here present the "House Divided" speech as intended, above all, to facilitate the creation of an effective and enduring antislavery electoral majority out of several constituencies that shared a distaste for slavery but otherwise had little in common.

In one sense (leaving out the special case of tie votes), a majority position on a contested question can always be manufactured if voters are presented with a one-round choice between two mutually exclusive options. But such decision constraints are often politically unrealistic. Whenever there are more than two policy options over which voters can express their preferences and the rules permit more than one round of voting, majorities can become unstable or even cyclical: option A defeats B, B defeats C, C defeats A. As noted in chapter 2, Lincoln identified the phenomenon of cyclical majorities in analyzing stances toward slavery in the territories. Similar obstacles to stable majorities emerged when immigration and slavery competed for voter attention in the free states.

Lincoln's "house divided" thesis facilitated the formation of a stable majority position on slavery by rejecting the middle position of popular sovereignty, thereby presenting voters with a choice between two mutually exclusive paths: one leading to the legalization of slavery everywhere in the United States, and the other leading to its ultimate extinction everywhere in the United States. Lincoln understood that the range of antislavery opinion from mildest to most radical, both among the electorate as a whole and within the Republican Party, was so wide that *only* by persuading voters they faced a dichotomous choice could a stable national antislavery majority be formed in the electorate and an effective Republican Party be organized to implement the will of that majority.

Consider several key features of the "House Divided" speech. First, the speech describes an inherently dichotomous decision on slavery: the nation will ultimately become "*all* one thing, or *all* the other." Second, Lincoln describes the current political situation as a "*crisis*" that must be "reached and passed." Finally, no *other* political issue besides slavery is mentioned in the speech.

On what basis did Lincoln claim that the slavery decision was inherently dichotomous? Any such claim should be critically examined because not every important public issue can be plausibly characterized this way. Most budgetary decisions, for instance, take the form of "more or less" rather than "all or nothing." Of course, individual dichotomous votes can be framed in nearly every field of policy. In budgetary politics, proposed amendments are voted up or down, and the same is true for the final budget package, but that does not make budgetary decisions inherently all one thing or all the other. In some fields of policy, the claim that a particular decision is all or nothing is transparently manipulative, such as when advocates of gun rights claim that *any* restrictions on firearms must ultimately lead to the prohibition and confiscation of *all* firearms. In fact, a wide range of coherent middle outcomes is possible in this domain and in most others.

Conversely, a public decision can be inherently dichotomous without rising to the level of an all-consuming political crisis. Whether the death penalty is permitted or prohibited is a dichotomous public choice (persons convicted of serious crimes cannot be *partially* executed), and that choice evokes strong moral passions on both sides. But it would be implausible to claim that political disagreement over this matter—with some states prohibiting the death penalty and others practicing it— generates a political *crisis* absorbing and dwarfing all other concerns. There had to be something peculiar about slavery as a political issue for Lincoln's claims in the "House Divided" speech to be plausible: that the slavery decision was inherently dichotomous, and that a national crisis had been reached with respect to which side would prevail.

The institution of slavery did have several features that lent plausibility to Lincoln's argument: the fact that unresolved sectional debates over slavery had been ongoing for decades, accompanied by threats of violence and disunion; the increasingly voracious demands by slaveholders for public policies affirming the rightness of slavery, accompanied by a sustained effort to suppress public expression of antislavery views; and the fact that slave owners claimed slavery was an absolute *property right* under the Constitution—a claim that, once accepted, implied its protection everywhere subject to the Constitution. Most comprehensively, at least in Lincoln's view, the institution of racial slavery was inconsistent with, and therefore undermined, the public commitment to natural equality and consent of the governed on which the American republican experiment depended. These features of the slavery dispute distinguished it from most other public issues in Lincoln's age, or any age.

Suppose, however, there was no coherent, sustainable middle position on slavery. That, by itself, did not guarantee that the question of slavery's future would be framed for voters in a dichotomous form ensuring a clear majority decision. Douglas's popular sovereignty policy may have represented an unprincipled and unstable middle position on slavery, but voters can and sometimes do register preferences for such unprincipled or unstable policies. An open-ended question (e.g., What should we do about slavery?), framed such that three or more responses were possible, would have resolved nothing and may have advantaged the advocates of slavery because they were the faction most unified and clearest on their goals. No matter how essentially dichotomous the slavery decision may have been in its essence, a clear majority position on slavery was possible only if political alternatives were deliberately presented to voters in dichotomous form.

It was precisely here that Lincoln's "house divided" thesis fulfilled a party-building and party-legitimating function. If the United States would ultimately become all free states or all slave states, and if the leaders of one major party (President Buchanan and Senator Douglas, both Democrats) were working, whether deliberately or unwittingly, toward legalizing slavery everywhere, then those who considered slavery wrong (a position Lincoln believed had majority support) deserved a political party whose platform and candidates enabled them to clearly express their opposition and thus redirect America's future toward the ultimate extinction of slavery. Douglas's popular sovereignty policy had to be electorally defeated, not only because it was morally empty and deliberately Janus-faced but also because its presence as a third, middle option prevented voters in both sections from clearly communicating which of these two starkly opposed futures with regard to slavery they preferred.

One of the functions of political parties, both individually and as components of a party system, is to reduce the potentially unlimited number of important political issues, and the potentially enormous range of possible actions on each issue, into a manageable subset of priority issues (on which rival parties divide) and a limited number of policy options with respect to each issue. Lincoln's efforts as a Republican Party builder to prioritize the slavery issue (on which he believed the northern public could unite) rather than immigration (which sharply divided the northern electorate) exemplify this selection among issues. Lincoln also engaged in issue selection in early 1855 when he urged his Whig supporters to back Lyman Trumbull for US Senate, thereby signaling that opposition to the Kansas-Nebraska Act should take precedence over other issues that had previously divided Whigs and Democrats. The Democratic and Whig Parties had practiced a different brand of issue selection during the 1830s and 1840s when they cooperated to suppress public agitation over slavery, even as they competed over banking, public lands, internal improvements, tariffs, and other issues. In a competitive party system, in short, parties agree to a large extent *which* issues require action, even as they advocate opposed policies with respect to those issues.

The manner in which political parties prioritize issues and define a limited range of possible actions is never neutral. This is one reason why many people, in Lincoln's day as well as our own, are suspicious of parties and demand a wider range of choices than the prevailing major parties offer. Party-defining issues can and do change over time, as parties decide to take up new issues or as new parties (e.g., the American and Republican Parties in the 1850s) form and realign party competition in fundamentally different ways. But at any given moment, the range of issues and policy options over which parties and candidates compete for votes will be limited. New issues can emerge and focus voters' attention only insofar as older issues are pushed into the background. This does not necessarily mean these older issues become obsolete or unimportant. They may continue to affect the interests and engage the passions of many voters, but they no longer structure and focus the competition between the major parties.

Lincoln's invocation of a *crisis* over slavery in the "House Divided" speech, and his systematic omission of all other issues, was an effort to refocus party competition, as described above. This is not to say that Lincoln was insincere in calling slavery a crisis. His public addresses as well as his private writings from the period indicate that his sense of crisis was genuine. He did believe slavery was on the way to becoming omnipresent and permanent in the United States unless deliberate action was taken to reverse current trends. Precisely because he believed the slavery crisis was real, he considered it essential to push all other issues—including tariffs, immigration, and temperance—into the background. To define a situation as a crisis and urge one's fellow citizens to unite to resolve that crisis does not mean that other issues suddenly disappear or lose their importance. It means only that, for the duration of that crisis, public contestation over other issues must be postponed or muted. Lincoln's phrasing in the closing section of the speech implicitly recognizes the legitimacy of these other concerns. "Two years ago the Republicans of the nation mustered over thirteen hundred thousand strong. We did this under the single impulse of resistance to a common danger, with every external circumstance against us. Of *strange, discordant*, and even, *hostile* elements, we gathered from the four winds, and *formed* and fought the battle through."[71] Lincoln's phrasing here tacitly acknowledged the continued existence—indeed, the naturalness and legitimacy—of the issues on which Republicans disagreed among themselves. Only the "single impulse of resistance to a common danger" was sufficient to prevent "the four winds" from blowing in different directions.

Finally, the "strange" and "discordant" elements composing the Republican Party could not be unified simply by enforcing party discipline or suppressing intraparty disagreement.[72] Lincoln was critical of the Democratic Party's internal autocracy, as exemplified by Stephen Douglas and James Buchanan making repeal of the Missouri Compromise a test of party loyalty in 1854, even though the party rank and file had never been consulted on the question (see chapters 3 and 4). (And by the time Lincoln gave his "House Divided" speech, Douglas himself had fallen victim to Democratic Party discipline, when President Buchanan made support for the admission of Kansas as a slave state a test of party loyalty.)[73] Because Republicans were still a fledgling party in 1858, Lincoln was in no position to enforce party orthodoxy by dispensing or withholding patronage, even if he had wanted to.

Instead, he had to genuinely persuade, not force, the diverse Republican Party constituencies to do two things. First, they had to draw a clear line between moral opposition to slavery and Douglas's stance of moral neutrality. Lincoln envisioned the Republican Party as a very large tent, but the wind could blow that tent away if it were stretched to include Douglas's "don't care" stance on slavery. Second, Republicans had to be willing to tolerate a wide range of intraparty disagreement about immigration, tariffs, abolitionism, colonization, racial equality, voting rights for Black Americans, and many other things. In short, for Lincoln in 1858, unifying the Republican Party required agreement on one thing: slavery was wrong. And it required its members to tolerate disagreement and intraparty debate on nearly everything else.

Necessity, Choice, and Individual Responsibility

The "House Divided" speech has been sharply criticized, at the time and subsequently by historians, for Lincoln's invocation of a "design" to make slavery "lawful in *all* the states, *old* as well as *new*—*North* as well as *South*"—which involved "concert of action, among its chief bosses." These bosses included Stephen Douglas, author of the Kansas-Nebraska Act; President Franklin Pierce, who helped ensure that the Kansas-Nebraska Act explicitly repealed the Missouri Compromise's slavery restriction, signed the act into law, and made it a test of Democratic Party loyalty; Roger Taney, chief justice of the US Supreme Court and author of the opinion in the *Dred Scott* case, which declared that slaveholders could bring enslaved persons into any federal territory; and President James Buchanan, who exhorted people in his inaugural address (March 4, 1857), two days before the *Dred Scott* decision was issued, "to abide by the forthcoming decision, *whatever it might be.*"[74]

Sympathetic interpreters have described Lincoln's "preconcert" charge as overstated and pointed out that his central claim—that the United States would eventually become all free or all slave—did not stand or fall on the existence of a deliberate conspiracy to nationalize slavery. Less sympathetic critics have called the charge "an absurd bogey," an expression of the "paranoid style" of American politics, or even deeply and fanatically dishonest. It has been characterized as an especially striking instance of the Republican fixation on a "slave power conspiracy" and, in that respect, as illustrative of Lincoln's rhetorical strategy, ideological appeals, and party-building methods, despite the implausibility of his argument. Some historians, however, maintain there was a real danger the US Supreme Court might rule in the future that slaveholders had a right to slave property in every US state as well as every territory and that, even if Lincoln's charge was inaccurate in some details, he was substantively correct that a small, well-organized group of powerful proslavery politicians had made increasingly extreme demands over the course of the decade.[75]

We can gain fresh perspective on Lincoln's much-discussed "design" charge by connecting it with a much more enduring theme in Lincoln's thought: the interplay between necessity and choice. This theme, too, has received attention from scholars, though in contexts other than the "House Divided" speech.[76] I argue that the most important feature of Lincoln's suggestion that a small group of powerful men acted in concert to perpetuate slavery was that he delineated a sphere of *personal* accountability amid a much larger, long-standing contest between two titanic sets of forces—those tending toward the ultimate extinction of slavery and those tending toward its perpetuation—that shaped the lives of millions of ordinary men and women. To a large degree, these clashing proslavery and profreedom tendencies were beyond the power of individuals to control: this was the realm of necessity. But at certain critical moments, these forces were so closely matched that the deliberate actions of individuals and small groups could tip the balance. Although "Stephen [Douglas] and Franklin [Pierce] and Roger [Taney] and James [Buchanan]" played with forces they did not understand and could not control, they had, in Lincoln's view, tipped the balance toward perpetuating slavery. Conversely, it was the duty of the Republican Party—and, most immediately, of the thousand or so party members who gathered at the Illinois statehouse on June 16, 1858—to tip the balance in the other direction while it was still possible: "If we stand firm, we shall not fail."[77]

Making this case requires some preliminary observations. First, I assume that Lincoln's "house divided" thesis, which was separable from the conspiracy charge, was plausible rather than paranoid, given the events and the evidence available to Lincoln and his contemporaries. If Lincoln had feverishly imagined (or dishonestly fabricated) the possible nationalization of slavery, his views on necessity and choice in this matter would be of little interest. I postpone to chapter 7 why, in my judgment, the continued expansion and ultimate nationalization of slavery in the United States was a real possibility, not "an absurd bogey."

Second, while Lincoln's "preconcert" allegation was specific to his 1858 contest with Stephen Douglas, Lincoln had reflected at all stages of his adult life, public and private, on questions of necessity and choice. He had long conjectured that the domain of necessity—that is, of causes and consequences lying beyond conscious human control—was quite large, while the range of matters subject to deliberate choice was comparatively narrow but by no means unimportant.[78] Necessity constrained political as well as personal life. The framers of the Constitution, Lincoln observed, had viewed slavery as an injustice, but because it already existed and was difficult to remove, they were "in a certain sense compelled to tolerate its existence. It was a sort of necessity. . . . They did what they could and yielded to the necessity for the rest."[79] Note here that Lincoln did not claim the framers' actions were completely constrained by necessity. Where choices about slavery were available, as in "territories where it did not exist" and the international slave trade, they took action. Lincoln's phrasing also suggests uncertainty about precisely where the line between necessity and choice was drawn: the framers were "in a certain sense compelled to tolerate" slavery, as it was "a sort of necessity." Necessity, as Lincoln described it elsewhere, was a kind of argument: "the argument of 'Necessity' was the only argument that [the framers] ever admitted in favor of slavery."[80] Not every such argument was equally plausible. In Lincoln's view, no plausible necessity required repeal of the Missouri Compromise in 1854. "There was no sort of necessity for destroying" the Missouri Compromise's slavery restriction in order "to organize these territories," Lincoln insisted during his 1858 debates with Douglas; Douglas could have simply "let that compromise alone."[81] Repealing the slavery restriction was instead an *act of choice* by Douglas and a few other powerful men.

During the Civil War, Lincoln reflected deeply on the theme of necessity and choice. Here too, he viewed the realm of necessity as large and the domain of choice as constricted, but choices were nevertheless possible and sometimes critical. In an oft-quoted passage from an 1864 letter, Lincoln wrote: "I claim not to have controlled events, but confess plainly that events have controlled me." Lincoln's point was not that events denied him any choice at all but rather that events during the war persuaded him it was necessary to make different choices than he had envisioned before the war or in its first two years. Early in the war, he had not considered it necessary to resort to military emancipation or to arm Black soldiers to fight against the Confederacy. But the border slave states' rejection of compensated emancipation and the prospect of "surrendering the Union, and with it, the Constitution" if the war was lost persuaded Lincoln that both military emancipation and the arming of Black troops *had* become "an indispensable necessity."[82] Thus, necessity constrained his range of choices but did not remove his discretion altogether (for he could have chosen *not* to employ Black troops and lost the war as a result). The letter also shows that, in Lincoln's view, both necessity itself and what political leaders *believe* to be necessary or unnecessary could change with circumstances. Necessity was not a constant, even though it was constantly at work.

The "House Divided" speech reflected Lincoln's thinking, before the war, about the interplay of necessity and choice with respect to his hope that slavery could be *peacefully* placed on the road to extinction. Here, as in other respects, the speech concisely framed the problem, for it described cause-and-effect relationships of two different kinds operating on very different scales. There was a push and pull between two sets of vast, largely impersonal forces, one that tended toward universalizing slavery and the other toward universalizing freedom. Enduring equilibrium between these two sets of forces was impossible; eventually, "it will become *all* one thing, or *all* the other." These powerful opposing tendencies with respect to slavery had been at work in the United States from the earliest years of the republic. Everyone's life was shaped by these forces, and no one, including powerful people in high office, could fully control them. Near the opening of the speech, Lincoln noted that for five years a series of leaders (including Douglas, Pierce, Buchanan, and Taney) had made the "*confident* promise" that their policies were "putting an end to slavery agitation," and yet "that agitation has not only, *not ceased,* but has *constantly augmented.*" Clearly, Douglas and these other powerful men deceived themselves that their words and actions could terminate the political, economic, social, and religious contest over slavery in the United States.[83]

In an early draft of the "House Divided" speech, Lincoln went into additional detail about how this clash of large forces affected the American political community at every level:

> Meanwhile, in those four years, there has really been more angry agitation of this subject, both in and out of Congress, than ever before. And just now it is perplexing the mighty ones as no subject ever did before. Nor is it confined to politics alone. Presbyterian assemblies, Methodist conferences, Unitarian gatherings, and single churches to an indefinite extent, are wrangling, and cracking, and going to pieces on the same question. Why, Kansas is neither the whole nor a tithe of the real question. *A house divided against itself cannot stand.*[84]

This was the domain of necessity, a clash of titanic forces connected with slavery that shaped the lives and actions of millions of Americans at all levels and in every sphere of activity. No individual, however powerful, could wish them away. Lincoln did not view these forces pushing and dividing Americans over slavery as something mindless and purely mechanical. They were the cumulative product of ordinary human motives, including but not limited to pecuniary self-interest, as they operated on thousands or millions of human beings under social, political, and economic circumstances shaped by the presence of slavery. There was nothing "conspiratorial" or "preconcerted" about the operation of such forces, which is what distinguished them from the deliberate actions of the small group of men responsible for repealing the Missouri Compromise.

Lincoln's most precise description of the larger social forces supporting the perpetuation of slavery came in his second inaugural address (March 4, 1865), where he observed that slavery constituted "a peculiar and powerful interest" and that this interest "was, somehow, the cause of the war"—a war neither side desired and whose magnitude and duration neither side expected.[85] Lincoln's phrase here, "a peculiar and powerful interest," though penned after the radical transformations of the war itself, was fully consistent with his prewar analysis of the human interests and motives that sustained slavery. This "peculiar and powerful interest" was implicit in Lincoln's October 16, 1854, speech on the Kansas-Nebraska Act, where he observed that "the Southern people . . . are just what we would be in their situation. If slavery did not now exist amongst them, they would not introduce it. If it did now exist amongst us, we should not instantly give it up."[86] In this sense, the "peculiar and powerful interest" sustaining slavery was, in Lincoln's view, *not* identical to the concept of a "slave power," insofar as the latter phrase referred to a small, specific group of powerful individuals deliberately promoting the political interests of slavery. For Lincoln, "Stephen and Franklin and Roger and James" may have constituted an arm of the slave power, but most slaveholders were not part of any such "conspiracy" or "preconcert." Instead, like nearly everyone else, they acted on and were constrained by interests whose cumulative force no one could fully control.

However, it did not follow that no one could shape the operation of such interests. Lincoln predicted in the "House Divided" speech that "a *crisis*" would soon be "reached, and passed" that would determine which set of opposed forces would ultimately prevail. To speak of a "crisis" in this context suggests that these opposed forces had become so closely matched that the deliberate acts of a relatively small number of prominent individuals might irreversibly shape their direction. Thus, Lincoln warned that although these individuals did not understand and could not control these larger proslavery and antislavery forces, they may have intervened just enough through their concerted action to tip the balance—that is, to give these forces a "*tendency*"—toward the eventual legalization of slavery everywhere. Conversely, under the same circumstances, the newly formed Republican Party had both the power and the duty to tip the balance the other way.[87]

Let us return to Lincoln's suggestion in the "House Divided" speech (he never claimed to know for certain) that some prominent individuals whose actions could tip the balance toward the nationalization of slavery acted in "preconcert." Lincoln's scenario was certainly "overstated" (to borrow Fehrenbacher's term) and inaccurate in some particulars. But insofar as his purpose was to hold certain powerful individuals accountable for specific actions critically affecting the future of slavery, Lincoln's blast was not widely off target. "Stephen and Franklin and Roger and James" conflated what were, at a minimum, two separate "preconcert" actions occurring at different times and whose cast of characters overlapped only in part. As noted in chapter 4, Douglas and Pierce met behind closed doors in 1854, along with the proslavery senators of the F Street Mess (whose participation Lincoln certainly would have included in the "preconcert" charge, had he known about it), the outcome of which was to add a clause to the Kansas-Nebraska Act explicit repealing the Missouri Compromise's slavery restriction, as the price of southern support for the bill.[88] Buchanan was overseas at the time, and Taney (whose *Dred Scott* decision lay three years in the future) was not physically present at the meeting. But one of the participating F Street Mess senators, Robert M. T. Hunter, had recently cited Taney's 1850 ruling in *Strader v. Graham* to argue that slaveholders had a constitutional right to bring and hold slaves in any federal territory.[89]

As for the *Dred Scott* decision (the other key event in Lincoln's "preconcert" allegation), Pierce had no role, and it is unlikely that Douglas was pushing behind the scenes for a judicial ruling that, as Lincoln acknowledged, threatened to destroy his doctrine of popular sovereignty. (Lincoln later characterized Douglas as the "dupe" of conspirators rather than the principal mover.)[90] But Lincoln's suspicion that, before his inaugural address, Buchanan had communicated with the justices and knew how the Supreme Court would rule in the *Dred Scott* case was substantially correct.[91]

Thus, Lincoln's preconcert charge was oversimplified and wrong on some details; it merged events from different times and places and was arguably unfair in its characterization of Douglas's purpose in agreeing to repeal the Missouri Compromise. What cannot be easily dismissed, however, was Lincoln's charge that the four men he named (among others) had acted in a way that triggered a political crisis over slavery, that they threatened the unchecked expansion of slavery, and that they could have acted otherwise.[92]

Conspiracy theories are endemic in politics. Many, perhaps most, of these theories cast suspicion on the democratic process itself. If there is some unelected, alien "shadow government" running the United States, how could it possibly be voted out? Conspiracy theories of this kind encourage fantasies of revolutionary resistance, and sometimes their adherents translate such fantasies into real-world violence.

Whatever well-founded criticism may be directed against Lincoln's "preconcert" allegation in the "House Divided" speech, at least this may be said in its favor: it was formulated to motivate peaceful, constitutional action to undo the pernicious acts of the "conspirators" and to reaffirm rather than erode faith in the democratic process. The remedy Lincoln urged was to vote out of office men like Stephen Douglas, Franklin Pierce, and James Buchanan and replace them with elected officials who would enact laws that were very different from the Kansas-Nebraska Act and appoint Supreme Court justices who were very different from Roger Taney. Lincoln ended his speech by saying, "*Wise councils* may *accelerate* or *mistakes delay* it, but, sooner or later the victory is *sure* to come."[93] He envisioned this as a peaceful victory, not a violent one.

6 | "The Plank Is Large Enough"

Lincoln on Race, Colonization, and Coexistence

Lincoln thought it was possible, though difficult, to build an effective, enduring antislavery electoral majority in the United States. This majority, in turn, would use its electoral victories to halt the expansion of slavery, squeeze it geographically and economically, and gradually extinguish it without bloodshed. At the time, only a small fraction of Black Americans enjoyed the right to vote, so this antislavery electoral majority would be composed almost entirely of white male citizens living in free states. Lincoln believed that most white Americans implicitly sensed that slavery was wrong and, moreover, could be persuaded that the expansion and perpetuation of slavery threatened their own rights and interests.

Herein lies the problem this chapter seeks to address. The same overwhelmingly white majority that Lincoln depended on to halt, shrink, and ultimately remove slavery from American soil was deeply prejudiced against Black Americans, whether enslaved or free, and was unwilling to accept them as social and political equals. In many respects, opposing slavery was politically less difficult, at least in free states, than advocating racial equality. If slavery could be abolished peacefully and without destroying the Union—a very big *if*—then nonslaveholding white northerners would lose comparatively little. Indeed, Lincoln argued that white workers would *gain* economically by the abolition of slavery. Social and political equality with Black Americans was a different matter. In this case, nonslaveholding white Americans would be asked not only to strip the slaveholding minority of its privileged status but to relinquish their own racial privilege as well.

White male citizens' near monopoly on political power was an injustice in itself, above and beyond slavery. But precisely because of this monopoly, any fundamental change (or at least any change accomplished without civil war) depended on the support of this same white majority.

In addition to demanding the immediate abolition of slavery everywhere in the United States, radical abolitionists advocated full civil and political equality, including citizenship and voting rights, for Americans of all races. Thus, abolitionists promised much more than Lincoln did, and their promises reflected the same natural right principles that Lincoln embraced. But abolitionists faced the same political dilemma. Barring civil war, their aims could be realized only by persuading a white majority, and they were less well positioned than Lincoln to do so because their promises were more far-reaching than his. Moreover, Lincoln had more skill and experience in building electoral majorities than abolitionists did, and he viewed such work as his calling in a way that most abolitionists did not.

Nor was civil war a magic bullet. A civil war initiated by political elites in the free states for the purpose of abolishing slavery and instituting full racial equality almost certainly would have failed on the battlefield, in the unlikely event it was even attempted. In a phrase often quoted today, abolitionist Frederick Douglass argued in 1857: "Power concedes nothing without a demand. It never did and it never will."[1] But unless victims of injustice already possess extralegal coercive force greater than the unjust power they seek to overthrow (which was not the case for Black Americans in the 1850s), oppressed persons and their allies, in demanding justice, must make effective use of existing political institutions and practices. In a democracy—even a deeply flawed democracy like the United States in Lincoln's time—persuasion was essential and election results mattered. Frederick Douglass realized this no less than Lincoln did.

In this chapter I examine Lincoln's prewar efforts to imagine a postemancipation racial future for the United States. Lincoln acknowledged sharing the racial prejudices of his white contemporaries to a certain degree, although he recognized that such feelings *were* prejudices, while most white Americans did not. But I suggest that the principal reason for Lincoln's unwillingness to implement in practice the full racial equality he endorsed in principle was not his racism but the political constraints under which he acted. These same constraints would have weighed with equal force on *any* candidate for elective office in Illinois or for president of the United States, even if that candidate were entirely free of prejudice.

Lincoln held that human beings of all races were naturally entitled to the rights and liberties promised in the Declaration of Independence.

These rights included not only "life, liberty, and the pursuit of happiness" but also "consent of the governed." Slavery conspicuously violated both the right to liberty and the right to consent. But to be legally free yet deprived of equal civil and political rights likewise violated the principle of consent. Lincoln forthrightly acknowledged that principle: "Allow ALL the governed an equal voice in the government, and that, and that only is self government."[2] What he claimed not to know was how this principle could be realized in practice for Black Americans residing in the United States.

During the 1850s Lincoln gave verbal support to "colonization"—the deeply impractical idea that, after emancipation, large numbers of Black Americans, under federal sponsorship, protection, and funding, would agree to emigrate from the United States to some other part of the world to form or join a self-governing political community free from what Lincoln believed was immovable white prejudice in the United States. During his presidency, Lincoln's small-scale colonization pilot projects quickly demonstrated their impracticality, and the "colonists" were rescued and returned to the United States.

Lincoln's support for colonization is among the most troubling aspects of his political career. But his embrace of colonization did not prevent him from acting against slavery at critical moments—not only during the war but also in early 1861, when, despite enormous political pressure, he refused to back down on his pledge to halt the spread of slavery to new territories. That Lincoln did not make colonization a *precondition* for the enactment of antislavery policies was of enormous importance. This distinguished him fundamentally from many other colonization advocates, including Thomas Jefferson and Henry Clay, who held that emancipation could not begin unless and until practical arrangements had been made for the removal of millions of persons of African descent from the United States. For Lincoln, emancipation *could* begin without colonization—not only the wartime emancipation he ultimately resorted to under radically transformed circumstances but also the gradual emancipation he envisioned during the 1850s.

In Lincoln's 1858 debates with Stephen Douglas, both candidates assumed that halting the geographic expansion of slavery would lead to greater numbers of free Blacks living and working in the United States, including in Illinois and other northern states. Douglas characterized this as a great danger, but Lincoln was relatively untroubled by it. What did trouble Lincoln was the prospect of Black Americans (many of them former slaves) living politically as "underlings," by which he meant persons legally free but lacking equal civil and political rights.[3] Unlike many of his contemporaries, including many other Republicans, Lincoln never argued that people of African descent were incapable of responsible self-government. His argument that full racial equality was impossible in the United States was based on his judgment that the vast majority of white Americans, including those who thought slavery was wrong, would refuse to accept Black Americans as their civil and political equals.

That such opposition existed is beyond dispute, although one might reasonably question Lincoln's judgment that white opposition was permanent and immovable. It is also true that Lincoln sometimes described this opposition in ways that reinforced it, as he certainly did in his 1858 debate with Stephen Douglas in Charleston, Illinois.[4] Nevertheless, I believe it is a mistake to treat Lincoln's racial prejudices as the principal reason he did not endorse full civil and political rights for Americans of all races. To make Lincoln's own prejudices the central explanatory fact implies that *if* he had been free of prejudice (and he was certainly far less prejudiced than Douglas) he could have been elected on a platform of full racial equality and could have effectively promoted that goal in office. In my judgment, it is more fruitful to focus on the political constraints and to ask to what degree any political leader enjoying significant support among the white electorate during the 1850s could have moved the needle of public opinion in the direction of racial equality.

Where Lincoln believed the needle of white public opinion *could* be moved—beyond persuading white Americans to squeeze slavery out of existence, a major task in itself—was toward accepting Black Americans' participation in free labor markets. This may seem a very minimal goal. But Lincoln believed it was important to confront head-on the widespread assumption that emancipated Black workers entering the free labor market would throw white workers out of work or pull down their wages. Lincoln argued that it was *slavery* that reduced the wages of white workers (because forced labor is cheap labor) and that emancipation would raise the wages of *both* white and Black workers, even if all formerly enslaved persons remained in the country. Thus, he assured white northerners that "the plank is large enough" to sustain both races, and there was "room enough for us all to be free."[5]

"I Can Just Leave Her Alone"

I begin with an important and often overlooked dimension of Lincoln's 1858 debates with Stephen Douglas. Both Douglas and Lincoln assumed that halting the expansion of slavery would weaken the institution politically and economically; this, in turn, would result in a gradual increase in the free Black population living and working in the United States, including in free states like Illinois. Douglas used this as an argument against supporting Lincoln and his party. Lincoln accepted it as a likely consequence of his policies and sought to reassure white Americans that they would suffer no great harm from it.

Douglas used Lincoln's opposition to the *Dred Scott* decision, and his insistence that "all men are created equal," to stoke the racial fears of Illinois voters about the dire consequences of electing Republicans like Lincoln to office. "Do you desire to turn this beautiful State into a free negro colony, in order that when Missouri abolishes slavery she can send one hundred thousand emancipated slaves into Illinois, to become citizens and voters, on an equality with yourselves?"[6] (Note that while Douglas was opposed to *introducing* slavery to Illinois, he was also opposed to *abolishing* slavery elsewhere, because some of the slaves emancipated in other states would migrate to Illinois.) Lincoln did not envision emancipation occurring as suddenly or as dramatically as in Douglas's race-baiting scenario; nor did Lincoln support voting rights for Blacks, as Douglas alleged. But Lincoln did not deny that the number of free Blacks living and working in the United States would increase if the policies he and his party supported went into effect. He and other Republicans did expect that border states like Missouri would be the first to abolish slavery once its expansion was halted and its profitability diminished.

Moreover, despite his support for colonization, Lincoln did not promise white Illinoisans that these newly emancipated Blacks would be transported to Liberia. On the contrary, he acknowledged that the *immediate* prospects for colonization were nonexistent, which meant that for a long time and perhaps permanently, most recently liberated former slaves would continue to live and work in the United States.[7] Nor did he deny that some of these newly emancipated persons would make their way to Illinois. His response to Douglas's race-mixing charges indicated that Lincoln expected Blacks and whites to cross paths frequently enough in free states for sexual relations between them to be possible, although he believed this would rarely occur where both races were free. Lincoln's stated opposition to interracial sex and marriage is often cited as evidence that he fully shared the racial prejudices held by most white Americans at the time.[8] Assuming that the "natural disgust" he expressed toward interracial marriage was genuine, his remarks clearly indicated racial prejudice of a specific type.[9] However, other, more important dimensions of his remarks about race and sex reveal a more racially egalitarian commitment, yet they have rarely been mentioned in commentaries on Lincoln.

On the surface, Lincoln and Douglas appeared to be taking the same stance on interracial sex and marriage in their 1858 debates—Douglas calling it shocking and bad, and Lincoln agreeing with him. Yet they emphasized very different real or supposed facts, and for that reason, they drew different practical conclusions. Douglas repeatedly emphasized the scenario of sexual relations between Black men, whom he portrayed as predators, and white women as their helpless or shameless victims. He knew this was the prospect his white male constituents would find most threatening. "If you, Black Republicans, think that the negro ought to be on a social equality with your wives and daughters, and ride in a carriage with your wife, whilst you drive the team, you have a perfect right to do so."[10] Though Douglas claimed to be neutral toward slavery, this nod-and-wink reference to supposedly predatory Black men activated one of the most powerful rhetorical weapons in the proslavery arsenal. If Black men were by nature sexual predators (the proslavery argument went), then only by keeping Black men enslaved could white women be protected and the white race saved from extinction.[11] Douglas did not need to spell this out. It followed that the best course of action, at least for Illinois, was to oppose the introduction of slavery there and to discourage its abolition elsewhere—especially in Missouri.

Lincoln, in contrast, in his remarks on interracial sex, emphasized predatory white male slaveholders subjecting enslaved Black women to "forced concubinage," thus making them "liable to become mothers of mulattoes in spite of themselves." Lincoln claimed this type of power relationship accounted for nine-tenths of "all the mixing of blood in the nation." He made his clearest statements on enslaved women's vulnerability to sexual violence in denouncing the *Dred Scott* decision, which (it is often forgotten) returned not only Dred Scott to slavery but also his wife and daughters, one of whom had been born in free territory.

Dred Scott, his wife and two daughters were all involved in the suit. We desired the court to have held that they were citizens so far at least as to entitle them to a hearing as to whether they were free or not; and then also, that they were in fact and in law really free. Could we have had our way, the chances of these black girls, ever mixing their blood with that of white people, would have been diminished at least to the extent that it could not have been without their consent. But Judge Douglas is delighted to have them decided to be slaves, and not human enough to have a hearing.

These remarks provide essential context for Lincoln's remarks about "race mixing," both in his 1857 speech on the *Dred Scott* case and in his 1858 debates with Douglas. "Now I protest against that counterfeit logic which concludes that, because I do not want a black woman for a *slave* I must necessarily want her for a *wife*. I need not have her for either, I can just leave her alone."[12] Lincoln repeated this argument the following year during his campaign against Douglas. Diana Schaub, one of the few scholars to emphasize this dimension of Lincoln's remarks on race, observes:

Lincoln avoids any mention of the black man/white woman pairing that is the surefire trigger for white outrage [and instead] turns his disavowal of race mixing into an endorsement of the essential equality and independence of women. Speaking of this hypothetical black woman, Lincoln says he need not "have her" as either a slave or a wife. He can just let her be, allow her to go about her business as a self-determining agent.[13]

Although Lincoln's opposition to sexual relations between the races in some respects reflected popular prejudice, in this respect it did not. There was no overwhelming demand among white voters in Illinois for protecting the personal autonomy of Black women.

Lincoln's perspective on sexual relations between the races carried different implications for racial coexistence than did Douglas's fixation on supposedly predatory Black men, about which Lincoln was conspicuously silent. Douglas's racial scaremongering functioned as a defense of slavery where it was already established and of strict racial separation where slavery was prohibited. Lincoln's conclusion—"I can just leave her alone"—carried a direct condemnation of slavery and, under conditions of freedom, did not require keeping Blacks and whites far apart. It did require, however, that Black women, no less than white women, be legally protected from unwanted sexual attention.

It also followed that sexual mixing of the races by itself furnished no strong rationale for colonization. This point deserves emphasis because some commentaries on Lincoln's racial views claim that his support for colonization was based principally on his horror of race mixing and, in particular, on his desire to prevent intermarriage.[14] But even if Lincoln was as horrified by consensual sexual relations between the races as he was by sexual violence inflicted on Black women under slavery (an unlikely assumption), interracial marriage could have been prevented by maintaining the preexisting laws forbidding it, without the enormous expense and economic disruption of a colonization scheme that Lincoln insisted Black Americans had the right to refuse in the first place.

Lincoln did say in his 1857 speech on the *Dred Scott* decision that "separation of the races is the only perfect preventive of amalgamation" and that "such separation, if ever effected at all, must be effected by colonization." This passage, taken in isolation, might appear to ground Lincoln's support for colonization entirely on opposition to race mixing. But the same speech also includes Lincoln's detailed description of the degree to which Black Americans, both enslaved and free, were trapped in a "prison house . . . bolted in with a lock of a thousand keys" and systematically deprived of the rights and liberties promised in the Declaration of Independence. In his closing, Lincoln compared colonization to the exodus of "the children of Israel," who "went out of Egyptian bondage in a body."[15]

Lincoln's phrase about colonization, "if ever effected at all," suggests that he regarded the whole project as unlikely. It is not my aim to defend Lincoln's endorsement of colonization, which, even in the voluntary form he proposed, would have been unjust as well as deeply impractical. But if the aim is to understand Lincoln's thinking in its full complexity, its weaknesses and contradictions as well as its strengths, we should not jump to the conclusion that Lincoln supported colonization simply because he was horrified at the prospect that men and women of different races might on occasion decide to marry one another.

"A Universal Feeling, Whether Well or Ill-Founded"

Did Lincoln's racial views explain his unwillingness to support full citizenship and voting rights for Black Americans? Here again, the question is not whether Lincoln was entirely free of racial prejudice. The "disgust" he expressed at the prospect of interracial sex and marriage indicates that he harbored some degree of prejudice. Even though he would not have compelled any formerly enslaved persons to leave the United States, his reference to Africa as the "native land" of Black Americans suggests that he had difficulty imagining the United States as a multiracial political community. His observation that "my own feelings" were opposed to living with Black Americans as social and political equals, that even "if mine would, we well know that those of the great mass of white people will not," and that "a universal feeling, whether well or ill-founded, can not be safely disregarded" can be plausibly read in more than one way.[16] Such statements can be interpreted to mean that he *did* share those "feelings" but, unlike most white Americans, recognized them as "ill-founded," or that he did *not* actually feel this strong opposition himself but regarded it as too deeply rooted to alter and for that reason declined to confront it. But under either interpretation, he cannot be classified as a strong advocate of racial equality, as many of the abolitionists were.

Lincoln never asserted that the white race was naturally superior in capacity to the Black race. Nor, however, did he definitely assert that all races of humanity were naturally equal in capacity—though he frequently affirmed that all human beings were equally entitled to the natural rights promised in the Declaration of Independence. On some occasions he suggested that whether the races were equal in all respects was a question to which he did not know the answer but that it did not affect his opposition to slavery one way or the other. The Black man, Lincoln observed, "is not my equal in many respects—certainly not in color, perhaps not in moral or intellectual endowment. But in the right to eat the bread, without leave of anybody else, which his own hand earns, *he is my equal and the equal of Judge Douglas, and the equal of every living man.*"[17] Here, Lincoln emphasized equality among all races in the capacity to labor and in the entitlement to the fruits of that labor, which meant that slavery was unjust regardless of one's stance on other dimensions of equality. "Color"—if this simply meant skin color—Lincoln elsewhere treated as a continuum, not a dichotomy, and he argued that it provided no rational foundation for inequalities of other kinds, especially slavery.[18] Inequalities of "moral or intellectual endowment" were important and often evident among *individuals*, but Lincoln neither affirmed nor denied that the Black and white *races* differed with respect to these qualities.

However, none of this reaches the question of whether Lincoln regarded persons of African descent as inferior to people of European descent in their capacity for responsible self-government and for *that* reason opposed extending to them full civil and political rights. Many critics assert that Lincoln did regard Blacks as inferior in the capacity for self-government. But he never said this or anything like it, even though many of his white contemporaries—including some prominent Republicans—expressed such a view confidently and often.[19] The only thing Lincoln definitely asserted was that white Americans, whether justly or unjustly, were *unwilling to accept* Black Americans as their social and political equals. Whether this was a good or bad reason for Lincoln's own unwillingness to press the issue is a separate question.

Participants in the debate over Lincoln's racial views often enlist supplementary evidence to fill in matters on which Lincoln himself was silent or evasive. Some argue that Lincoln's racial views can be inferred from the larger social and political context in which he lived and acted.[20] That is a questionable method of interpretation, however, for someone as complex as Lincoln, who was capable of voicing commonly held views in some respects and challenging them in others. Others more sympathetic to Lincoln make the contrary argument: that Lincoln's unwillingness to clearly affirm white supremacist doctrines during his 1858 contest with Douglas, while under intense political pressure to do so, indicates that he disagreed with such doctrines to a greater degree than he was willing to reveal.[21] Some of Lincoln's acquaintances recalled that he attended minstrel shows and sometimes engaged in racial humor, but what, if anything, this reveals about his unwillingness to support full social and political equality is unclear.[22] Lincoln himself typically treated the subject of race (and especially Douglas's charge that he and his party promoted "amalgamation" of the races) as a deliberate distraction from the main issue, which was the expansion and perpetuation of slavery.[23]

Psychological Roots of Race Prejudice

Lincoln's statements on race can be faulted on many scores. But he cannot be accused of overestimating the difficulty of creating a genuinely multiracial political community.[24] That most white Americans, North and South, would refuse to accept Black Americans as their social and political equals even after slavery had disappeared was one of Lincoln's most accurate and long-lasting predictions. But in my view, Lincoln can be justly criticized in at least two respects. First, under the circumstances, his unwillingness to directly challenge the white supremacist assumptions of the electorate in matters extending beyond the immediate question of slavery tended to *reinforce* those assumptions—though not to the degree Stephen Douglas did. Second, although Lincoln was a keen analyst of public opinion in many respects, his observations about the "universal feeling" against racial equality manifested by "the great mass of white people" were not accompanied by an explanation of *why* those feelings were so deeply rooted and what, if anything, might cause them to change.

If, in Lincoln's view, nearly universal white opposition "forever" (or "probably forever") prevented full social, civil, and political equality between "the white and black races" in America, we must ask why he described this disposition as permanent and unchangeable. He did not speak about slavery as permanent and unalterable, even though it too was deeply rooted and enormously difficult to remove. Moreover, as described in chapter 5, Lincoln had a keen sense of how public opinion about slavery could be transformed over time, in either a proslavery or antislavery direction, by the public statements and public acts of political leaders and political parties and their subsequent endorsement or rejection at the polls.

If white public opinion on slavery could, with effective leadership, shift over time in a decidedly antislavery direction, as Lincoln hoped, why could it not also shift over time, with effective leadership, toward greater acceptance of racial equality more generally? Conversely, if leaders like Stephen Douglas could perniciously mold public opinion to accept the perpetuation of slavery, as Lincoln charged, then it followed that Lincoln's public statements about white Americans' refusal to accept civil and political equality with Blacks might reinforce this refusal. That could happen even if Lincoln personally regarded such universal white opposition as "ill-founded" and unjust.

Even in his private writings, Lincoln did not analyze in depth *why* white Americans were so opposed to civil and political equality with Blacks. He was capable of great psychological insight in many respects. He perceptively analyzed how one slaveholder living in a community alongside nine (white) fellow citizens who were opposed to slavery could gradually turn his neighbors into defenders of slavery.[25] His fragment "On Proslavery Theology" examined in vivid terms the biased circumstances under which a slaveholding theologian, "Dr. Ross," sitting in the cool shade while the person he holds in bondage labors in the burning sun, deliberates on the question of whether it is God's will that the enslaved person remain enslaved or instead that Dr. Ross "walk out of the shade, throw off his gloves, and delve for his own bread."[26] At least in Lincoln's extant papers, there is no equivalent examination of the biased circumstances under which white, nonslaveholding Americans deliberated about whether free Blacks should be their social and political equals.

One possible explanation is that Lincoln could not critically examine white racial prejudices precisely because he shared those prejudices and was unable to think beyond them, just as Dr. Ross, relaxing in the cool shade, felt in his bones the rightness of slavery. Alternatively, Lincoln might have been free enough of white supremacist prejudices to recognize them *as* prejudices but not free enough to critically examine them in depth.

Lincoln did not leave any record, public or private, revealing whether he thought white Americans' opposition to social and political equality resulted from some innate, unalterable "racial instinct" (an interpretation I find improbable) or from specific and potentially alterable circumstances.[27] The word Lincoln used to describe white Americans' opposition to equality—he called it a "feeling"—is ambiguous. What we designate as "feelings" in ordinary usage covers a lot of ground. Feelings can have deep biological roots (sexual feelings, for example), or they can be responsive to specific, transitional experiences, such as the feeling of strangeness and dislocation one experiences upon arriving in a foreign country.

For comparison, consider some keen observations on white racism penned by Lincoln's contemporary, Black abolitionist and former slave Frederick Douglass, keeping in mind that Douglass's background, life experiences, and perspective were very different from Lincoln's. In the northern free states, Douglass observed and experienced racial discrimination and racially motivated violence on many occasions. He would not have disputed Lincoln's observation that the vast majority of white Americans were opposed to equality with Blacks. In 1850 Douglass described "prejudice against color" as "a feeling so universal and so powerful for evil,"[28] which anticipates Lincoln's 1854 phrase "a universal feeling." But Douglass specifically rejected the view that there existed "a natural, an inherent, and an invincible repugnance in the breast of the white race toward dark-colored people." He argued instead that the white man's unwillingness to associate on equal terms with Blacks was based largely on example setting: imitating what others do. Douglass was once the only Black man on a crowded train from Boston to Albany, and the only available seat was the one next to him. No white passenger was willing to sit beside him until the former governor of Massachusetts, who recognized him, sat down to talk with him for a while. After the governor left, other white passengers were eager to have the honor of sitting beside Douglass. "The governor had, without changing my skin a single shade, made the place respectable which before was despicable. . . . I am inclined to think that pride and fashion have much to do with the treatment commonly extended to colored people in the United States."[29] In other contexts, Douglass attributed white Americans' prejudice toward Blacks to another and arguably more enduring factor: fear of competition from an equal. But here too he argued that this attitude was alterable, though not as easily as the train episode might suggest. In an 1850 essay titled "Prejudice against Color," Douglass denied that white prejudice was driven by the *color* difference as such. White Americans had no problem being physically close to Blacks, so long as they were clearly of lower status: slaves, servants, waiters, buffoons. White Americans' angry insistence on their own superiority was unleashed precisely when Blacks exemplified "ennobling qualities of head or heart" that clearly merited their treatment as equal human beings. White Americans' rage against Black equality thus betrayed a bad conscience: "The fact that they fear an acknowledgment of our equality, shows that they see a fitness in such an acknowledgment." Whites did not display any comparable fear of being placed on equal footing with horses.[30] The antiequality motivations described by Douglass were unquestionably strong ones, but his observation that white Americans secretly recognized the "fitness" of race equality suggests the possibility of change.

What is intriguing about Douglass's argument that racial prejudice was founded at least in part on imitation—that is, a species of fashion— is that it parallels a passage in which Lincoln examined the operation of public opinion in another context. In his 1842 "Address to the Washington Temperance Society," Lincoln described the enormous influence of "*fashion* . . . the influence that *other* people's actions have on our own actions, the strong inclination each of us feels to do as we see all our neighbors do." He argued that making it *fashionable* to abstain from alcohol would accomplish much more for temperance than castigating and humiliating drinkers. Moreover, Lincoln argued that the influence of fashion was not "confined to any particular thing or class of things"; it was "just as strong on one subject as another."[31] However, Lincoln did not specifically apply that hypothesis to race relations in these reflections. Later in his career, when slavery and race became central concerns, he did not explain whether white Americans' "universal feeling" against Black equality exemplified the powerful hold of fashion (which would be difficult but not impossible to alter) or some other, more deeply rooted motive.

Lincoln clearly understood that white opposition to Black equality was partly rooted in fear of competition from Blacks on equal terms. He sought to mitigate such fears by assuring white Americans that it was *enslaved* Black labor, not *free* Black labor, that fundamentally threatened their rights and interests. A free person of color looking for work, Lincoln argued, threatened a white worker's economic interests no more or less than did competition from another white worker.

The fact that Lincoln believed Blacks and whites could coexist peacefully in the economic sphere but did not support full social and political equality for Black Americans has led some to conclude that, while he recognized Black people's natural right to the fruits of their labor, he saw no injustice in depriving them of civil and political rights.[32] It is easy to see how one might draw this conclusion. Nevertheless, I believe this reading is mistaken. I argue instead that Lincoln recognized that Black Americans were victims of both types of injustice. But he believed (accurately or inaccurately) that only the first of these injustices, depriving Black Americans of the fruits of their labor, could be remedied within the United States.

Natural Rights, Citizenship, and Voting

During the 1858 debates, Stephen Douglas repeatedly accused Lincoln of supporting full citizenship, including voting rights, for Blacks:

> If you desire negro citizenship, if you desire to allow them to come into the State and settle with the white man, if you desire them to vote on an equality with yourselves, and to make them eligible to office, to serve on juries, and to adjudge your rights, then support Mr. Lincoln and the Black Republican Party, who are in favor of the citizenship of the negro. . . . The Republicans say

that [the Negro] ought to be made a citizen, and when he becomes a citizen he becomes your equal, with all your rights and privileges.[33]

Douglas misrepresented some of the particulars, but he was correct that Lincoln had endorsed Black citizenship in some form. By the time of the 1858 debates, Lincoln was already on public record in support of some, though not all, citizenship rights for free Blacks. In his June 26, 1857, speech on the *Dred Scott* decision, Lincoln argued that Dred Scott, his wife, and his two daughters ought to have been recognized as citizens, "at least . . . to entitle them to a hearing." In his "House Divided" speech (June 16, 1858), Lincoln criticized the *Dred Scott* decision for summarily declaring that no person of African descent could ever be a citizen of any state or of the United States, thereby stripping Black Americans of the protections contained in the Constitution's privileges and immunities clause: "The citizens of each State shall be entitled to all privileges and immunities of citizens in the several states."[34] During the August 21, 1858, debate, Douglas specifically referred to what Lincoln had said about citizenship in the "House Divided" speech. "We are told by Lincoln that he is utterly opposed to the Dred Scott decision, and will not submit to it, for the reason that he says it deprives the negro of the rights and privileges of citizenship."[35]

In addition to keeping a record of what Lincoln had said about Black citizenship, Douglas made a persuasive argument about the *tendency* of Lincoln's commitments on race and natural rights. Douglas's argument in this respect was straightforward: because Lincoln held that Black people were no less entitled than white people to the natural rights promised in the Declaration of Independence, it followed that Lincoln was also committed to extending full citizenship, including voting rights, to Black Americans. As Douglas framed the issue: Lincoln maintained that, under the Declaration of Independence, "the negro is equal to the white man." For that reason, "it was rational for [Lincoln] to advocate negro citizenship, which, when allowed, puts the negro on an equality under the law." Douglas characterized Lincoln's denials on this point as no more than a hasty political retreat, in the face of voter backlash in southern Illinois, from the "rational" tendency of his previous public statements. Douglas, in contrast, claimed that Blacks were *not* included in the Declaration of Independence because they were "a race incapable of self government." But because Lincoln claimed Blacks *were* included in the Declaration (and never claimed they were incapable of self-government), there was no logical stopping point short of full citizenship.

Stephen Douglas may be justly criticized in many respects. But he was correct that Lincoln's natural rights arguments logically *tended* toward full civil and political rights for persons of all races—just as Lincoln was correct to argue that Douglas's neutral stance on slavery, and his denial that Blacks were included in the Declaration's "all men are created equal," *tended* toward the nationalization and perpetuation of slavery. In this matter, there was no principled stopping point in either direction. Civil and political rights are not the same as natural rights: the former vary from one political community to another, while the latter are, in theory, the same everywhere. But to permanently deny all or most civil and political rights to a person born in a territory and subject to its laws—to relegate them to "underling" status, in Lincoln's phrase—is to violate that person's natural rights.

The clearest arguments on this point came from Lincoln himself. Both in his 1854 speech on the Kansas-Nebraska Act and in the "prison house" passage from his 1857 speech on the *Dred Scott* decision, Lincoln acknowledged that for Black Americans to be deprived of political rights was a significant injustice in itself. In neither case, however, did he propose a practicable remedy. In his Kansas-Nebraska speech, Lincoln criticized Douglas's version of popular sovereignty as a perversion of democratic self-government because it presumed that the Black man was not a full human being. "But if the negro *is* a man, is it not to that extent, a total destruction of self-government, to say that he too shall not govern *himself?*" Lincoln called the principle of consent "the sheet anchor of American republicanism" and then quoted from the preamble of the Declaration of Independence, capitalizing for emphasis the phrase "DERIVING THEIR JUST POWERS FROM THE CONSENT OF THE GOVERNED." He closed this section by reaffirming the principle: "Allow ALL the governed an equal voice in the government, and that, and that only is self government."[36]

Lincoln's statement of political principle explicitly condemns slavery, which he described as "a total violation of this principle." But that principle was also clearly incompatible with permanently denying full civil and political rights, "an equal voice in the government," to any group of adults subject to the jurisdiction of the government and laws, whether or not those persons were enslaved. Lincoln's next sentence acknowledged this logical conclusion even as he distanced himself from its practical implications: "Let it not be said I am contending for the establishment of political and social equality between the whites and blacks. . . . I am not now combating the argument of NECESSITY, arising from the fact that the blacks are already amongst us."37 Lincoln here tacitly admitted that, in principle, full "political and social equality" *did* follow from what he just said, as did the complete abolition of slavery. But in both cases (slavery and denial of political rights) some practical "necessity" made it impossible, he argued, to fully and immediately act in accordance with the stated principle.

It is also clear that if enslaved Black Americans were emancipated, and if they chose to emigrate en masse from the United States to form or join a political community of self-governing equals elsewhere in the world, both the injustice of slavery and the injustice of unequal civil and political rights would be remedied. Yet *forced* emigration would violate this same principle of consent. Thus, Lincoln's own principles, together with his judgment about what was politically possible or impossible ("the argument of necessity"), boxed him into a corner, and the deus ex machina of Black Americans collectively deciding on a modern-day exodus to a new promised land appeared to be the only solution.

In the "let it not be said" passage that immediately follows the "Allow ALL the governed an equal voice," Lincoln invoked the "argument of necessity" both as a reason why slavery could not immediately be abolished, although its extension could be opposed, and as a reason why political and social equality was out of the question even for Black Americans not held in slavery. Yet the "necessities" preventing the immediate abolition of slavery in states where it existed were different from the "necessities" preventing free Black Americans from enjoying full civil and political rights in free states like Illinois. Slavery in the states was protected by the US Constitution; it was an enormous economic interest, and its abolition at least in the lower South would have required a complete reconstruction of the economy. Nearly everyone recognized that any direct attempt by the federal government to interfere with slavery in the states would trigger secession. In contrast, nothing in the US Constitution prevented Illinois from extending citizenship and voting rights to free persons of color residing in the state. White workers might fear the economic competition, but no new economic system would need to be created. In free states, the supposed "necessity" preventing social and political equality for persons of all races consisted entirely of what Lincoln described as "a universal feeling" among white Americans opposed to equality. Lincoln frequently referred to this obstacle, but he did not subject it to the kind of critical analysis he applied to the proslavery argument.

From the earliest years of his political career, before opposition to slavery became central to his agenda, Lincoln invested enormous energy and hope in the promise of popular self-government and feared its erosion or self-destruction. This provides context for the question he asked in his 1854 Kansas-Nebraska speech immediately after acknowledging the impracticality of colonization in the foreseeable future. "What then? Free them all, and keep them among us as underlings? Is it quite certain that this betters their condition? I think I would not hold one in slavery at any rate; yet the point is not clear enough for me to denounce people upon."[38] Lincoln did *not* say that it would be better for Blacks to remain in slavery, and his phrase "I would not hold one in slavery at any rate" makes it clear that the vulnerability of individuals lacking equal civil and political rights could not legitimately be used to justify their permanent enslavement. Overall, the passage suggests that Lincoln regarded "underling" status as better than slavery, though still very bad. Why, then, did he not clearly affirm that anything was better than slavery?

For persons formally free but who lacked civil and political rights, a wide range of scenarios was possible, from reasonably good (and much better than slavery) at one end of the spectrum to horrific at the other. At the better end, their status might approximate that of legal resident aliens, but without any route to citizenship. One would be able to own property, sign contracts, accept or quit a job, travel freely, marry legally, and do many other things; however, these freedoms would be enjoyed only at the discretion of the citizen body and thus were potentially revocable. Lacking the right to vote, emancipated Blacks would be far less secure in the possession and enjoyment of their private and personal rights than white citizens were. An uncertain, vulnerable situation of this kind would be the *best* possible outcome for a category of persons permanently deprived of civil and political rights.

Far worse postemancipation outcomes for Black Americans were imaginable and indeed were frequently voiced by defenders of slavery. Henry L. Benning of Georgia, who recognized that Lincoln called for gradual rather than immediate emancipation, nevertheless argued for secession in the wake of Lincoln's election on the grounds that emancipation plans in any form would trigger a racial war of extermination. "Abolition would be to the South one of the direst evils of which the mind could conceive. . . . The decree will excite an intense hatred between the whites on one side, and the slaves and the North on the other. Very soon a war between the whites and the blacks will spontaneously break out everywhere." Benning made it clear that, in his view, southern whites would be justified in exterminating free Blacks. But he predicted that, in the end, "our northern friends" would exterminate both former slaveholders and former slaves.[39]

Dire predictions of this kind were not confined to southern slaveholders. In their debates, Stephen Douglas argued that the implementation of Lincoln's policy to gradually extinguish slavery would also extinguish the Black race by making Blacks economically superfluous:

> He will hem them in until starvation seizes them, and by starving them to death, he will put slavery in the course of ultimate extinction. If he is not going to interfere with slavery in the States, but intends to interfere and prohibit it in the territories, and thus smother slavery out, it naturally follows, that he can extinguish it only by extinguishing the negro race, for his policy would drive them to starvation. This is the humane and Christian remedy he proposes for the great crime of slavery.[40]

Both of these postemancipation scenarios end in the extermination of Black Americans, and the racial assumptions driving them were undisguised: for Benning, emancipated Blacks were dangerous predators; for Douglas, they were shiftless and unproductive. Lincoln regarded both assumptions as false. But if significant numbers of white Americans *believed* this supposed racial struggle to the death, nightmare postemancipation scenarios could deliberately be initiated by fearful whites. Thus, it was not unreasonable for Lincoln to ask whether emancipation without equality might make formerly enslaved persons' situation worse, although he phrased it as a question, not as a definite conclusion.

Lincoln endorsed colonization at least in part because he believed it would be better, for Blacks as well as whites, than a society in which emancipated slaves lived as a political and social underclass. This is clear from the "prison house" passage in his June 26, 1858, speech on the *Dred Scott* decision. That speech contains Lincoln's most idealistic description of colonization, which, despite its idealism, remained wholly implausible. What is especially significant about the "prison house" passage is that "the heavy iron doors" behind which Black Americans were trapped referred not only to slavery but also to free Blacks' increasing legal and political disenfranchisement.

In the speech, Lincoln criticized Chief Justice Roger Taney's ruling in *Dred Scott*, among other things, for claiming "that negroes were no part of the people who made, or for whom was made, the Declaration of Independence, or the Constitution of the United States." Drawing from Justice Benjamin Curtis's dissenting opinion in the case, Lincoln responded that in five of the original thirteen states (New Hampshire, Massachusetts, New York, New Jersey, and North Carolina), "free negroes were voters, and, in proportion to their numbers, had the same part in making the Constitution that the white people had." Lincoln then criticized Taney's assumption that "the public estimate of the black man is more favorable *now* than it was in the days of the Revolution." Lincoln observed, "In some trifling particulars, the condition of that race has been meliorated; but, as a whole, in this country, the change between then and now is decidedly the other way; and their ultimate destiny never appeared so hopeless as in the last three or four years."[41]

Lincoln's first piece of evidence for this increasingly hopeless situation is the electoral disenfranchisement of free Blacks. "In two of the five States—New Jersey and North Carolina—that then gave the free negro the right of voting, the right has since been taken away; and in a third—New York—it has been greatly abridged; while it has not been extended, so far as I know, to a single additional State, though the number of the States has more than doubled." Lincoln then proceeds to the worsening situation, over the same period, for Blacks held in slavery, including greater legal obstacles to manumission and the ongoing extension of slavery to new territories. The final phase of the narrative addresses the increasing denial (by Stephen Douglas and Roger Taney, among many others) that the Declaration of Independence includes all members of the human family. The tone is unmistakably tragic and culminates in the following image of the oppression suffered by Black Americans, those who are legally free as well as those held in slavery:

> They have him in his prison house; they have searched his person, and left no prying instrument with him. One after another they have closed the heavy iron doors upon him, and now they have him, as it were, bolted in with a lock of a hundred keys, which can never be unlocked without the concurrence of every key; the keys in the hands of a hundred different men, and they scattered to a hundred different and distant places; and they stand musing as to what inventions, in all the dominions of mind and matter, can be produced to make the impossibility of his escape more complete than it is.[42]

Elsewhere in the speech, Lincoln mentions yet another lock keeping Black Americans in this prison: denial of legal due process. Lack of due process afflicted free Blacks as well as those held in slavery, and it increased the probability that a free person of color could be forced into slavery. The *Dred Scott* ruling, in Lincoln's view, exemplified precisely this danger. As noted earlier, Lincoln argued that Dred Scott and his family ought to have been declared citizens, "at least so far as to entitle them to a hearing."

Lincoln's 1857 *Dred Scott* speech also featured one of his most important and perceptive commentaries on the Declaration of Independence. To the argument that the authors of the Declaration "did not intend to include negroes, by the fact that they did not at once, actually place them on an equality with the whites," Lincoln responded that the authors "had no power to confer such a boon":

> They meant simply to declare the *right*, such that the *enforcement* of it might follow as fast as circumstances should permit. They meant to set up a standard maxim for free society . . . constantly looked to, constantly labored for, and even though never perfectly attained, constantly approximated, and thereby constantly spreading and deepening its influence, and augmenting the happiness and value of life to all people of all colors everywhere.[43]

Lincoln's phrase "as fast as circumstances should permit" was clearly relevant to his hope for the gradual extinction of slavery. But the passage also unmistakably applied to forms of civil and political inequality less extreme than slavery. The only justification for stopping short of full civil and political equality for all adult members of the community was that "circumstances" prevented it. And circumstances, by definition, are potentially alterable. Thus, Lincoln's "standard maxim" commentary on the Declaration of Independence cannot be reconciled with *permanently* denying equal civil and political rights to free Blacks.

The 1857 "prison house" passage confirms Douglas's claim that Lincoln's embrace of equal *natural* rights logically committed him to equal *civil and political* rights—if not immediately, then "as fast as circumstances should permit." Lincoln never described any *principled* stopping point between emancipation, on the one hand, and full social, civil, and political equality, on the other.[44]

"Wolf by the Ear"?

Lincoln did not believe the white majority could be persuaded to support equal civil and political rights for Black Americans. However, he considered it possible, though difficult, to persuade white Americans to coexist peacefully with Blacks as the latter were gradually released from slavery and entered free labor markets in increasing numbers. Lincoln sought to refute the view held by many white Americans that there existed some primordial racial struggle whereby one race could survive physically and economically only at the expense of the other. Such assumptions could be enlisted to support either continued enslavement or forced colonization of the kind Lincoln opposed. At the extreme, they fueled genocidal scenarios. In this respect, Lincoln's argument (both before and during the Civil War) that racial coexistence was possible and manageable on terms of mutual freedom was timely and important. He challenged an assumption that had long prevented many other political leaders, including Thomas Jefferson, from acting in accordance with their condemnation of slavery.

"All honor to Jefferson," Lincoln wrote in 1859, for inserting into the Declaration of Independence "an abstract truth, applicable to all men and all times, and so to embalm it there, that to-day, and in all coming days, it shall be a rebuke and a stumbling-block to the very harbingers of re-appearing tyranny and oppression."[45] Despite their differences in the field of political economy (Jefferson favored a minimal role for government, Lincoln a more active one) and their different life experiences (Jefferson was a wealthy slave owner; Lincoln started with little and never owned slaves), the political thinking of Jefferson and Lincoln exhibits some unmistakable similarities.[46] Both Jefferson and Lincoln embraced the theory of natural rights and government based on consent. Both considered slavery a violation of natural right and hoped for its ultimate disappearance from American soil. Both supported colonizing former slaves to Africa or some other part of the world, where they could become (as Jefferson phrased it) "a free and independent people," although Jefferson advocated compulsory colonization while Lincoln opposed it.[47] Many discussions of Jefferson and Lincoln emphasize their similarities on slavery, race, and colonization.[48] Here, I highlight their differences.

One important difference is that, after his presidency, Jefferson began to voice the implausible "diffusion" theory (whereby spreading slavery over a larger geographic area would facilitate its later extinction), which Lincoln decisively rejected in the 1850s as a "lullaby argument."[49] Nor did Lincoln share Jefferson's racial views. Jefferson argued in "Notes on the State of Virginia" that Blacks were moved by sensation rather than reflection, possessed no talent for either science or literature, and were generally "inferior to the whites in the endowments both of body and mind."[50] Many white Americans in Lincoln's time made racial assertions of this type. Lincoln, however, never said anything of the kind, either in public statements or in private writings. Moreover, Jefferson's proposed colonization of emancipated Blacks would be compulsory, not voluntary, while for Lincoln, colonization could proceed only with the consent of the persons being colonized. As president, Lincoln made this clear to associates who thought differently.[51]

Jefferson explained why, in his view, emancipation *must* be accompanied by colonization:

> It will probably be asked, Why not retain and incorporate the blacks into the state, and thus save the expence of supplying, by importation of white settlers, the vacancies they will leave? Deep rooted prejudices entertained by the whites; ten thousand recollections, by the blacks, of the injuries they have sustained; the real distinctions which nature has made and many other circumstances, will divide us into parties, and produce convulsions which will probably never end but in the extermination of the one or the other race.[52]

For Jefferson, colonization had to be compulsory because free Blacks who remained in the territory posed a grave danger to whites' very survival. This was the logic behind Jefferson's "wolf by the ear" analogy in his April 22, 1820, letter to John Holmes, written during the controversy over whether Missouri should be admitted to the Union as a slave state even though it lay north of the line that had previously divided free states and territories from slave states and territories. Jefferson's own 1784 "Report on Government for Western Territories" had stipulated that "after the year 1800 . . . there shall be neither slavery nor involuntary servitude" in those territories.[53] In 1820 Jefferson still hoped for "a general emancipation and expatriation" if it could be accomplished gradually. But he no longer supported federal restrictions on the territorial expansion of slavery or any policy that took decisions about the future of slavery out of the hands of slaveholders and slave states. Speaking for himself and his fellow slaveholders, Jefferson argued that their survival was at stake: "We have the wolf by the ear, and we can neither hold him, nor safely let him go. Justice is in one scale, and self-preservation in the other." He claimed that transporting slaves to new territories "would not make a slave of a single human being who would not be so without it," and he argued implausibly that diffusing enslaved persons over a greater territory would "facilitate the accomplishment of their emancipation."[54] Jefferson thus opposed what Lincoln and other Republicans later considered the essential first step in any plan of emancipation: halting the geographic expansion of slavery.

Jefferson's "wolf by the ear" described an apparently irreconcilable clash between conflicting natural rights claims. The clashing natural rights at stake, as Jefferson viewed it, were "justice"—meaning the enslaved person's natural right to freedom—on the one side, and "self-preservation" on the other. He believed that emancipated Blacks were far more dangerous, not only to former slave owners but to all whites living in the vicinity, than Blacks still held in bondage. In another 1820 letter on the Missouri controversy, Jefferson argued that if Congress were to "declare that the condition of all men within the US shall be that of freedom," then "all the whites South of the Patomak [*sic*] and Ohio must evacuate their States; and the most fortunate those who can do it first."[55]

Jefferson's "wolf by the ear," if accepted as a plausible characterization of the available options, effectively nullified the applicability of the Lockean version of natural right with respect to the Black and white races in the United States. Jefferson's scenario suggests instead a Hobbesian state of nature in which everyone has a natural right to do anything, including killing, enslaving, or forcibly deporting others, if one judges it necessary to one's own survival. Thus, in his later years, Jefferson's lifelong insistence that slavery was a violation of natural right and that there was no natural right to human property ceased to guide policy in any meaningful way. In practice, nearly every proslavery policy urged by those who did regard enslaved persons as property and called slavery a positive good could be urged with equal force by invoking Jefferson's plea of self-preservation, for there could be no meeting of minds between man and wolf, and the wolf remained a mortal threat whether the man held it or let it go. Lincoln, in contrast, specifically rejected the notion that the white and Black races, after the latter's emancipation, would necessarily become locked in a zero-sum struggle for survival if they remained on the same soil.

"Room Enough for Us All to Be Free"

Lincoln never directly responded to Jefferson's "wolf by the ear" passage. But he rejected two other images employed by white Americans to describe supposedly irreconcilable racial conflict that were broadly similar to Jefferson's life-and-death struggle between man and wolf. One was Stephen Douglas's image of a fight between a man and a crocodile. Douglas quipped that, in a struggle between a Black man and a crocodile, he sided with the Black man, while in a struggle between a white man and a Black man, he sided with the white man. Lincoln argued that Douglas's image dehumanized the Black man by implying that, "as the negro may rightfully treat the crocodile, so may the white man rightfully treat the negro." In response to this man-versus-crocodile image of racial conflict, Lincoln claimed: "There is no such struggle! It is merely an ingenious falsehood, to degrade and brutalize the negro. Let each let the other alone, and there is no struggle about it." Another image of racial struggle that was current in 1860 hypothesized two shipwrecked seamen, one white and one Black, "on a narrow plank, when each must push the other off or drown himself." Under these supposed circumstances, Lincoln conceded, "I would push the negro off or a white man either." But he denied this extreme scenario described the actual circumstances in the United States. "The plank is large enough for both. This good earth is plenty broad enough for white man and negro both, and there is no need of either pushing the other off."[56]

Lincoln made the same point in another 1860 speech: "The proposition that there is a struggle between the white man and the negro contains a falsehood. There *is* no struggle. *If* there was, I should be for the white man. If two men are adrift at sea on a plank which will bear up but one, the law justifies either in pushing the other off." Here too, Lincoln denied the premise that there existed some primordial winner-take-all racial struggle. "I never had to struggle to keep a negro from enslaving me, nor did a negro ever have to fight to keep me from enslaving him."[57]

The fable of two drowning men on one plank (which seemed to be familiar to Lincoln's audience) is significant because the white man and the Black man begin as equals (equally shipwrecked), without any history of personal enmity. This distinguishes it from Jefferson's "wolf by the ear" image, which expresses a slave owner's fear that emancipated slaves will try to settle the score. And unlike Douglas's comparison of Black men to crocodiles, both shipwrecked men are fully human and act on the same motives. Nevertheless, by adding the assumption of radical scarcity, the shipwreck fable renders equality and cooperation impossible and forces a life-and-death struggle for supremacy. Lincoln rejected precisely this assumption of radical scarcity: "The plank is large enough for both." Most obviously, Lincoln's statement challenged one commonly voiced economic argument for slavery: that white Americans' prosperity depended on keeping the Black race enslaved and poor. Less obvious but equally important, Lincoln's rejection of radical scarcity also undermined the argument for colonization of emancipated slaves—not only the compulsory colonization he rejected but also the voluntary colonization he endorsed.

To understand how Lincoln's rejection of the shipwreck fable undermined the case for colonization, it helps to identify the constituency he hoped to persuade. He directed his arguments in these speeches not to conscience-troubled slaveholders like Jefferson nor to slavery-friendly northerners who, like Douglas, viewed the territorial expansion of slavery with indifference. Instead, Lincoln addressed northern white working people (farmers, wage laborers, self-employed tradesmen, small business owners, and others) who were worried both by the expansion of slavery and by the prospect of economic competition with free Blacks. This was the constituency most susceptible to the argument that the presence of Blacks in their community, whether enslaved or free, threatened their livelihood and degraded their labor. Such fears would incline white working people to oppose the expansion of slavery (because it meant competing with enslaved Black labor) but also to oppose abolition (because it meant competing with free Black labor) and to demand that emancipation, *if* it occurred, be conjoined with the compulsory removal of free Blacks. Otherwise, Blacks would compete with whites for access to economic opportunities too scarce to sustain them both.

In response to such fears, Lincoln emphasized that it was not Black laborers but the institution of slavery that threatened the interests and degraded the status of white workingmen. In an 1859 speech in Ohio, Lincoln observed that Douglas's quip about siding with the white man against the Black man and with the Black man against the crocodile implied that "whoever is opposed to the negro being enslaved is in some way or other against the white man." To this, Lincoln replied:

> I say that there is room enough for us all to be free, and that it not only does not wrong the white man that the negro should be free, but it positively

wrongs the mass of the white men that the negro should be enslaved; that the mass of white men are really injured by the effect of slave labor in the vicinity of the fields of their own labor.[58]

Lincoln here emphasized an important distinction that many white northerners failed to make: it was not the presence of *free* Black workers but of *enslaved* Black workers that "injured" free white workers in the vicinity. It was not the Black worker's color but the fact that his labor was forced and unpaid that "positively wrongs the mass of the white men." Conversely, it was positively in the white man's interest "that the negro should be free." Lincoln knew that free Black workers would compete with white workers for employment opportunities, but this was no different from one free white worker competing with another. Free white workers competing with enslaved Black workers was a different matter altogether. That kind of competition devalued the labor and degraded the status of workers both Black and white.

Lincoln made this point again in a March 1860 speech in New Haven, Connecticut, where workers in the shoe industry were on strike. Lincoln remarked, "*I am glad to see that a system of labor prevails in New England under which laborers CAN strike* when they want to, where they are not obliged to work under all circumstances, and are not tied down and obliged to labor whether you pay them or not!" Lincoln praised free labor and the ideal of economic mobility in words that specifically included Black as well as white workers: "I want every man to have the chance—and I believe a black man is entitled to it—in which he *can* better his condition—when he may look forward and hope to be a hired laborer this year and the next, work for himself afterward, and finally to hire men to work for him!" But if the institution of slavery should expand and the state of Connecticut were to be seduced into welcoming slave-labor shoe manufacturing, then "you will get back the shoe trade—for what? You have brought owned labor with it to compete with your own labor, to under work you [i.e., produce at a lower cost], and to degrade you."[59]

Here again, it was enslaved labor, not the labor of free Black people, that threatened the rights and interests of white workers. Slavery was an all-or-nothing, zero-sum, winner-take-all economy—man versus crocodile, one man pushing another off the plank. A free-labor economy, in contrast, despite its inequalities and economic rivalries, was positive sum: the plank was large enough to hold everyone, and there was "room enough for us all to be free."

Where did this leave colonization? Lincoln's "room enough" statement could be taken to mean that there was room enough in the United States for emancipated Blacks who chose to remain in the country. Alternatively or additionally, he might have meant that there was sufficient unoccupied land and sufficiently bright economic prospects elsewhere in the world should emancipated Black Americans choose to emigrate in large numbers. He apparently considered both possibilities—emancipation with or without colonization—acceptable postslavery futures. But either way, "room enough for us all to be free" undermined the case for colonization by removing its supposed urgency. Colonization would be an essential counterpart to emancipation only if one embraced the theory, which Lincoln rejected, that a violent, primordial struggle between the white and Black races would necessarily persist or even escalate with the extinction of slavery.

Lincoln's "plank is large enough" and "room enough for us all to be free" statements from 1859 and 1860 anticipated an argument he made in greater detail as president on the eve of issuing the Emancipation Proclamation. In his December 1, 1862, message to Congress, a month before issuing the final Emancipation Proclamation, Lincoln proposed gradual, compensated emancipation in the slave states that remained in the Union (Delaware, Maryland, Kentucky, and Missouri) and thus were not subject to the Emancipation Proclamation. He included a separate proposal that Congress authorize funds "for colonizing free colored persons, with their own consent, at any place or places without the United States." He made clear that the proposed legislation "does not oblige, but merely authorizes, Congress to aid in colonizing such as may consent" and that colonization "comes to nothing, unless by the mutual consent of the people to be deported, and the American voters, through their representatives in Congress." Emancipation, in short, could be enacted with or without colonization.[60]

Lincoln then explained why, although he favored colonization, emancipation without colonization was also workable. He proceeded to argue, as he had before the war, that there was no inherent economic conflict between the races:

> I cannot make it better known than it already is, that I strongly favor colonization. And yet I wish to say there is an objection urged against free colored persons remaining in the country, which is largely imaginary, if not sometimes malicious.

It is insisted that their presence would injure, and displace white labor and white laborers. If there ever could be a proper time for mere catch arguments, that time surely is not now. In times like the present, men should utter nothing for which they would not willingly be responsible through time and in eternity. Is it true, then, that colored people can displace any more white labor, by being free, than by remaining slaves? If they stay in their old places, they jostle no white laborers; if they leave their old places, they leave them open to white laborers. Logically, there is neither more nor less of it. Emancipation, even without deportation, would probably enhance the wages of white labor, and, very surely, would not reduce them. . . .

But is it dreaded that the freed people will swarm forth, and cover the whole land? Are they not already in the land? Will liberation make them any more numerous? Equally distributed among the whites of the whole country, and there would be but one colored to seven whites. Could the one, in any way, greatly disturb the seven? There are many communities now, having more than one free colored person, to seven whites; and this, without any apparent consciousness of evil from it.[61]

Lincoln returned to the colonization theme later in this extended passage by observing that, by reducing the overall labor supply, colonization would further increase the demand and thus the wages of white labor.

But in practice, Lincoln's own arguments effectively undermined the case for colonization. If the economic fears driving white Americans' interest in colonization were largely imaginary (as Lincoln acknowledged in the passage just quoted), if fears of large-scale sexual mixing where both races were free were likewise imaginary (as Lincoln consistently argued before the war), if colonization had to be genuinely voluntary rather than compulsory, and if white American taxpayers had to cover the substantial costs of a successful large-scale Black colonization enterprise, then large-scale colonization became highly unlikely. Agreement by significant numbers of either Black Americans or white Americans to a compact of this kind was extremely improbable, and Lincoln must have suspected this.

The improbability of colonization did not prevent Lincoln from signing into law in April 1862 a bill abolishing slavery in the District of Columbia or from issuing the Emancipation Proclamation on January 1, 1863, freeing enslaved persons in states in rebellion against the United States.[62] In neither case did he make emancipation conditional on colonization. For Lincoln, colonization had to be genuinely voluntary, so by signing the Emancipation Proclamation he practically negated his own colonization scheme because, by signaling the impending death of slavery, the proclamation removed Black Americans' strongest motive for mass emigration and gave them renewed hope for their future in the United States.

That Lincoln did not make emancipation conditional on colonization furnishes essential context for evaluating his much-discussed and sharply criticized remarks to a delegation of Black leaders on August 24, 1862, five months before he signed the Emancipation Proclamation. At this meeting Lincoln sought unsuccessfully to persuade the delegation to take up the cause of colonization.[63] Some scholars characterize this meeting as evidence of Lincoln's irrevocable opposition to the prospect of a multiracial democracy.[64] Others—more persuasively, in my view—present it as a transitional stage in the process by which Lincoln listened, learned, and ultimately changed in response to the arguments of Black abolitionists.[65] Lincoln's principal argument in his effort to persuade the delegation to make the colonization cause their own was that, even after emancipation, white Americans would harbor ineradicable prejudices against Blacks: "Even when you cease to be slaves, you are yet far removed from being placed on an equality with the white race. . . . Go where you are treated the best, and the ban is still upon you." By emigrating, persons of color could join a political community where they would be "the equals of the best."[66] Lincoln's observations about white prejudice were not exactly news to Black Americans. In response to published accounts of the meeting, one Black abolitionist responded that Blacks were "fully conscious of the hatred to which you have adverted, they endure its consequences daily and hourly," but warned that Lincoln's remarks "may add fuel to the fire."[67]

On September 22, 1862, less than a month after his meeting with the Black delegation, Lincoln publicly announced his intention to issue an emancipation proclamation.[68] Colonization had not become any more practicable during that month, and the preliminary Emancipation Proclamation made colonization even more unlikely. Despite enduring prejudice, the vast majority of Black Americans preferred to remain in the United States, with slavery abolished, rather than emigrate. And as noted earlier, in December 1862 (four months after his remarks to the Black delegation), Lincoln publicly argued *against* the "imaginary" and "malicious" notion that emancipation depended on removing freed persons from the United States.

Lincoln did not relinquish his unrealistic colonization schemes all at once; they dissipated in stages as the war progressed. But even as he endorsed such schemes, both before the war and during its first two years, he sought to prepare white Americans for the probability that they would find more free persons of color living and working in their communities than in the past and to assure them that this was no great cause for alarm. In short, for Lincoln, advocating voluntary colonization and accepting racial coexistence on American soil were not mutually exclusive. In either case, the "plank" was large enough to sustain both races; there was room enough for all to be free.

Conclusion

Lincoln's stance on political equality was transformed by the Civil War. Black Americans' willingness to fight for the Union—thus helping to save the promise of popular self-government for *all* Americans—deeply impressed him.[69] He recommended that the franchise be extended to Blacks who had served in the military and to "the very intelligent" (which he did not define but likely would have included literacy), and he acknowledged more generally that "the colored man . . . desires the elective franchise," which he suggested would come in time but not all at once.[70] Measured by abolitionist standards, Lincoln's franchise proposal appears excessively cautious and conservative, but compared to his stance before the war, it marked a fundamental shift. Lincoln's change in attitude was facilitated by a simultaneous shift in what "the great mass of white people" (at least in the North) were willing to accept. During the 1850s, Lincoln believed white public opinion was permanent and immovable in its opposition to racial equality. By the war's end, white public opinion clearly could and had changed—though whether that change would be enduring or transient remained to be seen.

Yet Lincoln's stance on racial equality shifted during the war because the potential for a change in attitude was already present in his thinking before the war. A different president, faced during the war with the same opportunities and constraints, might have acted very differently. Another president, equally committed to saving the Union, might have declined to issue an emancipation proclamation or might have opposed a constitutional amendment permanently abolishing slavery. Lincoln's shift was not simply dictated by the exigencies of war. Instead, it built on his understanding of justice and his belief in the possibility of post-emancipation racial coexistence already evident in his prewar thinking.

From our perspective, it is natural to compare Lincoln with his contemporaries, both abolitionists and some radical Republicans, who took a more consistent and principled stance. Such a comparison is neither anachronistic nor unfair. Lincoln was aware of these radically principled men and women. He recognized that their efforts to shape public opinion were essential in the fight against slavery. He hoped to bring as many as possible under the Republican tent.

Lincoln also knew, however, that their principled stance on racial equality was strongly opposed by the vast majority of white Americans. Most of the political pressure on Lincoln in the 1850s, during the 1860 campaign, and amid the secession crisis following his election came from the other side: from those who could not imagine coexisting with free people of color in any form and who believed that Lincoln's stance on slavery needlessly inflamed the South. From this perspective, the relevant comparison is not how Lincoln differed from the abolitionists but how he differed from every other previous president in responding to the enormous and recurrent pressure to concede to slave states whatever they demanded as the price of remaining in the Union. Unlike previous national leaders, Lincoln did not back down. He was willing to act against slavery in the territories insofar as it lay in his power, and the slave-state leaders knew it.

Lincoln's willingness to act where previous national leaders had not was facilitated by his limited but significant commitment to racial equality. Though he favored colonization, he was willing to move against slavery without it. Though he knew postemancipation racial coexistence would be difficult, he did not consider it impossible, and he firmly rejected the argument that emancipation must be followed by a race war. He suspected that any danger of a race war came from fearful white Americans, not vengeful former slaves, and he was willing to tell white Americans that their fears were groundless.

Lincoln's mixed commitments to racial equality and his confined vision of postemancipation racial coexistence will strike many readers as woefully inadequate. In the context of the crisis he faced as president of the United States, they were critically important.

7 | "In Course of Ultimate Extinction"

Strategy for the Peaceful End of Slavery

Lincoln's inaugural address described a deliberate, constitutionally checked majority as "the only true sovereign of a free people." To call a decision maker "sovereign" implies the capacity to manage not only routine political questions but even those deep disagreements that could generate anarchy, despotism, or civil war if not resolved or at least contained. The future of slavery in the United States was clearly an extraordinarily difficult and divisive question. This chapter examines how Lincoln believed slavery could be peacefully, gradually, and constitutionally placed "in course of ultimate extinction" through the action of a determined national majority.[1]

I locate Lincoln's reasoning within broader currents of American antislavery thought and practice. In the late 1850s Lincoln was both a Republican Party spokesperson committed to organizing an enduring antislavery electoral majority and an individual thinker whose manner of reasoning and speaking about slavery differed, sometimes significantly, from that of other prominent Republicans. I describe the strategies, policies, and constitutional arguments Lincoln (and others) hoped would bring an end to slavery, as well as the formidable obstacles to their success. One of those obstacles was that proslavery leaders fully understood the strategy of ending slavery through a long, slow geographic squeeze and were willing to risk civil war to prevent the attempt.

This strategy can be summarized as follows.[2] Slavery as an institution had to either expand or die; on this point, Republicans and proslavery leaders agreed. For that reason, halting slavery's geographic, economic, and political expansion was the first step toward its extinction. Slavery's profitability would drop; its political power would shrink; and the ever-present threat of slave insurrections would increase as states with growing numbers of slaves were deprived of a westward outlet to keep their populations sufficiently free and white.[3] Eventually, slave states and slaveholders would accept compensated emancipation (perhaps financed by the federal government) to relieve them of an increasingly burdensome institution. In this way, slavery could be gradually and peacefully abolished without violating any express constitutional provisions.

To engage at length with a historical road not taken—the peaceful, gradual abolition of slavery in the United States—invites two fundamental objections: first, that such an outcome was impossible; and second, that even if it were possible, it would have been unjust because *gradual* abolition would have intolerably extended the life span of slavery. We cannot conclusively demonstrate that any historical event could have occurred differently. But in critically examining Lincoln's political thought and action, the relevant question is whether his hopes for the peaceful extinction of slavery were well-founded based on the evidence available to him at the time. Lincoln in the late 1850s believed at least three different outcomes were possible: (1) the full nationalization and perpetuation of slavery without disunion and civil war; (2) the gradual extinction of slavery without disunion and civil war; and (3) disunion and civil war over slavery, the outcome of which no one could predict with certainty. Given the tragic character of the first and third outcomes, I argue that it was morally responsible for Lincoln to press for the second outcome, so long as there appeared to be some chance of accomplishing it, even if it was significantly *less likely* than the other outcomes.

Gradual abolition of slavery had a precedent in the United States (though not at the federal level). This was the approach adopted by states north of the Mason-Dixon Line that phased out slavery in the decades following the American Revolution.[4] In some northern states, children born after passage of a state's emancipation act remained apprenticed to the slave owner until a certain age (in New York, age twenty-eight for men and twenty-five for women), which functioned as economic compensation to the slave owner.[5] Before independence, 20 percent of New York's population consisted of enslaved persons. In comparison, when Lincoln was elected president in 1860, the proportion of enslaved persons in Kentucky (which did not secede) was 23 percent; in Arkansas (which seceded after Fort Sumter), 20 percent, equivalent to New York in 1776; and in Missouri and Maryland (neither of which seceded), 13 and 12 percent, respectively.[6] Thus, phased emancipation, whatever its merits, was not an inherently unrealistic path to extinguishing slavery, at least for states with slave populations comparable to those in the upper South in 1860. Lincoln's 1849 proposal for gradual, compensated emancipation in the District of Columbia resembled these northern states' policies in many respects, although the legal and constitutional context was different. His proposal in late 1862 for gradual emancipation in slave states that remained loyal to the Union, with financial compensation to slave owners, likewise resembled northern states' post-Revolution emancipation acts.[7]

But the argument that peaceful abolition was impossible rests not on the logistical challenges of phasing out slavery but on its perceived *political* impossibility. The political circumstances of the 1850s were vastly different from those surrounding the northern states' post-Revolution gradual emancipations. Even as northern states moved gradually and haltingly toward abolishing slavery in the early decades of the republic, southern states and territories moved much more quickly and determinedly in the opposite direction, vastly expanding the territorial reach of slavery, its economic importance, and the number of enslaved persons. During this time, slave-state leaders defeated or evaded even minimal federal attempts to contain or slow the westward expansion of slavery—especially after the Louisiana Purchase opened vast new territories that were well suited to slave-based agriculture. After the Northwest Ordinance of 1787, which (incompletely) banned slavery in federal territories north of the Ohio River, and the 1808 termination of the legal (though not the illegal) international slave trade, no effective restrictions on the expansion of slavery were enacted at the federal level until the Missouri Compromise of 1820, which was arguably a slave-state victory. From the mid-1830s on, slave-state leaders repeatedly threatened secession whenever restrictions on slavery were discussed in Congress, even if those restrictions had no chance of becoming law. Moreover, by this time, slave-state leaders had shifted ideologically from defending slavery as a necessary evil to justifying it as a positive good. The latter argument was already voiced during the Missouri crisis of 1819–20, and it had become southern orthodoxy by the 1850s.[8] In sum, the political, economic, and ideological obstacles to peacefully extinguishing slavery in the United States as a whole in the late 1850s were much greater than those faced by northern states in the republic's early years.

Under the circumstances of the 1850s, several scenarios for extinguishing slavery could be eliminated as unrealistic. First, the institution of slavery was not going to die a "natural death," unassisted by antislavery political action. The thesis that slavery was an archaic economic form destined to be swept away by market capitalism was embraced by many mid-twentieth-century historians. Lincoln himself had voiced a version of the "natural death" thesis during the 1840s, but by the 1850s he realized that trends ran strongly in the opposite direction.[9] Second, abolitionists would not be able to persuade slaveholders en masse to free their slaves. Earlier in the century, many abolitionists had hoped that "moral suasion" would be sufficient to end slavery;[10] by the 1850s, few abolitionists still believed this. Some abolitionists, including William Lloyd Garrison, advocated free-state secession from the Union—principally to end free-state citizens' moral complicity with slavery, but also because they believed that slavery would be fatally weakened by eliminating federal assistance in suppressing slave insurrections and free states' constitutional obligation to return fugitive slaves.[11] Losing these federal props would have created some difficulties for the slave states, but the frequency with which slave-state leaders themselves threatened secession if the federal government took even mild antislavery action indicates that they did not regard the loss of federal protection as fatal to slavery. Finally, the notion that Congress could ignore constitutional limitations and directly abolish slavery in the states without triggering civil war or, alternatively, that a civil war commenced in this fashion would lead quickly and easily to northern victory and the abolition of slavery, was likewise unrealistic.

Between these implausible scenarios for slavery's extinction, on the one side, and the all-too-realistic prospects of free states' full capitulation to slaveholders' demands or slave-state secession and protracted civil war, on the other side, Lincoln believed there existed a narrow, difficult, but not impossible path to the peaceful and democratic extinction of slavery. Readers can judge for themselves whether such hopes were plausible or implausible.

Let us suppose, however, that extinguishing slavery over the course of several decades, with compensation paid to slave owners, could have been accomplished. That policy could be condemned as unjust, for at least two reasons. First, slavery was so great an injustice that to allow it to continue for a single year, much less several decades, was unconscionable; tens of thousands of men and women would die in slavery who might have drawn their last breaths in freedom. Second, paying compensation to slave owners for the loss of their supposed human property stood justice on its head; justice demanded that freedmen and freedwomen be compensated for their years of unpaid labor. This understanding of postemancipation justice was expressed in the Civil War–era phrase "forty acres and a mule."[12] However, the demand for paying compensation to enslaved persons (rather than slave owners) dates back to the American Revolution, when an enslaved woman in Massachusetts argued that she had been "denied the enjoyment of one morsel of that immense wealth, a part whereof had been accumulated by her own industry, and the whole augmented by her servitude."[13] These justice arguments are powerful on their own terms. Lincoln himself emphasized the natural right of every person "to eat the bread she earns with her own hand," which would certainly justify compensation to formerly enslaved persons for their unpaid labor.[14] However, Lincoln also argued that justice required not only that one's intentions be just but also that one take responsibility for the consequences of one's actions, even if one intended the opposite: "By the *fruit* the tree is to be known."[15] By this standard, Lincoln's gradualist approach would be judged not by its accordance with pure justice (where his stance inevitably rates poorly in comparison with abolitionists' stirring call for immediate emancipation and compensation to former slaves) but by its likelihood of producing a relatively more just outcome under circumstances in which pure justice was out of reach and far more unjust outcomes (including the continued expansion and nationalization of slavery) were real and imminent dangers.

Lincoln understood that abolitionists played an essential role in shaping public opinion on slavery. But he believed that if the Republican Party moved too far in an abolitionist direction, it would suffer irreversible electoral defeat and thus increase the strength of those committed to nationalizing and perpetuating slavery. Precisely how far Lincoln could have moved toward the abolitionist position without endangering the Republican Party's electoral prospects in 1860 can be debated. But in my judgment, Lincoln was fundamentally correct: given the political circumstances of the late 1850s and through the 1860 election, if the Republican Party had taken a significantly more radical stance, its ensuing electoral defeat would have increased the probability of slavery's nationalization and perpetuation in the United States.

To express this judgment is not to criticize abolitionists who stood up for justice regardless of popular opinion, for that too was essential. Slavery was so deeply entrenched in the United States that it could not have been abolished, whether peacefully or violently, without the combined forces of uncompromising abolitionists, direct resistance by enslaved men and women, and "calculating" politicians like Lincoln seeking to assemble an antislavery electoral majority. To adapt Lincoln's phrase from the "House Divided" speech: all three of these "*strange, discordant, and even, hostile* elements" had an indispensable role to play in breaking the power of slavery.[16]

Cordon of Freedom

Lincoln and other Republicans articulated a variety of scenarios for the peaceful, constitutional extinction of slavery. James Oakes observes that antislavery politicians believed that if it came to civil war, "the federal government would certainly have the power to free slaves as a military necessity" (which later grounded Lincoln's Emancipation Proclamation). But before the war, many antislavery leaders believed the ultimate extinction of slavery could be accomplished gradually and peacefully. The strategy was to weaken slavery through containment and slow suffocation. Slavery, the argument went, was inherently aggressive and expansive. If it did not continually extend into new territories, it would contract and ultimately die. According to Oakes, the strategy was to "withdraw all federal support for slavery, surround the South with a 'cordon of freedom,'" and pressure slave states to abolish the institution on their own. "'Like a scorpion girt by fire,' antislavery activists argued, slavery would eventually sting itself to death." In 1855, for example, William Seward (at the time a US senator from New York) claimed that slavery could be abolished "without violence . . . by the agency of the ballot box." Once it was surrounded by the "cordon of freedom," slavery would die "like the scorpion, by the poison of its own sting" or "as a poisoned rat dies of rage in its own hole."[17]

Proslavery leaders agreed that slavery would ultimately die if it could not expand, and they understood the cordon of freedom strategy. "We must expand or perish," Robert Toombs insisted during Georgia's November 1860 secession debate. Northerners "have told us for twenty years that their object was to pen up slavery within its present limits—surround it with a border of free States, and like the scorpion surrounded by fire, they will make it sting itself to death." Another Georgia advocate of preemptive secession, Thomas R. R. Cobb, made explicit the racial assumptions underlying the "scorpion's sting" image: "My friends, delay is dangerous, for ere long you will be imprisoned by walls of free States all around you. Your increasing slaves will drive out the only race that can move—the whites—and the masters who still cling to their father's graves, will, like the scorpion in a ring of fire, but sting themselves to die." For preemptive secessionists, the notion that slavery could be abolished through a slow geographic squeeze was a very plausible one. Therefore, there was good reason to secede before Lincoln and the Republicans had the opportunity to commence the experiment.[18]

The "slavery must expand or die" theory was not rooted exclusively in economic imperatives, such as maintaining profit margins and keeping slave property values high. Such economic considerations were certainly important, and high profits in particular helped reconcile slave owners and slave states to the ever-present fear of slave insurrection in a way that more modest profits might not have.[19] But in the 1850s there was still much room for slavery's profitable expansion in existing slave states such as Mississippi, Louisiana, and Texas, which contained extensive tracts of undeveloped land well suited to future slave plantations.[20] Yet proslavery leaders had an enormous *political* and *ideological* stake in expanding slavery northwest into Kansas (and beyond) or, if blocked in that direction, southward into the Caribbean, where they hoped to acquire Cuba as the first of several new slave states.[21] Every new slave state, even one formed out of a territory (like Kansas) where no one expected slavery to become the dominant mode of production, meant two additional slavery-friendly US senators and at least one additional slavery-friendly US House member, thus bolstering the political power of all slaveholders and all slave states at a time when slavery was increasingly subject to political attack. If Kansas entered the Union with a slave-state constitution, this would protect slavery at its most vulnerable flank: where slave states bordered free states, which permitted dangerous public expressions of antislavery opinion.[22]

Besides the economic, political, and ideological motivation for expanding slavery, there was an important demographic consideration: a growing slave population confined to a fixed or even shrinking geographic area would become increasingly dangerous.[23] This fear was central to Cobb's warning, noted earlier, that if slavery were "imprisoned" by a wall of free states, many white southerners would evacuate the slave states, leaving a shrinking number of white slave owners to confront an expanding and potentially violent population of enslaved Blacks. Under such circumstances (the cordon of freedom theory held), slaveholders themselves would ultimately consent to the extinction of slavery as the best way out of an untenable situation. Slaveholders, however, were unlikely to view such a fear-driven outcome as either morally or constitutionally legitimate.

Thus, the idea that slavery could be gradually squeezed out of existence, without disunion or civil war, was taken seriously by leaders on both sides of the slavery divide. One might reasonably doubt that slavery could have been extinguished this way in the United States. But it is important to underscore *why* such doubts are well-founded: not because the cordon of freedom strategy was unrealistic but because proslavery leaders fully understood the strategy, judged it to be realistic, and settled on preemptive secession as a countermeasure. Many antislavery leaders, for their part, too readily assumed that the prospect of wartime military emancipation would deter southerners from acting on their frequently voiced secession threats.

Moreover, the cordon of freedom strategy did not resolve the status of formerly enslaved persons after emancipation. Would they become full citizens with voting rights? Would they remain in the territory, exercising economic liberties but not political rights? Would they be colonized to some other part of the world? Such questions, on which antislavery leaders themselves were sharply divided, could be sidestepped during the early stages of implementing the cordon of freedom strategy. But if those early stages were successful in weakening the institution of slavery, it would become increasingly difficult to postpone questions about the future status of emancipated persons. It is conceivable that, if the slave states had remained in the Union rather than seceding and initiating civil war, Republicans' cordon of freedom strategy might have succeeded in its early stages but floundered later because of racial fear and intraparty differences.

In sum, the strategy of abolishing slavery through a long, slow majoritarian squeeze involved many difficulties and uncertainties. But one thing should be clear: peacefully and democratically halting the expansion of slavery (the principal plank of the Republican platform and the first stage of the cordon of freedom strategy) would not have been a toothless policy. Neither Republicans nor secessionists took the dismissive view (voiced by some historians) that halting the spread of slavery was a symbolic gesture devoid of practical significance, a mere vote-winning ploy, an empty dispute about "an imaginary Negro in an impossible place."[24]

Slavery-Shrinking Policies

Neither in 1858 nor in 1860 did Lincoln campaign on his own personal image, as has become standard practice today. He campaigned for the Senate and stood for election as president as a representative of a recently formed political party committed to halting the expansion of slavery and ultimately extinguishing it. Both supporters and opponents recognized that if voters elected Lincoln president, they would also legitimize the Republican Party and likely ensure its long-term future. Lincoln was fifty-two years old when he was inaugurated as president. He certainly would not have been president long enough, and probably would not have lived long enough, to witness the complete extinction of slavery accomplished peacefully and gradually. What mattered most was what the Republican Party stood for and what action it would take over a timeline extending beyond Lincoln's presidency and life span.

Moreover, if the seceding states had returned peacefully to the Union, as Lincoln urged them to, and if the Democratic Party had mended the internal divisions that contributed to Lincoln's election in 1860, then probably the most Lincoln and his party could have hoped to accomplish in his first term would have been to halt the spread of slavery to newly organized territories and to appoint Supreme Court justices who upheld the power of Congress to restrict slavery in areas under federal jurisdiction. Given the long winning streak enjoyed by proslavery forces during the 1850s, halting and reversing this political momentum would have been a difficult and significant accomplishment for a first-term Republican president. Furthermore, given Lincoln's analysis of the dynamics of public opinion (see chapter 5), these initial antislavery steps needed to be endorsed by the public in subsequent elections, which in turn would prepare Americans for additional and stronger antislavery actions. Electoral endorsements of this kind would accrue to Republican candidates at many levels, not just the president. Thus, every antislavery step depended not only on Lincoln's individual actions and views but also on what other Republican leaders thought and did.

For this reason, we should widen our perspective and describe the full range of Republican scenarios for the ultimate extinction of slavery. Some proposals were more radical than those publicly endorsed by Lincoln. His stances generally fell in the center of the Republican spectrum—not by accident but by design, for he worked to ensure that both radical and conservative elements of the Republican coalition stayed on board. What distinguished Lincoln from more radical members of his party were not fundamental differences of moral principle but his deliberate efforts to create a stable and coherent middle position within a new and deeply fractious party and his careful attention to establishing the wider democratic and constitutional legitimacy of the cordon of freedom policy on which Republicans of nearly all stripes agreed.

Proslavery leaders argued that slavery was a national institution that should be protected everywhere the American flag flew and that restrictions on slavery were merely local. Republicans (Lincoln included) insisted on the reverse: that freedom was national and slavery local.[25] They conceded that the antebellum Constitution prevented the federal government from directly abolishing slavery in the states where it currently existed. But once the principle was established that slavery was legitimized *only* where state law specifically authorized it, a whole range of policies designed to weaken and ultimately destroy slavery through a long, slow squeeze became imaginable. All of the following positions (drawn in part from Oakes's summary in *The Scorpion's Sting*) were advocated by at least some Republicans and many of them by Lincoln himself:[26]

1. Prohibiting slavery in all US territories that were not yet states, based on Congress's constitutionally authorized power "to make all needful Rules and Regulations respecting the Territory or other Property belonging to the United States." All Republicans, from the most radical to the most conservative, endorsed this position.
2. Restricting or prohibiting slavery on US military bases, including those located within the boundaries of slave states.
3. Using the US Navy to protect freedom on the high seas and effectively suppress the coastal slave trade.
4. Abolishing slavery in the District of Columbia, which, as the nation's capital, conveyed an important symbolic message with respect to slavery. (The slave trade in the District of Columbia had already been abolished as part of the Compromise of 1850.)
5. Restricting, or perhaps even prohibiting, the interstate slave trade, on the basis of Congress's Article I, section 8 power to regulate commerce "among the several states."
6. Refusing to employ the power of the federal government to recapture fugitive slaves—in other words, repealing the Fugitive Slave Act of 1850. Enforcement would therefore be exclusively local, which meant it would be weak or nonexistent in northern states.
7. Refusing to admit any new slave states to the Union.
8. Ultimately amending the Constitution to restrict or abolish slavery even in states where it had long existed. If several new free states and no new slave states were admitted to the Union, and if some

border states such as Maryland and Missouri decided to cut loose from an increasingly troublesome and unprofitable institution, the free states would eventually reach the three-fourths threshold necessary to amend the Constitution. As Oakes describes this scenario: "the number of free states would grow steadily and the number of slave states inexorably decline, shifting the balance of power in national politics from slavery to freedom. All it would take was a shift from slavery to freedom in half a dozen states to make an abolition amendment feasible."[27]

As for this final and most radical of the Republican proposals, Lincoln himself never publicly advocated an abolition amendment of this kind before the war. On the contrary, as he said in his August 21, 1858, debate with Stephen Douglas and repeated in his first inaugural address on March 4, 1861, "I have no purpose, directly or indirectly, to interfere with the institution of slavery in the States where it exists. I believe I have no lawful right to do so, and I have no inclination to do so."[28] Nevertheless everyone on both sides of the slavery issue understood that the probability of an amendment of this kind would rise significantly as soon as Lincoln and the Republicans blocked the flow of new slave states into the Union. Georgia secessionist Thomas L. Benning argued in November 1860 that the western territories would ultimately form twenty new states, all of which would be free states if Republicans restricted the expansion of slavery. Meanwhile, Delaware, Maryland, and Kentucky would eventually join the ranks of free states. "When that time comes, and indeed long before that time comes, the North—the Black Republican party . . . will have it in its power . . . to amend the Constitution, and take what power it pleases upon the subject of slavery."[29] Lincoln might not live to see such an amendment, but by restricting the expansion of slavery, he would accomplish the first essential step, and over time, his party would finish the job.

On some of the other Republican proposals listed above, Lincoln kept his options open: he denied that he was "pledged" to do many of these things, but neither did he pledge *not* to do them. In his second debate with Douglas (August 27, 1858), in response to the latter's interrogatories, Lincoln denied being "pledged" to the abolition of slavery in the District of Columbia. But he insisted that Congress had the power to do so, and he acknowledged that he "should be exceedingly glad to see slavery abolished in the District of Columbia." He proceeded to lay out the specific conditions on which he would support abolition there: "*First,* that the abolition should be gradual. *Second,* that it should be on a vote of the majority of qualified voters in the District, and *third,* that compensation should be made to unwilling owners." In this way, Lincoln concluded, Congress could "sweep from our Capital that foul blot upon our nation."[30]

Lincoln believed that the Constitution required paying compensation to "unwilling owners" when enslaved persons were emancipated. The Fifth Amendment stipulates that private property can be taken (from unwilling owners, if necessary) for "public use," but only if "just compensation" is paid to the owner. Lincoln held that abolishing slavery in the District of Columbia advanced a legitimate public purpose, but it had to follow the constitutional rules governing the taking of private property for public purposes.[31]

In his replies to Douglas's queries, Lincoln likewise stated, "I do not stand pledged to the prohibition of the slave-trade between the different States."[32] But neither did he pledge *not* to restrict the interstate slave trade. Nor does he appear to have doubted that restricting the interstate slave trade fell within the constitutional powers of Congress (a stance later reinforced in his Cooper Institute address). Slave-state leaders considered legislation of this kind an imminent possibility under a Republican-controlled federal government. Georgia secessionist Cobb cited as grounds for immediate secession the fact that "the inter-State Slave Trade is within the letter of the Constitution"; Lincoln and the Republicans could target it immediately, without waiting for a constitutional amendment specifically authorizing them to do so.[33] Lincoln's own follow-up remarks on abolition of the interstate slave trade would have confirmed Cobb's fears. Lincoln said he would "not be in favor of the exercise of that power unless upon some conservative principle . . . akin to what I have said in relation to the abolition of slavery in the District of Columbia."[34] Lincoln's "unless" qualification suggests that he had already considered how restrictions of some kind on the interstate slave trade might contribute to the gradual abolition of slavery itself. But if so, he was reluctant to announce that position too loudly, for any proposal to prohibit the interstate slave trade was political dynamite. Given the political climate of the 1850s, such a proposal almost certainly would have triggered slave-state secession. For this reason, many antislavery activists who were significantly more radical than Lincoln hesitated to publicly call for banning the interstate slave trade, even though they too believed Congress had the constitutional power to do so.[35]

In his Cooper Institute address (February 1860), Lincoln reported that in the early decades of the republic, Congress had enacted legislation restricting (but not banning) the domestic slave trade. In the 1804 act incorporating the Louisiana Purchase territory, although Congress did not prohibit slavery, it "did interfere with it—take control of it" in a "marked and extensive way." In addition to banning the importation of slaves from "foreign parts," Congress prohibited the importation of enslaved persons from any US state if those persons "had been imported into the United States since the first day of May, 1798." The act stipulated that "no slave should be carried into [the Louisiana territory], except by the owner, and for his own use as a settler; the penalty in all the cases being a fine upon the violator of the law, and freedom to the slave."[36] If this provision of the act had been enforced (in practice, it went unenforced), it would have restricted the domestic slave trade, for it limited slaveholders' power to sell or transport enslaved persons from a US state where slavery was legal to a US territory where slavery was also legal.[37] The precedent was not precisely parallel to restricting the slave trade between two slave states, but it was close enough to make such an extension imaginable. Lincoln thus made it clear that Congress was originally understood to have legitimate power to restrict the domestic slave trade.

Lincoln likewise denied that he stood "pledged against the admission of any more slave States into the Union." Here he made his thinking clear: personally, he would be glad to never admit another slave state. And he considered it highly unlikely that residents of a newly admitted state would subsequently vote to introduce slavery if slavery had been "kept out of the Territories during the territorial existence," such voters having been "uninfluenced by the actual presence of the institution among them." However, should the people of a free territory do something so "extraordinary" as to "adopt a slave Constitution" at the time of statehood, Lincoln would consider himself and his party obliged to admit that state into the Union.[38] But he was confident that if slavery was banned throughout the territorial stage, Republicans would never face this dilemma.

Conversely, Lincoln would have voted against the admission of Cuba as a new slave state. Proslavery leaders had their eyes on annexing the island, with Stephen Douglas's active encouragement.[39] But neither Cuba nor any other territories in the southward-expanding slave empire—which slaveholders were demanding as compensation for "losing"

Kansas and Nebraska—would have been free of slavery during the pre-statehood stage.

Lincoln was not among those Republicans calling for full repeal of the Fugitive Slave Act: "I do not now, nor ever did, stand in favor of the unconditional repeal of the Fugitive Slave Act." Return of fugitive slaves was a clearly expressed constitutional obligation, although many northerners had to "crucify their feelings" to fulfill it. Lincoln also recognized during the secession crisis that it was futile to insist that slave states respect their constitutional obligations unless free states also did so. Yet even here, Lincoln added qualifications designed to undermine the long-term viability of slavery. In his inaugural address, after acknowledging the constitutional obligation, Lincoln added that "any law upon this subject" ought to include "all the safeguards of liberty known in civilized and humane jurisprudence, so that a free man be not, in any case, surrendered as a slave"; it ought to ensure that "the citizens of each State shall be entitled to all privileges and immunities of citizens in the several States."[40] Lincoln's insistence on safeguards to prevent free Blacks from being forced into slavery was rooted in personal experience. In 1855 he and his law partner William Herndon intervened to rescue a young man from Springfield who had been illegally imprisoned and sold into slavery in New Orleans.[41]

Lincoln thus signaled that any fugitive slave law he would accept would have to guarantee persons suspected of being fugitive slaves the right to a fair trial, including the presumption of innocence and the right to testify in their own defense. He also affirmed that free persons of African descent could be citizens of the United States (which slave-state leaders denied) and thus were protected by the Constitution's privileges and immunities clause. These commitments stood in stark contrast to the actual provisions of the Fugitive Slave Act of 1850, which, as David Potter observes, "left all free negroes with inadequate safeguards against claims that they were slaves, and it exposed them to the danger of kidnapping."[42]

Lincoln conceded that Congress could not constitutionally abolish slavery in states where it already existed. But he argued that Congress could prohibit slavery in federal territories that were not yet states under its Article IV, section 3 power to "make all needful Rules and Regulations" for the territories. As noted earlier, he believed residents of a territory whose political institutions were "uninfluenced by the actual presence of the institution among them" would be unlikely to introduce slavery upon statehood. As more free territories entered the Union as free states, the slave states, as a bloc, would lose the rough political equality they had long enjoyed in the Union, including their veto power in the Senate. Banning slavery in the territories would magnify free states' future power to enact antislavery measures of other kinds.

The cordon of freedom that Lincoln and other Republicans envisioned would not have extinguished slavery quickly. But once enacted, such measures would transform slavery from a very profitable institution into an increasingly unprofitable one. For example, the value of slave property, by far the greatest economic asset in the southern economy, would immediately begin to fall as enslaved persons became riskier to transport and more difficult to sell. Turning slavery from an economic benefit into an economic burden was a critical step toward its ultimate extinction.

Lincoln was unpersuasive, however, when he insisted in his 1858 debates with Douglas, and again in his inaugural address, that "I have no purpose, directly *or indirectly*, to interfere with the institution of slavery in the States where it exists."[43] Lincoln could plausibly deny any intention to directly interfere with slavery in the states, but even this assurance required an understanding of the distinction between direct and indirect interference that differed from slaveholders' perceptions. Many slaveholders regarded prohibition in the territories and abolition in the District of Columbia as *direct* interference with slavery in the states. Suppose we reject slaveholders' expansive understanding of direct interference. The policies Lincoln envisioned to halt slavery's expansion constituted at least indirect interference, for he openly acknowledged his aim to halt the expansion of slavery, abolish it in the nation's capital, and mark it publicly as an injustice to be removed, not a morally neutral practice to be tolerated forever. Lincoln's denial that he intended "indirect" interference with slavery was not an act of deception. It revealed instead that each side sometimes understood words so differently that they talked past each other. If civil war over slavery was inevitable, as many historians believe, such mutual incomprehension was likely a contributing factor.

Moral and Constitutional Legitimacy

The differences between Lincoln's vision of ultimate extinction and that of other Republican leaders were not dramatic. Lincoln was more inclined than other Republicans to keep his tactical options open and his timing flexible. He also understood more clearly than most how enormously difficult even the first step would be: halting the *expansion* of slavery.

Lincoln differed significantly from some other Republicans, however, in his greater efforts to establish the moral and constitutional legitimacy of the cordon of freedom strategy. Lincoln never used dehumanizing metaphors, such as a scorpion stinging itself to death or a rat dying of rage in its own poisoned hole, to describe the gradual extinction of slavery. The alacrity with which defenders of slavery publicized Republican utterances of this kind is revealing. Enemies at war typically propagate dehumanizing images of the other side. But Republicans' hope to extinguish slavery *without* civil war depended on somehow reconciling white southerners to slavery's gradual disappearance. In this respect, cruel rhetoric that failed to recognize slaveholders' humanity—or that of enslaved persons, who would have been trapped in the same poisoned hole—was counterproductive.[44] As Lincoln remarked in another context, "If you would win a man to your cause, *first* convince him that you are his sincere friend." Lincoln's rhetoric toward the South—"We are not enemies, but friends. We must not be enemies"—respected this common humanity, though he too failed to dissuade secessionists.[45]

The scorpion's sting and poisoned rat images also reinforced white southerners' apocalyptic visions of a postemancipation race war. Slaveholders had long struggled to reconcile the enormous profits of slavery with its demographic dangers, and Republican policies threatened to eliminate the "safety valve" of western expansion. As the proportion of enslaved persons within a state continued to rise, and as nonslaveholding white southerners abandoned slave states, the slaveholders who remained faced escalating economic insecurity and physical danger. As Oakes describes the scenario: enslaved persons, "restless and increasingly anxious for their freedom, now pent up and concentrated in the cotton belt, would become rebellious and even revolutionary." Under such circumstances (according to cordon of freedom theory), slaveholders would be "awakened to the realization that their own future prosperity could only be ensured by shifting to free labor," at which point "the slave states would abolish slavery on their own."[46]

Several elements of this picture correspond with Lincoln's thinking. He too favored policies designed to make slavery less profitable, and he viewed a shift from slave labor to free labor as ultimately in everyone's interest, including former slaveholders. But on one critical point Lincoln's approach was distinctive: he did not consider it constructive to multiply white southerners' already significant fears. As noted in chapter 6, Lincoln knew that many white Americans, in free states as well as slave states, assumed (falsely, in his view) that Black Americans could survive and thrive only at the expense of white Americans. That fear was captured in the image of two shipwreck survivors clinging to a plank, each trying to push the other off. Unless such fears were allayed and the assumptions underlying them refuted ("the plank is large enough for both"), increasing misery and danger in the slave states were unlikely to persuade slaveholders to shift to free labor. Instead, such fears would fuel slaveholders' frequently voiced scenario of a race war ending in the annihilation of one race or the other. Paying compensation to slaveholders when enslaved persons were emancipated would (Lincoln hoped) counteract the fear and economic distress that might otherwise provoke white southerners to target Blacks with violence.

In the background of the cordon of freedom strategy for peacefully extinguishing slavery lay a powerful, high-stakes fallback: military emancipation if the slave states seceded and invited civil war rather than submit to peaceful, constitutional antislavery measures enacted by Congress (e.g., prohibiting slavery in the territories). The arguments legitimizing wartime military emancipation dated to the Revolutionary War, when the British emancipated and evacuated thousands of American slaves as a war tactic (even though the British Empire still practiced slavery and participated in the transatlantic slave trade). In response, some American revolutionaries advocated liberating slaves who consented to fight for American independence. The constitutional arguments supporting emancipation as an act of war power were later developed by John Quincy Adams, among others. According to Oakes, by the eve of the Civil War, wartime emancipation had become "a conventional proposition" accepted in principle "by radicals and conservatives alike." Wartime emancipation was not Republicans' aim, but it reassured them "that the South would never secede because that meant war and with war came military emancipation."[47]

Oakes reports that during the "secession winter" (the period between Lincoln's election on November 6, 1860, and his inauguration on March 4, 1861), "threats of military emancipation sprang up everywhere in the Republican speeches and editorials."[48] But Lincoln himself did not threaten military emancipation. In his inaugural address he

248 | CHAPTER 7

warned about "the momentous issue of civil war" but did not dwell on its possible consequences.[49] He certainly recognized that threatening military emancipation made it even more unlikely that the slave states would return to the Union. He also recognized that, despite tough talk about military emancipation in northern newspapers, there was little political support for an abolitionist war in March 1861—even if he wanted one, which he did not. He was determined that war, if it came, would be fought over the principle of respecting the results of free, constitutionally conducted elections—the principle that public issues must be decided by "peaceful ballots," not "bloody bullets." When abolishing slavery became an official war aim on January 1, 1863, it did not replace Lincoln's original aim of saving popular self-government but merged with it.

Lincoln believed that halting the spread of slavery and peacefully putting it on the road to extinction required deliberate action by Congress as the agent of a national antislavery majority. Only Congress had the constitutional authority to ban slavery in the territories—the indispensable first step. Only Congress could abolish slavery in the District of Columbia. Congress was also better positioned than state legislatures to make funds available for compensated emancipation. The later stages of the gradual abolition process would require antislavery action at the state level, but this would occur under political, economic, and legal circumstances already conditioned by congressional antislavery action. This entire process had two critical prerequisites: first, a persuasive argument that Congress possessed the constitutional authority to decide the status of slavery in the territories; and second, that Congress be willing to exercise such authority and ban slavery there.

Congress's authority over slavery in the territories had suffered a double hit during the 1850s: the Kansas-Nebraska Act (1854), whereby Congress denied itself power over slavery in newly formed territories (transferring responsibility to territorial legislatures, the federal judiciary, or both); and the Supreme Court's *Dred Scott* ruling (1857), which held (among other things) that neither Congress nor a territorial legislature could prohibit slavery in federal territories. But even in the early decades of the republic, when congressional authority to regulate slavery in the territories was widely accepted, Congress was unwilling or unable to exercise that authority to effectively halt the westward spread of slavery. Therefore, Lincoln's vision for the gradual extinction of slavery required both reestablishing the constitutional jurisdiction over slavery that Congress had exercised in the early republic and electing members of Congress who were willing to take much stronger antislavery action in the territories than Congress had ever taken before.

Such action had to be strong enough to fundamentally alter slavery's future but not so aggressive as to drive slave states to secession and civil war. Lincoln knew that slaveholders and slave-state leaders would not be persuaded in the foreseeable future to change their minds on slavery. But he hoped appeals to a shared Constitution, a shared political tradition, and shared respect for free elections might persuade them not to secede in response to antislavery legislation enacted in accordance with that shared Constitution. Effectively navigating this obstacle course would be extremely difficult and, in the end, proved impossible. But only by engaging with it can we reconstruct Lincoln's political and constitutional thinking before Fort Sumter irreversibly altered the circumstances. Moreover, only by taking seriously the prospect of gradual abolition can we understand the urgency secessionists felt to remove their states from the Union before Lincoln was inaugurated as president.

Constitutional Powers of Congress: The Cooper Institute Address

Article IV, section 2 of the Constitution stipulates that "the Congress shall have power to dispose of and make all needful rules and regulations respecting the territory or other property belonging to the United States." The clause did not specify whether slavery was subject to these "needful rules and regulations." Assuming that Congress did have jurisdiction of some type over slavery in the territories, the text did not clarify *which* slavery regulations were permissible or impermissible. In his inaugural address Lincoln, referring to this clause, asked: "*May* Congress prohibit slavery in the territories? The Constitution does not expressly say. *Must* Congress protect slavery in the territories? The Constitution does not expressly say." These constitutional questions were flash points for secession. Lincoln had publicly argued that Congress possessed the constitutional authority to *prohibit* slavery in the territories, while slaveholders insisted that Congress was constitutionally obliged to *protect* slavery in the territories. The 1860 platform of the Breckinridge-Lane faction of the Democratic Party held "that it is the duty of the Federal Government, in all its departments, to protect, when necessary, the rights of persons and property in the Territories, and wherever else its constitutional authority extends."[50] Here, "rights of persons and property" unmistakably referred to the supposed right of slave owners to hold enslaved persons as property everywhere the federal government had jurisdiction.

The passage in the inaugural address about important constitutional questions not "expressly" answered in the constitutional text led directly to Lincoln's defense of majority rule: "From questions of this class spring all our constitutional controversies, and we divide upon them into majorities and minorities."[51] The open-endedness of the constitutional text, even on points of great importance, was not, in Lincoln's judgment, a flaw in the Constitution. Instead, it gave substance to the people's right to govern themselves. In what follows, I examine the role of majority discretion—that is, the legitimate authority of a majority (in this case, a majority in Congress) to decide an important question either way—in Lincoln's constitutional thought. His reasoning differed dramatically from the proslavery stance that Congress was obliged to protect slavery in the territories. It also differed in subtle but important ways from the antislavery constitutional argument, best represented by Salmon Chase of Ohio, that Congress was constitutionally obliged to prohibit slavery in the territories. Lincoln's antislavery constitutionalism, which might appear weaker than Chase's, was in many respects stronger. Lincoln's interpretation was better rooted in history and less ideologically partisan, and it more persuasively grounded Congress's authority to determine national policy toward slavery.

Lincoln's historical narrative in the Cooper Institute address sought to demonstrate two things: that the framers of the Constitution understood Congress to have the authority to restrict slavery in the territories; and that the framers spoke and acted with respect to slavery in such a way as to mark it as "*an evil not to be extended, but to be tolerated and protected only because of and so far as its actual presence among us makes that toleration and protection a necessity.*"[52] On the first of these claims, which concerned the discretionary power of Congress (and where Lincoln made his principal contribution as a constitutional historian), his argument was persuasive. Lincoln's second claim, that the framers tolerated and protected slavery only where "its actual presence" made it "a necessity" (which was an article of faith among other Republicans, including Chase), was more open to dispute.

Commentaries on the Cooper Institute address often emphasize the second claim: that members of the founding generation regarded slavery as an evil, restricted it wherever they could, and tolerated it only where it was impossible to do otherwise. The founding generation, in short, had already placed slavery on the path of ultimate extinction; the Republican Party was simply continuing that work.[53] This was an overly generous construction of the founding generation's actual record on slavery.

Lincoln's more persuasive argument in the Cooper Institute address, and the one most closely connected with his defense of majority rule in the inaugural address, was that nothing in the text of the Constitution, nor in the understanding of those who framed that Constitution, "forbade Congress to prohibit slavery in the federal territory."[54] The negative form of this proposition is significant. Lincoln did not claim that either the constitutional text or the understanding of those who framed it specifically *obligated* Congress to prohibit slavery in the territories. He argued instead that neither the text of the Constitution nor the understanding of those who framed it *exempted* slavery from the "rules and regulations" that Article IV authorized Congress to make with respect to the territories. Phrased positively, Lincoln held that Congress had the discretionary authority to act in at least three different ways with respect to slavery in the territories: to tolerate it, to prohibit it, or to restrict it without prohibiting it. In summary: neither the Constitution nor its meaning as understood by those who drafted and ratified it prevented a congressional majority, acting in accordance with its own judgment, from restricting or prohibiting slavery in the territories.

Lincoln opened the address by quoting Stephen Douglas, who had declared in 1859, "Our fathers, when they framed the Government under which we live, understood this question [whether the federal government was prohibited from banning slavery in the territories] just as well, and even better, than we do now." Douglas argued that the framers intended the Constitution to prohibit the federal government from exercising "control as to slavery" in the territories. Lincoln proposed to establish the opposite: that the framers *did not* intend the Constitution to prohibit the federal government from exercising control over slavery in the territories; on the contrary, the framers clearly understood Congress to have authority to determine the status of slavery in the territories and acted in accordance with that understanding on several occasions. He made it clear that he did not treat the framers' own understanding of the Constitution as final and beyond challenge:

I do not mean to say we are bound to follow implicitly in whatever our fathers did. To do so, would be to discard all the lights of current experience—to reject all progress—all improvement. What I do say is, that if we would supplant the opinions and policy of our fathers in any case, we should do so upon evidence so conclusive, and arguments so clear, that even their great authority, fairly considered and weighed, cannot stand; and most surely not in a case whereof we ourselves declare [as Douglas did] they understood the question better than we.

In short: one may disagree with the framers and present an alternative argument. But if one invokes their authority in support of one's own view, one must get the facts straight. The Cooper Institute address was the fruit of Lincoln's own extensive research into the voting records and public statements of the thirty-nine men who signed the Constitution.[55]

Lincoln acknowledged that "the question of federal control of slavery in the territories, seems not to have been directly before the Convention which framed the original Constitution." But some of the delegates to the 1787 convention had served in the Continental Congress when it enacted the Northwest Ordinance. Other convention delegates were elected to Congress after the Constitution was ratified, and in that capacity they cast votes on federal legislation affecting slavery in the territories. Lincoln's research demonstrated that twenty-three of the thirty-nine framers, as members of the Continental Congress and/or as members of the US Congress, voted on federal legislation (or, in George Washington's case, signed legislation into law) that either prohibited slavery in a territory or restricted it in some manner short of prohibition. Twenty-one of the twenty-three voted at least once in favor of slavery restriction, indicating that "in their understanding," nothing in the "proper division between local and federal authority, or anything in the Constitution they had made themselves . . . forbade the Federal Government to control as to slavery in the federal territories." Two of the twenty-three voted against such legislation, but as Lincoln pointed out, the record does not indicate whether they opposed it as unconstitutional or for some other reason. Lincoln also observed that, of the sixteen framers who did not have occasion to cast votes on slavery in the territories, several (including Benjamin Franklin, Alexander Hamilton, and Gouverneur Morris) were outspoken critics of slavery in general and thus "would probably have acted just as the twenty-three did."[56]

The legislation Lincoln examined included the Northwest Ordinance passed by the Continental Congress in 1787 and the 1789 legislation enacted by the First Congress reconfirming and enforcing that slavery prohibition, which applied to territories comprising the future states of Ohio, Indiana, Michigan, Illinois, and Wisconsin. The First Congress's reconfirmation of the Northwest Ordinance's slavery prohibition was especially significant, Lincoln noted, because the 1789 legislation was introduced before, and passed after, the First Congress voted in favor of the Bill of Rights. This indicated that a majority of the First Congress (many of whom had been delegates to the federal convention) saw no incompatibility between slavery prohibition in the territories and the Bill of Rights. Thus, both Roger Taney's assertion in the *Dred Scott* opinion that the federal prohibition of slavery in the territories violated the Fifth Amendment guarantee against deprivation of "life, liberty, or property without due process of law" and Stephen Douglas's claim that congressional power over slavery in the federal territories violated the Tenth Amendment were at odds with the understanding of the members of the First Congress who passed both amendments.[57]

Besides the Northwest Ordinance and its reconfirmation, Lincoln examined three other laws affecting slavery in the territories on which some framers of the Constitution cast votes. The 1798 act organizing the Mississippi territory did not prohibit slavery in that territory, which had been ceded to the United States by the state of Georgia on the condition that the federal government not ban slavery there. However, the 1798 act gave Congress "control" over slavery in the territory by outlawing the importation of enslaved persons from foreign countries, authorizing legal penalties for violations of that ban, and "giving freedom to slaves so brought." The 1804 act organizing the vast Louisiana Purchase territories—which had not been ceded by any state, thus giving Congress a freer hand—likewise did not prohibit slavery there, even though Congress arguably could have done so, since slavery was firmly established only in New Orleans. But as Lincoln emphasized, Congress did "interfere" with slavery and "take control of it—in a marked and extensive way" by including a provision "that no slave should be carried into [the territory], except by the owner, and for his own use as a settler; the penalty in all cases being a fine upon the violator of the law, and freedom to the slave."[58] Don E. Fehrenbacher observes that this restriction on the domestic slave trade "was the strongest ever imposed on any part of the South before the Civil

War," but it was "highly unpopular among local residents, it lasted only a year and was probably never enforced." Fehrenbacher also notes: "It seems incredible that no one made an attempt to exclude slavery from the northern part of the Louisiana Purchase as an offset to allowing it in the southern part."[59] Nevertheless, as Lincoln pointed out, the restrictions on the domestic slave trade in the Louisiana bill demonstrated that Congress, including the two original framers serving at the time, perceived nothing in the Constitution that prevented Congress from restricting slavery in the territories.[60] Recall that during the 1858 debates, Douglas pressed Lincoln on whether he was "pledged" to prohibit the interstate slave trade. Lincoln denied being "pledged" to do so but indicated his willingness to support interstate restrictions of some kind as being conducive to the gradual abolition of slavery. His Cooper Institute address suggests he had no *constitutional* reservations about using Congress's authority over interstate commerce to restrict the domestic slave trade.

When the Missouri controversy erupted in 1819–20, only two of the thirty-nine original framers remained in Congress: Rufus King (originally from Massachusetts, now of New York), who consistently supported all slavery prohibitions, and Charles Pinckney of South Carolina, who voted against all slavery prohibitions. In the Cooper Institute address, Lincoln described the Missouri Compromise only briefly and did not emphasize its supposedly "sacred" character, as he had in his October 1854 speech on the Kansas-Nebraska Act. Perhaps because the Missouri Compromise was principally the work of a new generation (and the two remaining framers voted on opposite sides), Lincoln did not represent this episode as strong evidence of the framers' understanding of slavery in the territories.[61]

In sum: Lincoln made two principal arguments in the Cooper Institute address: that the framers understood Congress to have authority over slavery in the territories, and that they restricted slavery wherever it was possible to do so. The second claim is weak. In the years immediately following ratification of the Constitution, these same framers, as members of Congress, did little to slow the expansion of slavery in southern territories. Nevertheless, Congress did legislate on slavery in territories both north and south in these early years. In Lincoln's view, these precedents supported the authority of Congress to prohibit slavery in all federal territories, regardless of latitude.

Chase and Lincoln as Antislavery Constitutional Theorists

We can better grasp what was distinctive about Lincoln's constitutional argument in the Cooper Institute address by comparing it with Salmon Chase's antislavery constitutionalism, to which Lincoln and all Republicans were indebted. Chase pioneered a political-constitutional approach to slavery that differed from that of both Garrisonian abolitionists, who condemned the Constitution altogether as a "covenant with death," and certain anti-Garrisonian radical abolitionists, who claimed the Constitution authorized the abolition of slavery everywhere, including in long-established slave states. Chase instead argued for the "absolute and unqualified divorce of the federal government from slavery," the "denationalization of slavery," and the principle "freedom national, slavery sectional."[62] To "divorce" the federal government from slavery meant that in areas under the exclusive control of the states, slavery would be left alone, but in areas under federal jurisdiction (including the territories, the District of Columbia, and US ships in international waters, as well as foreign and interstate commerce), the federal government was not only authorized but also positively obligated to oppose slavery. In Chase's words, "Congress can neither create nor continue slavery anywhere, & in all places under the exclusive jurisdiction of Congress slavery is constitutionally impossible."[63] This divorce between the federal government and slavery, Chase and others argued, was precisely the one intended by the framers of the Constitution who, even as they "included securities for slavery in the text" of the document, studiously avoided using the words "slave" and "slavery" and "inserted their true libertarian aspirations into the Northwest Ordinance." By separating the federal government from slavery and enlisting the government for antislavery purposes wherever it had jurisdiction, slavery would be prevented from spreading, and states would be motivated to abolish slavery on their own. But (Chase and others claimed) the expectations of the framers had subsequently been "sadly betrayed" by an aggressive "Slave Power" that captured the federal government and used it aggressively to expand and perpetuate slavery.[64]

Among the conclusions Chase drew from this "absolute and unqualified divorce" between the federal government and slavery were (1) that Congress was authorized to ban slavery in federal territories, (2) that Congress was constitutionally prohibited from legalizing slavery in the territories, (3) that Congress was constitutionally obliged to prohibit slavery in the territories, and (4) that any federal fugitive slave law was unconstitutional because it breached the constitutionally prescribed divorce between slavery and the federal government. Slave states' own fugitive slave laws had no binding force outside their boundaries. In this way, Chase effectively repudiated the constitutional obligation (Article IV, section 2) to return a person held to "service or labor" who had fled to another state. Because slavery "can have no existence beyond the territorial limits of the state which sanctions it," Chase argued, "the moment a slave comes into [a free state] he acquires a legal right to freedom."[65]

For Chase, this divorce between the federal government and slavery was not merely a symbolic stance; it was essential for the goal of gradually squeezing slavery out of existence, as he believed the framers expected and intended. Chase interpreted the Constitution's language as broadly and flexibly as possible wherever it could be used for antislavery purposes and as narrowly as possible wherever it functioned to protect slavery. In this sense, Chase's rule of construction was the mirror image of the approach taken by proslavery constitutional theorists such as John C. Calhoun, who construed with enormous breadth the federal government's supposed constitutional obligation to protect and strengthen slavery wherever it had jurisdiction and narrowed, to the vanishing point, any power Congress might exercise to restrict slavery.[66] Thus, both Chase and Calhoun, coming from opposite directions, made constitutional construction purely instrumental to their stances on slavery.

In many respects, Lincoln's antislavery constitutionalism built on Chase's foundations. In the Cooper Institute address, Lincoln echoed Chase in denying that "the right of property in a slave is distinctly and expressly affirmed in the Constitution" (as asserted in Taney's *Dred Scott* opinion). This point was crucial because, as Lincoln observed in his 1858 debates with Douglas, if the federal Constitution "distinctly and expressly affirmed" the right to own slave property, then slaveholders would consequently have a right to hold slave property not only in federal territories but also in free states—for states, no less than territories, were obliged to respect the rights clearly affirmed in the Constitution. Lincoln feared this conclusion would be announced in a "second Dred Scott decision" declaring slavery "alike lawful in all the States—old as well as new, North as well as South." Lincoln also followed Chase in arguing that the framers deliberately avoided the words "slaves" and "slavery" in order to "exclude from the Constitution the idea that there could be property in man."[67]

Lincoln's interpretation of the Constitution's fugitive slave clause clearly differed from that of Chase and many other radical Republicans. Lincoln did not believe this clause could simply be repudiated, but he insisted that its execution include constitutional due process protections to prevent a legally free person from being forced into slavery. Lincoln personally regarded the Constitution's slavery-protecting features as serious flaws in the document; he called the fugitive slave clause "degrading" to the free states and the three-fifths clause "manifestly unfair."[68] But mutual respect, by both free states and slave states, for the Constitution's clearly expressed provisions and obligations was essential, in his view, not only to prevent disunion and civil war but also to preserve any hope that slavery could be peacefully and democratically abolished.

Lincoln and Chase also differed on the powers of Congress with respect to slavery in the territories. Chase believed that Congress was constitutionally prohibited from legalizing slavery in any territory (even though, in substance, it had done so multiple times as the nation expanded westward); at the same time, Congress was constitutionally obligated to ban slavery in every territory. In short, for Chase, Congress possessed little legitimate discretion with respect to slavery; its role in this area was narrowly circumscribed by constitutional prohibitions and obligations. In contrast, Lincoln sought to describe a shared Constitution, one whose powers and processes (including congressional power over the territories) had been exercised by supporters as well as opponents of slavery at various times; taken as a whole, the Constitution could not be simply reduced to either a proslavery or an antislavery instrument. The strength of Chase's interpretation of the Constitution was that it expressed a clear antislavery message, even if that message, as constitutional doctrine, was in many respects textually and historically implausible. The strength of Lincoln's interpretation of the Constitution was that it sought to establish legitimate space for antislavery action by the federal government within the wider functions that must be fulfilled by any constitution grounded in popular sovereignty. One of these wider functions is to enable deliberate, constitutionally checked majority rule. Another is to prevent deep political disagreements among the people from escalating into civil war.

Did the "Fathers" Act on Their Antislavery Principles?

Lincoln did not argue that the Constitution was inherently antislavery; he claimed only that its powers and processes could be legitimately exercised for antislavery purposes. It was essential for Lincoln's constitutional argument that the right to hold slave property was not "distinctly and expressly affirmed" in the Constitution and that the words "slave" and "slavery" were deliberately omitted in provisions alluding to slavery in order "to exclude . . . the idea that there could be property in man." If the Constitution had distinctly and expressly affirmed a right to slave property, then neither a majority in Congress nor a majority at any level of government—federal, state, or territorial—could constitutionally prohibit slavery. Beyond declining to specifically affirm "property in man," the Constitution furnished no strong antislavery principles. Those principles, Lincoln believed, were expressed in the Declaration of Independence, which was the "apple of gold," while the Constitution and the Union were the "picture of silver . . . subsequently framed around it. The picture was made, not to *conceal,* or *destroy* the apple; but to *adorn,* and *preserve* it." (Lincoln knew that some pieces of this "frame," such as the fugitive slave and three-fifths clauses, were wrought of lead, not silver, and did nothing to adorn and preserve the apple of gold.) He assumed that the "Fathers" (a group that included but extended beyond the thirty-nine who signed the Constitution) were guided in their words and actions by the principles of the Declaration of Independence and that they viewed slavery as an evil "to be tolerated and protected only because of and so far as its actual presence among us makes that toleration and protection a necessity."[69]

Most of those who declared and secured American independence, drafted and ratified the US Constitution, and breathed life into that document during its critical early decades acknowledged in principle that slavery was unjust. But the claim that, as a group, they consistently *acted* on this principle in making national policy and opposed slavery's expansion whenever it was within their power to do so is difficult to square with the historical record.[70] The founding generation's gulf between profession and action is most clearly revealed by what they did or did not do in the two decades following ratification of the Constitution. Some founding-generation leaders acted consistently with their antislavery commitments by supporting abolition in New York, Pennsylvania, and other northern states.[71] But the gradual pace of northern abolition during the early decades of the republic starkly contrasted with the speed and magnitude of slavery's expansion in southern states and territories during the same period. Lincoln might be criticized for his overly generous reading of the founding generation's historical record on slavery. My aim is to illuminate how Lincoln selectively appropriated their legacy to justify a *stronger* antislavery program than anything previously attempted by the founding generation or any of its successors.

In the Cooper Institute address, Lincoln observed that southerners claimed to be "conservative—eminently conservative," and they accused the Republican Party of being "revolutionary." He turned the charge around: "What is conservatism? Is it not adherence to the old and tried, against the new and untried?" In this sense, he argued, Republicans were conservative because they advocated "the identical old policy" with respect to slavery followed by "our fathers who framed the Government under which we live." The essence of that policy, according to Lincoln, was "federal prohibition of slavery in federal territories." In that sense, it was southerners who engaged in "innovation" and thereby "discarded the old policy of the fathers."[72]

I suggest that in this dispute both Lincoln and his southern critics were correct, in different ways. What made Lincoln and the Republicans radical, from slaveholders' perspective, was not their antislavery principles as such. Republicans were not radical abolitionists demanding immediate, uncompensated emancipation everywhere. Lincoln's southern contemporaries knew that George Washington, Thomas Jefferson, James Madison, James Monroe, and other slaveholding leaders of the founding generation had called slavery a violation of natural right and had spoken of its eventual disappearance in some indefinite future. Lincoln and the Republicans were revolutionary, in slaveholders' eyes, because they were finally willing to *act* on this principle. Slaveholders' past experience—from the federal convention of 1787 through the organization of the Louisiana territory, the Missouri crisis, the annexation of Texas, and the failed effort to ban slavery in territories acquired in the Mexican War—had been that, despite verbal condemnation and some political pushback, they had always gotten their way when it mattered most. No effective restrictions had been placed on slavery's expansion where slavery was profitable. Moreover (as noted in chapter 4), until the formation of the Republican Party, the political ground rules had been that any policies affecting slavery, including the Missouri Compromise's restriction on slavery north of 36° 30', had to be enacted *with the consent*

of slaveholders and slave states, not by a free-state majority over the opposition of slaveholders and slave states.[73] By the 1850s, the likelihood
that slave states would decide to abolish slavery on their own, without
intense outside pressure, had shrunk to zero. Slave-state leaders viewed
Lincoln and the Republicans as revolutionary because they proposed to
violate these long-standing unwritten political rules by enacting restrictions with practical effect, despite the vehement objections of slaveholders and slave states.

Lincoln argued that the founding generation, like the Republican
Party in 1860, had marked slavery "as an evil not to be extended" but to
be "tolerated and protected" only insofar as "its actual presence among
us makes that toleration and protection a necessity." It was in this sense
that Republicans sought to return slavery to where the "fathers" had
placed it—to "speak as they spoke, and act as they acted upon it." The
"fathers," in short, opposed slavery wherever it was in their power to do
so but tolerated it where "necessity" required. Necessity, however, can be
narrowly or expansively understood. The "necessity" of tolerating slavery
under given circumstances was not an elementary, transparent fact but a
certain kind of argument (elsewhere, Lincoln called it "the argument of
necessity"). Such arguments can be plausible or implausible; they can be
specific and restrictive or expansive to the point of emptiness. Proslavery
writers argued, for instance, that it was "necessary" for slavery to expand;
otherwise, it would die. A similarly tendentious argument, Lincoln observed, was voiced by Douglas, who claimed that "experience and the invention of the cotton-gin have taught us that the perpetuation of slavery
is a necessity." From Lincoln's perspective, the profitability of expanding
and perpetuating slavery did not establish its necessity. He sought instead
to restrict "necessity" to circumstances connected with slavery's "actual
presence among us." That justification was also potentially expansive, but
at least (Lincoln believed) it could not be used to justify planting slavery
in territories where it had never before existed. Among the many outrages of the Kansas-Nebraska Act was that "there was no sort of necessity"
for repealing the Missouri Compromise restriction and allowing slavery
to potentially expand to every US territory.[74]

Lincoln sought to establish that the founders tolerated slavery only
from necessity in this restrictive sense and that they prohibited slavery
wherever necessity did not stand in the way. (Lincoln provided two extended versions of this narrative—one from his October 1854 speech
on the Kansas-Nebraska Act and the other from his 1860 Cooper In-

stitute address. In what follows, I draw from both.) The centerpiece of Lincoln's argument was the Northwest Ordinance, which prohibited slavery in territories north of the Ohio River comprising the future states of Ohio, Michigan, Indiana, Illinois, and Wisconsin. In Lincoln's view, the Northwest Ordinance set a precedent for banning slavery in *all* federal territories, not just those north of a certain line, because the territory subject to the Northwest Ordinance was "the only territory owned by the United States" at that time.[75]

What about the US territories south of the Ohio River that comprised the future slave states of Kentucky, Tennessee, Alabama, Mississippi, and part of Florida? Fehrenbacher notes that the 1790 ordinance organizing the Southwest territory, "though similar in most respects to the Northwest Ordinance, omitted the ban on slavery." As a result, by 1790, Congress "had asserted and exercised its constitutional power to prohibit slavery in federal territory, but at the same time, it had renounced any intention of employing that power south of the Ohio River. . . . North of the river slavery was forbidden by federal law; south of the river it was silently permitted though not mandated by federal law."[76] On the one hand, this combination of policies supports Lincoln's argument that the framers of the Constitution intended Congress to exercise authority over slavery in the territories; on the other hand, it challenges Lincoln's argument that the political leaders of the early republic exercised that authority effectively to pursue antislavery aims, for it was in the territories south of the Ohio River that slavery commenced its enormous expansion in the two decades following ratification of the Constitution.

Lincoln resorted to a legalistic argument to support his thesis about the founders' antislavery record. North Carolina and Georgia ceded land to the federal government that was subsequently organized by Congress in the 1798 territorial act and became the states of Mississippi and Alabama. About this land, Lincoln observed: "In both deeds of cession it was made a condition by the ceding States that the Federal Government should not prohibit slavery in the ceded country. Besides this, slavery was then actually in the ceded country." He presented both these factors as "necessities" that prevented Congress from prohibiting slavery in these territories, although Congress did ban the importation of slaves from foreign countries.[77] In contrast, in the Northwest territory, where the ceding states (Virginia, New York, Connecticut, and Massachusetts) attached no such condition, Congress was free to prohibit slavery and did so.

But one might fairly ask: if the founding generation was so strongly motivated to restrict slavery, why did North Carolina and Georgia attach such conditions in the first place, and why did Congress so readily accept cession on those terms? Although one element of "necessity" was present—the existence of slavery in the territory—Lincoln placed greater emphasis on Congress's disposition to respect the wishes of the two slave states that ceded the land. Thus, the "necessity" to permit slavery in the territory was at least as much political as demographic. A Congress strongly motivated to halt the westward spread of slavery might have refused to accept land ceded on such terms.

Federal decisions affecting the Louisiana Purchase territories present even greater challenges to Lincoln's argument that the founding generation restricted slavery wherever no compelling necessity prevented them from doing so. The Louisiana Purchase included not only New Orleans and the surrounding area, where Lincoln acknowledged that slavery was already "thoroughly intermingled with the people,"[78] but also extensive lands to the north and west where slavery was absent or only minimally rooted. Because the Louisiana Purchase lands had not been ceded to the federal government by any state, no preconditions were attached, and Congress had a free hand to regulate slavery there. Political opposition to expanding slavery in the Louisiana territories was stronger than it had been when the Mississippi territory was organized. This opposition was motivated not only by principled objections to slavery but also by renewed attention to its dangers in the wake of the violent overthrow of slavery in St. Domingue (Haiti) in the 1790s and Gabriel's conspiracy in Virginia (1800). Because it was not yet a state, Louisiana's territorial government could not make policy on slavery without authorization from Congress; nor could it legally engage in the international slave trade (which, under the Constitution, states could do until 1808). Thus, despite slavery's existence in and around New Orleans, slavery's expansion in the territory could have been halted by blocking the importation of slaves from abroad and from other states. Moreover, Congress could have prohibited slavery altogether in the vast areas of the Louisiana Purchase where it had not yet spread.[79]

Congress did, at least initially, attempt to place some restrictions on the domestic slave trade in the Louisiana territory. And Lincoln emphasized these restrictions in his Cooper Institute address in an effort to demonstrate that Congress was widely understood to have the constitutional authority to regulate slavery in the territories. That part of his argument stands. But what is most striking about these restrictions is how limited, short-lasting, and weakly enforced they were. A proposal to emancipate adult slaves transported by their owners to Louisiana failed in the Senate.[80] Congress did enact legislation restricting Louisiana from importing slaves from other US states, in an unsuccessful effort to prevent the transshipment of enslaved persons trafficked by South Carolina, which had reopened the international slave trade on a massive scale before Congress could constitutionally close it in 1808.[81] Despite the prohibition on transporting slaves to Louisiana from outside the United States, immigrant slaveholders (many displaced by the overthrow of slavery in St. Domingue) were permitted to transport enslaved persons from the Caribbean and keep them in slavery in Louisiana.[82] Congress soon lifted the prohibition on Louisiana's importation of slaves from other states (many thousands of whom had been trafficked internationally).[83] Without the ability to import slaves, one Louisiana planter complained to Thomas Jefferson, this region of enormous economic promise would remain no more than a "vast swamp unfit for any creatures outside of fishes, reptiles, and insects."[84] Nor were regulations enacted to ban slavery in the northern part of the Louisiana Purchase territory. Jefferson, as the president responsible for the Louisiana Purchase and for overseeing administration of the territory, made some efforts to enforce the prohibition on the international slave trade, but he did not oppose Congress's decision to reopen the domestic slave trade and otherwise did little to stop the expansion of slavery in the territory.[85]

In the end, the "necessities" constraining federal slavery policy in the Louisiana territory were not limited to the difficulty of abolishing it where it was already established (the type of necessity Lincoln highlighted) but also included the enormous profitability of slavery in newly settled lands that were well suited to slave-produced sugar and cotton.[86] If Jefferson, his political party, or anyone else had stood in the way of this huge economic boon in the years following the Louisiana Purchase, they would have paid a high political price. In this sense, the perceived necessities that hindered attempts to restrict slavery in the Louisiana territory in the early 1800s resembled the expansive argument later voiced by Douglas and others that "experience and the invention of the cotton-gin" made the perpetuation of slavery a necessity.

This does not negate Lincoln's argument that the "fathers" (or most of them) regarded slavery as wrong, hoped for its ultimate extinction, and believed their own actions and policies could somehow be reconciled with that goal. Northern states' gradual abolition in the wake of the Revolution furnished Lincoln with an important precedent. But on the national level, and especially in the South, the founding generation's record on slavery offered little guidance for implementing the antislavery program to which Lincoln was committed. Lincoln and his party proposed to gradually squeeze out of existence an institution whose enormous economic importance and profitability no one denied, and to do so with or without the agreement of the slave states themselves. No American president, Congress, or major political party had ever before attempted this.

"The Tug Has to Come"

The obverse of Lincoln's hope that slavery could be abolished gradually, without civil war or disunion, was his fear that slavery might be nationalized and perpetuated, also without civil war or disunion, through a series of steps to which public opinion adjusted over time. Both possibilities were inherent in Lincoln's hypothesis that the "house divided" must ultimately resolve itself one way or the other. Neither outcome came to pass—at least not peacefully, as Lincoln had envisioned. He always recognized the possibility of disunion and civil war (in part because slaveholders so often threatened it), but like many of his contemporaries, he underestimated its likelihood until the lower South's secession made the prospect impossible to ignore. When he delivered his inaugural address (March 4, 1861), he was vividly aware of impending war, though he still hoped to avoid it.

But avoid war on what terms? Facing cascading secession and impending civil war, Lincoln retreated on some specific points, including abolition in the District of Columbia and restricting the interstate slave trade.[87] But he was unwilling to compromise "on the question of *extending* slavery" when some prominent Republicans expressed a willingness to do so.[88] The (failed) Crittenden Compromise, designed to stem the tide of secession and persuade already seceded states to return to the Union, consisted of six constitutional amendments. The key elements of the compromise that accounted for Lincoln's rejection of it were, first, that "in all territory, now held 'or hereafter acquired,' slavery was to be prohibited north of the line 36° 30' and protected south of it," and "no future amendment" could repeal or revise these amendments.[89] In substance, the Crittenden Compromise would have restored the Missouri Compromise line; extended it to the Pacific; invited and authorized the acquisition of additional territories south of 36° 30', including Cuba and other territories from the Caribbean and Latin America, designated as future slave states; and placed all these actions beyond the power of any future majority to alter, even the enormous supermajority required to amend the Constitution. The Crittenden proposals also would have written into the Constitution a positive endorsement of slavery, unlike the "all other persons" circumlocution employed by the framers to avoid legitimizing "property in man." One of Crittenden's proposed amendments announced, "In all the territory south of said line of latitude, slavery of the African race is hereby recognized as existing, and shall not be interfered with by Congress, but shall be protected as property by all the departments of the territorial governments during its continuance." Potter observes that this proposal "repudiated the oldest and most important plank of the Republican platform," which was to prohibit slavery in all federal territories; that it "seemed to invite expansion southward for the incorporation of more slave territory"; and that the concessions offered to slaveholders were "absolutely guaranteed against subsequent change."[90] And yet the Crittenden proposals did not go far enough for many slave-state leaders, who continued to insist that slavery must be legal and federally protected in *all* territories, regardless of latitude.

One dimension of Lincoln's preinauguration response to the secession crisis is especially important: his judgment that the Union could have been preserved and civil war avoided, but on terms he rejected as unacceptable because they would have fueled the continued expansion of slavery and subverted the results of a fair election. The subverted election dimension of the secession crisis reinforced Lincoln's determination not to compromise on slaveholders' demand to expand slavery to new territories.

In this regard, there is an intriguing thematic connection between Lincoln's prediction in the "House Divided" speech (June 1858) that "a *crisis* shall have been reached, and passed," and a phrase he repeated in two of his December 1860 letters opposing any compromise on extending slavery to new territories: "The tug has to come, & better now, than any time hereafter."[91] "The tug has to come" suggests a *necessary* crisis over slavery, not one that could be postponed indefinitely. Similarly, the "House Divided" speech invoked a necessary crisis whose outcome would determine in which direction the divided house ultimately fell. It is clear from the context of these December 1860 letters that in saying "the tug has to come" Lincoln did *not* mean that civil war was unavoidable. In this sense, too, the "tug" resembled the "crisis" of the "House Divided" speech, which looked to an electoral resolution, not a violent one. Of course, the political climate was very different in December 1860 than in June 1858. From the perspective of subsequent events, "the tug has to come" appears to predict a violent contest. But Lincoln's principal concern when he wrote these letters was that advocates of slavery would *threaten* secession, along with its violent consequences, to intimidate Republicans into renouncing their platform on slavery and agreeing to compromises that bound them to a proslavery political agenda that had already failed at the ballot box. In an electoral sense, the crisis had been "reached and passed" in November 1860, when Republicans won the presidency and made significant gains in Congress. But now the advocates of slavery were refusing to play by the rules.

That the "tug" referred to postelection pressure on Lincoln and the Republicans to renounce their political principles and relinquish in the face of threats what they had won at the ballot box is suggested by several passages from Lincoln's letters written in late 1860 and early 1861. In a December 11, 1860, letter containing the "tug has to come" phrase, Lincoln advised an Illinois congressman: "Entertain no proposition for a compromise in regard to the *extension* of slavery. The instant you do, they have us under again; all our labor is lost, and sooner or later must be done over." The phrase "they have us under again" appears to reference past episodes in which opponents of slavery backed down in the face of southern intransigence—a narrative that might readily include the federal convention of 1787, although Lincoln did not specify the frequency and dates of these previous episodes. In a December 15 letter to a North Carolina congressman who opposed secession but sought assurances from Lincoln that he could communicate to other southerners, Lincoln responded that such statements "would make me appear as if I repented for the crime of being elected, and was anxious to apologize and beg forgiveness." Despite his reluctance, Lincoln provided assurances on several secondary points but reaffirmed that "on the territorial question, I am inflexible," as he was on the moral point that slavery "is wrong and ought to be restricted." In a December 17 letter to an influential Republican strategist, Lincoln argued that if Republicans agreed either to extend the Missouri Compromise line or to adopt Douglas's popular sovereignty policy, it "would lose us every thing we gained by the election." What would follow next, Lincoln predicted, was "filibustering for all South of us, and making slave states of it"— meaning the expansion of US slave territory southward, into the Caribbean and Latin America. Lincoln repeated the southern expansion scenario as slaveholders' price for peace and a continued Union in a January 11, 1861, letter:

> We have just carried an election on principles fairly stated to the people. Now we are told in advance, the government shall be broken up, unless we surrender to those we have beaten, before we take the offices. In this they are either attempting to play upon us, or they are in dead earnest. Either way, if we surrender, it is the end of us, and of the government. They will repeat the experiment upon us *ad libitum*. A year will not pass, till we shall have to take Cuba [as a new slave state] as a condition upon which they will stay in the Union.

By acknowledging that advocates of slavery might be "in dead earnest," Lincoln now admitted the possibility of a violent contest, but he was unwilling to back down in the face of such threats. Lincoln wrote on February 1, 1861, to his secretary of state designee William Seward (who had recommended making additional concessions to the South), emphasizing, "I am inflexible" on "the territorial question," and warning against "any trick by which the nation is to acquire territory" that would "put us again on the high-road to a slave empire."[92]

The acquisition of Cuba as a US territory and prospective new slave state had been supported by presidents Franklin Pierce and James Buchanan and advocated vocally by Stephen Douglas, including in his 1858 debates with Lincoln. Both the regular Democratic Party platform of 1860 and the Breckinridge faction's platform endorsed the acquisition of Cuba.[93] For slavery-friendly politicians and parties, by the autumn of 1858, the Cuba issue had acquired increased prominence because of the "loss" of Kansas as a prospective slave state, despite the Buchanan administration's enormous efforts to impose a proslavery constitution on Kansas. Slaveholders feared that unless slavery could expand south and west, new free states entering the Union would greatly outnumber new slave states, thereby diminishing slavery's political power and its capacity to resist free-state efforts to squeeze it out of existence. The New Mexico territory (which included two future states—New Mexico and Arizona) had enacted a slave code in 1859, and slaveholders hoped for its admission to the Union as a slave state; however, its population was small (under 100,000 in 1860), and no one expected slavery to become the dominant mode of production there. Cuba's 1860 population exceeded 1.3 million. If it were acquired and admitted to the Union, it would have become the fourth or fifth largest state by population.

There were obstacles to acquiring Cuba, including the opposition of Spain, the opposition of free-state members of Congress, and the reluctance of Louisiana, a sugar-producing slave state, to compete in the US market with slave-produced sugar from Cuba.[94] But if free states had agreed to the southward expansion of slavery as the price demanded by slave states for refraining from secession and civil war, these practical obstacles to slavery's southward expansion could have been overcome. And even if Cuba or other Caribbean and Latin American territories were never acquired, it would signify a major political victory for slave states to get free states to endorse Cuba's acquisition as a foreign policy aim, for this would publicly communicate a powerful *national* proslavery statement. Lincoln certainly would have recognized the value to slaveholders of achieving symbolic victories of this kind.

Lincoln saw at least four different, mutually reinforcing factors tending toward what he called "*the perpetuity and nationalization of slavery*": (1) habituation, the process by which nonslaveholders living beside slaveholders gradually come to accept as normal practices that once shocked them; (2) slavery-friendly judicial rulings, most obviously the US Supreme Court's *Dred Scott* decision declaring the right to hold enslaved persons as property in any US territory, which Lincoln believed set a precedent for future judicial rulings upholding slaveholder rights in free states; (3) deliberate efforts by influential public figures— Stephen Douglas at the top of the list—to encourage Americans not to care about slavery; and (4) intense political pressure by slave states, including threats of secession and civil war, if their demands were not met.[95] In this final category is the pressure on Lincoln, after his election as president, to renounce his stance on slavery in the territories, based on the (doubtful) expectation that this would persuade seceded states to return to the Union.

Because many (though not all) historians have dismissed Lincoln's belief in the impending nationalization of slavery as paranoid, a political scare tactic, or both, it is important to understand what he did and did not mean by it.[96] I argue that, in the sense that Lincoln understood it, the nationalization of slavery was possible, even probable, in the absence of determined political opposition, and it was virtually certain if, as the price of peace and an intact Union, free states and slave states reached a postelection settlement along the lines of the Crittenden Compromise.

By the perpetuation and nationalization of slavery, Lincoln did not mean that the type of slave labor characteristic of the lower South would become the dominant mode of production in Illinois, Massachusetts, or any other northern or border state. This might seem too obvious to mention, were it not for the chorus of assurances in Lincoln's time that "climate"—otherwise known as the "isothermal line"—prevented the northward movement of slavery.[97] Climate certainly would have prevented Illinois from replacing family farms with slave-based sugarcane and rice production or Massachusetts from planting slave-produced cotton conveniently close to its textile mills. But climate did not prevent Missouri, on the same latitude as Illinois to the east and Kansas to the west, from becoming a slave state with a diversified economy similar in most respects to that of Illinois. Nor would climate prevent the use of slave labor in manufacturing and mining; slave labor had already been employed in these branches of production in the South. Lincoln rejected as a "lullaby" the argument that climate would prevent the northward spread of slavery. Proslavery ideologues likewise rejected the climate theory and saw no reason why slavery could not and should not move northward.[98] Even on its own terms, the isothermal theory anticipated at a minimum the perpetuation of slavery in the southern half of the United States and possibly its expansion southward in newly acquired territories.

But for Lincoln, the *presence* of slavery in a community mattered enormously for political, legal, psychological, and moral reasons, even if its economic impact was modest. In this sense, any regular, visible, and legally protected space for slavery in northern states and territories amounted to its nationalization, even if its presence was small and enslaved persons were classified as "temporary" residents or "in transit." The critical line in a previously free state or territory was crossed not when slavery became economically dominant (if it ever did) but when holding persons as property was legitimized in law and normalized in public opinion. In this sense, of course, the Constitution's fugitive slave clause had already partially nationalized slavery in important respects, and the Fugitive Slave Act of 1850 intensified that nationalization by legally obligating citizens of free states to assist in the recapture of fugitive slaves. Lincoln's concerns about the further legal incursion of slavery into free states focused on cases that could extend the *Dred Scott* precedent beyond the territories.[99] Justice Taney's *Dred Scott* opinion held that "the right of property in a slave is distinctly and expressly affirmed in the Constitution"; therefore, any act of Congress or of a territorial legislature "that prohibited a citizen from holding and owning property of this kind in the territory of the United States" was "not warranted by the Constitution and is therefore void."[100] Lincoln argued that if the right to slave property was indeed "distinctly and expressly affirmed in the Constitution" (which he denied), it logically followed that "nothing in the Constitution or laws of any State can destroy the right of property in a slave."[101] Lincoln did not claim that the Supreme Court would attempt to overturn the laws or constitutions of northern states that had outlawed slavery. Instead, he worried that cases involving slaveholders who were officially residents of slave states but who traveled through free states with their slaves or who resided "temporarily" (but potentially for extended periods) in free states while holding slaves there would provide the legal wedge to nationalize slavery.[102]

In a footnote to the published version of his Cooper Institute address (February 27, 1860), Lincoln identified the case of *Lemmon v. the People*, which involved a Virginia slaveholder who brought enslaved persons to New York, as potentially providing an opportunity for "the overthrow of our Free-State Constitutions." The slaveholder had argued:

> A citizen of Virginia has an immunity against the operation of any law which the State of New-York can enact, whilst he is a stranger and wayfarer, or whilst passing through our territory; and that he has absolute protection for all his domestic rights, and for all his rights of property, which under the laws of the United States, and the laws of his own State, he was entitled to, whilst in his own State.[103]

The New York court ruled against the slaveholder, on the grounds that under the laws of New York, the enslaved persons became free as soon as they crossed the state's border. The emancipated persons then migrated to Canada. The slaveholder appealed to the US Supreme Court, which (if civil war had not intervened) might have ruled in the slaveholder's favor and overturned the New York laws emancipating enslaved persons in transit from another state.[104]

Cases involving slave owners' demand for legal protection of their slave property while "temporarily" residing in free states likewise could have furnished legal avenues for the nationalization of slavery. Courts might have ruled that, under the Constitution's privileges and immunities clause, a citizen of one state cannot be deprived of his rights (in this case, the right to human property) while resident in another state, regardless of the length of that residence.

Lincoln did not believe, however, that judicial action alone could fully nationalize slavery without a supportive political climate and a corresponding shift of public opinion in favor of slavery, or at least a moral indifference toward it. His warnings about "the *next* Dred Scott" decision (applying the *Dred Scott* precedent to the states) were all conditional: if the political climate were favorable and if public opinion were prepared to accept it, the next step would come. He accused Douglas of "preparing the public mind for that new Dred Scott decision." But the converse was also true: if such a step met determined political opposition and if public opinion turned decisively against it, the trend toward nationalization of slavery could be halted and reversed. Lincoln stated, "My own opinion is, that the new Dred Scott decision, deciding against the right of the people of the States to exclude slavery, will never be made, if that party is not sustained by the elections."[105]

Secessionist leaders shared Lincoln's assessment of the judiciary's limited power, in practice, to ensure what slaveholders regarded as their constitutional right to bring and hold enslaved persons as property in free states and territories. Slaveholders likewise recognized the importance of the political climate and public opinion, and of course they sought to push it in the opposite direction from Lincoln and the Republicans. Moreover, defenders of slavery saw no essential distinction between the constitutionally guaranteed right to recover fugitive slaves and the right to bring enslaved persons who were not fugitives into free states, despite state laws to the contrary, and hold them there indefinitely. Slaveholders appeared to believe (and they may have been correct) that if their asserted right to slave property was not respected *everywhere*, including in free states, it would be secure *nowhere*—neither in the territories nor, in the long run, in the slave states themselves. By 1860, despite repeated assurances that they had no intention of imposing slavery on free states, slave-state leaders were placing conditions on their willingness to abstain from severing the Union, which reinforced Lincoln's fears about the push to fully nationalize slavery. On December 24, 1860, Jefferson Davis, then a US senator from Mississippi (which had not yet seceded), submitted the following resolution as a member of the Select Committee of Thirteen assigned to formulate a compromise to save the Union. Davis's proposed amendment read:

Resolved, That it shall be declared, by amendment of the Constitution, that property in slaves, recognized as such by the local law of any of the States of the Union, shall stand on the same footing in all constitutional and federal relations as any other species of property so recognized; and, like other property, shall not be subject to be divested or impaired by the local law of any other States, either in escape thereto or of transit or sojourn of the owner therein; and in no case whatever shall such property be subject to be divested or impaired by any legislative act of the United States, or of any of the Territories thereof.[106]

Davis here expressed the view that slaveholders had a constitutional right to "transit or sojourn" with their human property in and through free states as well as free territories, for indefinite spans of time, regardless of state or territorial laws to the contrary. This signified, from Lincoln's perspective, not merely a step toward the nationalization of slavery but its achievement. It is unlikely that Davis expected this resolution to pass. But in it, he set forth the conditions that must be met for Mississippi to remain in the Union and, if those conditions were not met, the justification for its secession.

That the free states, in the face of secession threats and possible civil war, would agree to such conditions to save the Union was precisely what Lincoln feared in November and December 1860. At this stage, he did not believe civil war was inevitable, or at least he did not say so. What he battled against was the oft-repeated cycle, over many decades, whereby every attempt to halt the spread of slavery was defeated by southern intransigence and secession threats. This time, the offensiveness of this oft-repeated extortion was heightened by the demand that the results of a free, fair, and constitutionally conducted election be effectively nullified. That had never happened before. Lincoln's *refusal* to renounce his and his party's stance on slavery in the territories was, under these circumstances, a stronger antislavery act than any president or major party had ever previously taken. This was true even though he had not yet been inaugurated as president.

Lincoln's election, together with his refusal to meet southern demands, potentially signified a fundamental shift in public opinion with long-term consequences, even if its immediate impact was limited. Secessionists recognized this. Robert Toombs in the Georgia secession debate, replying to those who believed they should wait to see what Lincoln would do as president, argued that the electoral endorsement of antislavery opinion was equivalent to antislavery action: "Surely no one will deny that the election of Lincoln is the indorsement of the policy of those who elected him, and an indorsement of his own opinions." Toombs and other advocates of preemptive secession understood that Lincoln and the Republicans would not immediately attempt to abolish slavery in the states. They recognized that the Republicans' aim was to "pen up slavery within its present limits" and slowly squeeze it to death. Because slavery had to either expand or die, penning it up would kill it over time. Electoral endorsement of Lincoln's opinions about slavery therefore amounted to a "war against slavery until there should not be a slave in America."[107] Lincoln and the Republicans, in short, would succeed in gradually extinguishing slavery unless the slave states exited the Union.

Lincoln did not believe his election as president amounted to a declaration of war on the South. He did, however, view the demand that he renounce the principles on which he had been elected as a declaration of war on popular self-government. When he wrote that "the tug has to come," he still hoped to avoid civil war. But if negating the outcome of a free election and nationalizing slavery were the price of peace and an intact Union, that was a price he was not willing to pay.

8 | "To Declare the *Right,* so that *Enforcement* Might Follow"

Lincoln's Reconstruction of Natural Right

Lincoln called on Americans to reaffirm the principles set forth in the Declaration of Independence: that "all men are created equal," regardless of race; that they possess certain unalienable rights, including liberty and the right to enjoy the fruits of their own labor; and that they cannot be justly governed without their consent. Slavery was "a total violation" of these principles.[1] He sought to reclaim the principles of the Declaration of Independence not only from John C. Calhoun and his followers, who openly rejected "all men are created equal" as a "self-evident lie," but also from men like Stephen Douglas and Roger Taney, who pretended to affirm those principles "in the sneaking way" of claiming that they applied exclusively to the white race.[2] Lincoln also had to challenge a perverse but politically consequential interpretation of natural right: that because slaves were property, and governments were instituted to protect property rights, no government at any level could legitimately deprive slaveholders of their human property.

On the other side of the slavery divide, Lincoln had to formulate an alternative to the abolitionist argument that taking natural rights seriously meant supporting the abolition of slavery immediately and everywhere.[3] Lincoln's stance of opposing the extension of slavery but tolerating it for an extended time where it was long established was a response to political necessity, not a distinction grounded in natural right. Natural rights were violated whether enslaved persons were kept in Alabama or transported to Kansas. Thus, natural rights theory would justify resistance, including violent resistance, by enslaved persons against those who held them in bondage. Lincoln regarded such resistance as natural and inevitable. But he did not believe slave insurrections could succeed on a large scale.[4]

Moreover, white Americans might acknowledge in the abstract that enslaved people had a natural right to resist without feeling obliged to assist them in those efforts—especially if doing so risked civil war. Most troubling of all, the theory of natural rights could generate apparently irreconcilable clashes of natural rights, as exemplified by Thomas Jefferson's "wolf by the ear" dilemma, whereby the enslaved person's natural right to liberty conflicts with the slaveholder's natural right to self-preservation. In this sense, even though natural rights theory could not without distortion justify the initial act of enslavement, once slavery was established, natural rights theory could arguably justify slaveholders' violent suppression of slave resistance in the name of self-preservation.

In contrast to both radical abolitionist and slavery-rationalizing appropriations of natural rights theory, Lincoln sought a peaceful, gradual, democratic, Union-preserving, Constitution-respecting extinction of slavery that secured life and liberty for former slave owners as well as for formerly enslaved persons. He also had to square his reaffirmation of natural rights with his commitment to majority rule. He knew that majorities could violate those rights, yet without majority support, there was no effective way to realize them in practice.

In this chapter I draw from John Locke's *Second Treatise of Civil Government* (1689) to illuminate Lincoln's efforts to revitalize natural rights in America and thereby enable a peaceful, democratic extinction of slavery. One might ask, why Locke? Lincoln does not appear to have had direct access to Locke's writings, although he was familiar with Lockean ideas from the Declaration of Independence, Thomas Jefferson's writings, Blackstone's *Commentaries*, and many other sources.[5]

It might seem best to focus on Lincoln's appropriation of those secondhand Lockean texts with which he was familiar. But it was precisely this secondhand American version of Lockean theory (best exemplified by the Declaration's preamble) that had hit the wall by Lincoln's time and split into irreconcilably opposed fragments with respect to slavery and race. Quoting the Declaration of Independence—though Lincoln did so frequently—was not sufficient to revitalize it. Its core ideas had to be reconstructed, retheorized, and reapplied in the light of history and present experience. The capsule version of Locke's *Second Treatise* in the Declaration's preamble invokes "consent of the governed" as a fundamental principle, but it says nothing about majority rule as a decision-making procedure when the people themselves have opposing views on important matters—including differing interpretations of the natural rights affirmed in the document. Instead, the Declaration speaks as though the American people were entirely of one mind about natural right and its violation by "the present King of Great Britain." This rhetorical assumption of unanimity was essential to the document's immediate purpose. But it left many postindependence questions unanswered, including the problem of clashing natural rights claims and the role, if any, of majority decision in resolving such clashes.

Locke's *Second Treatise* provides a richly articulated theory grounding the principles stated briefly and dogmatically in the Declaration of Independence, including a strong defense of majority rule for deciding matters on which the people are divided. Locke's defense of majority rule suggests that it is possible for democratic political action to remove or mitigate the conflicts of interest that generate clashing natural rights claims in the first place. I do not mean that Lincoln read and absorbed Locke's *Second Treatise* in some manner that has escaped the historical record. Nor would Locke's *Second Treatise* have resolved all of Lincoln's dilemmas, had he had access to the book. As we shall see, some of the slavery-related dilemmas Lincoln wrestled with were left conspicuously unresolved in the *Second Treatise*.

I argue in this chapter that Lincoln, in light of his own experience and drawing from Lockean ideas in secondhand form, independently reached conclusions about the relationship between natural right and majority rule that paralleled Locke's theory in important respects. Moreover, I suggest that in matters related to slavery—in particular, how to remove slavery where it was deeply entrenched and encoded in law—Lincoln employed majority rule to address problems Locke left unresolved. Finally, in opposition to the oft-voiced claim that Lincoln betrayed the principles of the Declaration of Independence by rejecting secession, I argue that this is where Lincoln was *most* faithful to the criteria justifying the dissolution of government as described by both Locke and the Declaration.

A Natural Right to Human Property?

The preamble of the Declaration of Independence was frequently invoked by Lincoln's fellow Republicans and was quoted in the party's 1860 platform.[6] Many abolitionists also quoted from it.[7] But the phrase "all men are created equal" was central to Lincoln's political thought to a greater degree than for many other Republicans who opposed slavery for a variety of reasons. Lincoln invoked "all men are created equal" both to condemn slavery, which became his primary concern after passage of the Kansas-Nebraska Act, and to express his broader lifelong commitment to the survival of popular self-government.

Yet the availability of natural rights theory for antislavery purposes was complicated by the frequently voiced *defense* of slavery on natural rights grounds, as an instance of the natural right to property. To defend slavery on natural rights grounds did not necessarily entail claiming a right by nature to enslave a free person. The argument instead was that once a property right was created, through whatever means, that property right rested *on the same foundation as all other property* and could not be infringed by any constitution or law. Article VII of the proslavery Lecompton Constitution for Kansas (1857) advanced the natural rights defense of slavery in stark form: "The right of property is before and higher than any constitutional sanction, and the right of the owner of a slave to such slave and its increase is the same and as inviolable as the right of the owner of any property whatever."[8] Property rights, according to this argument, existed prior to any constitution or laws (as they do in Locke's state of nature). The purpose of laws and constitutions was to better secure property rights. Therefore, an individual's natural right to hold slave property was as inviolable as his right to hold property of other kinds. The Lecompton Constitution's natural rights defense of slavery reproduced word for word Article XIII, section 1.3 of Kentucky's 1850 constitution.[9] The Southern State Convention that met in Mississippi in 1849 claimed that the right of property—specifically including slave property—"is coeval with the history of man" and "exists by a paramount law of nature."[10]

The supposed natural right to hold slave property was asserted with increasing vehemence in the 1840s and 1850s, but the claim had been made as early as the American Revolution. In response to Revolution-era abolitionists who insisted on enslaved persons' natural right to liberty, "proslavery advocates, North and South, saw property *in* slaves as a natural right, like property in any other commodity, which could not be abridged."[11] The efforts of South Carolina and Georgia at the 1787 Federal Convention to expressly affirm a constitutional right to slave property under the federal Constitution were defeated, but slaveholders continued throughout the antebellum period to insist that slavery was an inviolable federal constitutional right. By renewing the claim during the 1840s and 1850s that slave property was also an inviolable *natural* right (constitutions and laws to the contrary notwithstanding), defenders of slavery sought to ensure that all bases were covered.

Many educated slaveholders read Locke and considered themselves Lockeans. This group included not only anguished slaveholders like Thomas Jefferson but also unapologetic slaveholders like John C. Calhoun. As a youth, Calhoun had immersed himself in Locke's writings, and he knew that Locke had participated in drafting the fundamental constitutions of the Carolina colony. In his defense of slavery, Calhoun notoriously rejected the Lockean idea (codified in the Declaration of Independence) that all men were born free and equal.[12] But Calhoun embraced Locke's defense of property. Locke argued in the *Second Treatise*: "The reason why men enter into society, is the preservation of their property; and the end why they choose and authorize a legislative, is, that there may be laws made, and rules set, as guards and fences to the properties of all the members of the society."[13] In Calhoun's view, the Lockean right to property unquestionably included slave property.[14]

This explains why Lincoln considered it essential to deny that there could be "property in man," for once that premise was accepted, Locke's natural rights philosophy became a powerful ideological weapon for slaveholders. The right to slave property would then lie beyond the legitimate power of any political authority, including the will of the majority, to alter or abolish. Conversely, if "property in man" was not legitimate and enslaved persons counted as members of the community, it followed—also from Locke's principles—that slavery could be altered or abolished by the legislature, acting as the agent of the majority, when the common good of society required it.

A skeptic might understandably conclude that a natural rights theory open-ended enough to be enlisted on all sides of the slavery dispute was empty at the core. That was not Lincoln's view. He sought instead to rescue and revitalize natural rights theory, both to safeguard popular self-government against self-destruction and to legitimize peaceful, democratic antislavery action.

"A Standard Maxim for Free Society"

The elements of Lockean natural rights theory that Lincoln emphasized were, first, that human beings were by nature free and equal and not naturally subject to the authority of anyone else; and second, that political authority must be created by consent among these free, equal individuals. In his *Second Treatise*, Locke writes that "all men are naturally in

. . . a state of perfect freedom to order their actions, and dispose of their possessions and persons, as they think fit, within the bounds of the law of nature, without asking leave, or depending upon the will of any other man."[15] This resembles Lincoln's oft-repeated argument that everyone, regardless of race, had the same right "to eat the bread, without leave of anyone anybody else," produced by their own labor.[16]

This natural condition, according to Locke, is "a state also of equality, wherein all the power and jurisdiction is reciprocal, no one having more than another." Human beings are equal because they are "creatures of the same species and rank, promiscuously born to all the same advantages of nature, and the use of the same faculties."[17] Such passages mark as illegitimate the institution of slavery, which Locke defines elsewhere in the *Second Treatise* as "the state of war continued." Locke affirms that "all men" are born to this state of freedom and equality, not merely white men or Englishmen or Europeans. Moreover, the phrases "creatures of the same species or rank" and "use of the same faculties" indicate that natural equality holds, regardless of a person's social and political status. One can imagine defenders of racial slavery responding that persons of African descent, though of "the same species," were not of the same "rank" (and some even asserted that Blacks were a different species).[18] But if Locke had meant that human beings were naturally equal only insofar as they enjoyed equal social and political status, then such equality would be nullified even for white Englishmen, and the whole natural rights theory falls apart. In the chapter titled "Of Property," Locke remarks that "the wild Indian" is naturally entitled to "the fruit or venison" his labor has earned, to which "nobody has any right . . . but himself."[19] Though Locke held that natural liberty and equality applied to human beings of all races, including in the wilds of America, he was silent in the *Second Treatise* about the racial slavery English settlers had already introduced in the colonies.

The parallels are unmistakable between the preamble of the Declaration of Independence, which Lincoln never tired of quoting, and Locke's argument in the *Second Treatise* that human beings are born free and equal and subject to no authority except by their own consent. But there was a potentially important difference between Locke's state of nature and Lincoln's gloss on the Declaration of Independence. Locke's description of natural freedom and equality placed it in a hypothetical past (a time before government, written laws, and landed property). The state of nature also functioned for Locke (and the Declaration of

Independence) in the present, as a critical standard for evaluating the justice or injustice of existing governments and, in extreme cases, for dissolving oppressive governments and establishing new ones. Lincoln recognized both these employments of the state of nature idea. But for Lincoln, "all men are created equal" also carried a *future* application that was, at minimum, less emphasized by Locke or the Declaration's preamble. Roger Taney and Stephen Douglas, among others, had argued that if the authors of the Declaration had intended "all men are created equal" to apply to all races, they would have immediately abolished slavery and placed all Blacks "on an equality with the whites." Lincoln replied that the authors of the Declaration

> did not mean to assert the obvious untruth, that all were then actually enjoying that equality, nor yet, that they were about to confer it immediately upon them. In fact they had no power to confer such a boon. They meant simply to declare the *right*, so that the *enforcement* of it might follow as fast as circumstances should permit. They meant to set up a standard maxim for free society, which should be familiar to all, and revered by all; constantly looked to, constantly labored for, and even though never perfectly attained, constantly approximated, and thereby constantly spreading and deepening its influence, and augmenting the happiness and value of life to people of all colors everywhere.[20]

Here, the state of nature, as a condition of full liberty and equality, exists not in the past or in the present but in a hypothetical future. Neither Locke's *Second Treatise* nor the Declaration's preamble specifically rules out Lincoln's future-oriented application of "all men are created equal." But neither Locke nor the Declaration includes any counterpart to Lincoln's "standard maxim" passage.

Nor was Lincoln's modification a minor one. The narrative arc of both Locke's *Second Treatise* and the Declaration of Independence is one of a society consisting of free and equal property-owning citizens who are conscious of their rights and who establish a government to better secure those rights. But the rights of these citizens are now threatened by a despotic government plotting to reduce them to slavery, commencing with attacks on their property, followed by their life and liberty. These free, property-owning men first exhaust all legal avenues of redress, but when those fail, they realize that further delay could make their loss of liberty and property irreversible. So they band together to dissolve that government before it accomplishes its tyrannical design and establish a new one.

This Lockean–Declaration of Independence narrative matched reasonably well, in Lincoln's time, the fears of free, white, non-slave-owning citizens that an aggressive "slave power" would reduce them to servitude. But the narrative offers little hope for those already enslaved, who never enjoyed any political rights or any legal claim to the fruits of their labor and for whom violent resistance against oppression (which occurred periodically on a local scale) meant almost certain death. Moreover, successful resistance to enslavement might entail the death or exile of many, perhaps most, slaveholders, who (like Jefferson holding the wolf's ear) would prioritize their own natural right to life. In short, although the Lockean state of nature–government by consent–right of resistance narrative condemns the initial act of enslaving a free person, it provides little guidance for overthrowing deeply entrenched slavery on a mass scale. To adapt one of Locke's metaphors: if one discovers that the ship on which one is a passenger is headed not to one's expected destination but continually in the direction of Algiers (where pirates sold captives into slavery), one must seize control of the ship before it reaches port, for once one finds oneself in the slave markets of Algiers, it will be too late.[21]

Lincoln's reconstruction of natural right as a "maxim . . . constantly looked to, constantly labored for, and even though never perfectly attained, constantly approximated" was an effort to transform natural rights doctrine into a vehicle for the peaceful, gradual remediation of entrenched injustices. As such, it envisioned a more active and positive role for government than was likely intended by the signers of the Declaration of Independence. (Locke's theory, as noted below, is less hostile to active government.) Deliberate public action over a long period of time was necessary to better "enforce" and "approximate" the prescriptions of natural right.

Clashing Natural Rights

Lincoln's reformulation of "all men are created equal" as a future accomplishment, a proposition to which a political community "dedicates" itself (as he later phrased it in the Gettysburg Address), was designed, among other things, to remedy Jefferson's "wolf by the ear" dilemma. Jefferson presented a clash of natural rights: the enslaved human being's natural right to liberty versus the slaveholder's natural right to self-preservation. Life and liberty, along with property, are key Lockean natural rights. But if one looks to Locke's writings for a principled resolution of Jefferson's "wolf by the ear" dilemma, one finds none. Locke's discussion of slavery in the *Second Treatise* recognizes no legitimate clash of natural rights of the kind posed by Jefferson, and it prescribes no remedy for slavery other than driving away, killing, or (strangely enough) even enslaving the enslaver.

It is unclear whether or how Locke reconciled his practical involvement with slavery in the American colonies and his financial stake in the Royal African Company, which participated in the transatlantic slave trade, with the political theory set forth in the *Second Treatise of Civil Government*.[22] In any event, according to Locke's natural rights theory, slavery is not only illegitimate; it is the sum of all political evils. The attempt to establish and justify absolutist government, Locke's principal concern in the *Second Treatise*, amounted to a war on the life, liberty, and property of the people, with the aim of reducing them to slavery. "For nobody can desire to have me in his absolute power, unless it be to compel me by force to that which is against the right of my freedom, i.e., make me a slave. . . . So that he who makes an attempt to enslave me, thereby puts himself into a state of war with me." Slavery, in short, is "the state of war continued."[23] For this reason, enslaved persons, and those targeted for slavery but not yet reduced to it, have a natural right to resist, violently if necessary. Lincoln too, when he described "poisonings from the kitchen" and "assassinations in the field" as "the natural results of slavery," characterized slavery as the state of war continued.[24] Even slaveholders, despite their paternalistic rhetoric, betrayed their recognition that slavery was warfare by their spectacularly violent response to even unsubstantiated rumors of slave conspiracies.[25] Jefferson's "wolf by the ear" was another variant of slavery as the state of war continued.

Ironically, it is here, where Locke in principle is most strongly antislavery, that his theory offers little guidance for political leaders of a society where slavery has long been established and who hope somehow to abolish it. The conflict of natural rights that Jefferson posed, with "justice" on one side and "self-preservation" on the other, nowhere appears in Locke's discussion of slavery. For Locke, the would-be despot's intended victim, acting in self-defense, has "a liberty to kill the aggressor." There is no conflict of natural rights here because the aggressor, by his actions, has forfeited both life and liberty. Moreover—and here Locke's argument takes a strange twist—the aggressor's victim has a right to turn the tables and enslave the would-be enslaver. Because the latter has "forfeited his life" by an "act that deserves death," his intended victim "may (when he has him in his power) delay to take it, and make use of him to his own service, and he does him no injury by it."[26]

One may certainly dispute the justice of using for one's own service persons convicted of crimes against the life, liberty, or property of others. But even if slavery were justified for convicts, this could not justify slavery for persons who have *not* committed such crimes or for their children and descendants. Nor does Locke make any such claim; in fact, he argues the opposite. According to Locke, even in a just war (such as a war against an enslaving aggressor), forfeiture of life, liberty, and property rightly extends only to those directly responsible for acts of aggression, not to the population as a whole or their descendants, for "the miscarriages of the father are no faults of the children, and they may be rational and peaceable, notwithstanding the brutishness and injustice of the father."[27] Thus, under no circumstances could slavery be justly imposed in perpetuity on an entire race of human beings.

But once slavery has established itself (no matter how unjustly) and detailed codes of positive law have legitimated the practice of holding persons as property, Lockean principles of natural right provide no clear remedy. On the one hand, the injustices of slavery do not disappear. Slavery remains "the state of war continued," and every child born into slavery represents a new violation of natural right. Thus, Locke's natural rights theory could readily legitimize violent slave insurrections, although there is no evidence he intended it for that purpose. On the other hand, insofar as slave owners do not act lawlessly (at least with respect to public, written law), they do not resemble Locke's description of a tyrant, whose most prominent characteristic is lawless, arbitrary action. "Law-abiding" slaveholders would not regard themselves as tyrants, even if the persons they held in slavery viewed them as such. Instead, slave owners, as well as their nonslaveholding neighbors, would view slave insurrections as assaults on their own natural rights to life, liberty, and property.

Here we find conflicting natural rights claims: Jefferson's "wolf by the ear." But Locke does not clarify which natural rights should take precedence in such circumstances, and for whom. His statements on slavery make it difficult to acknowledge any conflict of principles. For Locke, either slavery is justified, because the enslaved person committed some act forfeiting his life and liberty, or it is not justified, in which case the persons responsible for the unjust act of enslavement could themselves be justly killed or enslaved. Locke's discussion of slavery (which focused on political tyranny in England, not plantation slavery in America) offers little in between.

Whatever the merits of Locke's argument that those who enslave others may justly be enslaved themselves, in the American context, such a stark dichotomy would have reinforced slaveholders' disposition to fight to the bitter end. One of American slaveholders' most frequently expressed fears, and one of the most effective arguments in the proslavery arsenal, was that abolition of slavery would produce not equality but a reversal of positions. John C. Calhoun warned: "Be assured that emancipation itself would not satisfy these fanatics—that gained, the next step would be to raise the negroes to a social and political equality with the whites; and that being effected, we would soon find the condition of the two races reversed. They and their northern allies would be the masters, and we the slaves."[28] Calhoun did not mean that white former slaveholders would literally become the chattel property of emancipated Blacks. But for slaveholders to fall from a position of power and public respect to one of political powerlessness, confiscation of property, and public disgrace was, in his view, equivalent to servitude and worse than death. This would be the fate of American slaveholders, Calhoun insisted, if they ceased to believe in the rightness of their cause. Locke was not responsible for every apocalyptic scenario voiced by southern leaders, but his discussion of slavery did little to dispel the dichotomous thinking (emancipating the slave entailed enslaving the slaveholder) that accentuated their fears.

For Lincoln, who sought the peaceful extinction of slavery, it was essential to resist characterizing all slaveholders as tyrants who had forfeited life and liberty. He distinguished between the "monstrous injustice" of slavery as an institution and the question of individual guilt for continuing the institution once established. He acknowledged there were "natural tyrants" incapable of recognizing the humanity of enslaved persons. Those engaged in "the African slave trade piracy" were tyrants of this kind, and they deserved death or imprisonment. The proslavery men invading Kansas waving "bowie-knives and six-shooters" acted tyrannically in many ways.[29] Lincoln's natural tyrant roughly corresponded to Locke's man who, either in the state of nature or in civil society, "attempts to get another man into his absolute power" and who knows "no other rule but that of force and violence."[30] From both Locke's and

Lincoln's perspectives, such persons were lawless at the core and could be justly punished.

But Lincoln argued that the proportion of "natural tyrants" was "no larger in the slave States than in the free." He believed that, for the majority of southerners, "If slavery did not now exist amongst them, they would not introduce it. If it did now exist amongst us, we should not instantly give it up."[31] Slavery as an institution was an extreme form of tyranny, but most individual slaveholders were not tyrants. This paradox underscores the difficulty of addressing the moral and political problem of slavery principally from the perspective of Lockean natural rights theory.

Locke's conception of action in the public good, however, offers a more promising avenue for addressing the problem of slavery and one that is more convergent with Lincoln's approach. For both Locke and Lincoln, action in the public good required the practice of majority rule, which is a political construction, not a natural right. A key function of majority rule is to resolve disagreements that neither the explicit text of constitutions nor the unwritten principles of natural right can resolve.

Locke, Lincoln, and Majority Rule

Locke's discussion of natural right did not address conflicts between an enslaved person's natural right to liberty and a slaveholder's natural right to self-preservation. But his *Second Treatise* presents not only a theory of natural right but also a theory of government, which Locke considered essential to remedy the "inconveniences" of living in a community with no rule of conduct other than natural right and natural law, which each person interprets and executes according to his own judgment. Peaceful coexistence requires an "established, settled, known law" and a "known and indifferent judge" to impartially execute that law.[32] Civil government and civil law do not annihilate natural right and natural law, which function both as moral standards guiding the construction of civil laws and governments and as last resorts when governments betray their legitimate purposes.

But the creation of civil government and civil law, through consent, introduces a new element that Locke calls "the common good" or "the public good of the people," which does not exist in the state of nature except in rudimentary form.[33] This public good is ascertained and pursued, as a matter of procedure, through majority rule: "For when any number of men have, by the consent of every individual, made a community, they have thereby made that community one body, with a power to act as one body, which is only by the will and determination of the majority."[34] Neither Locke nor Lincoln believed the majority was always right. Both for Locke and for Lincoln, the majority was morally obliged to respect the natural rights of society's members and to govern in accordance with natural law on matters where it provides clear guidance. Winning a war, for example, even one initiated unjustly by another country, does not give the victors the right to kill, dispossess, or enslave the entire population of the defeated enemy. Locke believed natural law was clear on this point.[35] But in many other matters, the prescriptions of natural right and natural law were *not* clear, and different individuals interpreted them in contrasting, self-interested ways, producing significant conflicts. This is why civil society governed by majority rule is necessary in the first place. In this respect, majority rule, although it should consult and be guided by natural right and natural law, in another sense determines what natural right and natural law prescribe in matters affecting "the public good of the people"—especially when natural right and natural law provide unclear or contradictory guidance.

Slavery, where long established, pushes the limits of what majority rule is capable of resolving. One might reasonably argue that slavery, as "the state of war continued," constitutes the kind of governance failure that justifies resort to the natural right of revolution or even the dissolution of government, regardless of what the majority thinks. Many abolitionists drew that conclusion in Lincoln's time. But in practice, Locke did not believe an oppressed minority, attempting revolution, could succeed without majority support. Even though individuals and minorities "have a right to defend themselves" against "manifest acts of tyranny" and to try to "recover by force what by unlawful force is taken from them," in the attempt to do so they are "sure to perish" unless they enlist the majority on their side. The majority, for its part, is unlikely to risk its own life and liberty by resorting to revolution unless "these illegal acts have extended to the majority of the people" or "the precedent and consequences seem to threaten all."[36] The right of revolution, in short, is a blunt, risky, and uncertain tool for remedying many types of injustice.

Majority rule as a decision-making procedure during "normal" times, however, presents a wider range of options for remedying injustice than are available during a revolutionary crisis. A functioning civil government responsibly exercising the powers entrusted to it is better able to address problems of every type than a government threatened with dissolution because it has abused those powers. Locke argued for entrusting the government, insofar as it expresses the will of the majority, with significant powers to act, even in the face of strong disagreement.[37] The need for effective government, despite disagreement, follows from the purposes for which human beings consent to leave the state of nature in the first place. In the state of nature, every individual possesses full "executive power" to interpret, act on, and punish violations of the law of nature. But everyone acting as judge and executor in his own case soon leads to a state of war, "wherein every the least difference is apt to end, where there is no authority to decide between the contenders." Violent quarrels could result even when men embraced the same principles of natural right. Two neighbors might agree on the natural right of private property but come to blows over where the property line is drawn. In consenting to form civil government, human beings transfer the "executive power they had in the state of nature, into the hands of the society, to be so far disposed of by the legislative as the good of the society shall require."[38] This transfer is not unconditional; it can be revoked if government engages in dangerous, deliberate, and persistent violations of this trust (Locke's famous "long train of abuses," a phrase repeated in the Declaration of Independence).[39] But unless and until this occurs, civil government exercises full powers to act in the public good; the exercise of this public trust cannot be held hostage to the will of individuals or a disaffected minority. This is Locke's rationale for majority rule. If every individual or minority were empowered to grant or refuse consent to laws and policies, civil society would be afflicted by the same "inconveniences" that characterize the state of nature. "And thus every man, by consenting with others to make one body politic under one government, puts himself under an obligation to every one of that society to submit to the determination of the majority, and to be concluded by it; or else this original compact, whereby he with others incorporate into one society, would signify nothing, and be no compact." For "the consent of every individual . . . is next to impossible ever to be had."[40] Lincoln's argument in the first inaugural address is parallel: "Unanimity is impossible; the rule of a minority, as a permanent arrangement, is wholly inadmissible; so that, rejecting the majority principle, anarchy, or despotism in some form, is all that is left."[41]

Locke said nothing about employing the powers of government to abolish slavery as practiced in Britain's North American colonies. But because, in his view, civil government possessed full powers to act in the public good, nothing in his theory of government would *exclude* a policy of abolition, so long as it was duly enacted by the legislative power and carried out impartially rather than arbitrarily. Nothing in Locke's theory suggests that he would accord the slaveholding minority veto rights over policies affecting slavery. In this sense, I argue, Lincoln's preferred policy of abolishing slavery gradually and democratically as an act in the public interest, with compensation paid to slaveholders but not enabling them to block emancipation, was consistent with Locke's understanding of the legitimate scope of government and majority rule. Moreover, Lincoln's preferred policy was consistent with the fundamental purpose of government according to Locke, which is to better secure the natural rights of all persons than is possible in the absence of government. As noted earlier, Jefferson's "wolf by the ear" dilemma cannot be resolved by any theory of natural right or natural law. There is no impartial way of deciding whether the liberty of the slave should take priority over the life of the slave owner, or vice versa; nor is there any synthesis of natural rights principles or overarching superprinciple that would resolve the dilemma. But it can be practically remedied if civil government, acting in the public interest, formulates laws and policies that cumulatively modify circumstances such that enslaved persons can be emancipated without depriving former slave owners of life or liberty. To adapt Lincoln's metaphor: if the plank is not large enough to save two shipwrecked sailors, an effective government might pull them both out of the sea or at least drop them a lifeboat large enough for two.

Thus, Locke's view of the legitimate purposes and scope of government was compatible with Lincoln's aim of extinguishing slavery through a long, slow majoritarian squeeze. This presupposes, however, that Locke's theory of natural rights does *not* include a natural right to hold human beings as property. But many of Lincoln's slaveholding contemporaries maintained that the Lockean natural right to property included *all* forms of property, including "property in man."

Lincoln, Locke, and Property

It might seem obvious that Locke's political theory permits no natural right to hold another human being as property. Human beings are born free, equal, and independent. To deprive others of their life, liberty, or property is a violation of natural law. *Self*-enslavement also violates natural law; no such compact is morally binding. Locke writes that a man "cannot, by compact, or his own consent, enslave himself to any one, nor put himself under the absolute, arbitrary power of another." Locke's discussion of property rights in the state of nature likewise excludes slavery. God "hath given the world to men in common." The original form of property is each man's "property in his own person," which "nobody has any right to but himself." At first, the earth and its fruits are held in common, so all property beyond the original right of self-ownership must come from the labor of one's own body. "Whatsoever then he removes out of the state that nature hath provided" and has "mixed his labour with" becomes one's property, and "no man but he can have a right" to it. Thus, property rights in the state of nature are incompatible with slavery in two different respects: one person cannot own the body of another, and one person cannot appropriate the fruits of another's labor.[42]

Not only "property in man" but also exclusive title to property in land—or at least more land than one can personally cultivate—is illegitimate in this original commons. "As much land as a man tills, plants, improves, cultivates, and can use the product of, so much is his property." This rule would "confine every man's possession to a very moderate proportion." At this stage, there could be no large, gated estates and no civil government to issue property titles, settle boundary disputes, and punish trespassers. Only later in the political and economic evolution of the human race did money and markets emerge, along with landed property in the modern sense whereby political communities "settled the bounds of their distinct territories, and by laws within themselves regulated the properties of the private men of their society." Political communities do not exist in the state of nature but instead are created "by common consent." At that point, "by positive agreement" they settle and define rights to landed property, "in distinct parts and parcels of the earth."[43] In the original commons, there was neither government nor landed property nor money nor slavery.

But herein lies the problem with respect to slavery. Locke argues that human beings establish governments and laws "for the mutual preservation of their lives, liberties, and estates, which I call by the general name property."[44] Locke does *not* say that governments and laws exist only to protect those forms of property that could have existed in a pure state of nature. Neither moneyed property nor landed estates existed in the original commons. Yet Locke clearly intended governments and laws to protect those forms of property no less than the fruits one has gathered or the fish one has caught from common lands and waters. Suppose the institution of slavery, or "property in man," has developed historically alongside money and estates. Under Locke's theory, would slave property be equally entitled to the protection of government, along with moneyed property and landed property and other types of property that did not exist in the original commons? To answer yes to this question, one would not need to claim a natural right to enslave another person; we have already seen that Locke's theory rules out any such claim. But one could insist that slave property, no matter how it emerged, be protected on the same basis as other forms of property, as asserted in the 1850 Kentucky constitution, the proslavery Lecompton Constitution, and many other documents of the time. The "unnaturalness" of slave property would not preclude its protection by government, any more than the unnaturalness of money or landed estates.

One might attempt to dismiss the problem by claiming that slavery cannot exist without a modern state, written laws, a law enforcement apparatus, and so on. However, while state institutions unquestionably reinforced the stability of slavery in the United States and elsewhere, it is inaccurate to claim that slavery cannot exist without them. Intriguingly, Stephen Douglas and Abraham Lincoln debated this question during the 1850s. Douglas in 1858 attempted to salvage his popular sovereignty doctrine in the wake of the Supreme Court's *Dred Scott* ruling by maintaining that "slavery cannot exist a day or an hour anywhere, unless it is supported by local police regulations," which "can only be established by the local legislature."[45] Lincoln, in contrast, had been arguing since 1854:

> Wherever slavery is, it has been first introduced without law. The oldest laws we find concerning it, are not laws introducing it; but *regulating* it, as an already existing thing. A white man takes his slave to Nebraska now; who will inform that negro that he is free? Who will take him before court to test the question of his freedom? In ignorance of his legal emancipation, he is kept chopping, splitting and plowing.

By the time formal laws are enacted, "the institution already in fact exists in the country, and cannot well be removed."[46] Lincoln here described how "property in man" could emerge early, before state institutions were fully developed and subsequently be codified into law, along with other forms of property. To convert the Lockean understanding of property into a strong antislavery instrument (which Lincoln aimed to do) required sharply distinguishing slave property from other forms of property, not only in long-superseded stages of economic development but also in modern commercial society.

Lincoln built on Lockean ideas about labor, property, and wealth but also transformed them, selectively emphasizing some and downplaying others. Lincoln's version of Lockean theory was exemplified in his criticism of the Democratic Party's understanding of liberty and property in the 1850s. The Democrats, Lincoln claimed, "hold the *liberty* of one man to be absolutely nothing, when in conflict with another man's right of *property*. Republicans, on the contrary, are for both the *man* and the *dollar*, but in cases of conflict, the man *before* the dollar."[47] This passage encapsulates what Lincoln kept and transformed in Lockean theory. The potential conflicts between "liberty and property," "the man and the dollar" that Lincoln invoked are hardly acknowledged, if at all, in Locke's discussion of property.

Locke's discussion (chapter 5 of the *Second Treatise*) of how property rights evolved as societies moved from hunting and gathering to landed property, money, and wage labor noticeably weakened the labor-property link he had strongly affirmed at earlier stages. In a passage frequently noted by his critics, Locke wrote that "the turfs my servant has cut . . . become my property" because "the labour that was mine, hath fixed my property in them."[48] Why are the turfs not the property of the servant who labored to cut them? Or if the landowner labored alongside the servant, why are the turfs not divided between them? Instead, the turfs belong to the landowner because he owns the land, which presupposes property titles and governments to enforce them; or they belong to the landowner because he paid the servant for his labor, which presupposes money. In short, Locke's landowner and servant interact at a later stage of economic development already characterized by "a disproportionate and unequal possession of the earth" and "an inequality of private possessions" for which the invention of money was essential.[49] Yet Locke nowhere suggests that the wealthy landowner is any less morally entitled to his landed and monied property (which might be enjoyed in comfortable idleness) than the fisherman is to the fish caught with his own hands in common waters. Whether Locke's turf-cutting passage functions as an ideological justification for capitalism (which hardly existed as an economic system when the *Second Treatise* was published) is a separate question.[50] The critical point is that the connection between the labor of one's own body and the ownership of the fruits of one's labor has become far less direct. Now the laws of the land, not the labor of one's body, determine what one owns. Civil laws (and the economic institutions they regulate) can be formulated in different ways, with correspondingly diverse consequences for the connection between individual labor and ownership of its fruits.

Locke does not discuss slavery in chapter 5 of the *Second Treatise*. But American slave owners (who often referred to enslaved persons as "servants") would have agreed, from their own perspective, with the statement that "the turfs my servant has cut" are "mine"—especially if that servant was also by law the slaveholder's property. Despite Locke's apparently unequivocal rejection of slavery in the state of nature, his discussion of property in modern states and commercial economies might be construed to support slaveholders' claim that the right to hold slave property was "as inviolable as the right of the owner of any property whatever."

I do not claim that this slavery-friendly conclusion was genuinely consistent with Locke's argument. But it expressed one politically influential current of Lockean thought in America. Some defenders of slavery had read Locke; others, like Lincoln, received Lockean ideas second- or thirdhand. But nearly all defenders of slavery regarded *all* forms of property, including "property in man," as equally entitled to the protection of government. Such was the stance Lincoln characterized as ranking "the dollar" before "the man."

Lincoln sought to restore, to the degree possible in a modern economy and a civil state, the direct link between labor and ownership of its fruits described in Locke's initial, precommercial discussion of property and labor. Lincoln wrote in 1847 that "inasmuch as most good things are produced by labour, it follows that all such things of right belong to those whose labour has produced them." Yet "in all ages of the world . . . *some* have laboured, and *others* have, without labour, enjoyed a large proportion of the fruits. This is wrong, and should not continue." For that reason, "to secure to each labourer the whole product of his labour, or as nearly as possible, is a most worthy object of any good government."[51] Before 1854, Lincoln enlisted this idea to advocate for protective tariffs; public investment in roads, canals, and railroads; public education; and, in general, an active role for government in supporting individuals' efforts to better their condition. The full fruits of one's labor ideal acquired additional force for Lincoln after 1854, when opposition to slavery became central to his political efforts.

Among the many reasons slavery was unjust was that it violated a human being's "natural right to eat the bread she earns with her own hands without asking leave of any one else." Slavery also undermined, for Americans of all races, what Lincoln regarded as a fundamental quality of free societies: that "every man . . . should have the chance— and I believe a black man is entitled to it—in which he *can* better his condition—when he may look forward and hope to be a hired laborer this year and the next, work for himself afterward, and finally to hire men to work for him! That is the true system."[52] The "true system," for individuals of all races, was to receive the full fruits of one's labor and, through sustained effort, to achieve economic independence. Slavery was manifestly incompatible with this system, but so was an economy that consigned large numbers of individuals, Black or white, to a life-time of low-paid wage labor and personal dependency. Locke's servant would never receive the full fruits of his labor nor achieve personal inde-pendence if he spent his entire life cutting turfs for wages on someone else's land.

One scholar has labeled Lincoln's ideal the "economics of the American dream." Scholars writing on the subject generally agree that Lincoln's ideal of free labor and individual self-advancement was not one of unbridled capitalism, with its enormous inequalities and rigid class divisions; however, they disagree on whether Lincoln articulated a workable alternative. Some characterize him as oblivious to how his policies, including his wartime actions as president, undermined this ideal of economic independence and upward mobility. Such debates underscore how Lincoln's reformulation of "all men are created equal" as a permanently relevant social and political ideal to constantly strive for, even if never fully attained, has implications well beyond the task of extinguishing chattel slavery.[53]

Here I emphasize a dimension of Lincoln's free-labor economics that is easily overlooked when one focuses on his relation to capitalism rather than his opposition to slavery. Lincoln's attempted resurrection, amid modern commercial economies and civil states, of a more direct connection between labor and entitlement to its fruits challenged the slavery-friendly claim that all forms of property are created equal and thus equally entitled to the protection of government. For Lincoln, human beings were created equal; categories of property were not. Those forms of property that enhanced laborers' natural right to the full fruits of their labor deserved to be reinforced and encouraged by public policies. Those forms of property that weakened—or, in the case of slavery, altogether negated—individuals' natural right to the fruits of their labor could be justly discouraged by public policies and, in some cases, squeezed out of existence if proper constitutional procedures were followed. This does not mean that Lincoln believed natural right and natural law directly overrode civil laws, as many abolitionists and some Republicans maintained. For Lincoln, civil laws had to be followed; he did not pretend the state of nature and the original commons could be restored. But civil laws affecting property could and should be altered. No *natural* right was violated by policies that treated slave property as morally illegitimate, sought to halt its accumulation, and gradually to extinguish it. Nor were any *constitutional* rights violated by such policies, because the US Constitution did not affirm the legitimacy of "property in man." Instead, such decisions were matters affecting the public good, and as such, they were rightfully vested in the majority.

Government had a moral responsibility to protect "the man" and his capacity to act and work and enjoy the fruits of his labor. Protecting "the dollar" (here symbolizing all forms of property separable from the working individual's mind and body) was typically necessary to support the efforts of the man. But in Lincoln's view, government had no moral or constitutional responsibility to uphold the dollar or any other form of property *at the expense* of individual human beings' powers to act and work and enjoy the fruits of their labors.

Secession and the Right of Revolution

We know historically, however, that slave-state leaders regarded any interference with slave property as a violation of their fundamental rights and thus justification for dissolving the Union. Indeed, in the lower South, even the *intention* to restrict the expansion of slavery was viewed as sufficient justification for secession. The seceding states did not rely primarily on the natural right to alter or abolish oppressive governments affirmed in the Declaration of Independence, although several secession statements quoted passages from the Declaration. Instead, especially in those states that seceded before Lincoln's inauguration, secession was justified by the claim that the Constitution permitted any state to exit the Union at any time and for any reason; further, nonseceding states were obliged, under that same shared Constitution, to treat secession as a legitimate act and offer no resistance to it.

Because my focus here is Lincoln's reconstruction of Lockean natural rights, I do not examine in detail the arguments for and against a right of secession under the US Constitution.[54] Instead, I describe the interplay between constitutional and natural rights arguments in the justifications advanced by preemptively seceding states. Few Americans (if any) believed that, once a slave state passed a secession ordinance, the federal government and all other states would recognize that act as legitimate and peacefully acquiesce in dismantling the Union. Lincoln and other Republican leaders (and many northern Democrats, including Stephen Douglas) publicly rejected the argument that states had a constitutional right to secede. The seceding states, for their part, prepared from the outset for a military confrontation. Despite slave-state leaders' repeated assertion of a constitutional right of secession, free states' refusal to recognize that supposed right forced secessionists to make natural right as well as constitutional arguments for secession. Both constitutional and natural rights arguments for secession were employed to sway public opinion, especially in the South.

There have long been critics who argue that Lincoln betrayed the revolutionary tradition and contradicted his professed reverence for the Declaration of Independence by refusing to acknowledge the South's right to secede. Richard Hofstadter, for example, argues that Lincoln failed to make the Declaration of Independence "a consistent part of his living work," insofar as he "suppressed secession and refused to acknowledge that the right of revolution he had so boldly accepted belonged to the South."[55] I argue, on the contrary, that Lincoln's response to secession was fully consistent with the Declaration's criteria concerning when resort to revolution is or is not justified. The Declaration's opening sentence acknowledges that "dissolving political bands" is an extraordinary act requiring public justification: "a decent respect to the opinions of mankind requires that they should declare the causes which impel them to the separation." The act of electing Lincoln president of the United States, in accordance with the constitutional rules, did not come close to meeting the Declaration's threshold for forcibly dissolving a government. I also bring the natural rights of enslaved persons into the discussion; historically, they have been (and continue to be) conspicuously erased in arguments defending southern states' supposed right to secede from the Union.

Lincoln acknowledged a right of revolution in his first inaugural address and admitted that, under certain circumstances, the right of revolution could justify secession. "If, by the mere force of numbers, a majority should deprive a minority of any clearly written right, it might, in a moral point of view, justify revolution—certainly would, if such right were a vital one." Southerners, like all human beings, had the right to alter or abolish a government that had systematically violated their fundamental rights. But Lincoln denied that southerners had suffered violations of this kind. "All the vital rights of minorities, and of individuals" were "plainly assured to them, by affirmations and negations, guaranties and prohibitions."[56] Nothing inflicted on the South rose to the level of what the Declaration of Independence, following Locke, called a "long train of abuses and usurpations" evincing "a design to reduce them under absolute despotism." Lincoln had not yet exercised any presidential powers. His antislavery acts, up to this point, had consisted entirely of words, public expressions of antislavery opinions not yet translated into policy. (As noted below, however, northern states' unwillingness to suppress antislavery speech was critical to slave states' justification for secession.)

In principle, secession could be framed as either a legal or an extralegal act. To invoke a natural right of revolution, as American colonists did in 1776, was an extralegal justification. Although the Declaration of Independence identified multiple violations of traditional English rights, it did not claim that the British constitution authorized the colonies' act of separation. The Declaration instead justified separation based on Britain's repeated violation of "unalienable rights" belonging to all human beings. As Lincoln pointed out in his inaugural address, any right-of-revolution justification for secession was weak under the circumstances of 1860–61. Moreover, a right-of-revolution justification was vulnerable because of the high regard for the Constitution professed by all sides in the slavery and secession crisis. Lincoln observed in his July 4, 1861, message to Congress that secessionists would have failed if their plan were seen as involving a *violation* of law; instead, they argued that secession could be effected "*consistently* with the national Constitution."[57] But the US Constitution was conspicuously silent on the question of secession. (So too was the constitution of the Confederate States of America.) Thus, any constitutional argument for secession necessarily took an extratextual form.

In the early 1850s South Carolina secessionist Robert Barnwell Rhett

proudly characterized southern secession as "revolution," but the rhetoric of revolution proved counterproductive and, with the help of Calhoun's constitutional theory, secessionists of all stripes learned to frame
secession as a constitutional act. Calhoun grounded a right of secession
in what he argued was the inherent logic of the process by which the US
Constitution was ratified. Because each state ratified the document individually and separately, and because each state could have chosen not to
ratify the Constitution and thus remain outside the Union, it necessarily
followed (Calhoun argued) that the states retained their sovereignty
throughout all stages of the process and could constitutionally revoke
their act of ratification and exit the Union at any time.[58]

Lincoln called such constitutional theory "an insidious debauching
of the public mind."[59] Whether debauched or not, the constitutional
argument worked, at least in the slave states. In 1860–61 most (but not
all) seceding states followed South Carolina's lead in framing secession
as a literal *unsigning* of the Constitution—that is, a revocation of the specifically dated act by which that state had ratified or otherwise affirmed
the US Constitution. South Carolina's December 20, 1860, secession
ordinance (a separate document from its declaration of causes) reads
in its entirety:

> That the Ordinance adopted by us in Convention, on the twenty-third day of
> May in the year of our Lord One Thousand Seven hundred and eighty-eight,
> whereby the Constitution of the United States of America was ratified, and
> also all Acts and parts of Acts of the General Assembly of this State, ratifying
> amendment of the said Constitution, are hereby repealed; and that the union
> now subsisting between South Carolina and other States, under the name of
> "The United States of America," is hereby dissolved.

Framing secession as a constitutional act was essential for enlisting
the constitutional reverence that Lincoln noted was still strong in all
sections of the country. Moreover, by keeping its secession ordinance
separate from its declaration of causes, South Carolina underscored its
claim that a state could secede for any reason; the declaration of causes
was explanatory but not constitutionally necessary. (Some slave states
followed South Carolina in issuing separate secession ordinances and
declarations of causes; others merged them into a single statement.)[60]

To portray secession as a constitutional act, rather than relying on
the natural right of revolution, was important for another reason: natural rights claims could likewise be made by enslaved persons and by abo-

litionists on their behalf. By the logic of natural right, enslaved persons had as much right to "secede" from slave owners as slave owners had to secede from the Union and to call on anyone they chose (including the Union army) for assistance in that effort. If the escalating logic of revolution took that course (and it eventually did), secession would defeat its intended purpose, which was to render slavery more secure. But if secession was framed as a constitutional right inhering not in individuals but in states as corporate bodies, enslaved persons could not make comparable claims.

Some secession declarations, including South Carolina's, opted for complete silence with respect to the inconsistency of demanding self-determination for oneself while radically denying it to the persons one held in bondage, as though even raising the question was unthinkable. Other declarations, most notably that of Texas, anticipated the natural rights objection by asserting as "undeniable truths" that the US government and the governments of every state "were established exclusively by the white race, for themselves and their posterity; that the African race had no agency in their establishment; that they were rightfully held and regarded as an inferior and dependent race, and in that condition only could their existence in this country be rendered beneficial or tolerable." Among the grievances Texas listed as justifying secession was that citizens of free states persisted in "proclaiming the debasing doctrine of equality of all men, irrespective of race or color—a doctrine at war with nature, in opposition to the experience of mankind, and in violation of the plainest revelations of Divine Law."[61]

Secession statements of this kind (and others could be cited) would appear to radically reject natural rights theory. In substance, this was the case. But politically, it was necessary for seceding states to pay rhetorical tribute to natural rights. Texas proclaimed that "all white men are and of right ought to be entitled to equal civil and political rights." This exemplified the perverted natural rights doctrine that Lincoln accused Douglas of promoting. But when secession declarations made natural rights arguments, they principally emphasized the right of property and, in particular, the right to hold slave property, which slaveholders viewed as both a natural and a constitutional right. South Carolina's declaration of the causes of secession, for example, charged that the people of "the non-slaveholding States" had "denied the rights of property established in fifteen of the States and recognized by the Constitution." Georgia's declaration of causes argued that inhabitants of free states had violated the principle that "property of every kind (including slaves)" must be "equally protected by public authority." The Mississippi declaration of causes charged that "hostility" to slavery in the North had "grown until it denies the right of property in slaves, and refuses protection to that right on the high seas, in the Territories, and wherever the government of the United States had jurisdiction." Violation of the supposed natural as well as constitutional right to hold slave property was thus a key component of secession justifications. The Declaration of Independence's broader affirmations—that "all men are created equal" and possess "inalienable rights" to "life, liberty, and the pursuit of happiness"—were either conspicuously absent from secession statements or (as in Texas) directly denied.[62]

It is instructive to compare the "long train of abuses" tending toward "absolute despotism" listed in the Declaration of Independence with its equivalent in the declarations of the preemptively seceding states. The Declaration of Independence attributes abuse of power to a specific, powerful political actor: "the present King of Great Britain." (This was a rhetorical simplification; Parliament was at least equally responsible for the specified abuses.) All the listed abuses referred to *actions* taken by that king: "He has dissolved Representative Houses repeatedly. . . . He has endeavored to make Judges dependent on his will alone. . . . He has plundered our seas, ravaged our Coasts, burnt our towns, and destroyed the lives of our people." Expressions of *opinion* by the king, members of Parliament, or the British public were not listed as grievances justifying separation. The British public was criticized for being "deaf to the voice of justice" and unwilling to "disavow" the king's "usurpations." But it was the king's usurpations, not the British public's indifference, that justified revolution. Many of the listed abuses were actions depriving American colonists of the normal, peaceful avenues for redressing grievances. It is difficult to resolve disputes peacefully when representative bodies have been dissolved, independent judiciaries corrupted, and civilian government replaced by military occupation. Such abuses were small compared with the despotism enslaved persons endured daily, during the Revolution as well as in Lincoln's time. But considered on their own terms, as stages in the impending destruction of a previously free system of government, the grievances highlighted in the Declaration were significant and presented a plausible case for resorting to the natural right of revolution.

The states that seceded before Lincoln's inauguration (South Carolina, Mississippi, Florida, Alabama, Georgia, Louisiana, and Texas) had experienced nothing comparable to the abuses cataloged in 1776. The two previous presidents, James Buchanan and Franklin Pierce, were northerners whose administrations had been conspicuously friendly toward slavery, as was the US Supreme Court. Lincoln and his party had expressed antislavery opinions, but Lincoln was a private individual before March 4, 1861, and the Republican Party was short of a majority in Congress. Congress as a body had not satisfied slaveholders' demand that it mandate a slave code for every US territory. But neither had it enacted any new restrictions on slavery. When Lincoln took office, no southern state legislatures had been dissolved, no defenders of slavery imprisoned, no martial law declared, no armed invasion carried out. At least with respect to *federal* action, slave states had suffered no long train of abuses; instead, they had enjoyed a long winning streak that ended with Lincoln's election.

Insofar as declarations of the preemptively seceding states referred to any "long train of abuses," they were actions taken by northern states, not the federal government. The first grievance listed by South Carolina was that "fourteen of the States have deliberately refused, for years past, to fulfill their constitutional obligations" to return fugitive slaves. Those states, with the active support of their citizens, had "enacted laws which either nullify the Acts of Congress or render useless any attempt to execute them." Thus the constitutional compact "has been deliberately broken," and "the consequence follows that South Carolina is released from her obligation."[63] All the preemptively seceding states identified the free states' obstruction of fugitive slave laws as a grievance justifying secession.

Mississippi's declaration echoed South Carolina's on several points, but whereas South Carolina identified "fourteen states" as the responsible agents, Mississippi referred vaguely to a "feeling" of "hostility" toward slavery. This "feeling of hostility" thereafter collapses into a kind of floating "it" responsible for all the supposed outrages against the South: "It has nullified the Fugitive Slave Law in almost every free State in the Union, and has utterly broken the compact which our fathers pledged their faith to maintain"; "It advocates negro equality, socially and politically, and promotes insurrection and incendiarism in our midst"; "It has invaded a State, and invested with martyrdom the wretch whose purpose was to apply flames to our dwellings, and the weapons of destruction to our lives."[64] "It" in this last clause clearly refers to John Brown's raid, which was the act of neither the federal government (which tried, convicted, and executed Brown) nor any state. Rather, it was carried out by a small band of private individuals whose action Lincoln and the 1860 Republican platform publicly condemned.[65] The offending agents in Texas's declaration were a similarly amorphous "they": "They have invaded Southern soil and murdered unoffending citizens" (referring to John Brown's raid). "By consolidating their strength, they have placed the slave-holding States in a hopeless minority in the federal congress" ("they" here referring to every northern citizen who supported Republican candidates for Congress). "They have sent hired emissaries among us to burn our towns and distribute arms and poison to our slaves for the same purpose" (in this case referring to no historically documented actors whatsoever but to a purely imaginary conspiracy).[66] Mississippi's and Texas's shadowy, shape-shifting actors *it* and *they* allegedly responsible for serious and repeated offenses against the slave states present a stark contrast to the Declaration's "present King of Great Britain," a specific, powerful actor officially responsible for the actions denounced in the document.

"Hired emissaries" delivering shipments of poison to Texas slaves exemplified the "ills you fly from" that "have no real existence" to which Lincoln referred in his inaugural address.[67] But it would be inaccurate to describe the grievances cataloged in the secession declarations as entirely imaginary. There was no plausible argument that slaveholders had been the victim of a "long train of abuses and usurpations." But neither would it be accurate to reduce their concerns to "light and transient causes." Lincoln's election was a real and long-lasting threat to slavery, if slow-moving in its execution. That threat inhered not in past public actions but in the real possibility that, if slave states accepted the legitimacy of Lincoln's election and remained in the Union, national public opinion would turn enduringly against slavery and support future public actions to extinguish it. In this respect, the preemptively seceding states' chief grievance was antislavery opinion expressed by their northern compatriots.

South Carolina's declaration stated: "Fifteen of the States . . . have assumed the right of deciding upon the propriety of our domestic institutions. . . . They have denounced as sinful the institution of slavery; they have permitted open establishment among them of societies, whose avowed object is to disturb the peace and eloign [carry off] the property of other states." Calhoun had argued in his final Senate speech (1850) that "the agitation of the slave question" must cease, and abolition societies must be suppressed by northern states that currently permitted them, if slave states were to remain in the Union. Abolitionist speech, writings, and pamphlets had obviously not been suppressed in northern states in the decade following Calhoun's death in 1850. Instead, as South Carolina's declaration noted, "this agitation has been steadily increasing" and has "now secured to its aid the power of the common Government"—meaning Lincoln's election as president. Though Lincoln had not yet been inaugurated, his "opinions and purposes are hostile to slavery"; he had declared that this government "cannot endure permanently half slave, half free" and announced that "the public mind must rest in the belief that slavery is in the course of ultimate extinction." South Carolina's declaration characterized Lincoln's position accurately and did not conflate him with John Brown. Nevertheless, the facts that northerners continued to denounce slavery as unjust, refused to suppress abolitionist societies, and used their votes to elect a president with known antislavery views were presented as compelling reasons to exit the Union immediately, before Lincoln could take office.[68]

Other preemptively seceding states likewise emphasized antislavery opinion in the North as justifying secession. Georgia's declaration observed: "The party of Lincoln, called the Republican party . . . is admitted to be an anti-slavery party . . . antislavery is its mission and its purpose. By anti-slavery it is made a power in the state." Mississippi's declaration charged that "it" (meaning opposition to slavery) had "enlisted the press, its pulpit and its schools against us, until the whole popular mind of the North is excited and inflamed with prejudice." Texas cited the "unnatural feeling of hostility" toward slavery harbored by northerners, who continued to proclaim "the debasing doctrine of equality of all men, irrespective of race or color," and characterized this as a "violation . . . of good faith and comity." Thus, widespread moral opposition to slavery by citizens of free states was viewed as sufficient justification for secession, even without overt antislavery acts by the federal government.[69]

Slave-state leaders viewed expressions of antislavery opinion as offenses justifying secession for at least three reasons. First, such expressions were insulting because they presumed that people of the free states were morally superior to slaveholders and citizens of the slave states— hence South Carolina's complaint that slavery had been denounced as "sinful." Second, if antislavery "books and pictures" somehow reached enslaved men and women, despite the barriers designed to prevent this, it could inspire, according to South Carolina, "servile insurrection."[70] Finally and perhaps most importantly, antislavery speech could cause white southerners to doubt both whether slavery was just and whether it was consistent with their own security. This particular worry was *not* voiced in secession declarations, which expressed no reservations about the wisdom or justice of slavery. But many public and private statements by slaveholders in the decades preceding the war revealed doubts about the institution's safety, justice, or both. Others, without harboring any such doubts themselves, worried that doubts would grow among their fellow southerners if abolitionist speech, writing, and petitions continued undiminished. It was on such grounds that Calhoun demanded in 1836 the immediate and forceful rejection of all abolitionist petitions submitted to Congress. Addressing other senators from slaveholding states who were willing to allow antislavery petitions but insisted that "whenever the attempt shall be made to abolish slavery, they will join with us to repel it," Calhoun responded that such petitions *were* abolition; antislavery words were themselves the principal weapons wielded by abolitionists.

> Do they expect that the abolitionists will resort to arms, and commence a crusade to liberate our slaves by force? Is this what they mean when they speak of the attempt to abolish slavery? If so, let me tell our friends of the South who differ from us, that the war the abolitionists wage against us is of a very different character, and far more effective. It is a war . . . waged, not against our lives, but our character. The object is to humble and debase us in our own estimation, and that of the world in general; to blast our reputation, while they overthrow our domestic institutions.

For this reason, Calhoun argued, "we must meet the enemy on the frontier. . . . Break through the shell, penetrate the crust, and there is no resistance within."[71] For Calhoun (who still hoped to preserve the Union), meeting the enemy on the frontier meant silencing antislavery speech at its source. By 1860–61, preemptive secessionists realized that such silencing would never happen, and meeting the enemy on the frontier meant exiting the Union before an antislavery president could take office. If slaveholders remained in a Union headed by a president who publicly voiced antislavery opinions, that would "humble and debase us in our own estimation," as Calhoun phrased it, and weaken southerners' will to resist the future antislavery actions that were certain to follow.

Lincoln recognized the full extent of the suppression of antislavery speech, press, and thought demanded by southerners as the price of an intact Union. "What will satisfy them?" Lincoln asked in his 1860 Cooper Institute address. "This, and this only: cease to call slavery *wrong*, and join them in calling it *right*. And this must be done thoroughly—done in *acts* as well as *words* . . . suppressing all declarations that slavery is wrong, whether made in politics, in presses, in pulpits, or in private. . . . The whole atmosphere must be disinfected from all taint of opposition to slavery, before they will cease to believe that all their troubles proceed from us."[72] From Lincoln's perspective, the issue was not free states exercising despotic power over slave states but slave states seeking despotic power over free states and their citizens.

To return to the broader theme of Lincoln and natural right: it was precisely in his response to the preemptively seceding states that Lincoln was most Lockean and most faithfully applied the natural rights theory set forth in the Declaration of Independence. To argue that the risky and potentially violent act of dissolving a government is justified if certain conditions are met implies that dissolving a government is not justified if those conditions do not hold. Lincoln knew there had been no "long train of abuses" of the kind detailed in the Declaration of Independence. He also recognized that sharply opposed views about slavery divided northern and southern public opinion and that these differences would not quickly disappear; he never claimed that the disagreements were "light and transient." But he did believe, perhaps naïvely, that clashing opinions could be managed peacefully if all Americans, North and South, trusted in the democratic process.

Lincoln was also convinced that no other attempted resolution—including formal separation, as demanded by the seceded states—would play out peacefully. Here, he had realism on his side: two newly separate American nations deeply opposed over slavery, both laying claim to common territories and eager to expand, both itching to exploit the other's internal divisions, sharing a boundary thousands of miles long through border states and territories where divisions over slavery had long been bitter and often violent, both demanding navigation rights on the same rivers, economically interconnected to a high degree, both continuing unabated their efforts to mobilize public opinion while harboring a large, oppressed, restive population of enslaved persons who would seek external allies in their liberation efforts wherever they could be found—none of these features indicated the likelihood of peaceful secession followed by harmonious side-by-side coexistence. If Lincoln's trust in the democratic process within a politically divided but not yet partitioned nation appears unrealistic, it was no more unrealistic—and arguably less unrealistic—than hopeful scenarios for peaceful separation of the kind expressed by some of Lincoln's contemporaries in late 1860 and early 1861 and still voiced by some today. If Lincoln and his contemporaries, deeply divided on matters of great importance, ultimately failed to coexist peacefully, separate peacefully, or reunite peacefully, we might ask ourselves how prepared we are to meet comparable challenges today.

Conclusion

This book has examined Lincoln's understanding of majority rule, and its connection with slavery, from his early career through his first inaugural address in March 1861. I have referenced documents from the war years only insofar as they illuminate his prewar thinking. The book's principal topics—majority rule, slavery, elections, political parties, public opinion, race, mob violence, and the survival of popular self-government—were ongoing concerns for Lincoln and his contemporaries during the Civil War and beyond. So why end in March 1861?

Besides space limitations, I close the narrative before the Confederate assault on Fort Sumter (April 12–13, 1861) because that event irreversibly altered the choices available on all sides. In the South, the Fort Sumter assault created a new and more powerful justification for secession. Indeed, that was its purpose. The argument that Lincoln's election was sufficient justification for preemptive secession carried the day in South Carolina, Florida, Georgia, Mississippi, Alabama, Louisiana, and Texas but failed in the later-seceding slave states of Virginia, North Carolina, Tennessee, and Arkansas, as well as in the never-seceding slave states of Delaware, Maryland, Kentucky, and Missouri.[1] As noted in chapter 8, at the time of Lincoln's inauguration, there had been no "long train of abuses and usurpations" by the federal government. There were no new federal policies affecting slavery, much less an invading army. It was northerners' antislavery *opinions* that secessionists regarded as the principal threat. The future action secessionists most feared before April 12, 1861, was not northern military invasion of the South but the "cordon of freedom" designed to peacefully squeeze slavery out of existence.

The Confederate assault on Fort Sumter exploited a fatal vulnerability in the stance of southern Unionists. Nearly all southern leaders who rejected preemptive secession embraced the doctrine that the federal government could never, under any circumstances, use force against a state. John C. Calhoun made that argument in 1833 during the nullification crisis, and by 1860 it had become constitutional orthodoxy in the

South.[2] If the federal government could *never* constitutionally employ force against a state, then it was barred from defending a federal fort against attack by the state in which that fort was located. Even a peaceful effort to resupply that fort signified, in states' rights theory, an act of military aggression against the state. In this way, South Carolina, in tandem with the newly formed Confederate States of America, assaulted Fort Sumter to leverage the secession of Virginia, North Carolina, Tennessee, and Arkansas, none of which had been persuaded that Lincoln's election was sufficient justification.

Popular historical memory of the Civil War obscures this fundamental difference between pre– and post–Fort Sumter secession. After Fort Sumter, Lincoln did raise an army to suppress secession. Southern "lost cause" tradition later falsely attributed that intention to Lincoln from the outset. Fort Sumter generated a new and more powerful secession justification. Secession and war could now be described as defense of white southerners' life, liberty, and property from a "war of Northern aggression." It was no longer persuasive to claim, as southern critics of secession had argued before Fort Sumter, that the institution of slavery was safer in the Union than out of it.

Fort Sumter also fundamentally altered Lincoln's choices, which shifted even more radically as the war progressed. That story is too complex to summarize here, but I will highlight two basic points. First, if Fort Sumter pushed the slave states of the upper South off the fence in one direction, it pushed the free states in the opposite direction and gifted Lincoln, at least initially, with bipartisan support for the war effort to a degree he could not otherwise have secured as the winner of a four-way presidential election with only 40 percent of the vote. Together with secession, which removed those members of Congress most opposed to his policies, this gave Lincoln's party (through 1862) majority support in Congress, which in the absence of secession would have depended on additional gains in future elections.

But because Lincoln viewed the Union as in principle still undivided, he recognized, more than many Republicans in Congress, the highly conditional status of this secession-gifted majority. This partly explains his intense concern for public opinion in the loyal slave states, which in the aggregate had sent only one Republican to Congress in 1861, and the importance he placed on those states emancipating slaves voluntarily rather than through federal compulsion. In the 1862–63 midterm elections (held amid the war's staggering death toll, sharp divisions over the Emancipation Proclamation, and concerns about civil liberties), Lincoln lost even this secession-gifted Republican majority in the House and subsequently depended on Unionist independents to supply the margin necessary to pass legislation in Congress.[3]

Second, the war transformed Lincoln's options by enabling him to attack slavery directly, as a military measure, which would not have been possible if he had succeeded in persuading the slave states to rejoin the Union peacefully. In this sense, the war strengthened Lincoln's hand. But for Lincoln himself, given his faith in the effectiveness of "time, discussion, and the ballot box" and his desire to restore peacetime democracy as soon as reasonably possible, the need to resort to military force, both to restore the Union and to abolish slavery, was tragic, above and beyond the death toll of the war. We cannot understand Lincoln's actions during the war—what he did or declined to do, and when— without acknowledging his conviction that the slavery and secession crises could and ought to have been resolved through peaceful democratic means.

After the war began, Lincoln's first significant public statement described, as a chief war aim, demonstrating to the world "that when ballots have fairly, and constitutionally, decided, there can be no successful appeal, back to bullets" and that "there can be no successful appeal, except to ballots themselves, at succeeding elections." His Gettysburg Address portrayed the war as "testing" whether "government of the people, by the people, for the people" shall or shall not "perish from the earth." Abolishing slavery was unquestionably part of this test, but reestablishing the primacy of ballots over bullets was equally critical to this great testing of American democracy.[4]

Lincoln never considered postponing elections during the war. For a time, when the war was going badly, he believed that he was likely to lose the 1864 presidential election and that, if he were defeated, the effort to restore the Union would fail. Yet he rejected all suggestions that the 1864 elections be canceled or postponed. "We can not have free government without elections, and if the rebellion could force us to forego, or postpone a national election, it might fairly claim to have already conquered and ruined us." Lincoln urgently wanted to restore the Union, but preserving free government took precedence.[5]

Lincoln's Legacy

Lincoln has long been one of the most admired figures in American history. But he has never lacked vehement critics. Unsurprisingly, many of them have been defenders of the Confederacy. Others, including admirers of Lincoln's Illinois rival Stephen Douglas, argue that Lincoln's "ultimate extinction of slavery" was an empty phrase designed to advance his political prospects and that it endangered the Union by needlessly alarming the South. Still others denounce his record on civil liberties during the war, his unwillingness to support full civil and political rights for Black Americans, his support for colonization, and his perceived tardiness in issuing the Emancipation Proclamation, among other things. Many of the issues raised by Lincoln's critics are legitimate. They help move the appraisal of Lincoln beyond what Merrill Peterson describes as his "apotheosis" in popular memory, where Lincoln's life and death echo the life and death of Christ, and also past the Carl Sandburg image of Lincoln as "the common man writ large," the personal embodiment of American democracy to whom men will "turn forever in unwearied homage." Such monumental idealizations obscure what was innovative or traditional, perceptive or blinkered, enduring or timebound in Lincoln's effort to revitalize the American promise of popular self-government, which is the theme of this book.[6]

Today, at one end of the political spectrum, many affiliates of "the party of Lincoln" now unapologetically display the Confederate flag; at the other end, any historical figure perceived as complicit with white supremacy is ripe for condemnation and erasure. Under these circumstances, Lincoln's public reputation is vulnerable from both sides: from resurgent admirers of the Confederacy who view Lincoln as perpetrating a war of northern aggression and from oppression-centered narratives of American history, some of which present Lincoln as principally a white supremacist hardly distinguishable in this regard from Jefferson Davis.[7]

Frederick Douglass's characterization of Lincoln as "pre-eminently the white man's president" in his April 15, 1876, speech at the Freedmen's Monument to Abraham Lincoln is among the most frequently quoted passages in current debates over Lincoln's legacy.[8] Often the phrase is quoted without mentioning Douglass's praise for Lincoln in the same speech. Douglass observed that, without "the powerful cooperation of his loyal fellow-countrymen," Lincoln's efforts to both "save his country from dismemberment and ruin" and "free his country from the great crime of slavery" would have failed.

> Viewed from the genuine abolition ground, Mr. Lincoln seemed tardy, cold, dull, and indifferent: but measuring him by the sentiment of his country, a sentiment he was bound as a statesman to consult, he was swift, zealous, radical, and determined. Though Mr. Lincoln shared the prejudices of his white fellow-countrymen against the negro, it is hardly necessary to say that in his heart of hearts he loathed and hated slavery.

Douglass here communicated a complex evaluation of Lincoln's limitations and strengths, including his capacity to change. Douglass also perceived the political obstacles Lincoln had to overcome to secure the support of the white majority so that the Union could be saved and slavery abolished. This contrasts with narratives of the American past that satisfy popular appetites for plaster saints and cardboard villains.[9]

What is most important from the perspective of this book is not whether one personally admires Lincoln. In his words and actions there is much to admire and much to criticize. Whatever one's view of Lincoln, I hope readers will take away from his life and thought the realization that great injustices will not disappear without organized, sustained public action and that, in a democracy, such action depends on cooperation among individuals and constituencies who in many respects have little in common. By recognizing the gigantic dilemmas Lincoln faced in his time and place without losing his faith in the capacity of American democracy to address them, we may better prepare ourselves to face the challenges of our own time.

Clinging to Power at Any Cost

In his June 16, 2022, testimony before the US House Select Committee to Investigate the January 6th Attack on the United States Capitol, retired federal appeals court judge J. Michael Luttig described January 6, 2021, as the "fateful day for the execution of a well-developed plan by the former president to overturn the 2020 presidential election at any cost, so that he could cling to power that the American People had decided to confer upon his successor."[10] On June 9, 2022, just before the House Select Committee opened its first public hearing, former president Donald Trump publicly stated: "January 6 was not merely a protest, it represented the greatest movement in the history of our Country to Make America Great Again. It was about an Election that was Rigged and Stolen, and a Country that was about to go to HELL."[11] Trump's continuing public endorsement of the January 6, 2021, insurrection, his ongoing efforts to obstruct investigations of the assault, and his endlessly repeated false claim that the 2020 presidential election was stolen from him reveal a *design* (as that word is used in the Declaration of Independence) to overturn the practice of free elections in the United States.

John Locke's *Second Treatise of Civil Government* likewise spoke of a "design" to establish tyranny, which he distinguished from "mistakes," "mismanagement," "wrong and inconvenient laws," and "slips of human frailty."[12] The Declaration of Independence similarly distinguishes between "light and transient causes" and despotic designs. For both Locke and the Declaration, despotic designs were revealed by *repeated* acts over time, "all tending the same way" (Locke) and "pursuing invariably the same Object" (Declaration). Luttig's phrase, "a well-developed plan . . . to overturn the 2020 presidential election," expresses the same idea.

Trump's words and actions before, during, and after the January 6 assault on the Capitol do not qualify as mere "mistakes" or "slips of human frailty." Nor was the January 6 insurrection, the purpose of which was to halt the constitutionally prescribed tabulation of electoral votes in Congress, a "light and transient" event. What we confront here is a formidable design for tyranny. The remedy for this attempted tyranny, however, is not to "dissolve" our democratic institutions (which was the insurrectionists' aim) but to safeguard and revitalize them.

What is shocking is not that an individual entrusted with the country's most powerful office would seek to perpetuate himself in that position. The framers of the Constitution were aware of this temptation. They believed they had provided adequate checks against the success of such efforts. And arguably those checks worked, insofar as the defeated incumbent's efforts to keep himself unconstitutionally in power beyond the term to which he had been elected ultimately failed. Despite enormous (and ongoing) pressure and threats in some jurisdictions,[13] election officials counted and reported the votes in accordance with standing rules.[14] Judges at both the federal and state levels repeatedly refused, given the lack of even remotely credible evidence, the Trump campaign's demand that hundreds of thousands of validly cast votes in key states be disregarded.[15] US military leaders, who take an oath to support the Constitution, clearly and publicly rejected the proposal, floated by several of Trump's close advisers, to declare martial law and hold a new presidential election conducted and supervised by the military.[16] The tally of electoral votes in Congress resumed late on the evening of January 6, after the Capitol was reclaimed from a violent (and potentially much deadlier) insurrection designed to halt the vote count and keep Trump in office.

Although the constitutional checks ultimately worked, suggesting the resilience of the American constitutional order, the picture becomes cloudier if we reflect on what Lincoln, in his 1838 Lyceum address, called "the strongest bulwark of any Government—I mean the *attachment* of its people."[17] The active and continuing support of Trump's false claims of a stolen election by a significant segment of the US population and his multiple efforts to overturn the election results before, during, and after the January 6 insurrection indicate that the American public's attachment (to employ Lincoln's word) to the practice of free, impartially conducted elections is significantly weaker than most observers had assumed.

The January 6 Committee presented persuasive evidence that Trump and his advisers knew he had lost the 2020 presidential election. Their efforts to reverse the results were at no point characterized by genuine attempts to ascertain the facts; they simply demanded that Trump be declared the winner, regardless of facts.[18] The message communicated to Trump supporters is that if one is powerful and brazen enough, one can refuse to accept election results that do not go one's way.

Embrace of the "stolen election" narrative is driven in part by attraction to one-man, extraconstitutional, authoritarian rule of a kind fundamentally irreconcilable with American political ideals and traditions. Beneath the apparently endless manufacture of new conspiracy theories, as previous ones are debunked, lies the assumption that Trump himself, an incumbent president seeking reelection, was the final judge of whether those election results were valid. In July 2020 he proposed that the elections be postponed, a stance he did not retreat from, despite intense public criticism, and that presumed he was the final judge of whether, when, and in what manner elections would be held.[19] His supporters' apparently unshakable conviction that his loss in 2020 resulted from mass election fraud is not, and has never been, based on an independent evaluation of the evidence but on his supporters' *personal* trust in their leader's statements about whether the election results were legitimate. Trump had been cultivating this frame of mind among his supporters, and fostering suspicion against any disconfirming evidence, for more than four years.[20]

The political crisis we confront in the United States today has no close counterpart in American history. The nearest parallel is the lower South's decision to secede rather than accept the results of the 1860 presidential election. But secessionists did not justify their act by falsely claiming the election had been stolen. Nor did secessionists assert the right to rule the United States, despite having lost the presidential election; instead, they sought to separate from it. During the war, neither the Union nor the Confederacy canceled elections or bowed before strongman rule. Elsewhere in the world, however, sowing distrust about the electoral process and falsely dismissing unfavorable election results as fraudulent are standard tactics in the authoritarian playbook. In many respects, the current threats to American democracy find closer parallels in the authoritarian experiences of other countries.[21]

But if the authoritarian trends we witness in the United States today echo episodes from beyond our shores, the political and moral resources essential to resist those trends must come from within: from our homegrown democratic institutions, flawed as they are, and the legacies of men and women in American history who struggled to make those institutions more just and inclusive. Lincoln's faith in "time, discussion, and the ballot box" to address enormously difficult problems and remedy entrenched injustice is one of the legacies on which we can draw at this critical time.

American Democracy's Uncertain Future

American democracy today is facing a crisis that is arguably greater than any since the 1850s—and that crisis ended in secession and civil war. Eroding public support for democracy and increasing attraction to political violence and authoritarian rule were evident well before Trump's presidency. Those trends are discernible at both ends of the political spectrum, and they are not limited to the United States; however, support for democracy has declined more steeply in the United States than in most other industrialized democracies.[22]

The current crisis, like that of the 1850s, has been developing for a long time. History never offers exact parallels; nor is any one historical period unequivocally the most appropriate for illuminating our current challenges. Other episodes from US history, including the mass suppression of African Americans' voting rights following Reconstruction, also offer essential perspective on the present.[23] Historical comparisons are fruitful precisely because parallels are *not* exact. Attention to both similarities and differences helps dislodge us from partisan habits of mind, enabling us to view the current situation in new ways. Thoughtful engagement with figures from the American past (including but not limited to Lincoln) can also facilitate bridge building among contemporary Americans, who too often view one another from opposite sides of a deep chasm across which voices can barely be heard.

Some similarities and differences between the antebellum crisis and our present political crisis are obvious; others are less so. Our own times are characterized by deep and growing ideological polarization. The same was true during the 1850s, although *ideological* polarization in the 1850s did not track *partisan* polarization as closely as it does today because the party system itself was in flux in the 1850s. Lincoln, who urged citizens of free states to hate "the monstrous injustice of slavery" without hating "the Southern people," observed that the power of slavery to divide Americans was not "confined to politics alone"; Christian churches of nearly every denomination were "wrangling, and cracking, and going to pieces on the same question."[24] This tendency for ideological polarization to divide Americans at every level of society—in choice of occupation, neighborhood, church affiliation, and many other dimensions beyond voting—has been noted by analysts of the contemporary United States. As political scientist Nolan McCarty observes, America's deepening "ideological, cultural, racial, regional, and economic divisions" became the subject of widespread reflection following Donald Trump's election in 2016, but "these fissures have been opening for several decades and are deeply rooted in the structure of American politics and society."[25]

While there is widespread agreement among political scientists that polarization is significant and increasing, there is less agreement on *why* this is happening.[26] There is no obvious contemporary counterpart to the polarizing impact of slavery, which was an overwhelming presence—legal, economic, political, constitutional, and demographic—in the antebellum United States. Without minimizing the injustice of slavery, it is not difficult to understand why citizens of slaveholding states—especially in the lower South, which was more deeply invested in slavery than the upper South—would risk everything rather than accept abolition in any form, no matter how gradual. Most contemporary hot-button issues, including immigration, same-sex marriage, and restrictions on high-capacity firearms, do not match slavery with respect to the moral and economic stakes involved. Nor can today's increasing polarization be plausibly attributed to divisions over abortion; public opinion on that issue has remained essentially constant, with only minor variation, for the last twenty-eight years.[27]

Race is another matter. Both persistent racial inequality and white Americans' anxiety about Black Americans' efforts to remedy those inequalities were present in the 1850s and continue today. Lincoln believed white Americans' opposition to racial equality was stronger, more enduring, and more geographically widespread, including in the free states, than support for the institution of slavery. He believed it was possible to build an enduring antislavery majority among an overwhelmingly white electorate. But he did not believe that same white majority could be persuaded to support full social and legal equality for Black Americans. Despite the transformative impact of the war on northern public opinion and ratification of the Thirteenth, Fourteenth, and Fifteenth Amendments, racism has proved far more enduring than slavery. Nor has the tendency of many white Americans to view Blacks' economic and social gains as coming at whites' expense disappeared over time. As noted in chapter 6, Lincoln sought to persuade white Americans that this zero-sum assumption—that one race can elevate itself only at the expense of the other, that the white man can save himself only by drowning the Black man—was false: "the plank is large enough" for both, Lincoln insisted. Economic life is no more inherently zero-sum today than it was in Lincoln's time. But when human beings of any race or background suffer chronic economic stress and fear for their future, they are susceptible to the argument that "you" (the group to which you belong) are suffering because "they" (the "others," however defined) have gained at your expense. A recent study by the Chicago Project on Security and Threats found that an estimated twenty-one million Americans believe insurrectionary violence is justified to restore Donald Trump to the presidency; of this group, 63 percent embrace the "great replacement" belief that "African American people or Hispanic people in our country will eventually have more rights than whites."[28]

Another frequently advanced explanation for polarization is persistent economic anxiety among Americans of all backgrounds at a time of stagnant or shrinking real incomes for most Americans, combined with steeply increasing economic inequality. In principle, economic inequality is a different polarizing factor than racial fear. In practice, however, economic inequality and anxiety cannot be easily disentangled from racial fear because many people (in the United States and elsewhere in the world) are susceptible to the argument that their own economic distress is caused by policies favoring racial or ethnic "others."[29] Political scientists Suzanne Mettler and Robert C. Lieberman argue that the convergence of three developments threatened democracy in the 1850s and that these same three factors—plus an additional one not present in the 1850s—place American democracy at risk today. The three factors common to both periods are deep political polarization, conflict over who should be included in the political community, and rising economic inequality. The new factor is concentration of power in the person of the president.[30]

Neither of the two major political parties of the 1850s anticipated, much less advocated, the enormous power American presidents now exercise, even in peacetime. During the Civil War, neither US president Abraham Lincoln nor Confederate president Jefferson Davis exercised such power; nor did they seek it. If they had sought it, their respective Congresses would have refused it. Proslavery ideologues in the decades preceding the Civil War threatened free government in many ways, including suppressing freedom of speech and the press, to which they believed abolitionists were not entitled. But they did not propagate cults of one-man rule. Many twentieth-century authoritarian movements elsewhere in the world did feature cults of personal power, which have now become a significant democracy-endangering factor in the United States.

Broken Branches and Rabid Partisans

Before his election as president, Lincoln was a strong advocate for the constitutional authority and political vitality of Congress, which he saw as the principal (though not exclusive) channel through which the will of the majority expressed itself on national questions. Lincoln opposed the Mexican War because, among other reasons, President James Polk deliberately misled Congress about the circumstances surrounding the initiation of hostilities. He denounced the Kansas-Nebraska Act and the

Dred Scott decision, both of which sought to strip Congress of its authority to decide the single most important question facing the American public: the future of slavery. And in the case of the Kansas-Nebraska Act, the wound was self-inflicted. Neither as a candidate for president nor in his first inaugural address did Lincoln claim extraordinary powers for the office of the president. Whether Congress had the authority to prohibit slavery in the territories was the central constitutional dispute. The Civil War was a genuine emergency that prevented Congress from safely meeting during the conflict's early stages, but Lincoln sought congressional endorsement after the fact for measures that would ordinarily require prior approval from Congress, and he acknowledged the authority of Congress to ratify, reject, or modify the emergency actions he had taken.[31] Which of Lincoln's discretionary actions were justifiable under the circumstances and which went too far in curbing civil liberties is an important debate that lies beyond the scope of this work.[32] Never, however, did Lincoln either exercise or assert the expansive presidential powers in all domains of policy, to the exclusion or marginalization of Congress, that many twentieth- and twenty-first-century presidents of both parties have routinely asserted and exercised.[33]

There is a large literature, both scholarly and popular, on the expansion of both presidential and judicial power at the expense of Congress, which is increasingly viewed as the "broken branch" of the federal government.[34] Many studies have observed that Congress itself is at least partly responsible for this development. The Senate's extraconstitutional filibuster rule, for example, is now employed as an all-purpose strategy, with little pretense of deliberation or compromise, to block legislation supported by a Senate majority—except when supporters of the legislation employ the parliamentary strategy of classifying a bill under one of the filibuster-circumventing rules. Whether and how Congress can be revitalized as an institution that is able and willing to responsibly and deliberately enact (not merely block) legislation addressing urgent issues of the present and future is an open question. Congress today is adept at conveying ideological stances but increasingly unable to govern effectively, which partly accounts for the ongoing flow of power and initiative from the legislative to the executive and judicial branches.

Congress did not always function in an exemplary manner in Lincoln's time either, as evidenced by the Mexican War, the Kansas-Nebraska Act, and the fact that Congress nearly admitted Kansas to the Union with a proslavery constitution strongly opposed by a large majority of its citizens.[35] Lincoln nevertheless believed that Congress could become an effective vehicle for gradually and peacefully extinguishing slavery. The historical record does not demonstrate that Congress failed at this effort; instead, secession prevented it from being seriously attempted.

Besides his attachment to the constitutional authority and political relevance of Congress, Lincoln strongly believed in political parties, as discussed in chapters 3 and 5. His faith in a strong Congress was interconnected with his faith in strong parties. For Lincoln, party competition made the abstract idea of popular self-government a living reality for voters because it gave the party's candidates and volunteers an electoral incentive "to see each man of his Section face to face."[36] Lincoln, like Martin Van Buren, opposed the idea that a political party should serve as an instrument for the political ambitions of one individual. On the contrary, for Lincoln, a political party that was properly organized and understood by its adherents ensured that its candidates stood for something beyond personal self-advancement. Even more fundamentally, in his view, political parties made majority rule itself possible by performing the difficult but essential work of converting a majority in sentiment into an electoral majority; by creating stable middle ground and a sense of common purpose among constituencies with extremely diverse backgrounds, interests, and views; by enabling complex issues like slavery to be addressed through a sequence of dichotomous votes on which majority and minority stances could be clearly ascertained; and by directing strong political passions into peaceful electoral channels when they might otherwise take violent, democracy-threatening paths. Lincoln did not claim political parties always functioned in this positive way, any more than he claimed that majority rule was always well informed or just. But parties at their best *could* accomplish this work, and Lincoln invested enormous time and energy during the latter half of the 1850s into building a Republican Party that was capable of doing so.

Today, neither major party is effective at performing the positive functions that Lincoln envisioned. Nor does the American public, either in its attitude toward parties or in its voting behavior, appear disposed to support or reward strong parties in Lincoln's sense. Instead, the American public tends increasingly to think and behave like *negative* partisans: to "dislike parties" and yet "behave like rabid partisans," as one recent study framed the paradox. Under conditions of negative partisanship, voters increasingly "align *against* one party instead of affiliating *with* the other." Voters' views of political parties in general—including their *own* party and its candidates—become increasingly negative. But because voter animosity toward the opposing party and its candidates is radically heightened, the consequence is increasingly partisan voting behavior at all levels of government.[37] Under such circumstances, it becomes increasingly difficult for parties to moderate political conflict by directing it into peaceful rather than violent channels. Insofar as negative partisans hold in contempt many of the "respectable" leaders of the party they are affiliated with, leaders become less capable of restraining their party's popular base from engaging in extreme rhetoric and extreme behavior. Those party leaders who are more inclined to extreme rhetoric and behavior thus increase their share of intraparty support. This is emphatically not how Lincoln intended the Republican Party to function with respect to slavery or any other issue.

Our contemporary political paradox—that is, Americans hate parties but behave like "rabid partisans"—helps explain why proposals to remedy hyperpartisanship branch off in contradictory directions, with some analysts insisting that parties must be weakened and others arguing that strengthening parties would have constructive consequences.[38] The dispute over whether parties should be weakened or strengthened is partly semantic because "strong" and "weak" carry a variety of meanings when describing the behavior of political parties. A party that wins elections by stoking the fear and resentment of its adherents but is incapable of enacting policies that effectively address the economic stresses and cultural anxieties driving that fear and resentment could be classified as a strong party by one standard and a weak party by another standard.

Dangerously negative polarization also characterized the 1850s, but as noted earlier, the ideological polarization of the 1850s did not correspond as closely with partisan polarization as we observe today. Instead, intraparty divisions over slavery helped destroy the Whig Party in the early 1850s, hindered the prospects of the anti-immigrant American Party, and fatally divided the Democratic Party in 1860. As noted in chapters 4 and 5, Lincoln believed that realigning major party competition around the slavery issue would actually have more peaceful consequences than persisting in failed efforts to neutralize the slavery question. If the Democratic Party had not fractured in 1860 over slaveholders' demand that Congress impose a slave code on all US territories, Lincoln's hope that two strong major parties offering contrasting proposals on slavery would have peaceful, system-stabilizing, and Union-preserving effects could have been put to the test. In this regard, it is worth noting that in the most recklessly proslavery state, South Carolina, party competition in any form had disappeared almost completely.

Putting Our Faith to the Test

In closing, I return to what has been for me personally the most haunting question: whether slavery could have been abolished in the United States without civil war. Some readers may ask: why spend so much effort thinking about a historical outcome that did not come to pass? In reply, I offer two straightforward reasons and one that is more open-ended.

First, to understand Lincoln's political thought, I believe it is essential to take into account his conviction that slavery could and should have been extinguished peacefully. It was not only the prospective carnage of war that motivated his efforts to visualize an end to slavery that was both peaceful and just. It was also that civil war over slavery signified that government of, by, and for the people had failed. Lincoln believed and hoped that popular self-government, at its best, was capable of resolving the most difficult problems, not just the easy ones. He may have been wrong about this. But we will better understand what he said and did, not only before the war but also during it, if we keep this conviction in mind.

Second, it bears repeating that many slaveholders, including those who insisted that slave states must secede before Lincoln took office, believed that abolishing slavery through a long, slow economic and geographic squeeze was possible and indeed likely to succeed if the slave states did not take immediate and forceful action. In this respect, understanding what did *not* happen better illuminates what *did* happen.

Finally, asking whether slavery could have been peacefully and democratically abolished puts our own faith in democracy to the test at a time when democracy in the United States, as well as worldwide, faces an increasingly uncertain future. It seems straightforward to conclude, as many people have, that slavery in the United States was too deeply entrenched to be abolished peacefully. That judgment has much evidence on its side. Any plausible counterargument is limited to claiming that peaceful extinction of slavery might have been possible, not that it was probable. And even if possible, it might have been accomplished on terms that were less just, from the perspective of enslaved persons, than the actual course of events.

I raise this question, however, with respect to our democratic present and future. If we maintain that slavery by its very nature was too difficult a problem to remedy peacefully and democratically in the United States, then we tacitly presume that there are two categories of political problems: those that can be resolved peacefully and democratically, and those that cannot. I do not believe a categorical distinction of this kind is sustainable as a premise of democratic theory; nor does it provide useful guidance for democratic citizens facing the enormously difficult challenges we face both nationally and globally. Only after the fact did it appear inevitable that slavery had to end violently in the United States. On the evidence available to him at the time—and this is the only kind of evidence anyone has when deliberating how to act—it was not unreasonable for Lincoln to believe that a peaceful, just, democratic resolution was possible, though very difficult.

Nor does the historical experience of other countries support a clear, categorical distinction between political conflicts that can be peacefully resolved and those that cannot. During the 1970s and 1980s, many people assumed that apartheid in South Africa could end only through racial civil war on a massive scale. That such an outcome was likely but not yet inevitable was precisely what motivated Nelson Mandela, while still in prison, to initiate secret, politically risky talks with the South African government in the hope of achieving a negotiated end to apartheid.[39] The odds were stacked against this effort; numerous factors could have derailed the process at many stages along the way. And if it had failed, we might now classify South African apartheid along with US slavery as textbook cases of conflicts with no peaceful solution.

In contrast, during the 1970s and 1980s, almost no one (including its own citizens) would have predicted that Yugoslavia's principal religious and national groups would engage in a horrifically savage three-way civil war. The partition of the country into its constituent republics was recognized as a possible outcome, but few anticipated that intergroup animosity and violence would become even worse after partition. During the late 1980s, few observers would have predicted that Yugoslavia in the 1990s, either intact or partitioned, would exhibit far higher levels of political violence (including horrific neighbor-against-neighbor violence) than South Africa in the same decade. Yet a nation with apparently unmanageable conflicts somehow managed them, and a nation with apparently manageable conflicts failed to do so.

I believe we are best served by assuming, with Lincoln, that any disagreement can turn violent if we do not consciously direct it into peaceful channels and that any disagreement, however contentious, is potentially resolvable, or at least containable, through peaceful democratic processes. Moreover, to speak as if some disagreements run so deep that they *cannot* be resolved except by violence is to hand a rhetorical weapon to those who would violently obstruct the democratic process.

In my view, what is most inspiring about Lincoln's life and words is that, amid a titanic clash of social, economic, and demographic forces that led many of his compatriots to despair of doing anything about slavery and others to preemptive violence, he did not succumb to this democratic despair—not before the war, nor during it, nor at its close in reflecting on its "fundamental and astounding" results.[40] He trusted that, despite the enormous forces at play and the flaws in America's democratic institutions and processes, those same institutions and processes were sufficiently responsive to the deliberate acts and choices of leaders and citizens to enable them to address the nation's most serious problems. Secession and civil war did not prove that votes do not matter. Instead, the events following the 1860 election demonstrated that, at critical times, votes can matter *so much* that powerful people resort to extreme measures to nullify their results. Let us today trust that our democratic institutions, flawed as they are, can be employed by men and women of good faith to address our most urgent challenges—among them ensuring the future of American democracy itself.

Acknowledgments

For much of my life, I have reflected upon Abraham Lincoln. I long contemplated writing a book about him but waited until I was sure I could add something new to the mountain of words already published. I concluded my own contribution would be, not unearthing some aspect of Lincoln hitherto lost in darkness, but better illuminating a matter right before our eyes yet mostly neglected in the literature: Lincoln's understanding of majority rule.

Early in my career, when I turned my attention to American political thought, my starting point was not Lincoln and the Civil War but the framing and ratification of the Constitution. This was how I came to know Alan Gibson and David Siemers, who became my friends, conversation partners, and collaborators in the field of American political thought. Thank you, Alan and David, for walking this road with me.

Through my engagement with James Madison's writings, I met Greg Weiner, who recognized and appreciated Madison's principled commitment to majority rule. Thank you, Greg, for our conversations as well as your writings, which helped me clarify what I aimed to accomplish with my book on Lincoln.

Alan Levine and I have been friends since our graduate school years, before either of us had turned our attention to American political thought. Alan persuaded me to write essays for two volumes he edited, one on the political thought of Ralph Waldo Emerson and the other on the political thought of the Civil War. Jim Stoner, coeditor of the Civil War volume, twice provided valuable feedback on my Lincoln presentations at conferences. Tom Merrill, third coeditor of that volume and a panelist with me at a 2019 symposium on the Missouri Compromise, helped me understand the political factors that discouraged Thomas Jefferson from taking stronger antislavery stances during his presidency and retirement.

During my stint as visiting professor at the University of California–Davis in 2008–2009, I met Michelle Schwarze, a scholar of the Scottish Enlightenment, and Jim Zink, who shared my interest in the political thought of James Wilson. Thank you to Michelle for arranging my presentation on Lincoln to the Political Theory Colloquium at the University of Wisconsin–Madison in 2018 and to Jim for organizing the "Missouri Crisis at 200" symposium at UW–Madison in 2019. Thanks also to the Center for the Study of Liberal Democracy at UW–Madison for hosting the event and to its director Rick Avramenko, who, as editor of the *Political Science Reviewer*, published the symposium essays in that journal. I am grateful to Michael McManus and Lucas Morel for their detailed feedback on my Lincoln essay (adapted from chapter 4 of my then book-in-progress) as manuscript readers for the journal.

I have twice given Constitution Day addresses focused on Lincoln: to James Madison College at Michigan State University in 2012 and to the Citadel in Charleston, South Carolina, in 2017. Thanks to Ben Kleinerman and Scott Segrest for enabling me to describe Lincoln's constitutional ideas on both sides of the Mason-Dixon Line.

Thank you to Bob Shoemake and Susan Anderson-Benson for inviting me to speak about Lincoln, on multiple occasions, to the Selim Center for Lifelong Learning at the University of St. Thomas and to Amy Sunderland and Sandy Larson for inviting me to present on Lincoln to participants in the Senior College Program at Alexandria Technical and Community College. Attendees' responses at these sessions confirmed for me that interest in Lincoln's defense of majority rule reached well beyond the ranks of academic specialists.

In 2016, at the invitation of Will Jordan and Charlotte Thomas, I gave a presentation on Lincoln at Mercer University to the "1776 at Home, Abroad, and in American Memory" conference, sponsored by the McDonald Center for America's Founding Principles. Fellow presenters Brian Steele and Diana Schaub provided especially helpful feedback. The conference presentations, including Diana's excellent essay "Lincoln and the Daughters of Dred Scott," were published in *When in the Course of Human Events*, edited by Will Jordan.

To Jon Schaff, who first read Lincoln as a student in my American Political Thought course: thank you for your book *Abraham Lincoln's Statesmanship and the Limits of Liberal Democracy*, as well as your comments on my own manuscript-in-progress.

Early in my career, before I was writing about Lincoln, Terry Ball invited me to speak to the Political Science Department at the University of Minnesota. Later, during the formative stages of the Lincoln book, Terry and his wife, Judith, hosted my wife and me several times at their cabin on Madeline Island, where we talked about Lincoln between hikes and kayaking. Thank you, Terry and Judith, for your friendship, conversation, and hospitality.

I presented selections of the book-in-progress to the American Political Science Association in 2013, 2019, 2020, and 2022; the Society for Historians of the Early American Republic in 2022; the Midwest Political Science Association in 2019; and the Montpelier Roundtable on James Madison and the American Constitution in 2016. Peter Mc-Namara, with whom I have taught American political thought courses several times under the Teaching American History program, invited me in 2013 to lecture on Lincoln at Utah State University, whose campus features a bust of Lincoln. Bill Pederson, who keeps the Lincoln flame burning in Louisiana, arranged for me to participate in a Lincoln conference in Chennai, India (many of whose founding leaders were admirers of Lincoln), in 2009, the 200th anniversary of Lincoln's birth. Maria Ganauser, president of the Austro-American Society of Salzburg, Austria, gave me the opportunity in 2019 to talk about Lincoln in the city of Mozart.

During more than a decade of working on this book, I received feedback in writing, conversation, or both from too many individuals to list here. In addition to those noted above, my thanks go to Steve Macedo, John Zumbrunnen, Karl-Friedrich Walling, Andrew Hertzoff, Greg Collins, and Alex Zakaras.

In 2010 I was invited to give the Alpheus T. Mason Lecture to the James Madison Program in American Ideals and Institutions at Princeton University, where I first presented the core ideas that grew into this book. Thank you to the program's executive director, Brad Wilson, and its director, Robert George, for this opportunity and to the Madison fellows for fruitful conversations following my presentation.

I have taught in the Political Science Department at the College of St. Benedict and St. John's University since 1988. Thank you to colleagues, students, alumni, and members of the St. Benedict's Monastery and St. John's Abbey for encouragement, conversation, and inspiration over the years. Thank you to the College of St. Benedict and St. John's University for a 2019 sabbatical that was indispensable to my completing this book.

My essay "From Calhoun to Secession" was published in *The Political Thought of the Civil War*, edited by Alan Levine, Thomas W. Merrill, and James R. Stoner Jr. (University Press of Kansas, 2018). Space limitations prevented its inclusion here, but my effort in that essay to view secession from the perspective of the slaveholding South informed my discussion of Lincoln throughout *Sovereign of a Free People*.

I am indebted to Fred Woodward, under whose leadership the University Press of Kansas has become a leading publisher of American political thought. He encouraged me to follow my book on John C. Calhoun's critique of majority rule with a book on Abraham Lincoln's defense of it. Jeremy Bailey and Susan McWilliams Barndt, American Political Thought series editors for the press, also encouraged the project, and Jeremy provided valuable feedback on a draft of chapter 2. Senior editor David Congdon supported the manuscript-in-progress, made helpful suggestions, and kept it moving forward under sometimes challenging circumstances. The two manuscript readers for the press reinforced my confidence that the book had something new and important to say about Lincoln. Thank you to Erin Greb for producing the maps.

My partner in life, Pia Lopez, has been there for me at every stage of this massive, life-absorbing project.

My parents, Herbert and Charlotte Read, taught me that American democracy, despite its flaws, can work if engaged citizens put in the effort. My brother, William Philo Read, genuinely believed in the equal worth of every human being, including those who begin life with several strikes against them. All three looked forward to reading the book but did not live to see me reach the finish line. To Mom, Dad, and Bill I dedicate this book, in love and remembrance.

Notes

Chapter 1. "The Only True Sovereign of a Free People"

1. Abraham Lincoln, "First Inaugural Address," March 4, 1861, in *Abraham Lincoln: Speeches and Writings, 1859–1865,* ed. Don E. Fehrenbacher (New York: Library of America, 1989), 220.

2. Nolan McCarty, *Polarization: What Everyone Needs to Know* (New York: Oxford University Press, 2019), 22–49.

3. Daniel A. Cox, "After the Ballots Are Counted: Conspiracies, Political Violence, and American Exceptionalism: Findings from the January 2021 American Perspectives Survey," Survey Center on American Life, February 11, 2021, https://www.americansurveycenter.org/research/after-the-ballots-are-counted -conspiracies-political-violence-and-american-exceptionalism/.

4. Fehrenbacher, *Speeches and Writings, 1859–1865,* 536.

5. Fehrenbacher, 249, 686–687.

6. Abraham Lincoln, "Message to Congress in Special Session," July 4, 1861, in Fehrenbacher, *Speeches and Writings, 1859–1865,* 261.

7. Abraham Lincoln, "Address to the Young Men's Lyceum of Springfield, Illinois," January 27, 1838, in *Abraham Lincoln: Speeches and Writings, 1832–1858,* ed. Don E. Fehrenbacher (New York: Library of America, 1989), 29, 32–36.

8. Abraham Lincoln to Joshua F. Speed, August 24, 1855, in Fehrenbacher, *Speeches and Writings, 1832–1858,* 361.

9. Abraham Lincoln, "Speech on the Kansas-Nebraska Act," October 16, 1854, in Fehrenbacher, *Speeches and Writings, 1832–1858,* 328.

10. "Speech on the Kansas-Nebraska Act," 334.

11. Abraham Lincoln, "Speech at Springfield, Illinois," July 17, 1858, in Fehrenbacher, *Speeches and Writings, 1832–1858,* 471.

12. For detailed results of both the 1856 and 1860 presidential elections, see Michael F. Holt, *The Election of 1860: "A Campaign Fraught with Consequences"* (Lawrence: University Press of Kansas, 2017), 191–199.

13. See, for example, the antisecession speeches of Alexander H. Stephens, Benjamin H. Hill, and Herschel V. Johnson during the Georgia secession debate of November 1860, in William W. Freehling and Craig M. Simpson, eds., *Secession Debated: Georgia's Showdown in 1860* (New York: Oxford University Press, 1992), 51–114.

328 | NOTES TO PAGES 7–15

14. Thomas R. R. Cobb's secessionist speech, November 12, 1860, in Freehling and Simpson, *Secession Debated*, 29.

15. Fehrenbacher, *Speeches and Writings, 1859–1865*, 111–130. The Cooper Institute address is also known as the Cooper Union address.

16. Freehling and Simpson, *Secession Debated*, 148.

17. Robert W. Johannsen, *Lincoln, the South, and Slavery: The Political Dimension* (Baton Rouge: Louisiana State University Press, 1993), 9.

18. "Speech on the Kansas-Nebraska Act," 324.

19. Douglas's deliberate lack of clarity on this critical point is discussed in chapter 4. See also Christopher Childers, *The Failure of Popular Sovereignty: Slavery, Manifest Destiny, and the Radicalization of Southern Politics* (Lawrence: University Press of Kansas, 2012).

20. "Speech on the Kansas-Nebraska Act," 334.

21. See, for example, Allen C. Guelzo, *Lincoln and Douglas: The Debates that Defined America* (New York: Simon & Schuster, 2008), xxvi.

22. Fehrenbacher, *Speeches and Writings, 1859–1865*, 221–222. On the near impossibility of a clean, peaceful separation between slave and free states, see Kenneth M. Stampp, *And the War Came: The North and the Secession Crisis, 1860–1861* (Baton Rouge: Louisiana State University Press, 1950), 204–238.

23. See, for example, James H. Huston, "Did the Tug Have to Come? A Critique of the New Revisionism of the Secession Winter," *Civil War History* 62, 3 (September 2016): 247–283; Timothy S. Huebner, *Liberty and Union: The Civil War Era and American Constitutionalism* (Lawrence: University Press of Kansas, 2016), x; John Burt, *Lincoln's Tragic Pragmatism: Lincoln, Douglas, and Moral Conflict* (Cambridge, MA: Harvard University Press, 2013), xiv.

24. James Madison to Edward Everett, August 28, 1830, in *James Madison: Writings*, ed. Jack N. Rakove (New York: Library of America, 1999), 849. See also Greg Weiner, *Madison's Metronome: The Constitution, Majority Rule, and the Tempo of American Politics* (Lawrence: University Press of Kansas, 2012).

25. See John C. Calhoun, "A Discourse on the Constitution and Government of the United States" and "Speech on the Veto Power," February 28, 1842, in *Union and Liberty: The Political Philosophy of John C. Calhoun*, ed. Ross M. Lence (Indianapolis: Liberty Fund, 1992), 121–131, 487–510.

26. See Calhoun, "Discourse on the Constitution" and "Speech on the General State of the Union," March 4, 1850, in Lence, *Union and Liberty*, 274–278, 599–601. See also James H. Read, *Majority Rule versus Consensus: The Political Thought of John C. Calhoun* (Lawrence: University Press of Kansas, 2009).

27. "Speech on the Kansas-Nebraska Act," 332.

28. Fehrenbacher, *Speeches and Writings, 1832–1858*, 426.

29. "Declaration of the Immediate Causes which Induce and Justify the Secession of South Carolina from the Federal Union," December 24, 1860, Avalon Project, https://avalon.law.yale.edu/19th_century/csa_scarsec.asp.

30. For a general account of this strategy, see James Oakes, *The Scorpion's Sting: Antislavery and the Coming of the Civil War* (New York: W. W. Norton, 2014). Lincoln's specific application of the strategy is described in chapter 7.

31. Abraham Lincoln, "First Joint Debate with Douglas," August 21, 1858, in Fehrenbacher, *Speeches and Writings, 1832–1858*, 512.

32. James Brewer Stewart writes that "immediate abolition" was demanded by "all fully committed abolitionists" because they shared the "fundamental conviction . . . that slavery itself was so heinous a crime in the eyes of God and so fundamental a violation of all principles of American freedom that it ought, by every measure of justice, to be destroyed in the twinkling of an eye." James Brewer Stewart, *Abolitionist Politics and the Coming of the Civil War* (Amherst: University of Massachusetts Press, 2008), 4. For Douglass's rejection of colonization, see David W. Blight, *Frederick Douglass: Prophet of Freedom* (New York: Simon & Schuster, 2018), 97–98, 370–377, 239–240; for his insistence on voting rights for all, regardless of race or sex, see Blight, 196, 273.

33. For a profile of Garrisonian abolitionism, see William W. Wiecek, *The Sources of Anti-Slavery Constitutionalism in America, 1760–1848* (Ithaca, NY: Cornell University Press, 1977), 228–248.

34. On abolitionists who made the strategic decision to work within the framework of the American political system, see Richard H. Sewell, *Ballots for Freedom: Antislavery Politics in the United States, 1837–1860* (New York: Oxford University Press, 1976); Corey M. Brooks, *Liberty Power: Antislavery Third Parties and the Transformation of American Politics* (Chicago: University of Chicago Press, 2016). Stanley Harrold describes the complex mix of hope and criticism with which many abolitionists viewed the Republican Party in general, and Lincoln in particular, during the 1850s. Stanley Harrold, *Lincoln and the Abolitionists* (Carbondale: Southern Illinois University Press, 2018), 49–74.

35. For Lincoln's advocacy of colonization "so far as individuals may desire"—that is, on the condition that it was genuinely voluntary—see his "Eulogy on Henry Clay," July 6, 1852, in Fehrenbacher, *Speeches and Writings, 1832–1858*, 270–271; "Speech on the Kansas-Nebraska Act," 316; "Speech on the Dred Scott Decision," June 26, 1857, in Fehrenbacher, *Speeches and Writings, 1832–1858*, 402–403. For Lincoln's wartime remarks on colonization, see his "Annual Message to Congress," December 3, 1861 (where the phrase "so far as individuals may desire" appears); "Address on Colonization to a Committee of Colored Men," August 14, 1862; and "Annual Message to Congress," December 1, 1862, in Fehrenbacher, *Speeches and Writings, 1859–1865*, 291–292, 353–357, 407–413.

36. See, for example, Lerone Bennett Jr., *Forced into Glory: Abraham Lincoln's White Dream* (Chicago: Johnson Publishing, 2000).

37. "Speech on the Dred Scott Decision," 402.

38. Abraham Lincoln, "Speech on Reconstruction," Washington, DC, April

11, 1865, in Fehrenbacher, *Speeches and Writings, 1859–1865*, 699–700. A year earlier Lincoln had privately expressed his support of voting rights for at least some formerly enslaved persons. Lincoln to Michael Hahn, March 13, 1864, in Fehrenbacher, 579.

39. Michael W. Kaufman, *American Brutus: John Wilkes Booth and the Lincoln Conspiracies* (New York: Random House, 2005), 209–210.

40. Although Illinois prohibited slavery, it also instituted harsh "black laws" that sought to bar free persons of color from entering the state; required those resident in the state to post a $1,000 bond; prevented them from serving on juries, testifying against white citizens, or serving in the state militia; and restricted public education to whites, in addition to denying Black persons the right to vote. See Leon F. Litwack, *North of Slavery: The Negro in the Free States, 1790–1860* (Chicago: University of Chicago Press, 1961), 66–71; Eric Foner, *The Fiery Trial: Abraham Lincoln and American Slavery* (New York: W. W. Norton, 2011), 8, 22–23, 119–120.

41. See, for example, Lincoln's "First Joint Debate with Douglas," 511, where he quoted from his October 16, 1854, "Speech on the Kansas-Nebraska Act."

42. "First Joint Debate with Douglas," 511.

43. "Speech on the Kansas-Nebraska Act," 316, 327–328.

44. "Speech on the Kansas-Nebraska Act," 329.

45. "Speech on the Kansas-Nebraska Act," 316.

46. Lincoln said: "My first impulse would be to free all the slaves, and send them to Liberia,—to their own native land. But a moment's reflection would convince me, that whatever of high hope, (as I think there is) there may be in this, in the long run, its sudden execution is impossible. If they were all landed there in a day, they would all perish in the next ten days; and there are not surplus shipping and surplus money enough in the world to carry them there in many times ten days." "Speech on the Kansas-Nebraska Act," 316.

47. According to David Blight, Douglass's first publicly recorded remarks occurred at an 1839 antislavery meeting where he spoke in favor of an anticolonization resolution that proclaimed: "We are *American citizens*, born with natural, inherent, just and inalienable rights." Blight, *Frederick Douglass*, 98.

48. Litwack, *North of Slavery*, 257–262.

49. For example, Hinton Rowan Helper, an antislavery white southerner from North Carolina, proposed that slave owners' wealth be confiscated and distributed to white non–slave owners, who, Helper argued, were the principal victims of slavery. As for enslaved persons themselves, Helper proposed that they all be forcibly deported within six months and dropped on the coast of Africa with $60 in their pockets. Hinton Rowan Helper, *The Impending Crisis of the South: How to Meet It* (New York: Burdick Brothers, 1857), 181–182.

50. Litwack, *North of Slavery*, 253.

51. Abraham, Lincoln, "Speech at New Haven, Connecticut," March 6,

1860, in Fehrenbacher, *Speeches and Writings, 1859–1865*, 139. See also Lincoln, "Speech at Hartford, Connecticut," March 5, 1860, in *The Collected Works of Abraham Lincoln*, 9 vols., ed. Roy P. Basler (New Brunswick, NJ: Rutgers University Press, 1953), 4:4–5.

52. To my knowledge, there are no full-length books on Lincoln's understanding of majority rule; nor have I found any journal articles focused on this theme. Mark A. Graber offers a brief but substantive and perceptive treatment of Lincoln and majority rule in *Dred Scott and the Problem of Constitutional Evil* (New York: Cambridge University Press, 2006), 179–198. Graber's account of Lincoln's majoritarianism is less sympathetic than the one I present here, but I share his view that Lincoln's majoritarianism represented a fundamental and disruptive challenge to the hitherto accepted ground rules of antebellum American politics.

53. On Lincoln's rhetoric, see Douglas L. Wilson, *Lincoln's Sword: The Presidency and the Power of Words* (New York: Vintage, 2006); Diana Schaub, *His Greatest Speeches: How Lincoln Moved the Nation* (New York: St. Martin's Press, 2021). On Lincoln's constitutional thought, see Daniel Farber, *Lincoln's Constitution* (Chicago: University of Chicago Press, 2003); Michael Les Benedict, "Lincoln and Constitutional Politics," *Marquette Law Review* 93 (2010): 1333–1366; Mark E. Neely, *Lincoln and the Triumph of the Nation: Constitutional Conflict in the American Civil War* (Chapel Hill: University of North Carolina Press, 2011). For Lincoln and public opinion, see Allen C. Guelzo, "'Public Sentiment Is Everything': Abraham Lincoln and the Power of Public Opinion," in *Lincoln and Liberty: Wisdom for the Ages*, ed. Lucas E. Morel (Lexington: University Press of Kentucky, 2014), 171–190; David Zarefsky, "'Public Sentiment Is Everything': Lincoln's View of Political Persuasion," *Journal of the Abraham Lincoln Association* 15, 2 (1994): 23–40.

54. See, for example, Phillip S. Paludan, "Lincoln and Democracy," in *Lincoln's Legacy: Ethics and Politics* (Urbana: University of Illinois Press, 2008), 1–12.

55. This theme is central to Gabor S. Boritt, *Lincoln and the Economics of the American Dream* (Urbana: University of Illinois Press, 1978).

56. Quoted in Paludan, "Lincoln and Democracy," 4. For the original fragment, unpublished in Lincoln's lifetime and conjecturally dated 1858, see Fehrenbacher, *Speeches and Writings, 1832–1858*, 484.

57. See, for example, William E. Gienapp, *The Origins of the Republican Party, 1852–1856* (New York: Oxford University Press, 1987). For Lincoln's earlier party-building efforts as an Illinois Whig, see Gerald Leonard, *The Invention of Party Politics: Federalism, Popular Sovereignty, and Constitutional Development in Jacksonian Illinois* (Chapel Hill: University of North Carolina Press, 2002), 245–249.

58. Harry V. Jaffa, *Crisis of the House Divided: An Interpretation of the Issues in the Lincoln-Douglas Debates*, 50th anniversary ed. (Chicago: University of Chicago Press, 2009), 184–185.

59. Michael I. Norton and Samuel R. Sommers, "Whites See Racism as a Zero-Sum Game that They Are Losing," *Perspectives on Psychological Science* 6, 3 (2011): 215–218.

60. See Robert Bray, "What Abraham Lincoln Read—An Evaluative and Annotated List," *Journal of the Abraham Lincoln Association* 28, 2 (Summer 2007): 28–81.

61. Jaffa, *Crisis of the House Divided*, 314–315.

62. Jaffa noted this problem in *Crisis of the House Divided* but left it largely unaddressed; see, for example, 326–327, 384–385. Jaffa suggests that Lincoln attempted to resolve Jefferson's "wolf by the ear" dilemma by adding an abstract principle: that is, in addition to enjoying a natural right to justice, one has a natural *duty* to do justice to others, irrespective of one's self-interest (327). Lincoln may have recognized such a duty, but unless this duty obligates human beings to sacrifice their lives for justice, it is not clear how adding natural duties to the mix resolves the dilemma as Jefferson framed it.

63. Thomas Jefferson to John Holmes, April 22, 1820, in *Thomas Jefferson: Writings*, ed. Merrill D. Peterson (New York: Library of America, 1984), 1434.

64. "Speech on the Kansas-Nebraska Act," 335.

Chapter 2. "We Divide into Majorities and Minorities"

1. Abraham Lincoln, "First Inaugural Address," March 4, 1861, in *Abraham Lincoln: Speeches and Writings, 1859–1865*, ed. Don E. Fehrenbacher (New York: Library of America, 1989), 219–220.

2. Fehrenbacher, 215.

3. Fehrenbacher, 220.

4. For example, South Carolina's Declaration of the Causes of Secession (December 24, 1860) lists specific grievances connected with all three disputed constitutional questions Lincoln posed in the inaugural address. The declaration condemned northern states' efforts to block federal enforcement of the Constitution's fugitive slave clause and asserted that the Constitution specifically recognized and protected "the right of property in slaves" under all circumstances (from which it followed that Congress *must* protect slavery in the territories). The declaration denounced the Republican Party's commitment that (as South Carolina phrased it) "the South shall be excluded from the common territory," or, as Lincoln framed it, Congress "*may* . . . prohibit slavery in the territories." "Declaration of the Immediate Causes which Induce and Justify the Secession of South Carolina from the Federal Union," Avalon Project, https://avalon.law.yale.edu/19th_century/csa_scarsec.asp.

5. Constitutional Union candidate John Bell, who received thirty-nine elec-

toral votes and 590,901 popular votes (12.6 percent), took no clear position on disputed slavery questions.

6. South Carolina's Declaration of the Causes of Secession names twelve northern states that "have enacted laws which either nullify the Acts of Congress or render useless any attempt to execute them. In many of these States the fugitive is discharged from service or labor claimed, and in none of them has the State Government complied with the stipulation made in the Constitution."

7. Fehrenbacher, *Speeches and Writings, 1859–1865*, 216. Lincoln called for revising the fugitive slave laws to include due process protections for persons accused of being fugitive slaves, but he considered enforcement of the clause in some form a constitutional obligation. On the Fugitive Slave Act of 1850, see David M. Potter, *The Impending Crisis, 1848–1861* (New York: Harper & Row, 1976), who observes that "the law left all free Negroes with inadequate safeguards against claims that they were fugitives, and it exposed them to the dangers of kidnapping" (131). Don E. Fehrenbacher, in *The Slaveholding Republic: An Account of the United States Government's Relations to Slavery* (New York: Oxford University Press, 2001), describes the law as "utterly one-sided, lending categorical federal protection to slavery while making no concessions to the humanity of African-Americans or to the humanitarian sensibilities of many white Americans" (232).

8. Fehrenbacher, *Speeches and Writings, 1859–1865*, 220.

9. Robert Bray, "What Abraham Lincoln Read—An Evaluative and Annotated List," *Journal of the Abraham Lincoln Association* 28, 2 (Summer 2007): 28–81. In Bray's coding system, he gives Blackstone's *Commentaries* an A+, denoting a work "attested by Lincoln himself in his writings, in such a way as to indicate more than passing awareness or mere quotation."

10. William Blackstone, *Commentaries on the Laws of England* [1765], book 1 (Oxford: Oxford University Press, 2016), 39. On the idea of popular sovereignty in the early American republic, see Bernard Bailyn, *The Ideological Origins of the American Revolution* (Cambridge, MA: Harvard University Press, 1967); Gordon S. Wood, *The Creation of the American Republic* (Chapel Hill: University of North Carolina Press, 1969); Edmund S. Morgan, *Inventing the People: The Rise of Popular Sovereignty in England and America* (New York: Norton, 1988).

11. Political scientist William Riker defines "populism" as the view that "the opinions of the majority *must* be right." William H. Riker, *Liberalism against Populism: A Confrontation between the Theory of Democracy and the Theory of Social Choice* (Prospect Heights, IL: Waveland Press, 1982), 14. Andrew Jackson wrote in his farewell address (1837): "Never for a moment believe that the great body of the citizens . . . can deliberately intend to do wrong." Quoted in Phillip S. Paludan, *Lincoln's Legacy: Ethics and Politics* (Urbana: University of Illinois Press, 2008), 3.

12. Abraham Lincoln, "Speech on the Kansas-Nebraska Act," October 16,

1854, in *Abraham Lincoln: Speeches and Writings, 1832–1858*, ed. Don E. Fehrenbacher (New York: Library of America, 1989), 326. On the challenges of converting the majority's antislavery sympathies into an antislavery electoral majority, see chapter 5. Lincoln's views on race are discussed in chapter 6.

13. J. David Greenstone, *The Lincoln Persuasion: Remaking American Liberalism* (Princeton, NJ: Princeton University Press, 1993), describes Lincoln as a "reform liberal," meaning that he was "concerned with the development of the faculties of individuals," in contrast to "humanist liberals" like Stephen Douglas, who "were concerned primarily with the satisfaction of the preferences of individuals" (6). Lincoln's perspective on the antislavery intuitions of the white majority was "developmental," in Greenstone's sense, because such intuitions had to be cultivated morally and channeled politically.

14. Fehrenbacher, *Speeches and Writings, 1859–1865*, 220–221.

15. Fehrenbacher notes the great irony that the Supreme Court's decision in the *Dred Scott* case was "an effort at judicial statesmanship, intended to bring peace but instead pushing the nation closer to civil war. . . . Peace on Taney's terms resembled the peace implicit in a demand for unconditional surrender." Don E. Fehrenbacher, *The Dred Scott Case: Its Significance in Law and Politics* (New York: Oxford University Press, 1978), 3.

16. For violations of constitutional process by the proslavery faction in Kansas, see William W. Freehling, *The Road to Disunion: Secessionists Triumphant, 1854–1861* (New York: Oxford University Press, 2007), 61–84, 123–144.

17. Fehrenbacher, *Speeches and Writings, 1859–1865*, 215.

18. "Speech on the Kansas-Nebraska Act," 331–332.

19. Fehrenbacher, *Speeches and Writings, 1859–1865*, 221.

20. Mark Graber observes that "Lincoln respected all previous constitutional compromises consented to by free-state representatives, whether these compromises were embodied in the Constitution or in legislation. . . . Lincoln insisted, however, that a free-state majority had no duty to accommodate any more slavery than plainly mandated by past settlements." Mark Graber, *Dred Scott and the Problem of Constitutional Evil* (New York: Cambridge University Press, 2006), 176.

21. See Calhoun's final address to the US Senate, March 4, 1850, in Ross M. Lence, ed., *Union and Liberty: The Political Philosophy of John C. Calhoun* (Indianapolis: Liberty Fund, 1992), 573–601. On Calhoun's understanding of the Constitution, see James H. Read, *Majority Rule versus Consensus: The Political Thought of John C. Calhoun* (Lawrence: University Press of Kansas, 2009), 85–117.

22. On secessions-within-secessions in the former Yugoslavia, see Susan L. Woodward, *Balkan Tragedy: Chaos and Dissolution after the Cold War* (Washington, DC: Brookings Institution, 1995); Robert M. Hayden, *Blueprints for a House Di-*

vided: The Constitutional Logic of the Yugoslav Conflicts (Ann Arbor: University of Michigan Press, 2000).

23. Fehrenbacher, *Speeches and Writings, 1859–1865*, 219.

24. Fehrenbacher, 221–224.

25. James Madison, Federalist 10, in *The Federalist*, ed. George W. Carey and James McClellan (Indianapolis: Liberty Fund, 2001), 43, 48.

26. Madison, 44. For an extended discussion of Madison's ultimate majoritarianism, see Greg Weiner, *Madison's Metronome: The Constitution, Majority Rule, and the Tempo of American Politics* (Lawrence: University Press of Kansas, 2012). Weiner argues persuasively that Madison's goal was not to stifle majority rule but to make it more deliberate and just by slowing down the pace of political decision.

27. Carey and McClellan, *The Federalist*, 270.

28. Carey and McClellan, 271.

29. Madison, Federalist 10, 48. For an analysis of Madison's belief that institutions could be designed to foster impartial behavior even in less-than-impartial human beings, see Alan Gibson, "Madison's 'Great Desideratum': Impartial Administration and the Extended Republic," *American Political Thought* 2, 2 (Fall 2012): 181–207.

30. See Richard Hofstadter, *The Idea of a Party System: The Rise of Legitimate Opposition in the United States, 1780–1840* (Berkeley: University of California Press, 1970); Lance Banning, *The Jeffersonian Persuasion: Evolution of a Party Ideology* (Ithaca, NY: Cornell University Press, 1980).

31. Fehrenbacher, *Speeches and Writings, 1832–1858*, 264–265.

32. On Lincoln's party building, see chapters 3 and 5.

33. In more complex scenarios, voters A and C might form a coalition if they agree to trade votes on unrelated issues or if one or both strategically conceal their actual preferences. See Riker, *Liberalism against Populism*, 137–168, for a discussion of these complications.

34. Abraham Lincoln, "Notes for Speeches at Columbus and Cincinnati, Ohio," September 16 and 17, 1859, in *The Collected Works of Abraham Lincoln*, 9 vols., ed. Roy P. Basler (New Brunswick, NJ: Rutgers University Press, 1953), 3:428.

35. Riker, *Liberalism against Populism*, 228–229.

36. "The paradox of voting is the coexistence of coherent individual valuations and a collectively incoherent choice by majority rule." Riker, 1.

37. See, for example, Barry R. Weingast, "Political Stability and Civil War: Institutions, Commitment, and American Democracy," in *Analytic Narratives*, ed. Robert H. Bates et al. (Princeton, NJ: Princeton University Press, 1998), 148–193.

38. William Riker, *The Art of Political Manipulation* (New Haven, CT: Yale Uni-

versity Press, 1986), 1–2. For Lincoln's question in context, see Fehrenbacher, *Speeches and Writings, 1832–1858*, 541–542.

39. Fehrenbacher, *Dred Scott Case*, 184–185. See also 198–199 for Douglas's unwillingness to resolve the ambiguity, even when specifically pressed to do so. The procedural incoherence of the Kansas-Nebraska Act is discussed in chapter 4.

40. Suppose, Douglas said, a slave owner brings his slaves to a territory where there is no law protecting his right to hold slaves. "He has no remedy if his slaves run away to another country: there is no slave code or police regulations, and the absence of them excludes his slaves from the territory just as effectually and as positively as a constitutional prohibition could." Fehrenbacher, *Speeches and Writings, 1832–1858*, 757.

41. On the negative consequences of Douglas's answer to Lincoln's Freeport question, see Allen C. Guelzo, *Lincoln and Douglas: The Debates that Defined America* (New York: Simon & Schuster, 2008), 145–164, 296–299. For the fateful split in the Democratic Party at its 1860 national convention, see Potter, *Impending Crisis*, 405–425; Michael F. Holt, *The Election of 1860: "A Campaign Fraught with Consequences"* (Lawrence: University Press of Kansas, 2017), 50–66; Freehling, *Road to Disunion: Secessionists Triumphant*, 288–322.

42. Riker, *Art of Political Manipulation*, 8.

43. Lincoln to Anson Miller, November 19, 1858, in Basler, *Collected Works*, 3:340.

44. See Arend Lijphart, *Democracy in Plural Societies: A Comparative Exploration* (New Haven, CT: Yale University Press, 1977); Adrian Guelke, *Politics in Deeply-Divided Societies* (Cambridge: Polity Press, 2012).

45. For a discussion of contemporary applications, direct or indirect, of Calhoun's diagnosis and proposed remedy for majority tyranny, see Read, *Majority Rule versus Consensus*, 196–226.

46. See Calhoun's critique of the protective tariff in his "Draft of the South Carolina Exposition" (1828) and "Fort Hill Address on the Relations of the States and Federal Government" (1831), in Lence, *Union and Liberty*, 313–362, 369–400. For the political context of the 1828 tariff, see William W. Freehling, *Prelude to Civil War: The Nullification Controversy in South Carolina, 1816–1836* (New York: Oxford University Press, 1966), 136–140; Harry L. Watson, *Liberty and Power: The Politics of Jacksonian America* (New York: Hill & Wang, 1990), 88–89.

47. John C. Calhoun, "Speech on the Force Bill," February 15–16, 1833, in Lence, *Union and Liberty*, 446–448.

48. See John C. Calhoun, "A Discourse on the Constitution and Government of the United States" (1850), in Lence, *Union and Liberty*, 260–269.

49. John C. Calhoun, "Speech on the General State of the Union," March 4, 1850, in Lence, *Union and Liberty*, 582–586.

50. John C. Calhoun to Anna Maria Calhoun Clemson, January 25, 1838, in *The Papers of John C. Calhoun*, ed. Clyde N. Wilson (Columbia: University of South Carolina Press, 1981), 14:107.

51. Calhoun described his proposed amendment in detail in his "Discourse on the Constitution" and mentioned it in his "Speech on the General State of the Union," March 4, 1850, in Lence, *Union and Liberty*, 274–277, 600.

52. John C. Calhoun, "Disquisition on Government," in Lence, *Union and Liberty*, 21–22, 49. For Calhoun's argument that slavery was "a great good" in the American setting, see "Speech on the Reception of Abolition Petitions," February 6, 1837, in Lence, 467–469.

53. Read, *Majority Rule versus Consensus*, 160–195.

54. Abraham Lincoln, "Fragment on Sectionalism," July 1856, in Fehrenbacher, *Speeches and Writings, 1832–1858*, 370.

55. South Carolina, Declaration of the Causes of Secession.

56. Fehrenbacher, *Speeches and Writings, 1832–1858*, 372.

57. Fehrenbacher, *Speeches and Writings, 1859–1865*, 120–121.

58. Fehrenbacher, *Speeches and Writings, 1832–1858*, 371–372.

59. Fehrenbacher, 370.

60. Abraham Lincoln, "Cooper Institute Address," February 27, 1860, in Fehrenbacher, *Speeches and Writings, 1859–1865*, 121.

61. "Cooper Institute Address," 120.

62. See William W. Freehling, *The Road to Disunion: Secessionists at Bay, 1776–1854* (New York: Oxford University Press, 1990), 98–118, 308–352; Freehling, *Road to Disunion: Secessionists Triumphant*, 330–341; William Lee Miller, *Arguing about Slavery: John Quincy Adams and the Great Battle in the United States Congress* (New York: Vintage, 1995); Daniel Walker Howe, *What Hath God Wrought: The Transformation of America, 1815–1848* (New York: Oxford University Press, 2007), 512–515, 609–611; Corey M. Brooks, *Liberty Power: Antislavery Third Parties and the Transformation of American Politics* (Chicago: University of Chicago Press, 2016), 47–72. That free states "have permitted open establishment" of abolitionist societies within their borders was one of South Carolina's central justifications for secession. South Carolina, Declaration of the Causes of Secession.

63. The infamous May 22, 1856, assault upon Charles Sumner of Massachusetts by South Carolina's Preston Brooks on the floor of the US Senate was not the only episode of proslavery violence and threatened violence in Congress. See Joanne B. Freeman, *The Field of Blood: Violence in Congress and the Road to Civil War* (New York: Farrar, Straus & Giroux, 2018).

64. Fehrenbacher, *Speeches and Writings, 1859–1865*, 120.

65. Daniel W. Crofts, *Reluctant Confederates: Upper South Unionists in the Secession Crisis* (Chapel Hill: University of North Carolina Press, 1989), 93–94.

66. Freehling, *Road to Disunion: Secessionists Triumphant*, 246–268.

67. For example, in 1854 Senator Davy Atchison of Missouri publicly ad-

vised "squatters in Kansas and the people of Missouri to give a horse thief, robber, or homicide a fair trial, but to hang a Negro thief or Abolitionist, without Judge or Jury." Freehling, *Road to Disunion: Secessionists Triumphant,* 72. Atchison's phrasing bore a striking resemblance to Lincoln's later observation in the Cooper Institute address: "You will grant a hearing to pirates or murderers, but nothing like it to 'Black Republicans.'"

68. "Speech on the Kansas-Nebraska Act," 315; "Fragment on Sectionalism," 372.

69. "Fragment on Sectionalism," 372.

70. Fehrenbacher, *Speeches and Writings, 1832–1858,* 326, 372.

71. Abraham Lincoln, "Message to Congress in Special Session," July 4, 1861, in Fehrenbacher, *Speeches and Writings, 1859–1865,* 259.

72. Abraham Lincoln, "Fragment on Slavery," in Fehrenbacher, *Speeches and Writings, 1832–1858,* 303.

73. Quoted in Vladimir Gligorov, "Is What Is Left Right? (The Yugoslav Heritage)," in *Transition to Capitalism: The Communist Legacy in Eastern Europe,* ed. Janos Matyas Kovacs (New Brunswick, NJ: Transaction Publishers, 1994), 158. Variants on this bitter joke turn up in many other histories and news reports on the Yugoslav conflicts.

74. "First Inaugural Address," 218.

75. Brian Barry, *Democracy, Power, and Justice: Essays in Political Theory* (Oxford: Oxford University Press, 1990), 34–36; Robert A. Dahl, *Democracy and Its Critics* (New Haven, CT: Yale University Press, 1991), 146–148.

76. Fehrenbacher, *Speeches and Writings, 1859–1865,* 217–218, 223.

77. Fehrenbacher, 261.

78. Abraham Lincoln, "Speech at Kalamazoo, Michigan," August 27, 1856, in Fehrenbacher, *Speeches and Writings, 1832–1858,* 381–382.

79. See, for example, Lincoln's "Speech at Cleveland, Ohio," February 15, 1861, in Fehrenbacher, *Speeches and Writings, 1859–1865,* 206–207. See also Kenneth M. Stampp, *And the War Came: The North and the Secession Crisis, 1860–1861* (Baton Rouge: Louisiana State University Press, 1950), 189–195.

80. On this theme, see Crofts, *Reluctant Confederates.*

81. The first actual shots by a seceding state against a federal military target occurred on January 9, 1861, before Lincoln's inauguration, when South Carolina troops fired on and hit the ship *Star of the West,* which was transporting troops to reinforce the federal garrison at Fort Sumter. No one was injured in the incident. The ship abandoned its effort to resupply the fort and returned to New York. Stampp, *And the War Came,* 84–86.

82. Fehrenbacher, *Speeches and Writings, 1859–1865,* 223.

83. Fehrenbacher, 215, 219.

84. Fehrenbacher, 218–219.

85. Fehrenbacher, 221, 224.

86. Fehrenbacher, 247–249.

87. Fehrenbacher, 260.

88. Fehrenbacher, 224.

89. Joshua Cohen, for example, writes that in a deliberative democracy, participants "give reasons with the expectation that those reasons (and not, for example, their power) will settle the fate of their proposal." Joshua Cohen, "Deliberation and Democratic Legitimacy," in *Deliberative Democracy: Essays on Reason and Politics*, ed. James Bohman and William Rehg (Cambridge, MA: MIT Press, 1997), 74.

90. See William W. Freehling and Craig M. Simpson, eds., *Secession Debated: Georgia's Showdown in 1860* (New York: Oxford University Press, 1992).

91. Potter, *Impending Crisis*, 501.

92. Quoted in Freehling, *Road to Disunion: Secessionists Triumphant*, 381.

93. Fehrenbacher, *Speeches and Writings, 1859–1865*, 215–216.

94. Daniel W. Crofts, *Lincoln and the Politics of Slavery: The Other Thirteenth Amendment and the Struggle to Save the Union* (Chapel Hill: University of North Carolina Press, 2016), 12.

95. See, for instance, Georgia secessionist Robert Toombs's November 13, 1860, speech, which accurately described the strategy of Lincoln and the Republicans to "pen up slavery within its present limits—surround it with a border of free States," and thereby effect its eventual extinction. Freehling and Simpson, *Secession Debated*, 41.

96. Quoted in Freehling, *Road to Disunion: Secessionists Triumphant*, 501.

97. Quoted in Potter, *Impending Crisis*, 475.

Chapter 3. "The Capability of a People to Govern Themselves"

1. Don E. Fehrenbacher, ed., *Abraham Lincoln: Speeches and Writings, 1832–1858* (New York: Library of America, 1989), 1–5.

2. Harry L. Watson, *Liberty and Power: The Politics of Jacksonian America*, 2nd ed. (New York: Hill & Wang, 2006), 42–72.

3. See Stephen M. Engel, *American Politicians Confront the Court: Opposition Politics and Changing Responses to Judicial Power* (New York: Cambridge University Press, 2011), 131–151.

4. See the discussion of this theme in chapter 2.

5. Abraham Lincoln, "Fragments on the Tariff," August 1846–December 1847, in Fehrenbacher, *Speeches and Writings, 1832–1858*, 153; "First Debate with Douglas, Ottawa, Illinois," August 21, 1858, in Fehrenbacher, 512; "Message to Congress in Special Session," July 4, 1861, in *Abraham Lincoln: Speeches and Writings, 1859–1865*, ed. Don E. Fehrenbacher (New York: Library of America, 1989), 259.

6. Insightful commentaries on Lincoln's Lyceum address include Diana Schaub, *His Greatest Speeches: How Lincoln Moved the Nation* (New York: St. Martin's Press, 2021), 1–58; Jon D. Schaff, *Abraham Lincoln's Statesmanship and the Limits of Liberal Democracy* (Carbondale: Southern Illinois University Press, 2019), 18–22; Lucas E. Morel, *Lincoln's Sacred Effort: Defining Religion's Role in American Self-Government* (Lanham, MD: Lexington Books, 2000), 23–44.

7. Edmund Wilson argued that in his Lyceum address, Lincoln "projected himself into the role against which he is warning." Edmund Wilson, *Patriotic Gore: Studies in the Literature of the American Civil War* (New York: W. W. Norton, 1994), 108. Two psychoanalytic studies of Lincoln, George B. Forgie's *Patricide in the House Divided: A Psychological Interpretation of Lincoln and His Age* (New York: W. W. Norton, 1979) and Charles B. Strozier's *Lincoln's Quest for Union: Public and Private Meanings* (New York: Basic Books, 1982), share Wilson's violent, self-projecting view of Lincoln, which they interpret as the unconscious expression of an unresolved Oedipal complex. For a critique of these and other aspiring-tyrant readings of Lincoln's Lyceum address, see Richard N. Current, "Lincoln after 175 Years: The Myth of the Jealous Son," *Journal of the Abraham Lincoln Association* 6, 2 (1984): 15–24; Schaff, *Abraham Lincoln's Statesmanship*, 18–22.

8. See Glen E. Thurow, *Abraham Lincoln and American Political Religion* (Albany, NY: SUNY Press, 1976), 20–37; Harry V. Jaffa, *Crisis of the House Divided: An Interpretation of the Issues in the Lincoln-Douglas Debates*, 50th anniversary ed. (Chicago: University of Chicago Press, 2009), 226–232; Morel, *Lincoln's Sacred Effort*, 12–44. For critique of Thurow's and Jaffa's emphasis on the religious at the expense of the civic and political dimensions of Lincoln's formulation, see William S. Corlett, "The Availability of Lincoln's Political Religion," *Political Theory* 10, 4 (November 1982): 520–540.

9. See Daniel Walker Howe, *The Political Culture of the American Whigs* (Chicago: University of Chicago Press, 1979), 269–271; Major L. Wilson, "Lincoln on the Perpetuation of Republican Institutions: Whig and Republican Strategies," *Journal of the Abraham Lincoln Association* 16, 1 (Winter 1995): 15–25. Both Howe and Wilson acknowledge that Lincoln was more democratic than most other Whigs of the age.

10. Daniel Walker Howe, *What Hath God Wrought: The Transformation of America, 1815–1848* (New York: Oxford University Press, 2007), 433, 437.

11. Abraham Lincoln, "Speech in the Illinois Legislature on the State Bank," January 11, 1837, in Fehrenbacher, *Speeches and Writings, 1832–1858*, 17.

12. Abraham Lincoln, "Amendment to an Act to Incorporate the Subscribers to the Bank of the State of Illinois," December 22, 1835, in *The Collected Works of Abraham Lincoln*, 9 vols., ed. Roy P. Basler (New Brunswick, NJ: Rutgers University Press, 1953), 1:43.

13. Fehrenbacher, *Speeches and Writings, 1832–1858*, 17.

14. David J. Siemers, "America's Machiavellian Moment," *Constitutionalist,*

December 15, 2020, https://theconstitutionalist.org/2020/12/15/americas-machiavellian-moment/. Siemers describes Donald Trump's evidence-free allegations of mass election fraud as a modern-day instance of calumny.

15. For example: "I have already appointed Senator SEWARD and Mr. BATES, of Missouri, and they are men whose characters I think the breath of calumny cannot impeach." Abraham Lincoln, "Remarks to a Pennsylvania Delegation," January 24, 1861, in Basler, *Collected Works*, 4:180.

16. Fehrenbacher, *Speeches and Writings, 1832–1858*, 29, 31.

17. Luke Mogelson, "A Reporter's Footage from Inside the Capitol Siege," January 6, 2021, https://www.youtube.com/watch?v=270F8s5TEKY&t=33s.

18. Lincoln to Joshua F. Speed, August 24, 1855, in Fehrenbacher, *Speeches and Writings, 1832–1858*, 361.

19. Abraham Lincoln, "Address to Young Men's Lyceum of Springfield," January 27, 1838, in Fehrenbacher, *Speeches and Writings, 1832–1858*, 30–31; Abraham Lincoln, "Speech on the Kansas-Nebraska Act," October 16, 1854, in Fehrenbacher, 334.

20. Fehrenbacher, *Speeches and Writings, 1859–1865*, 218.

21. Fehrenbacher, *Speeches and Writings, 1832–1858*, 29, 32–33.

22. Fehrenbacher, 31–33.

23. Fehrenbacher, 36.

24. See, for example, the portraits of Daniel Webster and Rufus Choate in Howe, *Political Culture of the American Whigs*, 210–237.

25. In 1858, referring to the *Dred Scott* decision, Lincoln remarked: "It so happens, singularly enough, that I never stood opposed to a decision of the Supreme Court till this." "Speech at Springfield, Illinois," July 17, 1858, in Fehrenbacher, *Speeches and Writings, 1832–1858*, 475.

26. Fehrenbacher, *Speeches and Writings, 1832–1858*, 33.

27. A notable exception is Lucas E. Morel, who acknowledges the difficulties connected with Lincoln's urging women and African Americans strictly to obey the law. Morel argues that Lincoln regarded their disenfranchisement as temporary and called on women and Blacks to trust "that the full blessings of self-government will come to them in time." Morel, *Lincoln's Sacred Effort*, 33–34. Even supposing this was Lincoln's ultimate intention as early as 1838, in my view, it is not clear, at least in the case of enslaved persons, how such a distant and uncertain future prospect could generate an obligation to strictly obey the law in the present.

28. In an 1836 public letter setting forth his principles as a candidate, Lincoln wrote: "I go for admitting all whites to the right of suffrage, who pay taxes or bear arms, (by no means excluding females)." "To the Editor of the Sangamo Journal," June 13, 1836, in Fehrenbacher, *Speeches and Writings, 1832–1858*, 5. At the time, Lincoln did not indicate support for extending suffrage to Blacks.

29. Lincoln observed that "occasional poisonings from the kitchen, and

open or stealthy assassinations in the field, and local revolts extending to a score or so" were "the natural results of slavery." "Address at Cooper Institute," February 27, 1860, in Fehrenbacher, *Speeches and Writings, 1859–1865*, 124.

30. Fehrenbacher, *Speeches and Writings, 1832–1858*, 328.

31. Robert W. Johannsen, *Lincoln, the South, and Slavery: The Political Dimension* (Baton Rouge: Louisiana State University Press, 1993), 9.

32. Lincoln's most forceful statement of this view came in his July 6, 1852, "Eulogy on Henry Clay," in Fehrenbacher, *Speeches and Writings, 1832–1858*, 265.

33. Lucas E. Morel notes that two key themes of Lincoln's Lyceum address, perpetuating American political institutions and the problem of mob violence, were formulated in part as responses to Martin Van Buren's public statements on those matters. Morel, *Lincoln's Sacred Effort*, 23–44.

34. On Van Buren's party building, see Joel H. Silbey, *Martin Van Buren and the Emergence of American Popular Politics* (Lanham, MD: Rowman & Littlefield, 2002); Richard Hofstadter, *The Idea of a Party System: The Rise of Legitimate Opposition in the United States, 1780–1840* (Berkeley: University of California Press, 1970).

35. Van Buren to Thomas Ritchie, January 13, 1827, quoted in Silbey, *Martin Van Buren*, 50.

36. For a perceptive comparison of Van Buren and Lincoln as theorists of party, see J. David Greenstone, *The Lincoln Persuasion: Remaking American Liberalism* (Chicago: University of Chicago Press, 1993), 154–185.

37. Silbey, *Martin Van Buren*, 15–82.

38. William G. Shade, "'The Most Delicate and Exciting Topics': Martin Van Buren, Slavery, and the Election of 1836," *Journal of the Early Republic* 18, 3 (Autumn 1998): 484.

39. On John Quincy Adams as an antislavery Whig congressman, see William Lee Miller, *Arguing about Slavery: John Quincy Adams and the Great Battle in the United States Congress* (New York: Vintage, 1995). Corey M. Brooks describes northern Whigs' complicated relationship to the abolitionist Liberty Party in *Liberty Power: Antislavery Third Parties and the Transformation of American Politics* (Chicago: University of Chicago Press, 2016), 15–103. On the competition between southern Democrats and southern Whigs over which group was the more committed and effective defender of slavery, see William J. Cooper Jr., *The South and the Politics of Slavery, 1828–1856* (Baton Rouge: Louisiana State University Press, 1978), 74–97.

40. See, for example, Abraham Lincoln, "Communication to the Readers of *The Old Soldier*," February 28, 1840: "With our own friends, we justify—we urge—organization on the score of necessity. A disbanded yeomanry cannot successfully meet an organized soldiery"; "Resolutions at a Whig Meeting," March 1, 1843: "*Resolved*, that we recommend to the whigs of all portions of this

State to adopt, and rigidly adhere to, the Convention System of nominating candidates"; "Campaign Circular from Whig Committee," March 4, 1843, which features Lincoln's first recorded use of the phrase "a house divided against itself cannot stand"—the house in this case being the Whig Party. Basler, *Collected Works,* 1:205, 308, 315.

41. "Lincoln's Plan of Campaign in 1840," January 1840, in Basler, *Collected Works,* 1:180–181.

42. In *The American Political Nation, 1838–1893* (Stanford, CA: Stanford University Press, 1991), 52–54, Joel H. Silbey quotes the full text of Lincoln's 1840 campaign plan and places it in the context of party mobilization throughout the United States that year. Silbey observes that "the similarity of Lincoln's plan of organization in 1840 and one circulated in the same year among New York Democrats is compelling" (71). On the turnout in 1840 compared to that in previous elections, see Michael McDonald, "National General Election VEP Turnout Rates, 1789–Present," United States Election Project, http://www.electproject.org/national-1789-present (accessed July 12, 2022).

43. Fehrenbacher, *Speeches and Writings, 1832–1858,* 36.

44. For Jackson's claim that his 1832 election victory represented a popular mandate to kill the bank, his belief that he was saving the Constitution by doing so, and his assertion that he alone (and not Congress) represented the American people as a whole, see Stephen M. Engel, *American Politicians Confront the Court: Opposition Politics and Changing Responses to Judicial Power* (New York: Cambridge University Press, 2011); Richard J. Ellis and Stephen Kirk, "Presidential Mandates in the Nineteenth Century: Conceptual Change and Institutional Development," *Studies in American Political Development* 9, 1 (Spring 1995): 117–186; Jeremy Bailey, "Opposition to the Theory of Presidential Representation: Federalists, Whigs, and Republicans," *Presidential Studies Quarterly* 44, 1 (March 2014): 50–71.

45. Abraham Lincoln, "Speech on the Subtreasury," December 26, 1839, in Fehrenbacher, *Speeches and Writings, 1832–1858,* 44–65; Lincoln to John T. Stuart, January 20, 1840, in Basler, *Collected Works,* 1:184. See also the *Sangamo Journal's* May 15, 1840, report of a campaign speech in which Lincoln "vindicated in a most triumphant manner" the constitutionality as well as the utility of the Bank of the United States. Basler, 1:210.

46. Fehrenbacher, *Speeches and Writings, 1832–1858,* 44–45, 55–56.

47. Fehrenbacher, 56–57.

48. Daniel Webster, "Second Speech on the Subtreasury," March 12, 1838 (Washington, DC: Gales & Seaton, 1838), 57, https://fraser.stlouisfed.org/title/3639.

49. It should be acknowledged, however, that in the conclusion of his December 1839 speech on the Subtreasury, Lincoln resorted to hyperbolically partisan rhetoric that mirrored the Democrats' tendency to delegitimize the

opposition: "I know that the great volcano at Washington, aroused and directed by the evil spirit that reigns there, is belching forth the lava of political corruption, in a current broad and deep." Fehrenbacher, *Speeches and Writings, 1832–1858*, 64. Full recognition of the legitimacy of an opposing party did not develop all at once, either in Lincoln's mind or in the minds of his contemporaries.

50. Stephen M. Engel argues—correctly, in my view—that Lincoln broke new ground in the first inaugural address by defining the majority "as a dynamic rather than static entity" and thus acknowledging "the possibility that multiple legitimate perspectives on meaning followed from the silences" of the Constitution. Engel, *American Politicians Confront the Court*, 181. But Engel presents this perspective as a late development in Lincoln's thinking, an "ideational innovation" motivated by "Lincoln's desperate attempts to stop secession" (189). I would argue that Lincoln's innovation was already present in rudimentary form in his 1839 speech on the Subtreasury.

51. Ellis and Kirk, "Presidential Mandates in the Nineteenth Century," 145–150, 162; Bailey, "Opposition to the Theory of Presidential Representation," 57–63.

52. Henry Clay, in rejecting Andrew Jackson's mandate claim, went to the opposite extreme of claiming that public officials should "make no effort to ascertain what messages their constituents might be trying to send them about appropriate public policies" and arguing that elections involved "little more than judgments about an individual's character or reputation." Ellis and Kirk, "Presidential Mandates in the Nineteenth Century," 155.

53. Abraham Lincoln, "Speech in the U.S. House of Representatives on the War with Mexico," January 12, 1848, in Fehrenbacher, *Speeches and Writings, 1832–1858*, 161–162; Lincoln to William H. Herndon, February 15, 1848, in Fehrenbacher, 175; Lincoln to Usher F. Linder, March 22, 1848, in Fehrenbacher, 178–179.

54. Abraham Lincoln, "'Spot' Resolutions in the U.S. House," December 22, 1847, in Fehrenbacher, *Speeches and Writings, 1832–1858*, 159; "Speech in the U.S. House of Representatives on the War with Mexico," 161–162, 166–168; Lincoln to John M. Peck, May 21, 1848, in Fehrenbacher, 184–185.

55. "Speech in the U.S. House of Representatives on the War with Mexico," 169.

56. Howe, *What Hath God Wrought*, 741.

57. Ellis and Kirk, "Presidential Mandates in the Nineteenth Century," 162; Polk, "Fourth Annual Message," December 5, 1848, quoted in Ellis and Kirk, 162.

58. Thomas Jefferson, "Opinion on the Constitutionality of a National Bank," February 15, 1791, in *Thomas Jefferson: Writings*, ed. Merrill D. Peterson (New York: Library of America, 1984), 421; James Madison, "Veto Message

on the National Bank," January 30, 1815, https://millercenter.org/the-presi
dency/presidential-speeches/january-30-1815-veto-message-national-bank.

59. Abraham Lincoln, "Speech in the U.S. House of Representatives on
Internal Improvements," June 20, 1848, in Fehrenbacher, *Speeches and Writings,
1832–1858*, 187–198.

60. Abraham Lincoln, "Speech on the Presidential Question," July 27, 1848,
in Fehrenbacher, *Speeches and Writings, 1832–1858*, 206–207.

61. "Speech on the Presidential Question," 207–208.

62. Abraham Lincoln, "What General Taylor Ought to Say," in Basler, *Collected Works*, 1:454. The editors assign this document a probable date of March
1848, which would place it before Lincoln's July 27, 1848, "Speech on the Presidential Question."

63. "What General Taylor Ought to Say," 1:454.

64. "Speech on the Presidential Question," 209. See also Lincoln's September 21, 1848, campaign speech on Taylor's behalf in Taunton, Massachusetts,
where Free-Soil sentiment was strong and Lincoln's antislavery characterization
of Taylor was met with skepticism. Basler, *Collected Works*, 2:6–9.

65. "Speech on the Presidential Question," 210–211.

66. Whig Party Platform, June 7, 1848, American Presidency Project,
https://www.presidency.ucsb.edu/documents/whig-party-platform-1848. The
platform praises Taylor as a hero of the Mexican War and makes no mention of
slavery, the Wilmot Proviso, tariffs, internal improvements, appropriate use of
the veto power, the justness of the Mexican War, or any other issues important
to Lincoln, other members of Congress, and the wider public.

67. For the founders' antiparty mind-set, see Hofstadter, *Idea of a Party System*. See also Engel, *American Politicians Confront the Court*, 131–169, who argues
that this mind-set endured longer than Hofstadter believed.

68. On the persistence of antiparty attitudes, especially among the Whigs,
see Gerald Leonard, *The Invention of Party Politics: Federalism, Popular Sovereignty,
and Constitutional Development in Jacksonian Illinois* (Chapel Hill: University of
North Carolina Press, 2014). Leonard notes that Lincoln's more positive view
of party organization was not shared by many Illinois Whigs and that Lincoln's
organizational efforts met significant intraparty resistance (245–249).

69. Zachary Taylor to Captain J. S. Allison, April 22, 1848, in *A Sketch of
the Life and Character of Gen. Taylor, American Hero and People's Man* (New York:
S. French, 1847), 13. The pseudonymous author of this candidate-authorized
campaign biography is listed as "The One-Legged Sergeant."

70. Lincoln quoted both the Democrats' platform resolution and Cass's
statement of support for it in his June 20, 1848, internal improvements speech.
Fehrenbacher, *Speeches and Writings, 1832–1858*, 187.

71. Fehrenbacher, 188.

72. "Speech on the Presidential Question," 208–209, 221.

73. Lincoln to Joshua F. Speed, August 24, 1855, in Fehrenbacher, *Speeches and Writings, 1832–1858*, 362–363.

74. Abraham Lincoln, "House Divided Speech," June 16, 1858, in Fehrenbacher, 434.

75. "Speech at Springfield, Illinois," 471.

76. Lincoln later claimed that during his term in Congress he voted for "The 'Wilmot Proviso' or the principle of it . . . at least forty times." Fehrenbacher, *Speeches and Writings, 1832–1858*, 312. For his January 10, 1849, "Proposal for Abolition of Slavery in the District of Columbia" (which he withdrew for lack of support), see Fehrenbacher, 227.

77. Stanley Harrold, *Lincoln and the Abolitionists* (Carbondale: Southern Illinois University Press, 2018), describes how abolitionists continually pushed Lincoln to take a stronger antislavery stance. Harrold is generally fair to Lincoln but understates his antislavery commitment during his Whig phase. Fred Kaplan's *Lincoln and the Abolitionists: John Quincy Adams, Slavery, and the Civil War* (New York: HarperCollins, 2017) misrepresents Lincoln on numerous points. Kaplan inaccurately claims that Lincoln and Dan Stone's March 3, 1837, "Protest in the Illinois Legislature on Slavery" held that "abolitionism . . . was as great an evil as slavery" (46) and that Congress should not abolish it in the District of Columbia, despite having the power to do so. In fact, their protest outlined the approach Lincoln and Stone believed Congress should follow in abolishing slavery in DC.

78. Fehrenbacher, *Speeches and Writings, 1832–1858*, 81–90. For a discussion of Lincoln's temperance address, see Schaff, *Abraham Lincoln's Statesmanship*, 22–25; Morel, *Lincoln's Sacred Effort*, 137–147.

79. Fehrenbacher, *Speeches and Writings, 1832–1858*, 89–90.

80. For debates among abolitionists over whether and in what manner to engage in electoral politics, see Brooks, *Liberty Power*, 15–46; James Brewer Stewart, *Abolitionist Politics and the Coming of the Civil War* (Amherst: University of Massachusetts Press, 2008), 3–31; Richard H. Sewell, *Ballots for Freedom: Antislavery Politics in the United States, 1837–1860* (New York: Oxford University Press, 1976), 24–42.

81. Howe, *What Hath God Wrought*, 512–515; Miller, *Arguing about Slavery*.

82. Basler, *Collected Works*, 1:75–76, editor's note.

83. Abraham Lincoln, "Protest in Illinois Legislature on Slavery," March 3, 1837, in Fehrenbacher, *Speeches and Writings, 1832–1858*, 18.

84. Harrold, *Lincoln and the Abolitionists*, 15; Kaplan, *Lincoln and the Abolitionists*, 12, 46.

85. For an in-depth examination of the "political abolitionists," see Brooks, *Liberty Power*.

86. Fehrenbacher, *Speeches and Writings, 1832–1858*, 447.

87. Lincoln to Mary Speed, September 27, 1841, in Fehrenbacher, *Speeches*

and Writings, 1832–1858, 74; Lincoln to Joshua F. Speed, August 24, 1855, in Fehrenbacher, 360–361.

88. Lincoln to Henry E. Dummer, November 18, 1845, in Fehrenbacher, *Speeches and Writings, 1832–1858*, 112.

89. Abraham Lincoln, "Speech on the Kansas-Nebraska Act," October 16, 1854, in Fehrenbacher, *Speeches and Writings, 1832–1858*, 339, 325.

90. Howe, *What Hath God Wrought*, 688–689.

91. Lincoln to Williamson Durley, October 3, 1845, in Fehrenbacher, *Speeches and Writings, 1832–1858*, 111–112,

92. Abraham Lincoln, "Speech at Worcester, Massachusetts," September 12, 1848, in Basler, *Collected Works*, 2:3–4; "Speech at Lacon, Illinois," November 1, 1848, in Basler, 2:14. Lincoln's distinction between "leaving the consequences to God" and acting upon "intelligent judgment of the consequences" anticipates Max Weber's distinction between "ethics of intention" and "ethics of responsibility." See Max Weber, "Politics as a Vocation," in *Max Weber: Selections in Translation*, ed. W. G. Runciman (Cambridge: Cambridge University Press, 1978), 212–225.

93. As a candidate for president in 1844, Clay initially opposed the "immediate annexation" of Texas, but in July 1844, in a bid for southern support, he declared he had "no personal objection to the annexation of Texas." William W. Freehling, *The Road to Disunion: Secessionists at Bay, 1776–1854* (New York: Oxford University Press, 1990), 435–436. On the difficulties Clay's reversal caused for antislavery northern Whigs' effort to hold off the Liberty Party challenge, see Brooks, *Liberty Power*, 94–103.

94. Brooks, *Liberty Power*, 47–72, 86, 124.

95. Brooks, for example, rejects the view that the Liberty Party was a minor party of little consequence, arguing instead that its "incredible achievement" was to make the Republican Party's accomplishments possible. Brooks, 213, 225.

Chapter 4. "Aroused Him as He Had Never Been Before"

1. "Autobiography Written for Campaign," June 1860, in *Abraham Lincoln: Speeches and Writings, 1859–1865*, ed. Don E. Fehrenbacher (New York: Library of America, 1989), 167; "Speech at Springfield, Illinois," July 17, 1858, in *Abraham Lincoln: Speeches and Writings, 1832–1858*, ed. Don E. Fehrenbacher (New York: Library of America, 1989), 471.

2. Michael F. Holt, *The Political Crisis of the 1850s* (New York: W. W. Norton, 1983), ix.

3. Stephen Douglas, "Speech at Chicago," July 9, 1858, in *The Lincoln-Douglas Debates*, ed. Robert W. Johannsen (New York: Oxford University Press, 1965), 22.

4. Abraham Lincoln, "Speech on the Kansas-Nebraska Act," October 16, 1854, in Fehrenbacher, *Speeches and Writings, 1832–1858*, 315.

5. "Speech on the Kansas-Nebraska Act," 328–329, 343.

6. "Speech on the Kansas-Nebraska Act," 334.

7. Christopher Childers, *The Failure of Popular Sovereignty: Slavery, Manifest Destiny, and the Radicalization of Southern Politics* (Lawrence: University Press of Kansas, 2012), 9–101; Don E. Fehrenbacher, *The Dred Scott Case: Its Significance in American Politics and Law* (New York: Oxford University Press, 1979), 87–113.

8. Childers, *Failure of Popular Sovereignty*, 40–73.

9. John C. Calhoun, "Speech on the Oregon Bill," June 27, 1848, in *Union and Liberty: The Political Philosophy of John C. Calhoun*, ed. Ross M. Lence (Indianapolis: Liberty Fund, 1992), 519; Jefferson Davis, "Remarks on Henry Clay's Resolutions," US Senate, January 29, 1850, in *The Papers of Jefferson Davis*, online archive, Rice University, https://jeffersondavis.rice.edu/archives/documents/jefferson-davis-remarks-henry-clays-resolutions.

10. For the events summarized in this paragraph, see Childers, *Failure of Popular Sovereignty*, 106–199; William J. Cooper, *The South and the Politics of Slavery, 1828–1856* (Baton Rouge: Louisiana State University Press, 1978), 225–317; David M. Potter, *The Impending Crisis, 1848–1861* (New York: Harper & Row, 1976), 63–120; Michael F. Holt, *The Fate of Their Country: Politicians, Slavery Extension, and the Coming of the Civil War* (New York: Hill & Wang, 2004), 19–91.

11. For the "all-too-malleable" doctrine of popular sovereignty as advocated by Lewis Cass in 1848, see Childers, *Failure of Popular Sovereignty*, 136–137, 147, 152. "But when the issue of *when* the people could decide became too explosive for Congress to address, Democrats called on the Supreme Court to determine the meaning of popular sovereignty" (Childers, 156). See also Mark A. Graber, *Dred Scott and the Problem of Constitutional Evil* (New York: Cambridge University Press, 2006), 44: "Judicial decisions often provide cover for political actors who cannot advocate certain policies directly. . . . Northern Democrats could accept Southern pretensions in the territories as long as they could do so indirectly by supporting a judicial decision rather than by expressing direct support for the policy."

12. For Douglas's railroad plans as motivation for the Kansas-Nebraska Act, see Robert W. Johannsen, *Stephen A. Douglas* (New York: Oxford University Press, 1973), 390–395; Potter, *Impending Crisis*, 145–167. On Douglas's personal financial stake, see Holt, *Fate of Their Country*, 95–96; Alice Elizabeth Malavasic, *The F Street Mess: How Southern Senators Rewrote the Kansas-Nebraska Act* (Chapel Hill: University of North Carolina Press, 2017), 72. On the status of the territory as Indian lands, see Malavasic, 65–78.

13. Fehrenbacher, *Dred Scott Case*, 184–185, 198–199.

14. Potter, *Impending Crisis*, 155, 158; Cooper, *South and the Politics of Slavery*, 347.

15. Malavasic, *F Street Mess*, 43–59, 90.

16. Potter, *Impending Crisis*, 159.

17. Cooper, *South and the Politics of Slavery*, 347.

18. Holt, *Fate of Their Country*, 101. See also Potter, *Impending Crisis*, 156–157.

19. Malavasic, *F Street Mess*, 91–92. See also Potter, *Impending Crisis*, 160.

20. Malavasic, *F Street Mess*, 97–98; Potter, *Impending Crisis*, 161–162.

21. Johannsen, *Stephen A. Douglas*, 426–427. See also Childers, *Failure of Popular Sovereignty*, 223.

22. See Nicole Etcheson, *Bleeding Kansas* (Lawrence: University Press of Kansas, 2004), who observes that Douglas's "provisions for expanded self-government in the territories were added piecemeal, not as part of a consistent program of promoting self-government" (21).

23. This is a far-from-exhaustive summary of the chaos that ensued in Kansas. For a full narrative, see Etcheson, *Bleeding Kansas*.

24. Abraham Lincoln, "House Divided Speech," June 16, 1858, in Fehrenbacher, *Speeches and Writings, 1832–1858*, 427. Harry V. Jaffa, in *Crisis of the House Divided: An Interpretation of the Issues in the Lincoln-Douglas Debates*, 50th anniversary ed. (Chicago: University of Chicago Press, 2009), argues that Douglas's principal failure was his inability to see that popular sovereignty depended on a moral commitment to human equality. But Jaffa presents Douglas as a principled democrat with respect to *process*, despite his blindness on natural rights. In my view, Douglas's thinking was no less flawed with respect to democratic process than it was with respect to democratic principles.

25. "Speech on the Kansas-Nebraska Act," 314–315, 321–322. "I am aware Judge Douglas now argues that the subsequent express repeal [of the Missouri Compromise restriction] is no substantial alteration of the bill. . . . He admits, however, that there is a literal change in the bill; and that he made the change in deference to other Senators, who would not support the bill without. This proves that those other Senators thought the change a substantial one; and that the Judge thought their opinions worth deferring to" (322).

26. Potter, *Impending Crisis*, 204.

27. Etcheson, *Bleeding Kansas*, 61–62.

28. Fehrenbacher, *Speeches and Writings, 1832–1858*, 361.

29. "Speech on the Kansas-Nebraska Act," 334; "House Divided Speech," 427. The rejected amendment Lincoln refers to was introduced by Senator Salmon Chase of Ohio.

30. William W. Freehling, *The Road to Disunion: Secessionists Triumphant, 1854–1861* (New York: Oxford University Press, 2007), 74.

31. "Speech on the Kansas-Nebraska Act," 320.

32. Lincoln to Joshua F. Speed, August 24, 1855, in Fehrenbacher, *Speeches and Writings, 1832–1858*, 303–304. See also Lincoln to John M. Palmer, September 7, 1854, in Fehrenbacher, 362–363: "You are, and always have been,

honestly, and *sincerely* a democrat; and I know how painful it must be to an honest sincere man, to be urged by his party to the support of a measure, which on his conscience he believes to be wrong." At the time, Palmer was a Democratic state senator in Illinois. He later joined the Republican Party.

33. Potter, *Impending Crisis,* 175; William E. Gienapp, *The Origins of the Republican Party, 1852–1856* (New York: Oxford University Press, 1987), 125–127.

34. See Stephen Douglas, "Speech at Chicago," July 9, 1858, in Johannsen, *Lincoln-Douglas Debates,* 30–31. Douglas argued that Lincoln's goal of ultimately extinguishing slavery everywhere could be accomplished only by "merging the rights and sovereignty of the States in one consolidated empire, and vesting Congress with the plenary power to make all the police regulations, domestic and local laws, uniform throughout the limits of the Republic."

35. "Speech on the Kansas-Nebraska Act," 324.

36. Etcheson, *Bleeding Kansas,* 107–112.

37. "Speech on the Kansas-Nebraska Act," 326.

38. Fehrenbacher, *Speeches and Writings, 1832–1858,* 324.

39. The track record of the Northwest Ordinance's slavery prohibition supports both Lincoln's claim that slavery could take root without positive authorization and his claim that slavery would become more deeply rooted where the law was silent than where slavery was legally prohibited. Because the Northwest Ordinance prohibition was inadequately enforced, slavery crept into Illinois and Indiana at the territorial stage, but much less extensively than in the bordering states of Kentucky and Missouri, where the law had been silent with respect to slavery during the territorial stage. See David Brion Davis, "The Significance of Excluding Slavery from the Old Northwest in 1787," *Indiana Magazine of History* 84, 1 (March 1988): 75–89.

40. Potter, *Impending Crisis,* 204; Fehrenbacher, *Dred Scott Case,* 462.

41. Abraham Lincoln, "Speech at Kalamazoo, Michigan," August 27, 1856, in Fehrenbacher, *Speeches and Writings, 1832–1858,* 377.

42. "I am naturally anti-slavery. If slavery is not wrong, nothing is wrong. I can not remember when I did not so think, and feel." Lincoln to Albert G. Hodges, April 4, 1864, in Fehrenbacher, *Speeches and Writings, 1859–1865,* 585.

43. Fehrenbacher, *Speeches and Writings, 1832–1858,* 326.

44. Fehrenbacher, 315.

45. Ralph Waldo Emerson, for example, in an 1851 speech urging resistance to the Fugitive Slave Act, described New Englanders as superior in civilization to white southerners, just as Englishmen were able to rule their empire through their superior degree of civilization. Ralph Waldo Emerson, "Address to the Citizens of Concord," in *Emerson's Political Writings,* ed. Kenneth Sacks (Cambridge: Cambridge University Press, 2008), 150–151.

46. Abraham Lincoln, "Address to the Washington Temperance Society of

Springfield, Illinois," February 22, 1842, in Fehrenbacher, *Speeches and Writings, 1832–1858*, 81–90.

47. Abraham Lincoln, "Draft of a Speech," [late 1857 or early 1858], in Fehrenbacher, *Speeches and Writings, 1832–1858*, 417–418. Lincoln's first recorded use of the phrase "a house divided against itself cannot stand" occurs in this document.

48. Fehrenbacher, *Speeches and Writings, 1832–1858*, 338.

49. In the draft document noted above, which functioned as the basis for the "House Divided" speech, Lincoln wrote: "I believe the government cannot endure permanently half slave and half free. I expressed this belief a year ago; and subsequent developments have but confirmed me." Fehrenbacher, *Speeches and Writings, 1832–1858*, 417. Although it is impossible to precisely date when Lincoln formulated the "house divided" idea, it clearly occurred several years after 1854.

50. Fehrenbacher, *Speeches and Writings, 1832–1858*, 307, 336.

51. "House Divided Speech," 426.

52. Fehrenbacher, *Speeches and Writings, 1832–1858*, 320–321.

53. For discussion of the Missouri controversy and Missouri Compromise, see Daniel Walker Howe, *What Hath God Wrought: The Transformation of America, 1815–1848* (New York: Oxford University Press, 2007), 147–160; Childers, *Failure of Popular Sovereignty*, 40–73; James Zink, "The Missouri Compromise at 200: Revisiting the Crisis and Its Aftermath" and "The Independence of the Declaration and Constitution: Disharmony and Divergence in the First Missouri Crisis," *Political Science Reviewer* 43, 2 (2019): 303–316, 379–414.

54. "Speech on the Kansas-Nebraska Act," 308; Abraham Lincoln, "Cooper Institute Address," February 27, 1860, in Fehrenbacher, *Speeches and Writings, 1859–1865*, 113–114.

55. Under the second Missouri Compromise, Missouri was admitted to the Union on the condition that it rescind the clause in its state constitution banning free Blacks from entering the state, which violated the privileges and immunities clause of the US Constitution. But Missouri subsequently violated this agreement without consequences. On this second, "less durable" Missouri Compromise, see Howe, *What Hath God Wrought*, 156–157.

56. "Speech on the Kansas-Nebraska Act," 312, 318–319.

57. For Clay's role in these three famous compromises, as well as the wider political context in which he operated, see Merrill D. Peterson, *The Great Triumvirate: Webster, Clay, and Calhoun* (New York: Oxford University Press, 1987), 59–66, 217–233, 455–462, 468–476.

58. Fehrenbacher, *Speeches and Writings, 1832–1858*, 264.

59. Peterson, *Great Triumvirate*, 455–462, 468–476; "Speech on the Kansas-Nebraska Act," 325. For a thoughtful comparison of Lincoln and Clay, see Kevin Vance, "Lincoln and Clay: What Is a Statesman to Do?" in *Lincoln and Democratic*

Statesmanship, ed. Michael P. Zuckert (Lawrence: University Press of Kansas, 2020), 58–99.

60. Mark A. Graber characterizes southern acceptance of the Missouri Compromise as follows: "The Southern demand for equality in the Union did not encompass the demand that Southern constitutional claims be fully honored. . . . At the end of the Missouri debates, prominent slave-state congressmen willingly surrendered the right to carry slaves into all American territory in exchange for Missouri statehood and better security for the right to carry slaves into some American territories." Graber, *Dred Scott,* 125.

61. For Calhoun's initial acceptance of the Missouri Compromise, see Calhoun to Charles Tait, October 26, 1820, in *The Papers of John C. Calhoun,* vol. 5, ed. W. Edwin Hemphill (Columbia: University of South Carolina Press, 1971), 412–414. For his later denunciation, see Calhoun, "Speech on the Oregon Bill," June 27, 1848, in Lence, *Union and Liberty,* 550.

62. Abraham Lincoln, "Drafts of Resolutions Recommending Amendment of the Kansas-Nebraska Act," January 4, 1855, in *The Collected Works of Abraham Lincoln,* 9 vols., ed. Roy P. Basler (New Brunswick, NJ: Rutgers University Press, 1953), 2:301; Lincoln to Joshua F. Speed, August 24, 1855, 362; Lincoln to George Robertson, August 15, 1855, in Fehrenbacher, 359–360.

63. Bruce Bueno de Mesquita and Alastair Smith use Lincoln's "no peaceful extinction of slavery" phrase to argue that "to fulfill his ambition and his beliefs Lincoln needed a civil war." Bruce Bueno de Mesquita and Alastair Smith, *The Spoils of War: Greed, Power, and the Conflicts that Made Our Greatest Presidents* (New York: PublicAffairs, 2016), xi, 118.

64. Lincoln to George Robertson, August 15, 1855, 359–360.

65. Cooper, *South and the Politics of Slavery,* 230, 240, 278–285, 339–344; Holt, *Political Crisis of the 1850s,* 119–159; Gienapp, *Origins of the Republican Party,* 37–67.

66. Lincoln to Joshua F. Speed, August 24, 1855, 363.

67. Childers, *Failure of Popular Sovereignty,* 259–268.

68. Rhett and other committed secessionists deliberately split the Democratic Party going into the 1860 election with the aim of ensuring a Republican victory, which would in turn provoke the slave states to secede from the Union. See Eric A. Walther, *The Fire Eaters* (Baton Rouge: Louisiana State University Press, 1992), 151. William W. Freehling argues that even in South Carolina the public show of unanimity in favor of secession in response to Lincoln's election masked significant divisions, and chance events may have tipped the balance. Freehling, *Road to Disunion: Secessionists Triumphant,* 375–426.

69. One of Stephen Douglas's central arguments against Lincoln and the Republican Party in the 1858 Senate contest was that a major political party having no presence in the South, and advocating principles that were strongly rejected in that section, was "revolutionary and destructive of the existence of this

Government." Douglas, "First Joint Debate," August 21, 1858, in Johannsen, *Lincoln-Douglas Debates*, 37, 44.

70. Fehrenbacher, *Speeches and Writings, 1859–1865*, 125.

71. Fehrenbacher, 127–130.

72. Stephen Douglas, "Speech at Chicago," July 9, 1858, in Johannsen, *Lincoln-Douglas Debates*, 29.

73. Abraham Lincoln, "Sixth Joint Debate," October 13, 1858, in Fehrenbacher, *Speeches and Writings, 1832–1858*, 742. See also "Seventh Joint Debate," October 15, 1858, in Fehrenbacher, 809.

74. "Draft of a Speech," 418.

75. On the 1860 Democratic split, see Potter, *Impending Crisis*, 405–416; Michael F. Holt, *The Election of 1860: "A Campaign Fraught with Consequences"* (Lawrence: University Press of Kansas, 2017), 50–66, 115–133.

76. Holt, *Political Crisis of the 1850s*, 2–3, 6, 8, 220–221.

Chapter 5. "Of Strange, Discordant, and Even, Hostile Elements"

1. Abraham Lincoln, "Speech on the Kansas-Nebraska Act," October 16, 1854, in *Abraham Lincoln: Speeches and Writings, 1832–1858*, ed. Don E. Fehrenbacher (New York: Library of America, 1989), 326. On economic self-interest obstructing the capacity to see enslaved persons as human beings, see Lincoln's "Speech at New Haven, Connecticut," March 6, 1860: "Whether the owners of this species of property [slavery] do really see it as it is, it is not for me to say, but if they do, they see it as it is through 2,000,000,000 of dollars, and that is a pretty thick coating." *Abraham Lincoln: Speeches and Writings, 1859–1865*, ed. Don E. Fehrenbacher (New York: Library of America, 1989), 135.

2. "Speech at New Haven, Connecticut," 135. See also Lincoln's "Fragment on Slavery," [1854], in which he shows that any argument used to justify the enslavement of another can be used to justify one's own enslavement. Fehrenbacher, *Speeches and Writings, 1832–1858*, 303.

3. John C. Calhoun, "Further Remarks in Debate on His Fifth Resolution," January 10, 1838, in *The Papers of John C. Calhoun*, vol. 14, ed. Clyde N. Wilson (Columbia: University of South Carolina Press, 1981), 104–106.

4. Fehrenbacher, *Speeches and Writings, 1832–1858*, 426.

5. See David M. Potter, *The Impending Crisis, 1848–1861* (New York: Harper & Row, 1976), 297–327; Kenneth M. Stampp, *America in 1857: A Nation on the Brink* (New York: Oxford University Press, 1992), 295–329.

6. William E. Gienapp, *The Origins of the Republican Party, 1852–1856* (New York: Oxford University Press, 1987), 3–4.

7. Fehrenbacher, *Speeches and Writings, 1832–1858*, 434.

8. See "Party Divisions in the House of Representatives, 1789 to Present,"

US House of Representatives, History, Art, and Archives, https://history.house
.gov/Institution/Party-Divisions/Party-Divisions/; Potter, *Impending Crisis*, 175–
176. For state-by-state results of the 1854 elections in the northern and western
states (including Illinois), see Gienapp, *Origins of the Republican Party*, 103–166.

9. Gienapp, *Origins of the Republican Party*, 78–80.

10. Lincoln to Ichabod Codding, November 27, 1854, in Fehrenbacher,
Speeches and Writings, 1832–1858, 349–350. See also Victor B. Howard, "The Illinois Republican Party: Part I; A Party Organizer for the Republicans in 1854,"
Journal of the Illinois State Historical Society 64, 2 (1971): 125–160; Victor B. Howard, "The Illinois Republican Party: Part II; The Party Becomes Conservative,
1855–1856," *Journal of the Illinois State Historical Society* 64, 3 (1971): 285–311.
According to Howard, these political abolitionists placed a high priority on enlisting Lincoln to the project, so they were patient with his hesitation and willing
to move partway in his direction.

11. Gienapp notes that "the Illinois Republican party existed only on paper
in 1854: Its state committee never met, its nominee declined, and the party
conducted no campaign." However, Owen Lovejoy, one of the organizers, possessed "a large measure of political pragmatism" and looked to fuse with a larger
antislavery coalition. Gienapp, *Origins of the Republican Party*, 122–124.

12. See Lincoln to Elihu B. Washburne, January 6, 1855, and Lincoln to
Richard Yates, January 14, 1855, in Fehrenbacher, *Speeches and Writings, 1832–
1858*, 352–354.

13. Gienapp, *Origins of the Republican Party*, 125.

14. Gienapp, 174.

15. Lincoln to Elihu Washburne, February 9, 1855, in Fehrenbacher,
Speeches and Writings, 1832–1858, 355–356. See also Gienapp, *Origins of the Republican Party*, 174–175.

16. The historical narrative in this paragraph draws from Michael F. Holt,
The Political Crisis of the 1850s (New York: W. W. Norton, 1983), 101–138, and
Gienapp, *Origins of the Republican Party*, 20–31, 37–67, 92–102.

17. "1852 Democratic Party Platform" and "Whig Platform of 1852," both
available on the American Presidency Project website: https://www.presidency.
ucsb.edu/documents/app-categories/elections-and-transitions/party-plat
forms. On Scott's bowing to southern pressure, see Gienapp, *Origins of the Republican Party*, 16–19. Michael F. Holt downplays the significance of slavery in
the Whigs' demise and places greater weight on the party's failure to respond
to nativist concerns and, more generally, on the Whigs' failure after 1850 to
distinguish themselves from the Democrats on any important issue. Holt, *Political Crisis of the 1850s*, 101–181. In contrast, John L. Brooke emphasizes how
deeply the Whig Party's endorsement of the Fugitive Slave Act of 1850 alienated
its supporters in the Northeast. John L. Brooke, "Party, Nation, and Cultural
Rupture: The Crisis of the American Civil War," in *Practicing Democracy: Popular*

Politics in the United States from the Constitution to the Civil War, ed. Daniel Peart and Adam I. P. Smith (Charlottesville: University of Virginia Press, 2015), 72–95.

18. Holt, *Political Crisis of the 1850s*, 155; Gienapp, *Origins of the Republican Party*, 155. Neither historian accepts this as an impartial assessment of voter opinion in 1854, but the statement suggests a high degree of uncertainty among Lincoln's contemporaries about the importance of slavery to northern voters.

19. On the Know-Nothing electoral successes in 1854–55 and the nature of their appeal to voters, see Holt, *Political Crisis of the 1850s*, 150–172; Gienapp, *Origins of the Republican Party*, 92–102.

20. Holt, *Political Crisis of the 1850s*, 170.

21. On this theme, see Gienapp's chapters "The Confusion of Fusion" and "The Failure of Fusion," in *Origins of the Republican Party*, 103–166.

22. Abraham Lincoln, "Address to the Washington Temperance Society of Springfield, Illinois," February 22, 1842, in Fehrenbacher, *Speeches and Writings, 1832–1858*, 81–90; Lincoln to Richard J. Oglesby, September 8, 1854, in Fehrenbacher, 304: "Other things being equal, I would much prefer a temperate man to an intemperate one; still I do not make my vote depend absolutely upon the question of whether a candidate does or does not *taste* liquor."

23. Lincoln to Joshua F. Speed, August 24, 1855, in Fehrenbacher, *Speeches and Writings, 1832–1858*, 363.

24. Lincoln to Owen Lovejoy, August 11, 1855, in Fehrenbacher, *Speeches and Writings, 1832–1858*, 357–358.

25. Gienapp, *Origins of the Republican Party*, 179–187.

26. Eric Foner, for example, challenges the view that "nativism and temperance, not antislavery, were responsible for the political upheaval of the 1850s." Eric Foner, *Free Soil, Free Labor, Free Men: The Ideology of the Republican Party before the Civil War* (New York: Oxford University Press, 1970), 227. See also Bruce Levine, "'The Vital Element of the Republican Party': Antislavery, Nativism, and Abraham Lincoln," *Journal of the Civil War Era* 1, 4 (December 2011): 481–505.

27. David Potter writes that "Abraham Lincoln kept very silent in public about his disapproval of Know-Nothingism." Potter, *Impending Crisis*, 253. Harry Jaffa claims that in contrast to Stephen Douglas, who forthrightly condemned anti-immigrant bias, Lincoln "kept almost silent about [the Know-Nothings] in public, expressing his strong hostility only privately." Harry V. Jaffa, *Crisis of the House Divided: An Interpretation of the Issues in the Lincoln-Douglas Debates*, 50th anniversary ed. (Chicago: University of Chicago Press, 2009), 42.

28. In response to Stephen Douglas's efforts to associate opposition to the Kansas-Nebraska Act with Know-Nothingism, Lincoln said in a speech on September 26, 1854, that "if such an organization, secret or public, as Judge Douglas had described, really existed, and had for its object interference with the rights of foreigners, the Judge could not deprecate it more severely than himself." Roy P. Basler, ed., *The Collected Works of Abraham Lincoln*, 9 vols. (New

356 I NOTES TO PAGES 166–167

Brunswick, NJ: Rutgers University Press, 1953), 2:234. See also Lincoln's February 22, 1856, speech in support of resolutions that "declared against Know-Nothingism, and in favor of 'liberty of conscience as well as political freedom.'" Basler, *Collected Works*, 2:333. These resolutions and Lincoln's speech in support of them were reported in both the *Decatur State Chronicle* and the *Peoria Weekly Republican*.

29. See Lincoln's June 30, 1858, letter to a committee of German Republicans from Chicago: To "*Our German Fellow-Citizens:*—Ever true to *Liberty*, the *Union*, and the Constitution," in Basler, *Collected Works*, 2:475. In Lincoln's widely publicized July 10, 1858, Chicago speech, he remarked that, based on Stephen Douglas's exposition of the Declaration of Independence's "all men are created equal" (by which Douglas meant merely that the people of America were equal to the people of England), "you Germans are not connected with it." Fehrenbacher, *Speeches and Writings, 1832–1858*, 456. Lincoln also personally arranged to have his "House Divided" speech translated into German. Basler, *Collected Works*, 2:536.

30. Abraham Lincoln, "Speech and Resolutions Concerning Philadelphia Riots," June 12, 1844: "*Resolved*, That we will now, and at all times, oppose as best we may, all attempts to either destroy the naturalization laws or to so alter them, as to render admission under them, less convenient, less cheap, or less expeditious than it is now," and "*Resolved*, That the guarantee of the rights of conscience, as found in our Constitution, is most sacred and inviolable, and one that belongs no less to the Catholic, than to the Protestant." Basler, *Collected Works*, 1:337–338. The *Illinois State Register* carried a report of Lincoln's speech in support of these resolutions.

31. Levine points out that although Lincoln avoided publicly "attacking nativist leaders or organizations by name," he made it clear to nativist leaders, both privately and publicly, that he did not share their views. For instance, at the 1856 meeting that launched the Illinois branch of the Republican Party, Lincoln publicly supported a plank that "opposed political discrimination on the basis of either birthplace or religion," and in a May 17, 1859, letter to Theodore Canisius (an immigrant from Germany), Lincoln criticized an anti-immigrant provision in the Massachusetts constitution. That letter was widely publicized and reprinted with Lincoln's permission. Levine, "'Vital Element of the Republican Party,'" 492–493. For Lincoln's letter to Canisius, see Fehrenbacher, *Speeches and Writings, 1859–1865*, 21–22.

32. Lincoln to Owen Lovejoy, August 11, 1855, 358.

33. "Address to the Washington Temperance Society," 83.

34. Gienapp, *Origins of the Republican Party*, 98, 176–178, 234, 236. The pro-immigrant plank of the 1860 Republican national platform read: "That the Republican party is opposed to any change in our Naturalization Laws or any State legislation by which the rights of citizenship hitherto accorded to immi-

grants from foreign lands shall be abridged or impaired; and in favor of giving full and efficient protection to the rights of all classes of citizens, whether native or naturalized, both at home and abroad." Quoted in Michael F. Holt, *The Election of 1860: "A Campaign Fraught with Consequences"* (Lawrence: University Press of Kansas, 2017), 200–205. Among the Pennsylvania, Indiana, New Jersey, and Connecticut delegations at the 1860 Republican convention, "former Know Nothings were simply too critical to Republican success to risk offending them by nominating Seward." Holt, 113.

35. Abraham Lincoln, "Speech to the Springfield Scott Club," August 14 and 26, 1852, and "Speech at Peoria, Illinois," September 17, 1852, in Basler, *Collected Works*, 2:135–159.

36. Fehrenbacher, *Speeches and Writings, 1832–1858*, 434. On Lincoln's 1856 "lost speech," see Richard Carwardine, *Lincoln: A Life of Purpose and Power* (New York: Vintage, 2007), 68–69.

37. In contrast to Lincoln's 1854–55 US Senate candidacy, which he announced only after the November 1854 elections and consisted of a letter-writing campaign among legislators, in 1858 he "came forward as an avowed candidate in June, five months *before* the election, and carried his subsequent campaign directly to *the people.*" Don E. Fehrenbacher, *Prelude to Greatness: Lincoln in the 1850s* (Stanford, CA: Stanford University Press, 1962), 49.

38. See chapter 3. As it turned out, Van Buren's Free-Soil candidacy may have drawn enough votes from northern Democrats to secure the election for Whig candidate Zachary Taylor.

39. See "Party Platforms," American Presidency Project, https://www.presidency.ucsb.edu/documents/app-categories/elections-and-transitions/party-platforms.

40. According to Corey M. Brooks, the label "political abolitionists" refers to those abolitionists who advocated direct engagement in electoral politics, with the aim of breaking slavery's hold on both major parties. Corey M. Brooks, *Liberty Power: Antislavery Third Parties and the Transformation of American Politics* (Chicago: University of Chicago Press, 2016), 15–16. Political abolitionists in this sense deviated from the principles of William Lloyd Garrison and his followers, who refused to vote at all under a Constitution that permitted slavery and advocated free-state secession from the Union.

41. Abolitionist Wendell Phillips, for example, condemned Lincoln as the "slave hound from Illinois" because Lincoln believed the Constitution's fugitive slave provisions had to be honored. Quoted in David Herbert Donald, *Lincoln* (New York: Simon & Schuster, 1996), 137. Frederick Douglass was also critical of Lincoln but alternated between sharp criticism and qualified support in a pragmatic way designed to push Lincoln and his party toward stronger antislavery action. On Lincoln and Douglass, see James Oakes, *The Radical and the Republican: Frederick Douglass, Abraham Lincoln, and the Triumph of Antislavery Politics*

(New York: W. W. Norton, 2008); David W. Blight, *Frederick Douglass: Prophet of Freedom* (New York: Simon & Schuster, 2018), 1–9, 321–460.

42. See Foner, *Free Soil, Free Labor, Free Men*, 103–148; Richard H. Sewell, *Ballots for Freedom: Antislavery Politics in the United States, 1837–1860* (New York: Oxford University Press, 1976), 343–365; Brooks, *Liberty Power*, 213–226.

43. Lincoln to Ward H. Lamon, June 11, 1858, in Basler, *Collected Works*, 2:458–459.

44. Foner, *Free Soil, Free Labor, Free Men*, 215–216.

45. William W. Freehling, *Becoming Lincoln* (Charlottesville: University of Virginia Press, 2018), 165, 191.

46. On Know-Nothings' anti-Catholicism, see Gienapp, *Origins of the Republican Party*, 365–367. On the irregular, sometimes violent electoral practices of immigrant political clubs in 1850s New York, see Tyler Anbinder, "'Peaceably if We Can, Forcibly if We Must': Immigrants and Popular Politics in Pre–Civil War New York," in Peart and Smith, *Practicing Democracy*, 196–221.

47. Gienapp, *Origins of the Republican Party*, 211–212, 418–421; Foner, *Free Soil, Free Labor, Free Men*, 232–237, 242–250. In some states, including Indiana, Republicans disagreed over how far to go in accommodating the concerns of Know-Nothings to enlist their support for the Republican ticket. For a narrative of Republican Party organizing in Indiana in 1855, see Gienapp, 281–286.

48. See Abraham Lincoln, "Notes for Speeches at Columbus and Cincinnati, Ohio," September 16 and 17, 1859, in Basler, *Collected Works*, 3:428.

49. On this phenomenon, see William J. Cooper Jr., *The South and the Politics of Slavery, 1828–1856* (Baton Rouge: Louisiana State University Press, 1978).

50. See, for example, Lincoln to Henry Asbury, November 19, 1858, in Fehrenbacher, *Speeches and Writings, 1832–1858*, 830–831.

51. Douglas's evasiveness on this point is discussed in chapter 4.

52. On Douglas's efforts, in the face of backlash from the Kansas-Nebraska Act, to make immigration the central issue and tie the Republicans to Know-Nothingism, see Stephen Hanson and Paul Nygard, "Stephen A. Douglas, the Know-Nothings, and the Democratic Party in Illinois, 1854–1858," *Illinois Historical Journal* 87, 2 (Summer 1994): 109–130. The authors observe that Douglas "tried to exploit the presence of the Know-Nothings between 1854 and 1856 as a means of dividing the anti-Democratic voters. Douglas was so convinced of the usefulness of nativism as a weapon to divide the opposition that he even provided financial support to the Know-Nothings in an effort to keep the organization alive after the American party began to break apart in 1856. His strategy helped make it impossible for the Republicans to form a majority coalition in Illinois" (110).

53. Both platforms are posted at the American Presidency Project, https://www.presidency.ucsb.edu/documents/republican-party-platform-1856, https://www.presidency.ucsb.edu/documents/1856-democratic-party-platform.

54. Fehrenbacher, *Speeches and Writings, 1832–1858*, 426.

55. In a July 9, 1858, speech, Douglas quoted from Lincoln's "House Divided" speech as evidence that "Mr. Lincoln advocates boldly and clearly a war of sections, a war of the North against the South, of the free States against the slave States—a war of extermination—to be continued relentlessly until the one or the other shall be subdued, and all the States shall either become free or become slave." Robert W. Johannsen, ed., *The Lincoln-Douglas Debates* (New York: Oxford University Press, 1965), 29. In reply, Lincoln denied "that I invite a war of sections." "Speech at Springfield," July 17, 1858, in Fehrenbacher, *Speeches and Writings, 1832–1858*, 469.

56. See Lincoln to George Robertson, August 15, 1855, in Fehrenbacher, *Speeches and Writings, 1832–1858*, 359, where Lincoln expressed the fear that "there is no peaceful extinction of slavery in prospect for us." But as noted in chapter 4, Lincoln wrote this letter after the collapse of the Whig Party and before the Republican Party had established itself as a major political party, which in Lincoln's view enabled "the judgment and feeling against slavery" to be directed into "the peaceful channel of the ballot box." "Address at Cooper Institute," February 27, 1860, in Fehrenbacher, *Speeches and Writings, 1859–1865*, 125.

57. See, for instance, from his debates with Douglas, Lincoln at Ottawa, August 21, 1958: "In this and like communities, public sentiment is everything. With public sentiment, nothing can fail; without it, nothing can succeed." Fehrenbacher, *Speeches and Writings, 1832–1858*, 525–526.

58. For an analysis of Lincoln and public opinion, see Allen C. Guelzo, "'Public Sentiment Is Everything': Abraham Lincoln and the Power of Public Opinion," in *Lincoln and Liberty: Wisdom for the Ages*, ed. Lucas E. Morel (Lexington: University Press of Kentucky, 2014), 171–190; David Zarefsky, "'Public Sentiment Is Everything': Lincoln's View of Political Persuasion," *Journal of the Abraham Lincoln Association* 15, 2 (1994): 23–40; Douglas L. Wilson, *Lincoln's Sword: The Presidency and the Power of Words* (New York: Vintage, 2006); Diana Schaub, *His Greatest Speeches: How Lincoln Moved the Nation* (New York: St. Martin's Press, 2021). For an analysis of the rhetorical structure of Lincoln's "House Divided" speech, see Michael C. Leff, "Rhetorical Timing in Lincoln's 'House Divided' Speech," in *The Van Zelst Lecture in Communication* (pamphlet) (Evanston, IL: Northwestern University School of Speech, 1983).

59. Fehrenbacher, *Speeches and Writings, 1832–1858*, 426.

60. "Speech at Springfield," 471.

61. Fehrenbacher, *Speeches and Writings, 1832–1858*, 426.

62. On this theme, William Gienapp observes that "men frequently do not perceive the full implications of their arguments, indeed often resist accepting them even when they are made clear." For example, many of the same slave-state leaders (including Jefferson Davis of Mississippi and Robert Toombs

of Georgia) who vociferously denied any intention to nationalize the institution of slavery supported policies and constitutional amendments that would have done exactly that. William Gienapp, "The Republican Party and the Slave Power," in *New Perspectives on Race and Slavery in America*, ed. Robert H. Abzug and Stephen E. Maizlish (Lexington: University Press of Kentucky, 1986), 69. See also Harry Jaffa, who argues that whether there was a "tendency" toward the nationalization of slavery is a separate question from whether such a tendency, if it existed, was caused by "some kind of plot or conspiracy." Jaffa, *Crisis of the House Divided*, 278.

63. Fehrenbacher, *Speeches and Writings, 1832–1858*, 427–428.

64. Fehrenbacher, 428.

65. Abraham Lincoln, "House Divided Speech," June 16, 1858, in Fehrenbacher, 432.

66. Abraham Lincoln, "Reply to Douglas at Galesburg Debate," October 7, 1858, in Fehrenbacher, 714.

67. "House Divided Speech," 432.

68. Eric Foner, for example, credits Lincoln's genuine moral commitment to "achieving slavery's 'ultimate extinction'" yet observes that "he had little idea how this could be accomplished." Eric Foner, *The Fiery Trial: Abraham Lincoln and American Slavery* (New York: W. W. Norton, 2011), 65. Mark E. Neely Jr. claims that "Lincoln's vagueness about the eventual 'extinction' of slavery . . . was perhaps the most intellectually dishonest part of his platform." Mark E. Neely Jr., *The Last Best Hope of Earth: Abraham Lincoln and the Promise of America* (Cambridge, MA: Harvard University Press, 1995), 41. Deak Nabers argues not only that Lincoln had no intention of ultimately extinguishing slavery but also that he was not serious about halting its extension. Deak Nabers, "Abraham Lincoln and the Self-Governing Constitution," in *The Cambridge Companion to Abraham Lincoln*, ed. Shirley Samuels (New York: Cambridge University Press, 2012), 111–116.

69. Fehrenbacher, *Speeches and Writings, 1832–1858*, 434.

70. Fehrenbacher, *Prelude to Greatness*, 74, 78–79, 83. Some nationally prominent Republican leaders, including William Seward of New York, had concluded that "a policy of nonintervention [meaning Douglas's popular sovereignty] if honestly applied, would be sufficient (along with the iron necessities of climate) to prevent the extension of slavery into the remaining Western territory" (78).

71. Fehrenbacher, *Speeches and Writings, 1832–1858*, 434.

72. In this respect, I disagree with Michael William Pfau, "The House that Abe Built: The 'House Divided' Speech and Republican Party Politics," *Rhetoric and Public Affairs* 2, 4 (Winter 1999): 625–651. Pfau argues that Lincoln's aspiration was to reproduce in the Republican Party the "military-like discipline" long practiced in the Democratic Party (628).

73. Stampp, *America in 1857*, 290–293.

74. Fehrenbacher, *Speeches and Writings, 1832–1858*, 426–428, 431.

75. Fehrenbacher, *Prelude to Greatness*, 80–81; Jaffa, *Crisis of the House Divided*, 278; David Brion Davis, *The Slave Power Conspiracy and the Paranoid Style* (Baton Rouge: Louisiana State University Press, 1970); M. E. Bradford, "Dividing the House: The Gnosticism of Abraham Lincoln," *Modern Age* 23 (Winter 1979): 10–24; Pfau, "House that Abe Built," 637–642; Gienapp, "Republican Party and the Slave Power," 67–69, 73–74.

76. Allen C. Guelzo, "Abraham Lincoln and the Doctrine of Necessity" in *Abraham Lincoln as a Man of Ideas* (Carbondale: Southern Illinois University Press, 2009), 27–48.

77. Fehrenbacher, *Speeches and Writings, 1832–1858*, 434.

78. See Lincoln's "Handbill Replying to Charges of Infidelity," July 31, 1846, where he acknowledged privately arguing "that the human mind is impelled to action, or held to rest by some power over which the mind itself has no control"; and "Address to the Washington Temperance Society," February 22, 1842, where he observed that those who do not fall victim to alcohol "have been spared more from the absence of appetite, than from any mental or moral superiority over those who have." Fehrenbacher, *Speeches and Writings, 1832–1858*, 139, 88.

79. "Speech at Springfield," 478.

80. Abraham Lincoln, "Speech on the Kansas-Nebraska Act," October 16, 1854, in Fehrenbacher, *Speeches and Writings, 1832–1858*, 337.

81. "Third Joint Debate with Douglas," September 15, 1858, in Fehrenbacher, 606.

82. Lincoln to Albert G. Hodges, April 4, 1864, in Fehrenbacher, *Speeches and Writings, 1859–1865*, 585–586.

83. Fehrenbacher, *Speeches and Writings, 1832–1858*, 426.

84. Abraham Lincoln, "Draft of a Speech," [December 1857], in Fehrenbacher, 413.

85. Fehrenbacher, *Speeches and Writings, 1859–1865*, 686.

86. Fehrenbacher, *Speeches and Writings, 1832–1858*, 315.

87. Fehrenbacher, 426–431.

88. For a detailed narrative, see Alice Elizabeth Malavasic, *The F Street Mess: How Southern Senators Rewrote the Kansas-Nebraska Act* (Chapel Hill: University of North Carolina Press, 2017).

89. Malavasic, 125–127.

90. "Under the Dred Scott decision, 'squatter sovereignty' squatted out of existence, tumbled down like temporary scaffolding." "House Divided Speech," 429. For Douglas as "dupe," see "Draft of a Speech," August 1858, in Fehrenbacher, *Speeches and Writings, 1832–1858*, 429, 490.

91. Don E. Fehrenbacher, *The Dred Scott Case: Its Significance in American Law and Politics* (New York: Oxford University Press, 1978), 307–314.

92. Michael F. Holt describes the repeal of the Missouri Compromise as the act of a small group of politicians that ultimately had enormous and lethal consequences for millions of ordinary Americans. Michael F. Holt, *The Fate of Their Country: Politicians, Slavery Extension, and the Coming of the Civil War* (New York: Hill & Wang, 2004), xi–xiv, 92–127.

93. Fehrenbacher, *Speeches and Writings, 1832–1858*, 434.

Chapter 6. *"The Plank Is Large Enough"*

1. Frederick Douglass, "The Significance of Emancipation in the West Indies" (1857), in *The Portable Frederick Douglass*, ed. John Stauffer and Henry Louis Gates (New York: Penguin, 2016), 288.

2. Abraham Lincoln, "Speech on the Kansas-Nebraska Act," October 16, 1854, in *Abraham Lincoln: Speeches and Writings, 1832–1858*, ed. Don E. Fehrenbacher (New York: Library of America, 1989), 328.

3. "Speech on the Kansas-Nebraska Act," 316.

4. Fourth Joint Debate with Douglas, Charleston, Illinois, September 18, 1858, in Fehrenbacher, *Speeches and Writings, 1832–1858*, 636–637.

5. Abraham Lincoln, "Speech at Cincinnati, Ohio," September 17, 1859, in *Abraham Lincoln: Speeches and Writings, 1859–1865*, ed. Don E. Fehrenbacher (New York: Library of America, 1989), 68; Abraham Lincoln, "Speech at New Haven, Connecticut," March 6, 1860, in Fehrenbacher, 139.

6. Stephen Douglas, First Joint Debate with Lincoln, Ottawa, Illinois, August 21, 1858, in Fehrenbacher, *Speeches and Writings, 1832–1858*, 504.

7. In his October 16, 1854, speech on the Kansas-Nebraska Act, Lincoln said that although he had "high hope . . . in the long run" for colonizing formerly enslaved persons in Liberia, "its sudden execution is impossible" due to a lack of funds and ships and because, "if landed there in a day, they would all perish in the next ten days." He repeated this passage during his 1858 debates with Douglas. Fehrenbacher, *Speeches and Writings, 1832–1858*, 316, 510. None of the practical obstacles to colonization Lincoln identified in 1854 had diminished by 1858.

8. See Stanley Harrold, *Lincoln and the Abolitionists* (Carbondale: Southern Illinois University Press, 2018), 54; Michael Lind, *What Lincoln Believed: The Values and Convictions of America's Greatest President* (New York: Anchor, 2006), 111–114.

9. Abraham Lincoln, "Speech on the Dred Scott Decision," June 26, 1857, in Fehrenbacher, *Speeches and Writings, 1832–1858*, 397.

10. Stephen Douglas, Second Joint Debate with Lincoln, Freeport, Illinois, August 27, 1858, in Fehrenbacher, *Speeches and Writings, 1832–1858*, 556.

11. See, for example, Henry L. Benning's speech at the Georgia legislature's

secession debate, November 19, 1860: "Abolition would be to the South one of the direst evils of which the mind can conceive. . . . It will be a war of man with man—a war of extermination. . . . And as for the women, they will call upon the mountains to fall on them." William W. Freehling and Craig M. Simpson, eds., *Secession Debated: Georgia's Showdown in 1860* (New York: Oxford University Press, 1992), 120.

12. "Speech on the Dred Scott Decision," 397–398, 401–402.

13. Diana Schaub, "Lincoln and the Daughters of Dred Scott: A Reflection on the Declaration of Independence," in *When in the Course of Human Events: 1776 at Home, Abroad, and in American Memory*, ed. Will R. Jordan (Macon, GA: Mercer University Press, 2018), 205–206.

14. Michael Lind writes that, for Lincoln, "the purpose of colonizing emancipated slaves as well as free blacks was to prevent the blending through intermarriage of the white and black populations in the United States." Lind, *What Lincoln Believed*, 111–112.

15. Fehrenbacher, *Speeches and Writings, 1832–1858*, 398–399, 402.

16. "Speech on the Kansas-Nebraska Act," 316.

17. Abraham Lincoln, First Joint Debate with Douglas, Ottawa, Illinois, August 21, 1858, in Fehrenbacher, *Speeches and Writings, 1832–1858*, 512. Lincoln repeated this passage word for word in his September 16, 1859, speech in Columbus, Ohio (Fehrenbacher, *Speeches and Writings, 1859–1865*, 32), and in substance many other times.

18. See "Fragment on Slavery," [1854], in Fehrenbacher, *Speeches and Writings, 1832–1858*, 303. Diana Schaub argues that Lincoln viewed all socially or politically important inequalities as individual characteristics, not class or racial characteristics. Schaub, "Lincoln and the Daughters of Dred Scott," 194–202.

19. Richard Striner provides some examples, including leading Republican William H. Seward, who said in 1860, when he was a US senator: "The great fact is now fully realized that the African race here is a foreign and feeble element like the Indians, incapable of assimilation." Richard Striner, *Lincoln and Race* (Carbondale: Southern Illinois University Press, 2012), 19. The quoted passage comes from Seward's September 4, 1860, speech titled "The National Divergence and Return."

20. See, for example, Paul D. Escott, *What Shall We Do with the Negro? Lincoln, White Racism, and Civil War America* (Charlottesville: University of Virginia Press, 2009), 84. Escott quotes a July 1863 *New York Times* column titled "The Social and Political Status of the Southern Negro," which opposed extending suffrage to freedmen on the grounds that "history and the African character proved that blacks were 'incapable' of exercising the suffrage . . . 'without danger to themselves and their neighbors.'" Escott implies that Lincoln, like the *Times*, opposed Black suffrage because he believed Blacks were incapable of participat-

ing responsibly in democratic self-governance. Whether Lincoln believed this in 1863 is debatable, but there is no record that he said it.

21. Richard Striner suggests that, as a "master politician," Lincoln strategically veiled his disagreement with white supremacist doctrines during the 1858 campaign. Striner, *Lincoln and Race*, 24–25. See also Joseph R. Fornieri, *Abraham Lincoln: Philosopher Statesman* (Carbondale: Southern Illinois University Press, 2014), 139.

22. For Lerone Bennett Jr., Lincoln's attendance at minstrel shows not only betrays his inveterate racism but also discredits his public statements about the natural equality of all races. Lerone Bennett Jr., *Forced into Glory: Abraham Lincoln's White Dream* (Chicago: Johnson, 2000), 91. In contrast, Henry Louis Gates Jr., though critical of Lincoln's racial humor, argues that Lincoln was an extraordinarily complex person and that his racial humor coexisted with a genuine hatred of slavery and deep sympathy for anyone unjustly deprived of the fruits of their labor. See Henry Louis Gates Jr., "Abraham Lincoln on Race and Slavery," and appendix, "Lincoln, Race, and Humor," in *Lincoln on Race and Slavery*, ed. Henry Louis Gates Jr. and Donald Yacovone (Princeton, NJ: Princeton University Press, 2009), 16–47, 263–267.

23. See, for instance, Lincoln's September 2, 1858, speech in Clinton, Illinois: "Judge Douglas is very much afraid that the triumph of the Republican party will lead to a general mixture of the white and black races. Perhaps I am wrong in saying that he *is* afraid; so I will correct myself by saying that he *pretends* to fear that the success of our party will result in the amalgamation of blacks and whites." Roy P. Basler, ed., *The Collected Works of Abraham Lincoln*, 9 vols. (New Brunswick, NJ: Rutgers University Press, 1953), 3:84.

24. Henry Louis Gates Jr. is critical of Lincoln on many levels, including colonization, but acknowledges that "it was certainly not unreasonable for Lincoln, and anyone else who took a moment to think about it, [to believe] that it would be extraordinarily difficult to assimilate this mass of former slaves into an integrated American society without extended social, political, and economic conflict." Gates, "Abraham Lincoln on Race and Slavery," 21.

25. Abraham Lincoln, "Speech at Kalamazoo, Michigan," August 27, 1856, in Fehrenbacher, *Speeches and Writings, 1832–1858*, 377. See the discussion in chapter 4.

26. Abraham Lincoln, fragment "On Proslavery Theology," [1858], in Fehrenbacher, *Speeches and Writings, 1832–1858*, 685. Lincoln's "Dr. Ross" was likely modeled on the Reverend Fred A. Ross of Alabama, author of the book *Slavery Ordained of God*.

27. I have found only two usages of the word "instinct" in Lincoln's papers, neither of them employed in a racial context. The principal antebellum purveyors of "racial instinct" theory, including Samuel George Morton, Josiah C. Nott, and George R. Gliddon, argued in favor of the scientific theory of "polygenesis,"

meaning that the various races of humanity had been separately created or separately evolved and thus differed in their essential natures, just as different species of animals did. They also argued that slavery was the natural condition of the Black race. See Alan Levine, "Scientific Racism in Antebellum America," in *The Political Thought of the Civil War*, ed. Alan Levine, Thomas W. Merrill, and James R. Stoner (Lawrence: University Press of Kansas, 2018), 98–132. The polygenesis theory was irreconcilably opposed to the theory of equal natural rights to which Lincoln subscribed.

28. Frederick Douglass, "Prejudice against Color," *North Star*, June 13, 1850, in Stauffer and Gates, *Portable Frederick Douglass*, 422.

29. Frederick Douglass, "Various Incidents," chap. 25 in *My Bondage and My Freedom* (New York: Miller, Orton & Mulligan, 1855), 312.

30. Douglass, "Prejudice against Color," 422–424.

31. Abraham Lincoln, "Address to the Washington Temperance Society," February 22, 1842, in Fehrenbacher, *Speeches and Writings, 1832–1858*, 88.

32. See, for example, Richard D. Brown, *Self-Evident Truths: Contesting Equal Rights from the Revolution to the Civil War* (New Haven, CT: Yale University Press, 2017), 134–135. Brown argues that Lincoln "saw no contradiction between defending race-based inequality and the Declaration's 'all men are created equal' doctrine," and that when he acknowledged the Black man's "right to eat the bread . . . which his own hand earns," Lincoln "in no way contradicted the emerging doctrine of white supremacy" because the natural rights promised in the Declaration "were not specific political rights." See also David M. Fredrickson, who writes: "Although Lincoln found slavery to be immoral and hoped for its demise, he made no comparable moral argument against political and social exclusion on grounds of race." David M. Fredrickson, *Big Enough to Be Inconsistent: Abraham Lincoln Confronts Slavery and Race* (Cambridge, MA: Harvard University Press, 2008), 64. I argue, in contrast, that Lincoln was fully aware of the injustice of political and social exclusion and *did* see deprivation of political rights as a violation of natural right.

33. Douglas, First Joint Debate with Lincoln, 504, 506.

34. Abraham Lincoln, "House Divided Speech," June 16, 1858, in Fehrenbacher, *Speeches and Writings, 1832–1858*, 429. The privileges and immunities clause is in Article IV, section 2, of the US Constitution.

35. Douglas, First Joint Debate with Lincoln, 504.

36. Fehrenbacher, *Speeches and Writings, 1832–1858*, 328.

37. Fehrenbacher, 328–329.

38. Fehrenbacher, 316.

39. Henry L. Benning's secessionist speech, November 19, 1860, in Freehling and Simpson, *Secession Debated*, 119–120.

40. Stephen Douglas, Sixth Joint Debate with Lincoln, October 13, 1858, in Fehrenbacher, *Speeches and Writings, 1832–1858*, 753.

41. Fehrenbacher, *Speeches and Writings, 1832–1858*, 395–396.

42. Fehrenbacher, 396–397.

43. Fehrenbacher, 398.

44. Although Lincoln acknowledged in 1857 that Black Americans' electoral disenfranchisement was an important stage in their worsening oppression, earlier in his career he seemed indifferent to Black voting rights. See "Speech at Tremont, Illinois," May 2, 1840, in Basler, *Collected Works*, 1:210, where Lincoln sought to embarrass Democratic presidential nominee Martin Van Buren by revealing that he had supported Black voting rights in New York.

45. Abraham Lincoln to Henry L. Pierce and others, April 6, 1859, in Fehrenbacher, *Speeches and Writings, 1859–1865*, 19.

46. Gabor S. Boritt argues that, in contrast to Jefferson, Lincoln interpreted the Declaration's "all men are created equal" as a commitment to "equality of opportunity to get ahead in life," which required a more activist government than Jefferson envisioned. Gabor S. Boritt, *Lincoln and the Economics of the American Dream* (Urbana: University of Illinois Press, 1978), 158.

47. Thomas Jefferson, "Query XIV, Notes on the State of Virginia," in *Thomas Jefferson: Writings*, ed. Merrill D. Peterson (New York: Library of America, 1984), 264. See also Peter S. Onuf, *Jefferson's Empire: The Language of American Nationhood* (Charlottesville: University of Virginia Press, 2000), 147–188.

48. Harry V. Jaffa characterizes Lincoln's approach to race and colonization as broadly similar to Jefferson's. Henry V. Jaffa, *Crisis of the House Divided: An Interpretation of the Issues in the Lincoln-Douglas Debates*, 50th anniversary ed. (Chicago: University of Chicago Press, 2009), 384–386. Paul D. Escott also emphasizes similarities between Jefferson and Lincoln on colonization and is deeply critical of both. Escott, *What Shall We Do with the Negro?* 25–26, 36–37. Kevin R. C. Gutzman quotes Jefferson's line that emancipation without colonization would "produce convulsions which will probably never end but in the extermination of one or the other race." He suggests that Lincoln shared this view—overlooking Lincoln's specific arguments *against* that thesis. Kevin R. C. Gutzman, "Abraham Lincoln, Jeffersonian: The Colonization Chimera," in *Lincoln Emancipated: The President and the Politics of Race*, ed. Brian R. Dirck (De Kalb: Northern Illinois University Press, 2007), 45–72.

49. Fehrenbacher, *Speeches and Writings, 1832–1858*, 325. For Jefferson's embrace of "diffusion" theory, which he employed to *oppose* territorial restrictions on the spread of slavery similar to those he had supported earlier in his career, see Lacy K. Ford, *Deliver Us from Evil: The Slavery Question in the Old South* (New York: Oxford University Press, 2009), 74–77.

50. Jefferson, "Query XIV, Notes on the State of Virginia," 264–270.

51. During a September 24, 1862, cabinet meeting called to discuss the Emancipation Proclamation, Lincoln's attorney general Edward Bates argued in favor of the compulsory deportation of emancipated slaves. Secretary of the

navy Gideon Welles recorded in his diary that Lincoln replied: "Their emigration must be voluntary and without expense to themselves." Don E. Fehrenbacher and Virginia Fehrenbacher, *Recollected Words of Abraham Lincoln* (Stanford, CA: Stanford University Press, 1996), 474–475.

52. Jefferson, "Query XIV, Notes on the State of Virginia," 264.

53. Thomas Jefferson, "Report on Government for Western Territories," March 1, 1784, in Peterson, *Thomas Jefferson: Writings*, 377.

54. Thomas Jefferson to John Holmes, April 22, 1820, in Peterson, *Thomas Jefferson: Writings*, 1434.

55. Thomas Jefferson to Albert Gallatin, December 26, 1820, in Peterson, *Thomas Jefferson: Writings*, 1449.

56. "Speech at New Haven, Connecticut," 139. Lincoln repeated his criticism of Douglas's crocodile image in several other public speeches in late 1859 and early 1860.

57. Abraham Lincoln, "Speech at Hartford, Connecticut," March 5, 1860, in Basler, *Collected Works*, 4:10.

58. "Speech at Cincinnati, Ohio," 68.

59. "Speech at New Haven, Connecticut," 144.

60. Abraham Lincoln, "Annual Message to Congress," December 1, 1862, in Fehrenbacher, *Speeches and Writings, 1859–1865*, 407, 412.

61. Lincoln, "Annual Message to Congress," 407, 412–413.

62. Abraham Lincoln, "Message to Congress," April 16, 1862, in Fehrenbacher, *Speeches and Writings, 1859–1865*, 316. Lincoln signed the bill even though it differed in some particulars from his own preferred approach to abolition in the District of Columbia.

63. Abraham Lincoln, "Address on Colonization to a Committee of Colored Men," August 24, 1862, in Fehrenbacher, *Speeches and Writings, 1859–1865*, 353–357.

64. See, for example, Escott, *What Shall We Do with the Negro?* 53–55.

65. Manisha Sinha, "Allies for Emancipation? Lincoln and Black Abolitionists," in *Our Lincoln: New Perspective on Lincoln and His World*, ed. Eric Foner (New York: W. W. Norton, 2008): 180–196.

66. "Address on Colonization," 353, 357.

67. George B. Vashon quoted in Sinha, "Allies for Emancipation?" 185.

68. Abraham Lincoln, preliminary Emancipation Proclamation, September 22, 1862, in Fehrenbacher, *Speeches and Writings, 1859–1865*, 368–370.

69. Abraham Lincoln to James C. Conkling, August 26, 1863, in Fehrenbacher, *Speeches and Writings, 1859–1865*, 499.

70. Abraham Lincoln, "Speech on Reconstruction," April 11, 1865, in Fehrenbacher, *Speeches and Writings, 1859–1865*, 699–700.

Chapter 7. "In Course of Ultimate Extinction"

1. Abraham Lincoln, "First Inaugural Address," March 4, 1861, in *Abraham Lincoln: Speeches and Writings, 1859–1865*, ed. Don E. Fehrenbacher (New York: Library of America, 1989), 220; Abraham Lincoln, "House Divided Speech," June 16, 1858, in . *Abraham Lincoln: Speeches and Writings, 1832–1858*, ed. Don E. Fehrenbacher (New York: Library of America, 1989), 426.

2. Here I draw from James Oakes, *The Scorpion's Sting: Antislavery and the Coming of the Civil War* (New York: W. W. Norton, 2014), which describes a strategic vision for the peaceful extinction of slavery shared by Republicans of varying political perspectives and degrees of radicalism.

3. Lacy K. Ford, *Deliver Us from Evil: The Slavery Question in the Old South* (New York: Oxford University Press, 2009), describes slaveholders' chronic fear that their state's free white population would fall too low to enable the state to effectively suppress a slave uprising. Such fears diminished during boom times in the slave economy but returned in full force whenever slaveholding became less profitable.

4. Arthur Zilversmit, *The First Emancipation: The Abolition of Slavery in the North* (Chicago: University of Chicago Press, 1967); Gary B. Nash and Jean R. Soderland, *Freedom by Degrees: Emancipation in Pennsylvania and Its Aftermath* (New York: Oxford University Press, 1991).

5. State of New York, "An Act for the Gradual Abolition of Slavery" (1799), New York State Archives, http://www.archives.nysed.gov/education/act-gradual-abolition-slavery-1799.

6. "Selected Statistics on Slavery in the United States," collected from 1860 US Census by Kathryn L. MacKay, Weber State University, https://faculty.weber.edu/kmackay/selected_statistics_on_slavery_i.htm.

7. Abraham Lincoln, "Proposal in the U.S. House of Representatives for Abolition of Slavery in the District of Columbia," January 10, 1849, in Fehrenbacher, *Speeches and Writings, 1832–1858*, 227–230; Abraham Lincoln, "Annual Message to Congress," December 1, 1862, in Fehrenbacher, *Speeches and Writings, 1859–1865*, 408–411.

8. For the long process culminating in the positive-good, "paternalistic" proslavery argument, see Ford, *Deliver Us from Evil.*

9. Lincoln to Williamson Durley, October 3, 1845, in Fehrenbacher, *Speeches and Writings, 1832–1858*, 111–112.

10. James Brewer Stewart, *Abolitionist Politics and the Coming of the Civil War* (Amherst: University of Massachusetts Press, 2008), 6–7, 17–18.

11. See, for example, William Lloyd Garrison, "No Compromise with Slavery: An Address Delivered in the Broadway Tabernacle, New York, February 14, 1854." Garrison argued that, "In itself, Slavery has no resources and no strength. Isolated and alone, it could not stand an hour" (31). The full text

has been posted by the Library of Congress at https://www.loc.gov/resource /rbaapc.11000/?st=gallery.

12. Sarah McCammon, "The Story behind 'Forty Acres and a Mule,'" *All Things Considered*, NPR, January 12, 2015, https://www.npr.org/sections/code switch/2015/01/12/376781165/the-story-behind-40-acres-and-a-mule.

13. Belinda's Petition, Massachusetts General Court, 1782, quoted in Manisha Sinha, *The Slave's Cause: A History of Abolition* (New Haven, CT: Yale University Press, 2016), 71. Sinha notes, "The General Court granted Belinda's petition, partly because her master, Isaac Royall Jr. was a Loyalist, and allotted her an allowance for a year."

14. Abraham Lincoln, "Speech on the Dred Scott Decision," June 26, 1857, in Fehrenbacher, *Speeches and Writings, 1832–1858*, 398.

15. Lincoln to Durley, October 3, 1845, 111–112. Lincoln admitted that he, too, bore responsibility for the unintended consequences of his actions. Responding to accusations that his "House Divided" speech invited a war between North and South, Lincoln denied any such intention but acknowledged that if his words or actions *did* bring about such a war, "It is just as fatal to the country, if I have any influence in producing it, whether I intend it or not." Abraham Lincoln, "First Joint Debate with Douglas," August 21, 1858, in Fehrenbacher, *Speeches and Writings, 1832–1858*, 515.

16. Fehrenbacher, *Speeches and Writings, 1832–1858*, 434. Lincoln described the Republican Party as composed of "strange," "discordant," and "hostile elements" united by their opposition to the expansion and perpetuation of slavery. The range of discordance among Republicans, abolitionists, and enslaved persons resisting their bondage was even greater, although these three groups did not have to agree on a shared political platform, as the Republicans did.

17. Oakes, *Scorpion's Sting*, 13, 36.

18. Speech by Robert Toombs, November 13, 1860, and speech by Thomas R. R. Cobb, November 12, 1860, in *Secession Debated: Georgia's Showdown in 1860*, ed. William W. Freehling and Craig M. Simpson (New York: Oxford University Press, 1992), 29, 40.

19. On the necessity of high profits and "the rising value of capital invested in slaves" to reconcile white Southerners to "the difficulties of slave control," see Ford, *Deliver Us from Evil*, 6.

20. See William W. Freehling, *The Road to Disunion: Secessionists Triumphant, 1854–1861* (New York: Oxford University Press, 2007), 19–26, for a snapshot of slavery's "economic bonanza" in the 1850s in Alabama, Mississippi, Louisiana, Texas, and Arkansas. Slaveholders there purchased large numbers of slaves from border South and middle South slave states. The consequence of slavery's expansion southward, however, was a declining proportion of slaves in politically critical border states such as Missouri, which might conceivably become

a free state in the not-too-distant future if Kansas entered the Union as a free state (63–66).

21. Key leaders of the Democratic Party—not just southerners but also Franklin Pierce, James Buchanan, and Stephen Douglas—repeatedly endorsed US expansion into the Caribbean. In his 1858 debates with Lincoln, Douglas argued that "the time may come, indeed has now come, when our interests would be advanced by the acquisition of the island of Cuba. . . . So, when it becomes necessary to acquire any portion of Mexico or Canada, or of this continent or the adjoining islands, we must take them as we find them, leaving the people free to do as they please, to have slavery or not, as they choose." Fehrenbacher, *Speeches and Writings, 1832–1858,* 601. Slave-state leaders, however, made it clear that, from their perspective, the whole point of US expansion into the Caribbean was to acquire future slave states.

22. William Freehling describes why proslavery extremists in South Carolina were so determined that Kansas enter the Union as a slave state. South Carolina congressman Preston Brooks (who assaulted Massachusetts senator Charles Sumner on the floor of the US Senate in 1857) argued that if Kansas entered the Union as a free state, "Abolitionism will become" Missouri's "prevailing sentiment. So with Arkansas—so with Upper Texas," at which point slaveholders would have to "put our house in order to die by inches." But if establishing slavery in Kansas became "a point of honor with the South," then the "slavery question" would be "settled, and the rights of the South are safe." Freehling, *Road to Disunion: Secessionists Triumphant,* 81.

23. The danger inherent in a growing enslaved Black population combined with a shrinking free white population is a central theme in Ford, *Deliver Us from Evil.*

24. The original phrase comes from James G. Blaine, *Twenty Years of Congress from Lincoln to Garfield,* vol. 1 (Norwich, CT: Henry Hill, 1884), 272. The phrase has been repeated by historians who endorse the thesis that the "ultimate extinction" idea had no practical function except to help Republicans win elections in northern states.

25. For discussion of how the "freedom national" principle shaped policy from the outset of Lincoln's presidency, see James Oakes, *Freedom National: The Destruction of Slavery in the United States, 1861–1865* (New York: W. W. Norton, 2012).

26. Oakes, *Scorpion's Sting,* 30–32.

27. Oakes, 33–34.

28. Fehrenbacher, *Speeches and Writings, 1832–1858,* 512; Fehrenbacher, *Speeches and Writings, 1859–1865,* 215.

29. Freehling and Simpson, *Secession Debated,* 118–119.

30. Fehrenbacher, *Speeches and Writings, 1832–1858,* 540.

31. For Lincoln's "hopeless" 1849 proposal to gradually abolish slavery in

the District of Columbia, see Don E. Fehrenbacher, *The Slaveholding Republic: An Account of the United States Government's Relations to Slavery* (New York: Oxford University Press, 2001), 78, 82. Lincoln's remarks on the subject during his debates with Douglas indicate that he did not consider the prospect hopeless in 1858.

32. Fehrenbacher, *Speeches and Writings, 1832–1858*, 539.

33. Freehling and Simpson, *Secession Debated*, 15.

34. Fehrenbacher, *Speeches and Writings, 1832–1858*, 541.

35. On the "revolutionary" proposal to ban the interstate slave trade, which was "politically delicate" even among antislavery radicals, see Corey M. Brooks, *Liberty Power: Antislavery Third Parties and the Transformation of American Politics* (Chicago: University of Chicago Press, 2016), 8, 18–19, 214.

36. Abraham Lincoln, "Cooper Institute Address," February 27, 1860, in Fehrenbacher, *Speeches and Writings, 1859–1865*, 114.

37. Ford, *Deliver Us from Evil*, 112–121.

38. Abraham Lincoln, "Second Joint Debate with Douglas," August 27, 1858, in Fehrenbacher, *Speeches and Writings, 1832–1858*, 538–540.

39. On Douglas's support for annexing Cuba as a new slave state, see Robert W. Johannsen, *Stephen A. Douglas* (New York: Oxford University Press, 1973), 147, 326–327, 528–529, 683, 692. On Douglas's endorsement of Cuban annexation in the 1858 Lincoln-Douglas debates, see Fehrenbacher, *Speeches and Writings, 1832–1858*, 601.

40. "Second Joint Debate with Douglas"; Lincoln to Joshua F. Speed, August 24, 1855, in Fehrenbacher, *Speeches and Writings, 1832–1858*, 361, 538; "First Inaugural Address," 216–217.

41. Lincoln and Herndon were contacted by Polly Mack, the mother of John Shelby, a young Black man from Springfield who worked on a Mississippi River steamboat. In New Orleans, Shelby had been arrested for failing to carry "free papers," then sold into slavery when he could not pay his fine. Lincoln paid out of his own pocket to purchase Shelby's freedom. Sidney Blumenthal, *All the Powers of Earth: The Political Life of Abraham Lincoln, 1856–1860* (New York: Simon & Schuster, 2019), 305–306. The original source is Herndon's *The Life of Abraham Lincoln* (1889).

42. David M. Potter, *The Impending Crisis, 1848–1861* (New York: Harper & Row, 1976), 131.

43. "First Joint Debate with Douglas," 512; "First Inaugural Address," 215, emphasis added.

44. Oakes notes the dissonance here: "But wasn't there something irreducibly violent in the metaphor of the scorpion's sting?" Oakes, *Scorpion's Sting*, 36.

45. Abraham Lincoln, "Address to the Washington Temperance Society," February 22, 1842, in Fehrenbacher, *Speeches and Writings, 1832–1858*, 82; "First Inaugural Address." See also Lincoln to Alexander Stephens, December

22, 1860: "I wish to assure you, as once a friend, and still, I hope, not an enemy."
Fehrenbacher, *Speeches and Writings, 1859–1865*, 194, 224.

46. Oakes, *Scorpion's Sting*, 35.

47. Oakes, 15–21, 104–156.

48. Oakes, 156.

49. "First Inaugural Address," 223.

50. Democratic Party Platform (Breckinridge faction) of 1860, American Presidency Project, https://www.presidency.ucsb.edu/documents/democratic -party-platform-breckinridge-faction-1860.

51. Fehrenbacher, *Speeches and Writings, 1859–1865*, 220.

52. "Cooper Institute Address," 120, emphasis in original.

53. See Harold Holzer, *Lincoln at Cooper Union: The Speech that Made Abraham Lincoln President* (New York: Simon & Schuster, 2004). For Holzer, the central message of Lincoln's speech is clear: "the gods of America's secular heaven had ordained a limit to the spread of slavery with the hope and expectation of its eventual demise" (123). See also Lucas E. Morel, *Lincoln and the American Founding* (Carbondale: Southern Illinois University Press, 2020), 18–20, 103–105.

54. Fehrenbacher, *Speeches and Writings, 1859–1865*, 113.

55. Fehrenbacher, 111–113, 119. On Lincoln's research and writing process for the Cooper Institute address, see Holzer, *Lincoln at Cooper Union*, 50–54.

56. Fehrenbacher, *Speeches and Writings, 1859–1865*, 112, 115–117.

57. Fehrenbacher, 117–118.

58. Fehrenbacher, 114–115.

59. Fehrenbacher, *Slaveholding Republic*, 260–261.

60. "Cooper Institute Address," 114–115.

61. Fehrenbacher, *Speeches and Writings, 1859–1865*, 115; Fehrenbacher, *Speeches and Writings, 1832–1858*, 319.

62. See Brooks, *Liberty Power*, 84–85, 143; William W. Wiecek, *The Sources of Antislavery Constitutionalism in America, 1760–1848* (Ithaca, NY: Cornell University Press, 1977), 191–193, 208–219, 228–275.

63. Chase to Lewis Tappan, March 18, 1847, quoted in Wiecek, *Sources of Antislavery Constitutionalism*, 209.

64. Wiecek, *Sources of Antislavery Constitutionalism*, 209–211.

65. "Speech of Salmon P. Chase, in the Case of the Colored Woman, Matilda" (1837), quoted in Wiecek, *Sources of Antislavery Constitutionalism*, 191–192.

66. For Calhoun's proslavery constitutionalism, see James H. Read, *Majority Rule versus Consensus: The Political Thought of John C. Calhoun* (Lawrence: University Press of Kansas, 2009), 85–117.

67. "Cooper Institute Address," 118, 127; "First Joint Debate with Douglas"; Abraham Lincoln, "Fifth Joint Debate with Douglas, Galesburg, Illinois," October 7, 1858, in Fehrenbacher, *Speeches and Writings, 1832–1858*, 527, 714. On the unwillingness of the Constitution's framers to legitimize "property in man,"

see Sean Wilentz, *No Property in Man: Slavery and Antislavery at the Nation's Founding* (Cambridge, MA: Harvard University Press, 2018), 85–86, 95–99.

68. Abraham Lincoln, "Speech on the Kansas-Nebraska Act," October 16, 1854, in Fehrenbacher, *Speeches and Writings, 1832–1858*, 331–332.

69. "Cooper Institute Address," 120, 126–127; "Fragment on the Constitution and the Union," ca. January 1861, in *The Collected Works of Abraham Lincoln*, 9 vols., ed. Roy P. Basler (New Brunswick, NJ: Rutgers University Press, 1953), 4:169.

70. Wilentz, *No Property in Man*, makes as strong a case for the founders' antislavery commitments as the historical record permits. For a much more negative view of the founders, see Paul Finkelman, *Slavery and the Founders: Race and Liberty in the Age of Jefferson*, 3rd ed. (Armonk, NY: M. E. Sharpe, 2014), 3–45. Michael Zuckert summarizes the scholarly debate and seeks a coherent middle position in "Slavery and the Constitution in Madisonian Perspective," *Starting Points*, November 4, 2021.

71. This list would include Benjamin Franklin, Benjamin Rush, and Thomas Paine of Pennsylvania and Alexander Hamilton and John Jay of New York. Those most directly responsible for abolition in the North, however, were lesser known men and women, including enslaved persons who pressed freedom suits. See Zilversmit, *First Emancipation*; Sinha, *Slave's Cause*, 65–96.

72. Fehrenbacher, *Speeches and Writings, 1859–1865*, 122.

73. This point is emphasized by Mark A. Graber in *Dred Scott and the Problem of Constitutional Evil* (New York: Cambridge University Press, 2006), 91–153. Graber traces these ground rules back to the framers themselves, including James Madison, who regarded slavery as unjust and hoped for its ultimate extinction. "The framers understood that slavery might be restrained or even abolished under the constitutional arrangements agreed upon in 1787, but they believed that would happen only when many Southerners thought such policies desirable" (92).

74. "Cooper Institute Address," 120; "Speech on the Kansas-Nebraska Act"; Abraham Lincoln, "Third Joint Debate with Douglas," September 15, 1858, in Fehrenbacher, *Speeches and Writings, 1832–1858*, 328, 604, 606.

75. "Cooper Institute Address," 112–113.

76. Fehrenbacher, *Slaveholding Republic*, 256.

77. "Cooper Institute Address," 113–114.

78. "Cooper Institute Address," 114.

79. See Adam Rothman, *Slave Country: American Expansion and the Origins of the Deep South* (Cambridge, MA: Harvard University Press. 2005), 26–35; Fehrenbacher, *Slaveholding Republic*, 259–263; Ford, *Deliver Us from* Evil, 112–130.

80. Rothman, *Slave Country*, 30–31; Ford, *Deliver Us from Evil*, 110–111.

81. Ford, *Deliver Us from* Evil, 102–111.

82. Ford, 129; Rothman, *Slave Country*, 90–92.

83. Rothman, *Slave Country*, 34.

84. Quoted in Rothman, 31.

85. Fehrenbacher, *Slaveholding Republic*, 259–263; Ford, *Deliver Us from Evil*, 112–115; Finkelman, *Slavery and the Founders*, 214–215.

86. Rothman, *Slave Country*, 31–34, 73–95; Ford, *Deliver Us from Evil*, 104, 135–136.

87. See Lincoln to John A. Gilmer, December 15, 1860, and Lincoln to William H. Seward, February 1, 1861, in Fehrenbacher, *Speeches and Writings, 1859–1865*, 190–192, 197–198. Lincoln also indicated his willingness to accept a constitutional amendment, which passed Congress on the eve of his inauguration, explicitly securing slavery in the states (though not in the territories) against federal interference. On this "other" thirteenth amendment (which was never ratified by the states), see Daniel W. Crofts, *Lincoln and the Politics of Slavery: The Other Thirteenth Amendment and the Struggle to Save the Union* (Chapel Hill: University of North Carolina Press, 2016).

88. See Lincoln's letters to Lyman Trumbull, December 10, 1860; William Kellogg, December 11, 1860; John A. Gilmer, December 15, 1860; Thurlow Weed, December 17, 1860; John D. Defrees, December 18, 1860; James T. Hale, January 11, 1861; and William H. Seward, February 1, 1861, in Fehrenbacher, *Speeches and Writings, 1859–1865*, 190–193, 195–198.

89. Kenneth M. Stampp, *And the War Came: The North and the Secession Crisis, 1860–1861* (Baton Rouge: Louisiana State University Press, 1950), 130.

90. Potter, *Impending Crisis*, 531–532.

91. Lincoln to Trumbull, December 10, 1860. Lincoln used the same phrase, with minor alterations, to make the same point in his December 11, 1860, letter to William Kellogg. Fehrenbacher, *Speeches and Writings, 1859–1865*, 190.

92. Lincoln to Kellogg, December 11, 1860; Gilmer, December 15, 1860; Weed, December 17, 1860; Hale, January 11, 1861; and Seward, February 11, 1861, in Fehrenbacher, *Speeches and Writings, 1859–1865*, 190–197.

93. Both platforms are posted by the American Presidency Project: https://www.presidency.ucsb.edu/documents/1860-democratic-party-platform; https://www.presidency.ucsb.edu/documents/democratic-party-platform-breckinridge-faction-1860.

94. Freehling, *Road to Disunion: Secessionists Triumphant*, 145–167.

95. "First Joint Debate with Douglas," 514; "Speech at Kalamazoo, Michigan," August 27, 1856, in Fehrenbacher, *Speeches and Writings, 1832–1858*, 377; "First Joint Debate with Douglas," 524; "Fifth Joint Debate with Douglas," 716–717. On violent threats against the practice of free elections, see Lincoln's Cooper Institute address: "But you will not abide the election of a Republican President! In that supposed event, you say, you will destroy the Union; and then, you say, the great crime of having destroyed it will be upon us!" Fehrenbacher, *Speeches and Writings, 1859–1865*, 127.

96. For a survey of dismissive responses to Lincoln's nationalization scenario, followed by a persuasive case for the well-grounded character of Lincoln's fears, see William E. Gienapp, "The Republican Party and the Slave Power," in *New Perspectives on Race and Slavery in America*, ed. Robert H. Abzug and Stephen E. Maizlish (Lexington: University Press of Kentucky, 1986), 69–74.

97. For example, many supporters of popular sovereignty under the Kansas-Nebraska Act claimed that an isothermal line would prevent slavery from establishing itself in Kansas, even though its latitude was the same as Missouri's, a bordering slave state. Christopher Childers, *The Failure of Popular Sovereignty: Slavery, Manifest Destiny, and the Radicalization of Southern Politics* (Lawrence: University Press of Kansas, 2012), 259.

98. "Speech on the Kansas-Nebraska Act," 323. On proslavery advocates' similar rejection of the climate theory and their confidence that mining and other industrial enterprises could be profitably based on slave labor in any latitude, see the editorial in the March 31, 1860, edition of the *Charleston Mercury* (posted at the American Historical Association website), rejecting the notion that any isothermal line made Kansas unsuited to slavery. "It turns out now, not only that Kansas is a fine hemp and tobacco country, but abounding in mines which may make it the rival of California in the production of gold." The Pike's Peak gold rush of the late 1850s occurred in what was then Kansas territory and now the state of Colorado.

99. For the argument that slavery could have been effectively nationalized through an accumulation of judicial decisions, see Paul Finkelman, *An Imperfect Union: Slavery, Federalism, and Comity* (Chapel Hill: University of North Carolina Press, 1981), 313–343.

100. Dred Scott v. Sandford, 60 U.S. 393 (1857).

101. "Fifth Joint Debate with Douglas," 714–715.

102. One troubling episode from Lincoln's law career came in 1847, when he represented Kentucky slaveholder Robert Matson. Matson was trying to recover the enslaved Jane Bryant and her family, whom Matson had brought to Illinois to work on farmland he owned there. Bryant insisted that under Illinois law she was free, and she won her case in court. This is often incorrectly characterized as a fugitive slave case. Lincoln's motivation in taking Matson's case has been debated. The episode occurred before the Kansas-Nebraska Act placed opposition to slavery at the center of his career and thought. By the late 1850s, Lincoln clearly viewed slaveholders' supposed right to temporarily reside in or travel through a free state with persons they held in slavery as one of the paths by which slavery could be imposed on free states through judicial decree. In this respect, his experience with the Matson case would have reinforced Lincoln's later fears about the nationalization of slavery. On the Matson case, see Roger D. Billings Jr., "Abraham Lincoln and the Duty of Zealous Representation: The Matson Slave Case," *Connecticut Public Interest Law Journal* 14, 2 (2015): 179–206.

103. Basler, *Collected Works*, 3:548, 550n37. Lincoln did not prepare the notes, but he approved them for the published version of the address.

104. Paul Finkelman writes: "By 1860 an appeal in *Lemmon* to the Taney court seemed imminent, and it took little imagination to predict how that court would decide the case. Even if the Taney court found only a limited right of slave transit, that would have provided the opening wedge Republicans feared. And, given the court's sweeping decision in *Dred Scott*, it is hard to deny that an appeal in *Lemmon* would not have led to some form of slavery in the North." Finkelman, *Imperfect Union*, 322–323.

105. "Fifth Joint Debate with Douglas," 715.

106. Records of the Senate of the United States, 36th Congress, 2nd session, December 24, 1860.

107. Speech by Toombs, 46.

Chapter 8. *"To Declare the* Right, *so that* Enforcement *Might Follow"*

1. Abraham Lincoln, "Speech on the Kansas-Nebraska Act," October 16, 1854, in *Abraham Lincoln: Speeches and Writings, 1832–1858*, ed. Don E. Fehrenbacher (New York: Library of America, 1989), 328.

2. Abraham Lincoln, "Seventh Joint Debate with Douglas," October 15, 1858, in Fehrenbacher, 794–795.

3. See, for example, Frederick Douglass, "What to the Slave Is the Fourth of July?" July 4, 1852, in *The Portable Frederick Douglass*, ed. John Stauffer and Henry Louis Gates (New York: Penguin, 2016), 195–222.

4. Abraham Lincoln, "Cooper Institute Address," February 27, 1860, in *Abraham Lincoln: Speeches and Writings, 1859–1865*, ed. Don E. Fehrenbacher (New York: Library of America, 1989), 124.

5. See Robert Bray, "What Abraham Lincoln Read—An Evaluative and Annotated List," *Journal of the Abraham Lincoln Association* 28, 2 (Summer 2007): 28–81. Bray judges it "highly unlikely" that Lincoln read Locke's *Second Treatise of Civil Government.*

6. The second plank of the 1860 Republican platform quoted at length from the Declaration's preamble and added that these principles were "essential to the preservation of our Republican institutions." American Presidency Project, https://www.presidency.ucsb.edu/documents/republican-party-platform-1860.

7. William Lloyd Garrison wrote: "I am a believer in that portion of the Declaration of American Independence in which it is set forth, as among self-evident truths, 'that all men are created equal; that they are endowed by their Creator with certain inalienable rights; that among these are life, liberty, and the pursuit of happiness.' Hence, I am an abolitionist." William Lloyd Garrison,

"Address before the Anti-Slavery Society," New York City, February 14, 1854, in *The American Debate over Slavery, 1760–1865: An Anthology*, ed. Scott J. Hammond, Kevin R. Hardwick, and Howard Lubert (Indianapolis: Hackett, 2016), 252.

8. *Transactions of the Kansas State Historical Society, 1883–1885* (Topeka: Kansas Publishing House, 1886), 445.

9. Constitution of Kentucky, 1850, https://www.wordservice.org/State%20 Constitutions/usa1040.htm.

10. Quoted in James L. Huston, "Property Rights in Slavery and the Coming of the Civil War," *Journal of Southern History* 65, 2 (May 1999): 262.

11. Sean Wilentz, *No Property in Man: Slavery and Antislavery at the Nation's Founding* (Cambridge, MA: Harvard University Press, 2018), 39.

12. John C. Calhoun, "Speech on the Oregon Bill," June 27, 1848, in *Union and Liberty: The Political Philosophy of John C. Calhoun*, ed. Ross M. Lence (Indianapolis: Liberty Fund, 1992), 566–567.

13. John Locke, *Second Treatise of Civil Government*, chap. 19, sec. 222, in *Two Treatises of Government and a Letter Concerning Toleration*, ed. Ian Shapiro (New Haven, CT: Yale University Press, 2003), 197.

14. On Calhoun and Locke, see Robert Elder, *Calhoun: American Heretic* (New York: Basic Books, 2021), 10–11, 22, 180, 286–287. Elder describes a conversation with John C. Calhoun that John Quincy Adams recorded in his diary during the 1820 Missouri controversy. "Where Adams believed that slaves were part of Locke's community of the governed whose assent was a precondition of legitimate government, Calhoun viewed slaves as property, which, according to Locke, it was one of the fundamental purposes of government to protect" (179–180).

15. Locke, *Second Treatise*, chap. 2, sec. 4, 101.

16. Abraham Lincoln, "First Joint Debate with Douglas," August 21, 1858, in Fehrenbacher, *Speeches and Writings, 1832–1858*, 512. Elsewhere, Lincoln specifically emphasized that a Black woman had an equal "natural right to eat the bread which she earns with her own hands without asking leave of any one else." Abraham Lincoln, "Speech on the Dred Scott Decision," June 26, 1857, in Fehrenbacher, 398.

17. Locke, *Second Treatise*, chap. 2, sec. 4, 101.

18. Alan Levine, "Scientific Racism in Antebellum America," in *The Political Thought of the Civil War*, ed. Alan Levine, Thomas W. Merrill, and James R. Stoner (Lawrence: University Press of Kansas, 2018), 98–132.

19. Locke, *Second Treatise*, chap. 5, sec. 26, 111.

20. "Speech on the Dred Scott Decision," 398.

21. Shapiro, *Two Treatises*, 193.

22. James Farr observes that, according to Locke's *Second Treatise*, the only form in which slavery is legitimate as punishment for crimes against the life,

liberty, and property of others does not remotely match the reality of racial slavery in the Americas, and that Locke nowhere asserts any doctrine of racial inferiority to justify slavery. Farr concludes that Locke made no attempt to reconcile his political theory with his financial stake in the slave trade and that his principal concern was preventing the enslavement of free Englishmen by an absolutist government. James Farr, "'So Vile and Miserable an Estate': The Problem of Slavery in Locke's Political Thought," *Political Theory* 14, 2 (May 1986): 263–289. Other scholars have argued that Locke implausibly applied "convict labor" or "just war" justifications to New World slavery or that he justified slavery as an adjunct to colonial conquest. For an analysis of scholarly debate on the implications of Locke's financial stake in colonial slavery, see Wayne Glausser, "Three Approaches to Locke and the Slave Trade," *Journal of the History of Ideas* 51, 2 (April–June 1990): 199–216.

23. Locke, *Second Treatise*, chap. 3, sec. 17, chap. 4, sec. 24, 107, 110.

24. "Cooper Institute Address," 124.

25. Lacy K. Ford, *Deliver Us from Evil: The Slavery Question in the Old South* (New York: Oxford University Press, 2009), 205–237.

26. Locke, *Second Treatise*, chap. 3, sec. 19, chap. 4, sec. 23, 108, 110.

27. Locke, chap. 16, sec. 182, 181.

28. John C. Calhoun, "Speech on the Reception of Abolition Petitions," February 6, 1837, in Lence, *Union and Liberty*, 475.

29. "Speech on the Kansas-Nebraska Act," 326, 334.

30. Locke, *Second Treatise*, chap. 3, secs. 16 and 17, 107.

31. "Speech on the Kansas-Nebraska Act," 315–316, 326.

32. Locke, *Second Treatise*, chap. 9, secs. 124 and 125, 155.

33. Locke, chap. 9, sec. 131, 156–157.

34. Locke, chap. 7, sec. 96, 142.

35. Locke, chap. 16, 178–187.

36. Locke, chap. 18, secs. 208 and 209, 192.

37. Ian Shapiro describes how Locke's emphasis on majoritarian rather than individual consent minimizes the obstacles to government action, in contrast to contemporary libertarian theorists, who prioritize individual consent and reduce the scope of government action to a minimum, even when such action has majority support. "John Locke's Democratic Theory," in Shapiro, *Two Treatises*, 309–340.

38. Locke, *Second Treatise*, chap. 3, sec. 21, chap. 9, sec. 131, 156.

39. Locke, chap. 19, sec. 225, 199.

40. Locke, chap. 8, secs. 97 and 98, 142.

41. Abraham Lincoln, "First Inaugural Address," March 4, 1861, in Fehrenbacher, *Speeches and Writings, 1859–1865*, 220.

42. Locke, *Second Treatise*, chap. 4, sec. 23, chap. 5, secs. 26 and 27, 110, 111.

43. Locke, chap. 5, secs. 32, 36, and 45, 113, 115, 117.

44. Locke, chap. 9, sec. 123, 154–155.

45. Stephen Douglas, "Second Joint Debate with Lincoln," August 27, 1858, in Fehrenbacher, *Speeches and Writings, 1832–1858*, 552.

46. "Speech on the Kansas-Nebraska Act," 324.

47. Lincoln to Henry L. Pierce and others, April 6, 1859, in Fehrenbacher, *Speeches and Writings, 1859–1865*, 18.

48. Locke, *Second Treatise*, chap. 5, sec. 28, 112.

49. Locke, chap. 5, sec. 50, 121.

50. See C. B. Macpherson, "Locke on Capitalist Appropriation," *Western Political Quarterly* 4, 4 (December 1951): 550–566. With respect to Locke's "turfs my servant has cut," Macpherson remarks: "Had Locke not been taking the wage relationship entirely for granted, his inclusion of 'my servant's labor' in 'the labour that was mine' would have been a direct contradiction of the whole case he was there making" (560).

51. Abraham Lincoln, "Fragments on the Tariff," 1847, in Fehrenbacher, *Speeches and Writings, 1832–1858*, 153.

52. "Speech on the Dred Scott Decision," 398; Abraham Lincoln, "Speech at New Haven, Connecticut," March 6, 1860, in Fehrenbacher, *Speeches and Writings, 1859–1865*, 132.

53. Gabor S. Boritt examines Lincoln's understanding of labor, value, and the worker's entitlement to the full fruits of his labor in *Lincoln and the Economics of the American Dream* (1978; reprint, Urbana: University of Illinois Press, 1994), 109–128. Jon D. Schaff argues that Lincoln's free-labor political economy was a carefully considered alternative to unrestrained capitalism on one side and socialism on the other; for Lincoln, *wage* labor, though far more just than *slave* labor, was not the same as *free* labor. Jon D. Schaff, *Abraham Lincoln's Statesmanship and the Limits of Liberal Democracy* (Carbondale: Southern Illinois University Press, 2019), 121. In contrast, Richard Hofstadter describes Lincoln as blissfully ignorant as he "presided over the social revolution that destroyed the simple equalitarian order of the 1840s, corrupted what remained of its values, and caricatured its ideals." Richard Hofstadter, *The American Political Tradition & the Men Who Made It* (1948; reprint, New York: Vintage, 1974), 136. Phillip S. Paludan portrays Lincoln as a genuine believer in the ideal of affording all men "an unfettered start and a fair chance in the race of life" but argues that, as president, Lincoln supported legislation "that undercut the position of the working class." Phillip S. Paludan, "Commentary on 'Lincoln and the Economics of the American Dream," in *The Historian's Lincoln: Pseudohistory, Psychohistory, and History*, ed. Gabor S. Boritt (Urbana: University of Illinois Press, 1988), 120.

54. For an examination of arguments for and against a constitutional right of secession, see Daniel Farber, *Lincoln's Constitution* (Chicago: University of Chicago Press, 2003), 70–91. Farber also discusses whether slave-state secession could plausibly be grounded on the natural right of revolution (101–112).

55. Hofstadter, *American Political Tradition*, 130–131.

56. "First Inaugural Address," 219.

57. Fehrenbacher, *Speeches and Writings, 1859–1865*, 254–255.

58. On Rhett's shift from secession as "revolution" to echoing Calhoun's constitutional justification, see James H. Read, "From Calhoun to Secession," in Levine, Merrill, and Stoner, *Political Thought of the Civil War*, 142–146. Calhoun maintained the constitutionality of secession in "A Discourse on the Constitution and Government of the United States," in Lence, *Union and Liberty*, 81–101, 212–213.

59. Abraham Lincoln, "Message to Congress in Special Session," July 4, 1861, in Fehrenbacher, *Speeches and Writings, 1859–1865*, 255.

60. See the Digital History archive of secession ordinances, https://www.digitalhistory.uh.edu/disp_textbook.cfm?smtID=3&psid=3953. Georgia, Virginia, and North Carolina—which, like South Carolina, were among the original states ratifying the Constitution—followed South Carolina's lead in framing their secession ordinances as a revocation of that specifically dated act. The secession ordinances of Louisiana, Texas, and Arkansas—not among the original states ratifying the Constitution—used a similar format but substituted the dated act by which their territorial legislatures resolved to accept the authority of the US Constitution. The secession ordinances of Florida, Alabama, Tennessee, and Mississippi did not take the form of revoking any specific past act of ratification.

61. State of Texas, "A Declaration of the Causes which Impel the State of Texas to Secede from the Federal Union," February 2, 1861, Texas State Library and Archives Commission, https://www.tsl.texas.gov/ref/abouttx/secession/2feb1861.html.

62. Texas, "Declaration of the Causes"; State of South Carolina, "Declaration of the Causes of Secession," https://avalon.law.yale.edu/19th_century/csa_scarsec.asp; State of Georgia, "Declaration of the Causes of Secession," https://avalon.law.yale.edu/19th_century/csa_geosec.asp; State of Mississippi, "Declaration of the Causes of Secession," https://avalon.law.yale.edu/19th_century/csa_missec.asp.

63. South Carolina, "Declaration of the Causes of Secession."

64. Mississippi, "Declaration of the Causes of Secession."

65. For Lincoln's observations on John Brown's raid, see "Cooper Institute Address," 122–125. The 1860 Republican platform states: "we denounce the lawless invasion by armed force of the soil of any state or territory, no matter under what pretext, as among the gravest of crimes."

66. Texas, "Declaration of the Causes." For the false but widely believed rumor that abolitionists had stirred up Texas slaves to commit widespread acts of arson and to poison wells with strychnine, see William W. Freehling, *The Road to Disunion: Secessionists Triumphant, 1854–1861* (New York: Oxford University Press, 2007), 331–336.

67. Fehrenbacher, *Speeches and Writings, 1859–1865*, 219.

68. South Carolina, "Declaration of the Causes of Secession"; John C. Calhoun, "Speech on the General State of the Union," March 4, 1860, in Lence, *Union and Liberty*, 600.

69. Georgia, "Declaration of the Causes of Secession"; Mississippi, "Declaration of the Causes of Secession"; Texas, "Declaration of the Causes."

70. South Carolina, "Declaration of the Causes of Secession."

71. John C. Calhoun, "Speech on Abolition Petitions," March 9, 1836, in *The Papers of John C. Calhoun*, vol. 13, ed. Clyde N. Wilson (Columbia: University of South Carolina Press), 104–105.

72. Fehrenbacher, *Speeches and Writings, 1859–1865*, 128–129.

Conclusion

1. For the upper South's rejection of secession before Fort Sumter, see Daniel W. Crofts, *Reluctant Confederates: Upper South Unionists in the Secession Crisis* (Chapel Hill: University of North Carolina Press, 1989).

2. John C. Calhoun, "Speech on the Force Bill," February 15–16, 1833, in *Union and Liberty: The Political Thought of John C. Calhoun*, ed. Ross M. Lence (Indianapolis: Liberty Fund, 1992), 403–460. In a December 30, 1860, letter, Alexander Stephens urged Lincoln under no circumstances to attempt to preserve the Union by force: "This great object can never be obtained by force. . . . An error on this point may lead to the most disastrous consequences." Richard Malcolm Johnson and William Hand Browne, *Life of Alexander H. Stephens* (Philadelphia: J. B. Lippincott, 1884), 371. For an examination of arguments for and against the constitutionality of the federal government's use of armed force against a state, see Daniel Farber, *Lincoln's Constitution* (Chicago: University of Chicago Press, 2003), 92–114.

3. William E. Gienapp, "Abraham Lincoln and the Border States," *Journal of the Abraham Lincoln Association* 13, 1 (1992): 13–46; Jamie L. Carson, Jeffery A. Jenkins, David W. Rohde, and Mark A. Souva, "The Impact of National Tides and District-Level Effects on Electoral Outcomes: The U.S. Congressional Elections of 1862–1863," *American Journal of Political Science* 45, 4 (October 2001): 887–898. The lone Republican elected to the US House in 1860 from a loyal slave state represented St. Louis, Missouri, and surrounding areas. No Republicans were elected to the US House from Kentucky, Maryland, or Delaware, and no Republican US senators were selected in the loyal slave states.

4. Abraham Lincoln, "Message to Congress in Special Session," July 4, 1861; "Gettysburg Address," November 19, 1863, in *Abraham Lincoln: Speeches and Writings, 1859–1865*, ed. Don E. Fehrenbacher (New York: Library of America, 1989), 260, 536.

5. Abraham Lincoln, "Memorandum on Probable Failure of Re-election," August 23, 1864; "Response to a Serenade," November 10, 1864, in Fehrenbacher, *Speeches and Writings, 1859–1865*, 624, 640. Benjamin A. Kleinerman argues that, despite his embrace of the concept of *military* necessity, Lincoln regarded holding scheduled elections during wartime as a *constitutional* necessity. Benjamin A. Kleinerman, "Executive Power and Constitutional Necessity," in *Lincoln and Democratic Statesmanship*, ed. Michael P. Zuckert (Lawrence: University Press of Kansas, 2020), 204–207.

6. Merrill D. Peterson, *Lincoln in American Memory* (New York: Oxford University Press, 1994), 3–35, 273–275; M. E. Bradford, "Against Lincoln: An Address at Gettysburg," in *The Historian's Lincoln: Pseudohistory, Psychohistory, and History*, ed. Gabor S. Boritt (Urbana: University of Illinois Press, 1988), 107–115; Robert W. Johannsen, *Lincoln, the South, and Slavery* (Baton Rouge: Louisiana State University Press, 1991), 58–68; Carl Sandburg, *Abraham Lincoln: The Prairie Years and the War Years*, 1 vol. ed. (New York: Harcourt Brace Jovanovich, 1954), viii.

7. See, for example, Lerone Bennett Jr., *Forced into Glory: Abraham Lincoln's White Dream* (Chicago: Johnson, 2000), which makes many assertions at variance with the historical record, including the claim that Lincoln opposed the Thirteenth Amendment. In fact, Lincoln strongly supported that amendment, and his efforts were essential to securing its passage in Congress. Nikole Hannah-Jones presents a more historically accurate but still, in my view, unduly negative picture of Lincoln in *The 1619 Project: A New Origin Story* (New York: One World, 2021), 22–27.

8. See, for example, DeNeen L. Brown, "Frederick Douglass Delivered a Lincoln Reality Check at Emancipation Memorial Unveiling," *Washington Post*, June 27, 2020.

9. Frederick Douglass, "The Freedmen's Monument to Abraham Lincoln," April 15, 1876, in *The Portable Frederick Douglass*, ed. John Stauffer and Henry Louis Gates (New York: Penguin, 2016), 372–373. For discussion of Douglass's Freedmen's Memorial speech and its wider context, see David L. Blight, *Frederick Douglass: Prophet of Freedom* (New York: Simon & Schuster, 2018), 1–9.

10. J. Michael Luttig, Opening Statement at January 6 Select Committee Hearing, June 16, 2022, *Politico*, https://www.politico.com/news/2022/06/16/j-michael-luttig-opening-statement-jan-6-hearing-00040255.

11. Trump's statement was posted on his social media platform Truth Social. See "Donald Trump Goes on the Offensive Ahead of Capitol Riot Hearing," *Newsweek*, June 9, 2022, https://www.newsweek.com/donald-trump-january-6-hearing-criticism-truth-social-1714308.

12. John Locke, *Second Treatise of Civil Government*, chap. 19, sec. 225, in *Two Treatises of Government and a Letter Concerning Toleration*, ed. Ian Shapiro (New Haven, CT: Yale University Press, 2003), 199.

13. Election officials received many death threats immediately after the 2020 presidential election, and as of June 2022, those threats were ongoing. "'There Is Nowhere I Feel Safe': Election Officials Describe Threats Fueled by Trump," *New York Times*, June 21, 2022.

14. For the US Department of Homeland Security's statement that the 2020 election "was the most secure in American history," see "Joint Statement from Elections Infrastructure Government Coordinating Council and the Infrastructure Sector Coordinating Executive Committees," November 12, 2020, https://www.cisa.gov/news/2020/11/12/joint-statement-elections-infrastructure-government-coordinating-council-election. Many studies have found no evidence of mass voter fraud in the 2020 election. See, for example, Andrew C. Eggers, Haritz Garro, and Justin Grimmer, "No Evidence for Voter Fraud: A Guide to Statistical Claims about the 2020 Election," Hoover Institution, February 3, 2021, https://www.dropbox.com/s/0120sormtbw9w10/fraud_extended_public.pdf?dl=0.

15. For one of the many lawsuits filed by the Trump campaign or its supporters asking that hundreds of thousands—or in this particular case, more than a million—votes be invalidated, see *Donald J. Trump for President v. Secretary, Commonwealth of Pennsylvania*, U.S. Court of Appeals, No. 20-3371 (3d Cir. 2020), decided November 27, 2020. For a tabulation of lawsuits seeking to overturn the election results in Pennsylvania, see "Trump and His Allies Tried to Overturn Pennsylvania Election Results for Two Months: Here Are the Highlights," *Philadelphia Inquirer*, January 7, 2021. Similar multiple efforts were made in Wisconsin, Michigan, Georgia, Arizona, and Nevada and rejected by federal or state courts.

16. "Calls for Martial Law and U.S. Military Oversight of New Presidential Election Draws Criticism," *Military Times*, December 2, 2020, https://www.militarytimes.com/news/your-military/2020/12/02/calls-for-martial-law-and-us-military-oversight-of-new-presidential-elections-draws-criticism/.

17. Abraham Lincoln, "Address to Young Men's Lyceum of Springfield, Illinois," January 27, 1838, in *Abraham Lincoln: Speeches and Writings, 1832–1858*, ed. Don E. Fehrenbacher (New York: Library of America, 1989), 31. On the diverse ways antebellum political leaders sought to "attach" Americans to their republican political institutions, see Emily Pears, *Cords of Affection: Constructing Constitutional Union in Early American History* (Lawrence: University Press of Kansas, 2021).

18. "Panel Ties Trump to Fake Elector Plan, Mapping His Attack on Democracy," *New York Times*, June 21, 2022.

19. "Trump Defends 'Delay the Election' Tweet, Even Though He Can't Do It," *New York Times*, July 30, 2020.

20. "Donald Trump Won't Say if He'll Accept Result of Election," *New York Times*, October 19, 2016. In speeches to his supporters during both the 2016

and 2020 campaigns, Trump made it clear that he would accept the results only "if I win."

21. For an examination of how apparently stable democracies can fail or deteriorate significantly, see Steven Levitsky and Daniel Ziblatt, *How Democracies Die* (New York: Crown, 2018). For a bleak assessment of the US context, see Steven Levitsky and Lucan Way, "America's Coming Age of Instability: Why Constitutional Crises and Political Violence Could Soon Be the Norm," *Foreign Affairs,* January 20, 2022.

22. The organization Bright Line Watch (https://brightlinewatch.org/) monitors contemporary threats to American democratic norms and institutions, as well as countervailing factors indicating democracy's resilience in the face of these threats. For Americans' eroding faith in democracy before Trump's presidency, see Roberto Stefan Foa and Yascha Mounk, "The Danger of Deconsolidation: The Democratic Disconnect," *Journal of Democracy* 27, 3 (July 2016): 5–17; Gerhard Feierherd, Noam Lupu, and Susan Stokes, "A Significant Minority of Americans Say They Could Support a Military Takeover of the U.S. Government," *Washington Post*, February 18, 2018, which analyzes polling data from 2010, 2012, 2014, and 2017.

23. See Suzanne Mettler and Robert C. Lieberman, *Four Threats: The Recurring Crises of American Democracy* (New York: St. Martin's Griffin, 2020).

24. Abraham Lincoln, "Speech on the Kansas-Nebraska Act," October 16, 1854; "Draft of a Speech," ca. December 1857, in Fehrenbacher, *Speeches and Writings 1832–1858*, 315–316, 417.

25. Nolan McCarty, *Polarization: What Everyone Needs to Know* (New York: Oxford University Press, 2019), 1. McCarty emphasizes that ideological polarization and partisan polarization, though often connected in practice, are different concepts and that ideological polarization may or may not align closely with major party competition (8–13).

26. For a description of several different theories about the causes of contemporary polarization, see McCarty, *Polarization*, 69–100.

27. Gallup Historical Trends: Abortion, https://news.gallup.com/poll /1576/abortion.aspx, accessed June 30, 2022. Gallup's most recent posted survey findings on abortion are dated May 2022.

28. Robert Pape, "Why We Cannot Afford to Ignore the American Insurrectionist Movement," University of Chicago, Chicago Project on Security and Threats, August 6, 2021.

29. Alan Abramowitz and Jennifer McCoy argue that racial and ethnic resentment on the part of white voters is the strongest driver of contemporary polarization and negative partisanship in the United States, although they acknowledge that "racial resentment and economic discontent" are closely connected, given that many white voters have been persuaded that their own worsening economic prospects are the result of policies favoring "undeserving"

ethnic and racial minorities. Alan Abramowitz and Jennifer McCoy, "United States: Racial Resentment, Negative Partisanship, and Polarization in Trump's America," *Annals of the American Academy of Political and Social Sciences* 68 (January 2019): 146, 150–151.

30. Mettler and Lieberman, *Four Threats.*

31. For Lincoln's defense of his actions in the early months of the war, see "Message to Congress in Special Session," 246–261. For discussion, see Farber, *Lincoln's Constitution,* 115–143.

32. For a critical but nuanced treatment of this theme, see Mark E. Neely Jr., *The Fate of Liberty: Abraham Lincoln and Civil Liberties* (New York: Oxford University Press, 1991).

33. Jon D. Schaff argues that, on matters less directly related to the conduct of the war, Lincoln neither stiff-armed Congress nor passively deferred to it. Instead, he exercised "modest" presidential leadership in a manner consistent with the Whig principles articulated earlier in his career, and he acknowledged the primacy of Congress in this domain. Jon D. Schaff, *Abraham Lincoln's Statesmanship and the Limits of Liberal Democracy* (Carbondale: Southern Illinois University Press, 2019), 180–205.

34. "Broken branch" comes from Thomas E. Mann and Norman J. Ornstein, *The Broken Branch: How Congress Is Failing America and How to Get It Back on Track* (New York: Oxford University Press, 2008). The authors' more recent work presents Congress as even more broken. See Thomas E. Mann and Norman J. Ornstein, *It's Even Worse than It Looks: How the American Constitutional System Collided with the New Politics of Extremism,* expanded ed. (New York: Basic Books, 2016).

35. David M. Potter, *The Impending Crisis, 1848–1861* (New York: Harper & Row, 1976), 315–325.

36. "Lincoln's Plan of Campaign in 1840," January 1840, in *The Collected Works of Abraham Lincoln,* 9 vols., ed. Roy P. Basler (New Brunswick, NJ: Rutgers University Press, 1953), 1:180–181. See the discussion in chapter 3.

37. Alan I. Abramowitz and Steven W. Webster, "Negative Partisanship: Why Americans Dislike Parties but Behave Like Rabid Partisans," *Advances in Political Psychology* 39, suppl. 1 (2018): 119–135. Abramowitz and Webster note that a variety of explanations have been offered for the steep rise in negative partisanship, including the impact of partisan media outlets, "divisive cultural issues such as abortion and gay rights," and "increasingly expensive and negative campaigns." However, they argue that "the single most important factor underlying the rise of negative partisanship has been the growing racial divide between supporters of the two parties" (123).

38. For the argument that major party rivalry in a two-party system is the root of the problem, see Lee Drutman, *Breaking the Two-Party Doom Loop: The Case for Multiparty Democracy in America* (New York: Oxford University Press,

2020). For the counterargument that party weakness is a significant factor driving polarization, see Frances McCall Rosenbluth and Ian Shapiro, *Responsible Parties: Saving Democracy from Itself* (New Haven, CT: Yale University Press, 2018); Daniel Schlozman and Sam Rosenfeld, "The Hollow Parties," in *Can America Govern Itself?* ed. Francis E. Lee and Nolan McCarty (New York: Cambridge University Press, 2019), 120–154.

39. For discussion of this case and the critical role of risk-taking leadership, see James H. Read and Ian Shapiro, "Transforming Power Relationships: Leadership, Risk, and Hope," *American Political Science Review* 108, 1 (February 2014): 40–53.

40. Abraham Lincoln, "Second Inaugural Address," March 4, 1865, in Fehrenbacher, *Speeches and Writings, 1859–1865*, 686.

Selected Bibliography

Abramowitz, Alan I., and Steven W. Webster. "Negative Partisanship: Why Americans Dislike Parties but Behave Like Rabid Partisans." *Advances in Political Psychology* 39, suppl. 1 (2018): 119–135.

Bailey, Jeremy. "Opposition to the Theory of Presidential Representation: Federalists, Whigs, and Republicans." *Presidential Studies Quarterly* 44, 1 (March 2014): 50–71.

Barry, Brian. *Democracy, Power, and Justice: Essays in Political Theory.* Oxford: Oxford University Press, 1990.

Basler, Roy P., ed. *The Collected Works of Abraham Lincoln.* 9 vols. New Brunswick, NJ: Rutgers University Press, 1953. Searchable text has been posted online by the Abraham Lincoln Association. https://quod.lib.umich.edu/l/lincoln/.

Blight, David L. *Frederick Douglass: Prophet of Freedom.* New York: Simon & Schuster, 2018.

Boritt, Gabor S. *Lincoln and the Economics of the American Dream.* Urbana: University of Illinois Press, 1978.

Brooks, Corey M. *Liberty Power: Antislavery Third Parties and the Transformation of American Politics.* Chicago: University of Chicago Press, 2016.

Carwardine, Richard. *Lincoln: A Life of Purpose and Power.* New York: Vintage, 2007.

Childers, Christopher. *The Failure of Popular Sovereignty: Slavery, Manifest Destiny, and the Radicalization of Southern Politics.* Lawrence: University Press of Kansas, 2012.

Cooper, William J., Jr. *The South and the Politics of Slavery, 1828–1856.* Baton Rouge: Louisiana State University Press, 1978.

Crofts, Daniel W. *Reluctant Confederates: Upper South Unionists in the Secession Crisis.* Chapel Hill: University of North Carolina Press, 1989.

Dahl, Robert A. *Democracy and Its Critics.* New Haven, CT: Yale University Press, 1991.

Ellis, Richard J., and Stephen Kirk. "Presidential Mandates in the Nineteenth Century: Conceptual Change and Institutional Development." *Studies in American Political Development* 9, 1 (Spring 1995): 117–186.

Etcheson, Nicole. *Bleeding Kansas: Contested Liberty in the Civil War Era.* Lawrence: University Press of Kansas, 2004.

Farber, Daniel. *Lincoln's Constitution.* Chicago: University of Chicago Press, 2003.

Fehrenbacher, Don E., ed. *Abraham Lincoln: Speeches and Writings, 1832–1858.* New York: Library of America, 1989.

———, ed. *Abraham Lincoln: Speeches and Writings, 1859–1865.* New York: Library of America, 1989.

———. *The Dred Scott Case: Its Significance in American Law and Politics.* New York: Oxford University Press, 1978.

———. *Prelude to Greatness: Lincoln in the 1850s.* Stanford, CA: Stanford University Press, 1962.

———. *The Slaveholding Republic: An Account of the United States Government's Relations to Slavery.* Completed and edited by Ward M. McAfee. New York: Oxford University Press, 2001.

Finkelman, Paul. *Slavery and the Founders: Race and Liberty in the Age of Jefferson.* 3rd ed. Armonk, NY: M. E. Sharpe, 2014.

Foner, Eric. *The Fiery Trial: Abraham Lincoln and American Slavery.* New York: W. W. Norton, 2011.

———. *Free Soil, Free Labor, Free Men: The Ideology of the Republican Party before the Civil War.* New York: Oxford University Press, 1970.

Ford, Lacy K. *Deliver Us from Evil: The Slavery Question in the Old South.* New York: Oxford University Press, 2009.

Freehling, William W. *The Road to Disunion: Secessionists Triumphant, 1854–1861.* New York: Oxford University Press, 2007.

Freehling, William W., and Craig M. Simpson, eds. *Secession Debated: Georgia's Showdown in 1860.* New York: Oxford University Press, 1992.

Freeman, Joanne B. *The Field of Blood: Violence in Congress and the Road to the Civil War.* New York: Farrar, Straus & Giroux, 2018.

Gates, Henry Louis, Jr., and Donald Yacovone, eds. *Lincoln on Race and Slavery.* Princeton, NJ: Princeton University Press, 2009.

Gienapp, William E. *The Origins of the Republican Party, 1852–1856.* New York: Oxford University Press, 1987.

———. "The Republican Party and the Slave Power." In *New Perspectives on Race and Slavery in America,* ed. Robert H. Abzug and Stephen E. Maizlish, 51–78. Lexington: University Press of Kentucky, 1986.

Graber, Mark A. *Dred Scott and the Problem of Constitutional Evil.* New York: Cambridge University Press, 2006.

Harrold, Stanley. *Lincoln and the Abolitionists.* Carbondale: Southern Illinois University Press, 2018.

Holt, Michael F. *The Election of 1860: "A Campaign Fraught with Consequences."* Lawrence: University Press of Kansas, 2017.

———. *The Political Crisis of the 1850s.* New York: W. W. Norton, 1978.

Howe, Daniel Walker. *What Hath God Wrought: The Transformation of America, 1815–1848.* New York: Oxford University Press, 2007.

Jaffa, Harry V. *Crisis of the House Divided: An Interpretation of the Issues in the*

Lincoln-Douglas Debates. 50th anniversary ed. Chicago: University of Chicago Press, 2009.

Lence, Ross M., ed. *Union and Liberty: The Political Philosophy of John C. Calhoun.* Indianapolis: Liberty Fund, 1992.

Leonard, Gerald. *The Invention of Party Politics: Federalism, Popular Sovereignty, and Constitutional Development in Jacksonian Illinois.* Chapel Hill: University of North Carolina Press, 2002.

Levine, Bruce. "'The Vital Element of the Republican Party': Antislavery, Nativism, and Abraham Lincoln." *Journal of the Civil War Era* 1, 4 (December 2011): 481–505.

Levitsky, Steven, and Daniel Ziblatt. *How Democracies Die.* New York: Crown, 2018.

Malavasic, Alice Elizabeth. *The F Street Mess: How Southern Senators Rewrote the Kansas-Nebraska Act.* Chapel Hill: University of North Carolina Press, 2017.

McCarty, Nolan. *Polarization: What Everyone Needs to Know.* New York: Oxford University Press, 2019.

Mettler, Suzanne, and Robert C. Lieberman. *Four Threats: The Recurring Crises of American Democracy.* New York: St. Martin's Griffin, 2020.

Morel, Lucas E. *Lincoln's Sacred Effort: Defining Religion's Role in American Self-Government.* Lanham, MD: Lexington Books, 2000.

Oakes, James. *The Scorpion's Sting: Antislavery and the Coming of the Civil War.* New York: W. W. Norton, 2014.

Paludan, Phillip S. *Lincoln's Legacy: Ethics and Politics.* Urbana: University of Illinois Press, 2008.

Potter, David M. *The Impending Crisis: 1848–1861.* Completed and edited by Don E. Fehrenbacher. New York: Harper & Row, 1976.

Read, James H. *Majority Rule versus Consensus: The Political Thought of John C. Calhoun.* Lawrence: University Press of Kansas, 2009.

Riker, William H. *Liberalism against Populism: A Confrontation between the Theory of Democracy and the Theory of Social Choice.* Prospect Heights, IL: Waveland Press, 1982.

Schaff, Jon D. *Abraham Lincoln's Statesmanship and the Limits of Liberal Democracy.* Carbondale: Southern Illinois University Press, 2019.

Schaub, Diana. *His Greatest Speeches: How Lincoln Moved the Nation.* New York: St. Martin's Press, 2021.

———. "Lincoln and the Daughters of Dred Scott: A Reflection on the Declaration of Independence." In *When in the Course of Human Events: 1776 at Home, Abroad, and in American Memory,* ed. Will R. Jordan, 189–210. Macon, GA: Mercer University Press, 2018.

Sewell, Richard H. *Ballots for Freedom: Antislavery Politics in the United States, 1837–1860.* New York: Oxford University Press, 1976.

Silbey, Joel H. *Martin Van Buren and the Emergence of American Popular Politics.* Lanham, MD: Rowman & Littlefield, 2002.

Sinha, Manisha. *The Slave's Cause: A History of Abolition.* New Haven, CT: Yale University Press, 2016.

Stampp, Kenneth M. *And the War Came: The North and the Secession Crisis, 1860–1861.* Baton Rouge: Louisiana State University Press, 1950.

Stauffer, John, and Henry Louis Gates, eds. *The Portable Frederick Douglass.* New York: Penguin, 2016.

Striner, Richard. *Lincoln and Race.* Carbondale: Southern Illinois University Press, 2012.

Wiecek, William W. *The Sources of Anti-Slavery Constitutionalism in America, 1760–1848.* Ithaca, NY: Cornell University Press, 1977.

Wilentz, Sean. *No Property in Man: Slavery and Antislavery at the Nation's Founding.* Cambridge, MA: Harvard University Press, 2018.

Zuckert, Michael P., ed. *Lincoln and Democratic Statesmanship.* Lawrence: University Press of Kansas, 2020.

Index